Canyoning in the Pacific Northwest

A Technical Resource

Kevin Clark

Canyoning in the Pacific Northwest
A Technical Resource

ISBN: 978-1-7367869-0-1.

All photos and illustrations used with permission. Rigging diagrams were created with *vRigger*.

Cover: Wim Aarts rappelling Parkett Falls, Ore. (Photo: Wade Hewitt)
Frontispiece: Wade Hewitt on a first descent of Panther Creek, Ore. (Photo: Kevin Clark)
Title: Kendra Kallevig and Lisa Ripps descending East Canyon Creek, Wash. (Photo: Kevin Clark)

Canyoning in the Pacific Northwest

A Technical Resource

Author
Kevin Clark

Editor
Sarah Bradham

Illustrations
Bruce Wyse

Photography
Wim Aarts
Sean Brady
Kevin Clark
Annalisha Cox
Karl Helser
Wade Hewitt
Andy Sorensen
Leah Sorensen

Table of Contents

Preface

This manual is about intermediate-level recreational *canyoning* (or *canyoneering*) in the Pacific Northwest.[1] We'll touch on a few topics relevant to the sandstone canyons of the American Southwest (mainly to be filed under "good things to know when visiting"), but this manual's primary focus is local *aquatic canyons*.[2]

What this manual is ...

Aquatic canyoning is well-established in Europe, but is only just arriving in this corner of the United States. Interest in the sport is on the rise and, within the last few years, local canyoning has really started to take off. Today, more organizations are offering classes in aquatic canyon techniques, and there's a small, but growing, dedicated community. Information in the public domain has also increased in the form of online classes, articles, videos, and internet forums.[3] Canyon reference books (at least those written in English), however, have lagged behind. Only a handful cover aquatic techniques in significant detail.

The goal of this project is to create a useful and practical resource for intermediate-level aquatic canyoning; one that's tailored to the Pacific Northwest. Hopefully, this manual will answer a lot of the big questions and help others along in their journey.

Like most technical manuals, very little of the material presented herein is unique or original. All of the techniques we use to descend canyons have been fine-tuned over many years by those who came before us. We stand on their shoulders and share the benefit of their collective experience and hard-earned wisdom.

Getting the most out of this manual ...

Be aware: this manual is not intended for true beginners. An assumption is made that the reader is already:

- o   A competent rappeller.
- o   Reasonably well-versed in anchor building, belaying and rope management.
- o   Familiar with the common knots used in ropework (ex: overhand, figure-8 on a bight, clove hitch).

Those with a decent technical background will get the most out of this manual. If you're lacking this background, don't expect to pick it up on the fly. This manual skips over some huge important topics, such as how to rappel, anchor basics, wilderness navigation, and more. One of the best ways to get started is to take an introductory-level canyon or climbing class. This will lay down a solid foundation that you can build on. *Do it ... It'll be fun!* Education and training increases safety and confidence.

For more experienced folks: reading this manual will not magically transform you into an expert canyoneer. Some forms of canyon rigging appear simple at first glance, but there are many easily-missed subtleties. Also, things somehow become surprisingly complicated when hanging on a rope 30m (~100ft) above the ground in the middle of a waterfall. Nothing beats hands-on training from a qualified instructor. Some skills, especially rescue techniques, can't be learned by reading alone.

It should be stressed that this manual is a reference only. It's intended to complement instruction and training, not replace it. Taking a class or three is highly recommended.

---

[1] FAQ: Is it *canyoning* or *canyoneering*? Some canyoneers use the terms interchangeably, whereas others see a distinction between wet and dry canyons. I've decided to go with canyoning as that's the term used internationally.
[2] An aquatic canyon is any canyon with significant flowing water.
[3] Use caution when seeking out information online. There are great resources out there, including a number of forums hosted by expert canyoneers who, very generously, share their knowledge and answer questions. Other sites, however, are less than stellar, with some promoting faulty, incomplete, or even dangerous information.

What to expect …

Be aware: the information in this manual may or may not be relevant outside the Pacific Northwest. Canyons throughout the world are extremely diverse, so it makes sense that rigging systems, techniques, and best practices will also be different. The skills needed to run a canyon safely will vary depending on where you are in the world and how much water is present. Running aquatic canyons requires a different slate of skills and techniques.

Also note: this manual is not intended to be an encyclopedia of all possible rigging options. The methods presented here are just one solution and should not be interpreted as being "the only way" or "the right way." Quite often, there'll be multiple ways to solve a given problem. How you go about it will depend on the situation, your training, your experience, available resources, and personal preference. So, if you disagree or do things differently than what's presented here, that's not unexpected. The wide variety of solutions and interesting nuances will continue to stir passionate debate on the internet for years to come.

The bottom line with all techniques: evaluate and find a safe solution that works for you.

What is Canyoning?

Canyoning is the sport of exploring canyons using a variety of techniques such as scrambling, climbing, wading, swimming, and rappelling.[4] The term is most often used to describe the descent of technical canyons requiring ropes, harnesses, and other specialized gear. Like mountain peaks, canyons are extremely diverse and vary widely in level of difficulty. Dry canyons are generally easier in terms of rigging and preparation compared to those with flowing water. The more water that's present, the more difficult the canyon.

Canyoning is practiced all over the world, but is most well known in Europe and the United States. It's a sport that is rapidly growing in popularity. In North America, most people associate canyoning with the famous slot canyons of the Colorado Plateau, although it's also being practiced in the Rocky Mountains, the Sierra Nevada, Arizona, British Columbia, Mexico, Hawaii, and here in the Cascade Range. The Pacific Northwest possesses one of the greatest concentrations of waterfalls in the world, making canyoning a natural fit.

Canyoning involves problem-solving, anchor creativity, route-finding, efficient rope management, and rappelling in unusual circumstances (ex: awkward starts, confined spaces, through waterfalls). Water adds new dangers to the rappel equation, and water protection will likely be required for both you and your gear. The ability to swim is critical in some canyons; in others, canyoneers must negotiate swiftwater hazards and strong current. Canyoning often involves venturing into remote rugged areas and, like climbing and technical caving, demands a high level of self-sufficiency.

---

[4] Rappelling is known as *abseiling* in the United Kingdom, Australia, New Zealand, and other parts of the world. Rappelling is the French term; abseiling comes from the German.

Chapter 1: Planning & Best Practices

Always learn as much as possible about the canyons you plan to visit. A little advance research will help set your expectations and could save your bacon out there if you get into trouble. In this chapter, we'll take a look at the planning process, discuss best practices, and talk about common pitfalls and hazards.

Canyon Ratings

How difficult are these canyons? What are my options? The *American Canyoneering Association (ACA)* has developed a rating system that has been widely adopted throughout the United States. A given rating includes at least three pieces of information: how technical the canyon is, how much water is present, and the time required to complete the canyon. Sometimes, other information is added, such as an indicator of the canyon's level of risk, perceived fun factor, and so on.

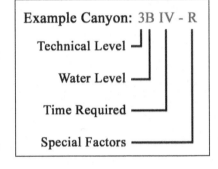

A canyon's rating is not definitive; it's intended to provide a general sense how difficult the canyon is under "normal conditions." This means the rating is for the time of year when the canyon is normally visited. The rating also assumes the canyon is being run by a small competent party. The rating is for the most difficult part of the canyon.

For aquatic canyons, the rating is particularly subjective as the amount of water that's present will change with the year and the season. A canyon that's rated class C2 in May might be a C1 in August, or even A if it's a seasonal creek that runs dry. Water levels can also change after big precipitation events. For this reason, you can sometimes find the same canyon given strikingly different ratings depending who ran it and when. The canyon's rating should be regarded as a starting point for setting your expectations.

Technical Level

1	Non-technical	An easy hike-through canyon. Ropes are unnecessary.
2	Scrambling	Easy downclimbs. A rope might be used as a hand line or for lowering packs. Exiting up-canyon is feasible without ropes.
3	Intermediate	Rappels or technical downclimbing. Exiting up-canyon requires setting ropes.
4	Advanced	Difficult anchoring or complex ropework. Aid climbing, multi-pitch rappels, or high-risk downclimbing. Requires solid canyoning experience.

Water Level (volume & current)

A	Dry or little water	Dry falls. Expect wading in up to waist-deep pools.
B	Water is present	Very light to no current. Falls are dry or running at a trickle. Expect deep pools and swimming.
C	Significant water with current	Waterfalls, deep pools, and swimming. Advanced skills and judgement required. Class C canyons are sometimes subdivided as follows: ○ C1: Light to moderate current. Easy to negligible water hazards. ○ C2: Strong current. Swiftwater hazards (such as hydraulics) may be present. ○ C3: Very strong current. Dangerous swiftwater hazards. Experts only. ○ C4: Extreme current. Hazards may be difficult even for experts.

Dry Canyon: Class A (a1)

Calm Pools: Class B (a2)

Light Flow: Class B/C (a3)

Moderate Flow: Class C1 (a4)

Time Required (approximate car-to-car time by a small competent party)

I	A couple hours	
II	Half day	
III	Most of a day	
IV	Long day	Start early and bring a headlamp. Be prepared for an overnight bivy.
V	More than a day	Usually two days.
VI	Two or more days	

Special Factors

--	*No rating*	Normal level of risk.
R	Risky	Additional risk above and beyond the norm. Solid technical skills and judgement required. Not appropriate for beginners even with competent leadership.
X	Extreme	Multiple risk factors. Errors may lead to injuries or death. Experts only.

Always choose a canyon that matches the skill and fitness level of your group. Hikers will enjoy 2A and 2B canyons. Alpine climbers will gravitate toward 3A and 3B, although good judgement and proper gear are still required. Being a competent swimmer is a good prerequisite for all Class B and C canyons.

- Class B (a2)
  Depending on the air/water temperature and how much swimming is expected, a wetsuit may be required.

- Class C (a3+)
  A wetsuit will likely be required. Significant flow and deep pools change the technical requirements of the canyon. Different techniques may be required; we'll discuss these in later chapters.

> **The International Rating System**
> The *French Federation for Mountaineering and Climbing* (FFME) has also developed a canyon rating system that is the standard in Europe and the rest of the world. The International System is a little better for describing aquatic canyons. The rating is composed of three factors:
>
> - **Vertical:** A numerical rating of 1–7 describing how technical the canyon is.
> - **Aquatic:** A numerical rating of 1–7 describing how much water is present.
> - **Time Required**: A Roman numeral from I to VI indicating the commitment level of the canyon.
>
> Our example canyon (*3B IV – R*) would be rated *v5a3 IV* under the International System. This rating can be abbreviated as *5.3 IV*.

Acquiring Beta

Guidebooks, forums, and websites can provide a wealth of information about canyons, including route descriptions, ratings, photos, and trip reports. Also, check in with local canyoneers who may have visited the area recently. They can provide suggestions and firsthand reports on current conditions. Some good information to track down:

- What's the height of the tallest rappel in the canyon?
- How many rappels are expected?
- Are there any special hazards to be aware of?
- How high is the flow currently?

Be aware: the canyon environment is a dynamic one, so the most recent/up-to-date information is always preferred. Don't assume that everything will be exactly as described in the guidebook or even the same as the last time you visited. A canyon full of logs could get swept clean by winter floods. Giant boulders can get moved around. Pools can be created, or filled in by rocks and sand. Anchors and bolt stations may be missing or damaged. Canyons are continually subject to erosion; be prepared for landslides, fallen trees, and rockfall. Fierce winter storms can bring down all manner of branches and woody debris to clog the watercourse. Wildfires can create unstable conditions that can persist for many years. In mountainous terrain, you may have avalanche debris to deal with. A one-year-old trip report may already be out of date.

- If possible, try to corroborate beta from multiple sources. It's good to see where various sources agree or disagree with one another. Two individuals might describe the same canyon quite differently depending on their level of experience and training.

- Take all beta with a grain of salt. *Don't rely on it unduly.* Crowd-sourced information may not be accurate and guidebook authors can make mistakes. The height of a given rappel might be someone's best guess. Depending on what anchor you use, you might need more or less rope.

Red Tape

Does this canyon require permits or have any special regulations? Are there any issues with private property? It's a good idea to check in with local land managers to learn about access and regulations. If a given canyon is closed seasonally for wildlife or due to a forest fire, it's best to learn about it in advance. Driving four hours to the trailhead to find out the hard way is non-optimal. As of this writing, canyon-specific regulations are few and far between in the Pacific Northwest, but that may change as interest in the sport continues to grow.

Navigation

Once in the canyon, it's difficult to become lost (i.e., head downstream), but maps are useful for planning your approach and exit. Some canyons are easy to access, whereas others require hours of bushwhacking and serious navigation. Beware placing too much reliance on technology to navigate. There may be no reception in deep valleys and tight canyons. Batteries can go dead, and your phone may become a useless piece of junk if it gets wet. Bring a map and compass, and know how to use them. Wilderness navigation is a great support skill.

- If the canyon proves too much and you need to bail out, what's your escape plan? Is it possible to retreat upstream or exit mid-canyon? Study the map ahead of time and identify possible escape routes.

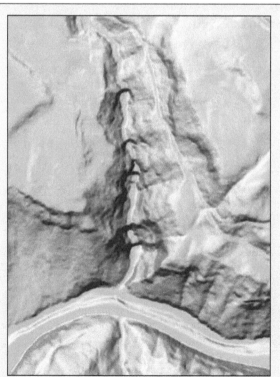

Light Detection and Ranging (LIDAR)
Lidar is a surveying technology that uses lasers to produce high-resolution terrain maps. *Google Earth*, when backed with lidar data, is a powerful tool for pinpointing waterfalls and measuring their height with surprising accuracy. Online mapping tools are a great way to identify likely canyon prospects from the comfort of your own home.

Disadvantages
- Lidar map data is not available everywhere.

- Lidar may not accurately depict tight slots and other places where the lasers were unable to penetrate the forest canopy.

Lidar map of Stafford Creek in the Oregon Coast Range. The waterfalls are clearly visible. (Map courtesy of the *State of Oregon Department of Geology and Mineral Industries*.)

Documenting Canyons

Here are some common abbreviations that are used to describe canyons:

- There's often a need to denote which side of the canyon something is located on, such as the anchor for a given rappel. A shorthand similar to *DCL* or *DCR* is used. This means when facing down-canyon, the anchor is located on your left or right.

- Rappels are often prefixed by "R". The number that follows may indicate the sequence, or, sometimes, the height of the pitch.

> **Sample Beta: Goat Creek**
> - *Downclimb a low-angle ramp about 50m. The DCL side is easier.*
> - *R1: 20m from a bolt station DCL into a pool.*
> - *Low angle ramp. Downclimb another 30m.*
> - *R2: 35m. There's a logjam at the bottom that is easily bypassed DCR.*
> - *R3: 20m.*
> - *Downclimb 50m to a short jump. Walk a short distance to R4.*
> - *R4: 40m.*
> - *At the bottom, the canyon widens and you can exit up to the road.*

Canyon Topos

Canyon beta can also be represented pictorially. This is a form often found in guidebooks; it's a visual cheat-sheet for the canyon. Advantage: The beta can be instantly understood without needing to read a long description. Be sure to include a legend as there's no universal standard for symbols. Given the dynamic nature of canyons, make sure to include the date when topo was created.

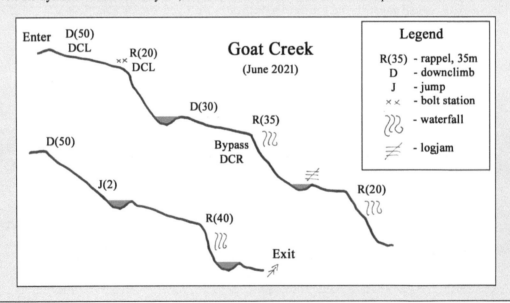

Estimating Water Levels

Maps are also useful for determining the size of the canyon's watershed (aka collection area). This is a good way to estimate how much water you're likely to find out there. Generally, the bigger the watershed, the more aquatic the canyon and the longer it'll take for flows to diminish heading into late summer. Canyons with smaller collection areas will have less water and are more likely to open earlier in the season.

Some other factors affecting flow rate would include the local terrain (mountains vs. hills), geology, ground saturation, prevalence of springs, current snowpack, and how much annual precipitation the area receives.

- Weather

  Keep an eye on the weather the week before your trip. How much rainfall has there been? Have there been any big storms lately? Check the weather again the morning of your trip and reassess throughout the day. Be prepared to change your plans if conditions prove unfavorable.

- Checkpoints & Reference Photos

  Reference photos are another tool for assessing conditions. Every time you run a canyon, take a photo to document the water levels. The photo should be labeled with the date you ran the canyon and a brief description of the conditions you found within (e.g., low water, moderate, high, extreme).

  Ideally, reference photos should be taken at the same location and from a place that's easy to access (i.e., you can get there without committing to the canyon). This location is called a *checkpoint*. Prior to running the canyon, visit the checkpoint and compare today's conditions with any reference photos to get an idea of what you're in for. The more photos you have, the better the prediction. When reference photos are posted online, they can benefit the entire canyon community.

- Water Gages

  The United States Geological Survey (USGS) maintains automated flow monitoring stations throughout the country. This information is publicly available and updated in real time. While gages are generally placed on large creeks and rivers, this information is still useful for getting a ballpark idea of water levels in the neighborhood. You can also check historical trends. Flow rate in the United States is measured in cubic feet per second (*cfs*). (See also "Flow Rate" in Chapter 19.)

- Areas downstream of dams and reservoirs may be subject to controlled water release. Check in with the local authorities before running such canyons.

- In alpine regions, streams originating from glaciers and snowmelt will become higher as the day progresses. They'll be at their lowest early in the morning.

FAQ: What's the best time of year to run canyons …

… in the Pacific Northwest?
Canyon season in the Pacific Northwest typically starts in May or June and lasts until the first big rainstorms of the fall (mid-September to early October). Rain can fall any time of the year, but the dry season usually begins in late June or early July. Water levels reach their lowest in late August to early September. While summer is the most comfortable time of year, canyoning can be pursued all year round. It's all about having adequate water protection and running canyons with reasonable flow.

… in the American Southwest?
Spring and fall are the best times to visit the Desert Southwest. Avoid the summer months as the heat can be scorching. Beware thunderstorms and flash floods. The rainy season in Utah is roughly mid-July through mid-September. The driest time of the year is in June.

Time Required

It can be difficult to predict how long it'll take to run a given canyon. The canyon's rating is a good place to start, but the actual time required will vary significantly. Canyoning tends to be slow. Depending on the terrain, obstacles, and conditions, traveling even a single mile could be an all-day adventure. If a group is overdue, it's often because the descent took longer than expected.

A small experienced team who knows the canyon well will move faster than a group of canyoneers who are visiting for the first time. In technical sections, experienced teams will move faster than a group of beginners. It's never a bad idea to get an early start and give yourself a healthy time margin for safety.

- Tip: Allow some extra time for setting up shuttles, the approach, the exit, rest breaks, etc.

Scouting

If you only have limited beta, consider scouting the canyon first. You can scope out the area, check out the entrance and exit, locate the waterfalls, and, perhaps, even rappel into the middle of the canyon (planning to climb back out via the same rope) to get an idea of what you're in for. Sometimes, you might do a series of dry rappels alongside the canyon, taking a peek into the drainage every so often to check things out. If the canyon is especially committing, one or more fixed ropes could be set along the rim. These *rim ropes* will then provide opportunities to escape if you should need them during your descent.

Canyon Hazards

Canyoning is a lot of fun, but things can get serious fast. Just being aware of common hazards is a good first step towards avoiding many problems.

Limited Escape

Canyons are notoriously committing. They're often easy to enter, but difficult to escape from due to sheer walls and steep terrain. In the world of alpine climbing, you can often turn around and go back when the going gets tough. In the canyon world, however, once you've pulled your rope after the first rappel, you may be committing to the entire descent. So, what happens when you're in the middle of a canyon and your only rope gets stuck?

- Canyons can be a special trap for beginners. It's easy for the inexperienced to rappel in, then suddenly realize they've gotten in over their heads.

Terrain

In aquatic canyons, expect everything underfoot to be uneven, loose, and slippery. There may be numerous obstacles to climb over, under, around, and through. Significant bushwhacking may be required just to reach the canyon. Slipping, falling, strains, sprains, and impalements are no fun. Minor injuries can become major problems for the entire team. (See "Common Injuries" in Chapter 25.)

- Log Dams & Logjams
  Logs falling into a creek frequently get lodged in narrow constrictions. More debris washes in behind them to create natural dam-like structures. Use caution as sometimes these dams can be undercut. You may unknowingly be walking across a weak floor subject to collapse. Logjams can be also be dangerous if a log shifts suddenly when weighted.

- Downclimbs
  Even a simple downclimb can be treacherous in an aquatic canyon. Don't hesitate to request assistance or use a rope. Requesting a rope might slow progression momentarily, but a broken ankle could end today's fun for everyone.

- Falling
  Use caution when moving around above a drop. Even minor slips can have major consequences. The party line says everyone should be clipped in (or otherwise belayed) when within a body-length of an edge where a fall could cause injury. In aquatic canyons, traverse lines are used more frequently to protect an exposed approach to an anchor. (See "Safety Lines" in Chapter 14.)

Rockfall

Falling rocks are always a danger. Rocks might be knocked loose by a rappeller or dislodged by the action of the rope moving around above you. Rappelling in or immediately adjacent to the watercourse may be the safest place as most loose debris will have been swept out in flood events. Rocks, however, are not the only flying objects to watch out for. Beware ropes, rope bags, packs, dropped gear, and retrievable systems.

- Always wear a helmet. It's usually put on when first entering the creek. Slipping and banging your head on a boulder is just as detrimental as getting struck by rockfall from above.

Water
The more water that's present, the more difficult and dangerous the canyon.

- Drowning
  In canyons with significant water, everyone on the team should know how to swim. If there's a deep pool (e.g., too deep to stand) at the bottom of the pitch, excess rope in the water can become an entanglement hazard. Getting stuck under a waterfall in the middle of a rappel (ex: jammed descender) can be a life-threatening situation. Special techniques have been developed to mitigate these risks. We'll talk more about them in later chapters.

  If lots of swimming is expected, consider bringing additional flotation.

- Water Levels
  The flow rate on a given creek can vary dramatically from year to year and season to season. A canyon that's beginner-friendly in August could be suicidal to enter in February. Flow in the Pacific Northwest reaches its lowest in late summer, but water levels will increase during and after big precipitation events.

  Before committing to the canyon, evaluate the flow. Does it match your expectations? How experienced is your team? Given today's conditions, can your team run the canyon safely? Avoid succumbing to "canyon fever." Fatal accidents have occurred when groups were unwilling to back off from an objective, even though they knew the flow was too high. Always try to have a Plan B in your back pocket.

  If you're on the fence about entering the canyon, it's better to err on the side of safety. Why not come back another day when there'll be less stress and more fun?

March 2017 – High Flow

May 2016 – Moderate-Low Flow

Stafford Creek (Ore.) at different times of the year.
This is the same waterfall.

- Temperature

  Jumping into pools and rappelling through waterfalls is marvelous fun on a hot summer day, but can be a serious hypothermia risk at other times of the year. According to *Rescue 3 International*, cold water saps heat from the human body 25 times faster than air. This is an effect that's magnified in fast-moving water.[5] Having proper insulation (i.e., a full-body wetsuit) makes a huge difference in your canyon comfort. It's the difference between a fun romp vs. a "let's get the hell out of here" freeze-fest. Well-protected canyoneers will be floating in every pool they can find, whereas the unprepared will be having a bad day and doing their utmost to stay out of the water.

  Hypothermia sets in quickly; it's a condition that leads to fumbling, stumbling, and poor decision-making. This is not a road you want to be on while descending a technical canyon. Inadequate water protection has led to fatal accidents.

- Flash Floods

  Flash floods are usually caused by heavy rain associated with thunderstorms and are more common in desert environments. The ground is unable absorb the rainwater, so it runs off all at once. A dry canyon is transformed into a raging torrent. Note that flash floods are not always instantaneous. Depending on the terrain and conditions, there can be a considerable lag between the storm and the arrival of the flood. In the Desert Southwest, people have been killed under blue skies by a flood from a storm that took place 30km (~20mi) away. Even beginner-friendly canyons can become death traps.[6]

**A minor drainage scoured by a debris flow.
Note the lack of vegetation on the canyon walls.**

Always check the forecast before entering the canyon: both the local forecast and, if applicable, that of the headwaters. If you have any doubts, play it safe and don't go.

In the Desert Southwest, the Golden Rule is:
If inclement weather threatens, go somewhere else!
It's not worth your life.

Flash floods can happen in the Pacific Northwest too, but are less common in the Cascades. Forested areas will generally have a slower run-off with water levels rising and falling over an extended period of time. Floods in the mountains are more likely to be the result of a hillside or natural dam giving way. In alpine areas, flooding could be the result of a glacial release.[7]

Even apart from the threat of flooding, running canyons in the rain may not be the best of ideas. Rainy days are colder, and everything's a little more slippery. While it might be possible to run the canyon, why not come back on a nicer day when you'll have more fun?

---

[5] Rescue 3 International. *Water and Flood Rescue Manual - v4.2*. Rescue 3 International, 2015.

[6] Schaffer, G. "Special Report: The Keyhole Seven." *Outside Online* (May 2016).
https://www.outsideonline.com/2072666/special-report-keyhole-seven

[7] Columbia Gorge News. "One dead in Mt. Hood NF flash flood." *Columbia Gorge News* (August 2014).
https://www.columbiagorgenews.com/news/one-dead-in-mt-hood-nf-flash-flood

> **Flash Floods**
>
> Warning signs: a sudden increase in water level, often accompanied by floating debris and clouds of sediment. The sound of roaring water may be heard upstream. Big floods can carry along enormous logs and boulders. Floods usually kill by trauma, not drowning.
>
> Never attempt to outrun a flash flood. Go for the high ground immediately; the higher the better. Ditch your pack if you have to. The inside of a creek bend may be safer than the outside. Large trees and well-established vegetation may indicate places of safety as they haven't been affected by previous floods. Once in a safe place, wait patiently for the water levels to subside. Depending on the nature of the event, it may take hours or days to return to normal.

- Swiftwater Hazards

  As the amount of water in the canyon increases, other water hazards will start to appear. Hydraulics, a basin filled with recirculating water, can appear at the foot of waterfalls. Strong hydraulics can trap and hold floating objects, such as an unwary swimmer. Overcoming such obstacles requires training and advanced canyon techniques. We'll talk more about swiftwater hazards in Chapter 19.

Poison Oak

Devil's Club in winter

Local Flora & Fauna

Here are a few local hazards found in the Pacific Northwest:

- Poison Oak

  Some fortunate few are not allergic, but everyone should learn to recognize and avoid. The plant actually looks quite different depending on the season. Poison oak prefers partial sun and generally doesn't grow in drainages with significant water. It's more likely to be found when entering or leaving the canyon. A reaction to poison oak occurs 24–72 hours after exposure and persists for about two weeks. To avoid, wear long pants, long sleeves, gloves, and rinse off any contaminated garments as soon as possible.

- Devil's Club
A big-leafed plant species found in swampy drainages throughout the Pacific Northwest. Both the leaves and stems are covered in nasty-looking spines that break off easily on contact. As with poison oak, avoid with long pants, long sleeves, and gloves.

- Rattlesnakes
Encountered more frequently in desert areas and on the eastern slopes of the Cascades. Snakes generally want nothing to do with you and will move away if they sense you coming. Don't surprise them.

- Yellowjackets
In late summer, western yellowjackets begin nesting in dry rotting logs and ground burrows. Keep a sharp eye out when entering/leaving a canyon and leave some space between party members. If allergic, carry appropriate medications and let the team know ahead of time.

- Ticks
Nasty parasites found increasingly throughout the Cascades. They can carry a variety of diseases. DEET is an effective deterrent, but is not recommended in aquatic canyons as it'll wash off into the creek. Best advice: wear long pants and check yourself thoroughly post-trip.

Desert Southwest
Sandstone canyons have some unique features/hazards that are worth a mention for familiarity. Avoidance is probably the best plan until you've gained more experience.

- Keeper Potholes[8]
A pothole is a basin or pit carved by falling water at the foot of a drop. Potholes can be dry or contain water. Keepers are a dangerous subcategory that can trap an unwary canyoneer. When full, a keeper is not really a threat – one can hop in and swim right across. Later in the season, its true nature becomes apparent. You can rappel in, only to find that escape is impossible due to sheer featureless walls. In some keepers, the remaining water may be too deep to stand which complicates an exit. Pothole escapes may require aid-climbing, advanced canyon techniques, or climbing up on the shoulders of a partner.

- High Stemming
Some slot canyons are so narrow that it's physically impossible to walk along the bottom. It might be less than 15cm (~6in) from wall to wall. Canyoneers use chimneying, bridging, and counterforce moves, sometimes traveling 6m (~20ft) or more above the canyon floor. High stemming is slow, strenuous, and does not lend itself to wearing a pack. If you have a pack at all, it's usually small and is clipped to your harness with a tether. The pack either hangs below you, or is moved along behind you as you climb. High stemming can quickly become complicated if the canyon bells out underneath you. Some skinny canyons require expert rock-climbing skills.

Best Practices

Physical Fitness
Before running a canyon, make sure you're in shape to do so. Canyoning is surprisingly demanding and strenuous. A long approach or exit (compounded with bushwhacking) can wear you out, but the canyon itself will also take a toll. In aquatic canyons, everything underfoot is loose and slippery, requiring constant attention and balance. It's a full-body non-aerobic workout, made even harder if carrying a pack. It's never a bad idea to get out there well in advance of your trip for some solid conditioning.

---

[8] Keeper potholes are rare in the Pacific Northwest. In 2018, one was discovered at Curly Creek Falls in southern Washington State. It's believed to have formed where the creek cut through an underlying lava cave.

Have Sufficient Training

Aquatic canyons are not the place to be rappelling for the very first time. It's much safer to learn techniques in a dry environment and become fully proficient. Continue to build your skill set by taking classes and going on trips with more experienced canyoneers. When starting off in your canyon career, it's best to start with easy canyons and work your way up from there.

- **Beginners "leading" beginners is a major cause of accidents in canyoning.** Enthusiasm is not a substitute for training.

- Be aware: descending popular canyons in places such as Zion National Park will not teach you much about canyoning. Similarly, running dry canyons will not prepare you for those with significant water. Canyons with a little flowing water will not prepare you for serious swiftwater. Taking a class or three is highly recommended. It's fun and you'll learn a lot.

- Support skills such as navigation, wilderness first aid, and swiftwater rescue are also valuable.

- Keep practicing. Skills that you don't use frequently will slip away.

- Techniques, technology, and best practices change with the times. It's good to keep up with the latest developments. Don't make the mistake of assuming you've seen everything.

Bring the Right Gear

Do your homework and bring the gear you need for the canyon. In the Pacific Northwest, you'll almost certainly want a wetsuit. If you only have limited beta, extra ropes and gear may provide an additional margin of safety. We'll go into a lot more detail on proper attire, water protection, and what to carry in Chapter 3.

- Bringing the right gear doesn't do you a lot of good if you don't know how to use it.

- Before the trip, make sure your gear is in good working order.

- Verify everyone has the gear they need before departure. This includes both your personal kit (e.g., wetsuit, helmet, harness, headlamp, food, and water) and group gear (e.g., sufficient ropes, anchor material, group first aid kit, and an emergency beacon).

Know Your Team

Get to know your teammates ahead of time, especially their background, experience, and skill level. Do they know how to self-rescue? Could they rescue someone else in an emergency? What level of medical training, if any, do they have? Running canyons with several expert canyoneers and a Wilderness First Responder (WFR) is quite different from a group of beginners that you just met on the internet. Always choose a canyon that's appropriate for the experience level of your team.

- Does anyone have any medical conditions that the group should know about? If, for example, you carry an epinephrine kit, it's good to let the team know. (See also "Before Entering the Canyon" in Chapter 25.)

Keep It Simple

Follow the KISS principle: Keep It Safe & Simple. Avoid overly-complicated rigging, anchors, and rappel systems. The more steps that are involved in a given process, the greater the potential for human error.

- Simple systems are also easier to inspect.

Avoid Complacency

Rappels are performed so frequently when canyoning that they start to become routine. Don't get complacent about it. Try to avoid taking shortcuts. Some examples include:

- Assuming pre-existing anchors are "bombproof" and forgoing inspection.
- Not clipping into an anchor, using a safety line, or being belayed while moving around above a drop.

o   Not double-checking ropework systems.
o   Skipping safety checks when setting up to rappel.
o   Not paying attention while rappelling. (Does your rope actually reach the bottom?)

Bad habits are reinforced through repetition. "Well, nothing bad happened last time …" Resist the temptation to cut corners and instead try to develop good habits to promote safety for you and your team. Don't let your guard down. Rappels must be set up correctly every single time.

Be Smart
Use caution and avoid getting in over your head. Play it safe and don't take unnecessary risks. Don't go down canyons you're not ready for. Be flexible and ready to change plans if the weather deteriorates or water levels are too high. Don't go alone.

- Always tell someone where you're going. Leave a route description and the approximate time that you'll be back. This might be the only way you'll get rescued if you get stranded mid-canyon.

- Take responsibility and try to be as self-sufficient as possible. If you run into a problem, be prepared to fix it. Deep in the canyon, outside help may be many hours, or even days, away.

- Most important of all: **You are responsible for your own safety!**

After the Trip
Canyoning has a way of beating up both you and your gear. Inspect your ropes, harness, and other gear on a regular basis for signs of wear, abrasion, and damage. Retire your gear before your gear retires you.

Keith Campbell rappelling Stafford Falls, Ore.
(Photo: Karl Helser)

Chapter 2: Leave No Trace

Most readers will already be familiar with the principles of *Leave No Trace* (LNT). *Leave No Trace* is a set of guidelines formalized in the 1990s to promote outdoor conservation and ethics. They're intended to be adapted to any recreational activity. With the increasing popularity of canyoning in the Pacific Northwest, it's important to establish good practices to minimize impact. By minimizing our impact, we can continue to visit these beautiful places in a sustainable manner.

Preparation & Planning Ahead

We've already discussed this aspect of *Leave No Trace* quite a bit already in the previous chapter. Advance planning increases group safety and helps avoid many problems. Knowing the height of the tallest rappel, for instance, helps ensure that the team brings enough rope. Conversely, poor planning and being unprepared can lead to becoming lost, getting stranded mid-canyon, hypothermia, accidents, etc. In a rescue, safety will take priority over environmental concerns, so, by making good plans, we can avoid rescues and also protect the environment.

- In popular canyons, try to avoid times of high use. Consider visiting during the off-season, mid-week, or get an early start to avoid the crowds.

- Always try to have a backup plan in case your first choice falls through. "If the flow's too high to run the canyon today, we'll go over here and run this other canyon instead." If you have a backup plan already queued up, your trip will never be a failure.

The Problem with Large Groups

Canyoning is definitely a team sport, but there is such a thing as too many people. It depends on the difficulty of the canyon and current conditions, but 4–6 is often a nice size. Smaller groups allow for reasonable speed and can still comfortably carry all the ropes and gear the party requires.

Big groups are slower, noisier, and have a greater environmental impact. If you have a large team and sufficient leadership, consider splitting into two (or more) smaller groups instead.

- How long will it take? Let's say this canyon has ten rappels and each person requires three minutes to set up, rappel, and disconnect at the bottom of the pitch:

Group of four:	4 x 10 x 3 = 2 hours.
Group of ten:	10 x 10 x 3 = 5 hours.

  There are some ways to speed things up, but … *ouch!* Note that this calculation is rappel time only and doesn't include the approach, exit, or travel between rappels, all of which will take longer with a big group. This calculation also assumes that everyone is competent and everything goes well on every rappel. Big groups and long/complex canyons may not mix well.

- Big groups will require more time to get through technical sequences, so this may mean more time spent standing around and more opportunities to get cold.

Travel on Durable Surfaces

When hiking off-trail, it's important to stay on durable surfaces to minimize impact. The riparian environment of aquatic canyons is fragile. It doesn't take many people hiking along the bank or detouring around obstacles before a social trail gets worn in. The going may be slower, but the best way to avoid impact is to stay in the watercourse. If land travel is necessary, for time or other considerations, try to spread out rather than concentrating your impact in a single area. It's not always possible, but an even better solution would be to exit the canyon entirely.

- Use roads and existing trails as much as possible to enter/exit the canyon. Consult maps to find ways in and out that minimize erosion. Smaller side drainages are often a good means of access.

- As with established trails, light maintenance in the canyon is permitted under *Leave No Trace*. When practical, branches and other storm debris can be cleared away to encourage visitors to stay in the watercourse. This is a particularly good thing to do in popular canyons.

- Desert Southwest: Avoid hiking in areas of cryptobiotic soil. Damage to the fragile crust (ex: footprints) can take years to fully recover.

When possible, try to stay in the watercourse … **… even when on rappel.**

Rappelling in the Watercourse

When conditions and anchors permit, try to rappel in the watercourse or adjacent to it. Canyon walls in the Pacific Northwest are frequently covered with lush mosses, hanging ferns, and other delicate vegetation. Rappelling out of the water increases the risk of trampling plant life and leaving ugly streaks of torn moss. It doesn't take many rappellers before a "vertical trail" gets created down the pitch.

- When water levels are high, safety will dictate that rappels take place out of the water.

- Teams lacking adequate water protection (i.e., no wetsuits) are more likely to rappel out of the water. This can increase the odds of environmental damage.

- When rappelling outside the watercourse, do your best to practice good rappel technique. Trust the anchor and slt back in your harness. Ideally, your feet should be about shoulder-width apart with your legs perpendicular to the rock surface. This stance allows for deliberate foot placement. Try to avoid dragging your feet and crushing the fragile vegetation. (See also "Rappel Stance" in Chapter 15.)

Desert Southwest: Rope Grooving

One impact problem unique to sandstone environments is rope grooving. Sandstone is a relatively "soft" sedimentary rock and a moving rope coming in contact with it can quickly etch out deep permanent grooves. In addition to being unsightly, these grooves can trap ropes during the pull (i.e., one rope strand pinching the other). Grooving is considered extremely bad form in the Desert Southwest. When running sandstone canyons, try to use anchors that will minimize the rope's contact with rock surfaces.

Courtesy anchors, edge protection, and retrievable rigging can all be used to help reduce groove formation. (We'll introduce these techniques in Chapters 4 and 13 respectively.)

An extreme case of grooving caused by canyoneers wrapping their rope directly around a sandstone boulder. The sling was added later, after the damage was done.

What We Leave Behind

Leave No Trace espouses a "pack it in / pack it out" ethic. If you bring it into the canyon, take it out with you. Some schools of thought suggest that organic biodegradable material is okay to discard, but it's not good for wildlife and, often, takes a surprisingly long time to fully decompose. It's best to pack it out too. Don't leave pistachio shells scattered around the rappel station for the next party. Not cool.

- Try to minimize the use of sunscreen, lotions, and insect repellent which can wash off into the creek. Even biodegradable options can affect water quality.

- Sanitation: do your business at least 60m (~200ft) away from the water or, better yet, not in the canyon at all. Nobody wants to be hiking through "TP flowers" in a tight slot canyon. Yack.

- Please pack out any trash and leave the canyon cleaner than you found it. Lost party balloons are the author's special nemesis. They're a great way to send litter deep into the backcountry.

- It's good to check on local environmental issues. In some countries, there are concerns about canyoneers transporting invasive species between creeks.[9] Accidental transportation can often be avoided by cleaning your gear and letting it dry completely between outings. As of this writing, there are no known issues regarding invasive species in Pacific Northwest canyons.

- Gear is cheap, but life is not. While we strive to follow *Leave No Trace* and leave the canyon clean, all gear is expendable if it means getting home safely. Sometimes, abandoning gear is only a temporary measure. Make a plan to come back and retrieve it at a later date.

---

[9] One example is *Didymosphenia germinata* (aka Didymo), an invasive alga that can be carried on wetsuits and footwear. It's a serious problem for New Zealand canyoneers. It's native to North America.

American Dipper nest hidden behind a waterfall.

Respect Wildlife

Occasionally, you'll encounter wildlife during canyon forays; from the errant frog to the more charismatic mega-fauna such as deer, elk, or bears. Cascade drainages are also home to some unique and interesting species, such as the Pacific Giant Salamander. Sometimes, you'll find fish living in the pools between the waterfalls.

Avoid getting too close to animals, touching them, or picking them up. It's better to observe from a distance and avoid stressing them. Do not grab the wildlife.

- Some species of birds, such as the American Dipper, make their nests behind waterfalls. If you encounter a nest while rappelling, try to avoid it. If possible, signal the team to move the anchor to another location.

- Bears and cougars are not a serious threat in the Cascades and will usually run away before you can get your camera out. Consider yourself lucky to see one.

Be Courteous to Other Visitors

We're not alone out there. Canyons are visited by many others, including hikers, hunters, fishermen, photographers, and, sometimes, a family out for a swim on a hot summer day. Canyoning is still in its infancy in the Pacific Northwest and other wilderness users can sometimes react negatively; perhaps voicing opinions that rappelling is extremely dangerous and you should not be doing it. Consider taking a moment to assuage their concerns. Be friendly and answer any questions they might have about what you're up to. Poor encounters can lead to complaints, which, in turn, leads to more rules and regulations for canyoneers by the local authorities. When talking with others, you're also representing the local canyon community.

- Try to avoid rappelling *show waterfalls* (i.e., waterfalls that see high numbers of tourists, hikers, and photographers). Individuals climbing, rappelling, or slack-lining on or around such falls are far more likely to garner negative reactions and complaints from the general public. Sometimes, it's viewed as being disrespectful. If you must rappel such falls, try to visit early in the morning or on weekdays when the number of other visitors will be low.

- If you encounter other canyoneers, allow the faster party to move on by and give them some space. Try to avoid bottlenecking at rappel stations.

- Keep the volume down. Consider hand signals instead of shouted rappel commands. Bellowing "OFF RAPPEL!" at the top of your lungs will not endear you to other canyon visitors.

- While drones have some benefits from a canyoning perspective (e.g., scouting and taking reference photos), be aware that some people find them highly obnoxious. Check on local regulations too. Drones are illegal in Wilderness areas and most National Parks.

- Avoid putting on a show for other visitors and change in/out of your wetsuit somewhere out of sight.

Anchors & Minimizing Impact

Like alpine climbing, canyoning is one of the few outdoor sports where it's acceptable to leave anchors and other gear behind in order to permit a safe descent.

- Try to use dull, natural-colored webbing that blends in with the environment. Black webbing (the color of shadows) is best as it can be used anywhere in the world. Brightly-colored webbing sticks out like a sore thumb and is particularly obnoxious to waterfall photographers.[10]

- Avoid leaving anchors where they're visible or easily accessed by the general public. The presence of anchors may encourage the inexperienced to try to follow you. Ghosting techniques (see below) can sometimes be used to avoid leaving anything behind. Alternatively, consider hiking back up to the top afterward to clean the anchor.

- If leaving an anchor, don't use more material than you need to. Avoid leaving fixed ropes.

Bolts

Bolting is something of a dilemma under *Leave No Trace* as it's a more-or-less permanent addition to the canyon. Some would argue, however, that the goal in climbing and canyoning is to minimize impact, not avoid it completely, so therefore bolting, when necessary, is an acceptable practice.[11] Bolting is also a practice which is easily abused. Installing a bolt station right next to a bombproof tree is clearly bad form. There are good reasons to bolt and good reasons not to bolt. We'll talk more about the ethics of bolting in Chapter 6.

The *Leave No Trace Center for Outdoor Ethics* takes the following stance on bolts:

- Prior to placing hardware, check in with local land managers to get familiar with any rules and regulations.
- If specific rules are lacking, default to local bolting practices.

Deep in a canyon, it's unlikely that anyone will see the bolts except other canyoneers. In places visited by the general public, however, bolts should be placed where they're hidden or unobtrusive. Sometimes, the first rappel into the canyon is deliberately left unbolted to deter the unprepared.

Ghosting

Ghosting is the ability to descend a canyon and leave nothing behind. Basic ghosting includes downclimbing, slides, and jumps. Advanced ghosting involves the use of *retrievable systems* (i.e., a rigging or anchor system that can be recovered from the bottom of the pitch). Retrievable rigging, however, is inherently riskier and requires a greater degree of judgement and experience to use. Ghosting is a great thing to strive for, but don't take it to extremes. It has limits, and safety comes before ethics.

- Retrievable systems are used less frequently in aquatic canyons. The more water that's present, the more you should look to alternate rigging techniques.

---

[10] An observant reader will note that brightly-colored webbing is used in many examples throughout this manual. This is done for visual clarity and is not an endorsement of the practice.

[11] It should be noted that rock climbers have been bolting remote crags for decades.

Benefits of Ghosting

- Ghosting is a good idea in places that are visible or easily accessed by the general public. The lack of anchors makes it harder for the inexperienced to follow you.

- Conservation of anchor material. The same anchor/rigging system can be used again and again while descending the canyon. If an anchor must be left behind, ghosting techniques can sometimes be used to reduce the amount of material required. This is useful on first descents.

- Minimize environmental impact. Ghosting can protect trees from rope abrasion and reduce grooving in sandstone environments.

- Keeps the canyon clean and allows others to share the same experience that you did.

- In some cases, ghosting is faster than building a fixed anchor.

When to Avoid Ghosting

- Traditional fixed anchors are a better choice when rappelling in high flow or if the pitch is full of brush/obstacles.

- Ghosting isn't a good idea in popular canyons. Removing pre-existing anchors and ghosting the drops may cause beginners to get into trouble.

- If the team is exhausted or in a rush to get out of a canyon (ex: trying to get out before dark), ghosting may not be a great idea. Follow the KISS principle and keep rappelling simple.

Ghosting sounds great, but, surprisingly, it isn't always the most environmentally-friendly solution. Let's imagine the team arriving at the top of a rappel. There's a great tree for an anchor here, but reaching it requires scrambling up a 3m (~10ft) vegetated embankment. If everyone visiting the canyon is sending someone up to rig an anchor, it doesn't take long before a trail gets worn in. Even a fixed anchor on the tree isn't a great solution as someone will need to go up and inspect it. From an environmental standpoint, the best anchor is one that doesn't require leaving the watercourse at all.

What About a Virtual *Leave No Trace*?

This is the Age of the Internet. Posting detailed beta, blog entries, GPS tracks, videos, and photos of that awesome canyon you ran last weekend leads to increased awareness which has both pros and cons. Adding beta to public forums is a great way to give back to the local canyon community and allows others to share your experience. Ideally, with more awareness comes a greater desire to protect these special places and increased support for conservation. On the other hand, increased awareness can also be detrimental if it unleashes a flood of careless visitors. Posting beta of any kind can have a definite impact on the real world. When providing information online, always be aware of your audience. Websites, print media, and television can reach even larger audiences.

- Most modern cameras and phones will capture your GPS coordinates when taking a photo. This information is included automatically in the photo's digital headers. Consider turning this feature off.

- Instead of "checking in" or tagging specific locations, consider tagging an entire region or state.

Zach Kiefer rappelling Thunder Falls, Wash.
(Photo: Kevin Clark)

Chapter 3: Gear

Before heading out to run a canyon, there's a lot to know about proper gear and attire. Your kit will vary depending on the nature of the canyon, current conditions, experience level, group size, personal preference, and other factors. If you're just getting into canyoning, it's wise to borrow or rent gear at first. See how you like the sport before making any big investments.

- Be aware: this chapter is tailored to the Pacific Northwest and may not be relevant for canyons elsewhere.

- Bringing the right gear doesn't do you a lot of good if you don't know how to use it.

Proper Attire

Clothing & Layers

Proper canyon attire is synthetic and quick-drying, suitable for wading and swimming. Avoid expensive apparel as canyons can be hard on gear.

- Long sleeves and long pants will keep you from getting shredded while bushwhacking.

- Bring a rainshell. An old shell, paddle jacket, or dry top worn over a wetsuit is surprisingly effective at keeping you a little warmer. The shell reduces convective heat loss.

- It's not be a bad idea to carry some extra dry layers (e.g., wool, fleece, or polypro). Extra layers become important if the team needs to stop for an extended period of time (i.e., an emergency or an unexpected overnight bivy in the canyon).

Wetsuit

A wetsuit will greatly increase your canyon comfort, especially on chilly days and in cold water. The best wetsuits are the full body variety (either one or two piece) with long sleeves/pants and reinforced elbows/knees. A 4/3mm is the recommended minimum. Go with thicker neoprene if you run cold. Thick wetsuits are pretty much mandatory for high mountain creeks or when running canyons in the off-season. Wetsuits should be snug, but not restrict movement. An ill-fitting or baggy wetsuit will only provide limited insulation as more water can get inside. A number of companies make canyon-specific wetsuits.

- FAQ: "What's worn under a wetsuit?" Your preference: a swimsuit, skivvies, or nothing. Extra layers of rash guard or neoprene might be worn over or under the wetsuit for extra insulation.

- Shorties and Farmer John/Jane style wetsuits are not recommended unless it's really hot. Similarly, thin wetsuits (2–3mm) are unlikely to provide adequate insulation.

- Thick wetsuits sometimes come with an integrated hood. Hoods will keep you warmer, but can limit your hearing. Some canyoneers will wear a thin neoprene skull cap or balaclava under their helmet.

- A rainshell worn over your wetsuit will help block evaporative cooling.

- In some canyons, you might be able to get away without a wetsuit on a blazingly hot summer day. You still might be more comfortable with one, however.

- Drysuits (with sufficient fleece) provide superior warmth, but may not always be the best choice in the Pacific Northwest. Local forests and canyons tend to be full of sharp pointy things. If your drysuit gets punctured, water will start to seep in and your canyon comfort will plunge. Additionally, drysuits don't provide as much buoyancy in deep water. They're also expensive and require periodic maintenance.

FAQ: "Do I really need a wetsuit?"
In the Pacific Northwest: most likely, yes. The party line says: wear a wetsuit if the combined air and water temperature is less than 50° C (~120° F). Some other factors that may influence your decision: how much water is present, how much swimming is expected, if you'll be rappelling through waterfalls, the size of your group, weather, local snowpack, etc. Tight canyons are often deep, shaded, and chilly. Adequate water protection makes the trip a lot more fun.

- Avoid hiking around in a wetsuit on a hot summer day. Neoprene doesn't breathe and it becomes a total sweat-fest. (See also "Thermoregulation" in Chapter 25.)

- Desert Southwest: Pools at the bottom of tight slot canyons receive little-to-no sunlight. It's almost impossible to believe how cold the water is until you experience it for yourself. If a significant amount of water is present, a wetsuit is probably a good plan.

Care & Feeding of your Wetsuit
The canyon environment is a harsh one on gear. While wetsuits act like body armor to a degree, they're not indestructible. If you have a nice wetsuit or are renting one, it's good to take steps to avoid unnecessary abuse. It'll last a lot longer.

- Avoid bushwhacking in your wetsuit. It'll eventually tear the legs to ribbons. If significant off-trail travel is expected, it's better to change out of your wetsuit first.

- Canyon-specific harnesses usually come with an integrated polyvinyl-chloride (PVC) seat that will protect the wetsuit when sliding around on abrasive rock. Other companies make similar seat products that fit most harnesses.

- Wearing a pair of shorts over your wetsuit is another way to prevent damage. Some canyoneers take it a step further by wearing hiking pants or a caving-style coverall.

- If lacking seat-protection, try to minimize how much sliding you do.

Kneepads
Kneepads are nice on difficult rappel starts and will help prevent wetsuit damage. Cheap volleyball kneepads work quite well; they're soft and are pulled on right over the joint. A larger size may be required if worn over a wetsuit. Some canyoneers wear shin guards for added protection.

- Desert Southwest: Kneepads (and, sometimes, elbow pads) are pretty much mandatory in tight slots with lots of stemming and chimney moves. Consider them part of your battle armor.

Footwear
Most approach shoes or light hiking boots are fine, provided they're sturdy, synthetic, and have decent tread and ankle support. Open-toe footwear and thin-soled recreational water shoes should be avoided: your toes will get mashed. Footwear with openings along the sides should also be avoided; they'll let in all manner of small rocks, jabbing sticks, and irksome debris.

Combine your footwear with a pair of neoprene socks (2–7mm).[12] Some canyoneers prefer heavy synthetic or wool socks, but neoprene will keep your feet warmer. If your feet feel like blocks of ice, that's a clear sign that it's time to upgrade. More insulation will be required on chilly days, in mountain creeks, and during the off-season.

---

[12] Some neoprene booties will not fit inside a standard hiking boot. It's a good idea to test your footwear solution at home before entering the canyon.

- Felt-soled waders are one solution used by fishermen. Con: They're illegal in some parts of the United States as they've been shown to be a vector for transporting invasive species. Check on local regulations.

- A number of companies make canyon-specific footwear. The sticky rubber sole usually provides excellent traction, but they're expensive. Even with the best footwear available, it can still feel like being at the ice rink. Some creeks are more slippery than others.

Gloves

Some canyoneers like wearing gloves; others do not. Leather gloves will protect your hands while bushwhacking and rappelling. Note that canyons will slowly destroy them, so cheap leather gardening gloves are preferred. Some canyoneers wear neoprene gloves with reinforced palms.

- Sometimes, gloves will keep your hands a little warmer. If the water's really cold, however, wet gloves can work against you (i.e., continuing to pull heat from your hands long after you're out of the water).

- Con: Wearing gloves makes it harder to tie knots. Fingerless gloves might be a compromise.

Eyewear

Swim masks and goggles are useful for scouting pools (i.e., checking the depth for a jump) and can make rappelling through waterfalls a little more comfortable.

- Falling water and pools can be problematic for anyone with corrective lenses. Leashes can be used to avoid losing eyeglasses. For contact lens wearers, a pair of swim goggles might be a good solution. If you wear corrective lenses (glasses or contacts), be sure to bring an extra pair.

- Sunglasses generally aren't worn in aquatic canyons. They're easily lost or broken.

A variety of ways to keep things dry.

Packs & Keeping Things Dry

In aquatic canyons, there are many things that need to be kept dry: any extra layers, the map, canyon beta, first aid kit, electronics, and your lunch. Typically, such gear is stored in kegs or dry bags inside your pack.

Backpacks

For packs, 40–50 liters is a good size to shoot for. Canyons are hard on gear, so go durable over cheap. A narrow pack profile is superior for bushwhacking and squeezing through tight spaces. Avoid external pockets and strapping things to the outside. Packs should be large enough to carry a rope bag cinched down under the lid or stored inside.

- Be aware: a standard backpack (i.e., a non-canyon specific pack) can fill with water when swimming or passing through a waterfall. You'll need to dump it out afterwards. A quick and dirty solution: install a set of grommets in the sides and bottom to facilitate drainage.[13]

- A kayak portage pack is a large dry bag with backpack straps. These might seem a good solution for canyoning, but will seep after prolonged immersion. If a portage pack gets punctured, it's immediately compromised.

- A number of companies make specialized canyon packs. These are generally quite burly, drain well upon exiting the water, and are designed to float. They're often equipped with quick-release buckles, internal loops for racking gear, and other special features. In aquatic canyons, vinyl packs are generally preferred as they don't absorb as much water.

Dry Kegs

Kegs provide superior water protection, but are bulky and expensive. Fragile items should be well-padded to avoid damage. Always make sure the lid is closed securely so that jumps and/or bag tosses won't unseat it.

- Wide-mouth Nalgene bottles make great mini-kegs for snacks and other small items.

Dry Bags

Dry bags come in many shapes and sizes. Read the fine print carefully as some are only water resistant. Prolonged immersion will result in seepage. Go for durable and waterproof.

- Be aware: overstuffed dry bags can rupture on a hard impact. This might happen when tossing packs into a pool or jumping.

- Mission-critical items can be double-bagged for added security. Con: This increases the amount of time required to access such items.

Electronics

Canyons are hard on electronics. Phones, cameras, car-key fobs, watches, GPS devices, radios, and emergency beacons may all require water protection. The author and his friends have lost more than a few cameras and phones between them. Waterproof pouches, kegs, and dry boxes are the way to go. If you get seriously into canyoning, consider investing in a waterproof phone/camera. It's a good idea to test your water protection systems before using them in the field.

- Don't place too much reliance on technology. High canyon walls will block reception, and some electronics will become useless if they get wet. Do you have a backup copy of the beta?

- If you carry an emergency beacon, it's a good idea to test its ability to transmit when deep in a canyon. Some beacons will not transmit unless they can first establish a GPS position.

---

[13] Packs lacking adequate drainage can be dangerous. If your pack fills while rappelling through a waterfall, it can become heavy and threaten to flip you on the rope. (See "Rappelling Through Waterfalls" in Chapter 15.)

Ropes

Static and semi-static (i.e., low-stretch) ropes are the standard in canyoning.[14] Minimal stretch makes rappelling and ascending easier, and gives the rope better abrasion resistance. Con: Static ropes don't take shock loading well. Using a static rope to belay above an anchor is not recommended.

Static ropes for canyoning generally range from 8–10mm. Skinny ropes are lighter in weight/bulk and absorb less water, but also require more care as they're less durable and cut-resistant. More rope management will be required. The 8mm end of the spectrum is probably best for experienced canyoneers, whereas the 9mm range seems to be the sweet spot between durability and weight. Larger diameter ropes will require less care and will stand up better to use and abuse.

- Brightly colored ropes are good for visibility. They're easier to spot in the middle of a waterfall or pool. It's also easier to spot tangles when using different colored ropes.

- New ropes are often highly twisted (e.g., a byproduct of being pulled off a spool) and prone to tangling. They can often be slippery on the first few rappels due to a coat of lubricant adhering to the rope fibers.

- It may be harder to untie knots in skinny pliable ropes.

- Beginners are more apt to damage ropes, so a larger diameter may be preferred when training.

---

[14] Static and semi-static ropes may have up to 5% stretch. For comparison, some dynamic ropes (those used by climbers) can stretch by as much as 25–35%.

- Beware tape, printed labels, and plastic caps on the ends of your rope.[15] Their presence can increase the odds of getting a rope stuck during deployment or retrieval.

- Desert Southwest: In sandstone environments, wet ropes will pick up a tremendous amount of silt which gets worked into the sheath. Dirty ropes can do an impressive amount of damage to your rappel device, its carabiner, and other gear in a very short period of time. A dynamic rope used in more than a few canyons should be retired from lead climbing.

FAQ: "How much rope do we need?"

The party line says: take the height of the tallest rappel and multiply by three. Bring at least that much rope. So, if the tallest rappel in the canyon is 30m (100ft), we should bring a minimum of 90m (300ft). This might seem excessive, but it's actually an insurance policy. If a rope gets damaged or stuck, you'll still have enough rope to escape the canyon.

Okay, let's say we bring 90m of rope. Let's look at some options:

➢ *Bring a single 90m rope.*
This works, but it's a lot of weight for one person to carry. If the rope gets stuck during the pull, you'll likely need to cut it order to escape the canyon.

➢ *Bring one 60m rope and one 30m rope.*
Two ropes are better for distributing weight and provide more options for speed. Sometimes, multiple rappels could be rigged, allowing the team to get down faster. Alternatively, one rope could be sent ahead to rig the next rappel while the team is still coming down the last one. Note that the 60m rope will be required to rig the big pitch.

➢ *Bring two 60m ropes.*
Another good option for speed. You have more rope than you need, but that's not necessarily a bad thing. Pack weight generally isn't much of a concern unless you have a small team or are running a very remote canyon. With two equal length ropes, you also don't need to worry about having a specific one available for the big rappel. This is a good choice when you have multiple *rigging teams* and are leap-frogging. (We'll introduce these topics later in Chapter 9.)

➢ *Bring three 30m ropes.*
This also works and provides options for speed. Note that two ropes must be tied together for any pitch greater than 15m (~50ft) which may slow you down a little.

- When running canyons with limited beta (ex: first descents), you may not know the height of the tallest pitch ahead of time. In this case, it's good to bring extra rope. Not having enough rope risks getting stranded mid-canyon.

- Extra ropes provide more options for speed and safety. If you're on a day outing and have a large group, there's really no real downside to carrying an extra rope. Some canyoneers will bring an extra rope equal to the height of the tallest pitch; this rescue rope always stays at the back. The same pack might also contain additional rescue gear and a group first aid kit.

- Don't believe everything you read. The beta might be correct that the tallest rappel in the canyon is 30m, but more rope will be required if the anchor is located 3m (~10ft) back from the top. In this case, a doubled 60m rope will not reach the ground. Different guidebooks will sometimes list wildly different heights for the same rappel.

---

[15] Technora has an extremely high melting point, so plastic caps are often placed on the rope ends by the manufacturer to prevent fraying. Caps can sometimes cause problems (ex: getting stuck in cracks). Consider removing them and applying a thin coat of superglue to the ends of the rope.

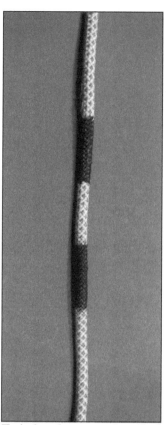

**Twin bands – a good method
of middle marking.**

Rope Marking & Shrinkage

It's a good idea to middle mark your ropes. Even on single-strand rappels it's handy to know where the mid-point is. Check with the manufacturer on the preferred method of marking. There are concerns that some marking methods can weaken or damage the rope fibers.

Repeated wet/dry cycles and regular use will cause some ropes to shrink significantly; sometimes by as much as 5–10% of their original length. Your rope, initially measured at 60m (~200ft), may now be 55m (~180ft). If the manufacturer does not pre-shrink their ropes, it's a good idea to get the rope thoroughly wet and let it dry before marking.

- Tip: One possible middle mark is a pair of black bands (each about 5cm or 2in wide) placed about 5cm apart at the center of the rope. If the rope length changes for any reason (e.g., shrinkage, or if the rope was damaged and had to be cut), the gap between the bands can be filled in and a new pair of bands established at the new mid-point.

- Markings will fade with time and wear. Re-mark as needed. It's good to check your ropes occasionally to ensure the mid-mark really is at the middle.

- Bi-color ropes are another solution, although marking may still be necessary if the rope shrinks or needs to be cut.

- Some canyoneers mark the rope ends with a series of symbols or color-coded tape to indicate the length. If a rope has a dedicated rope bag, the length could be written on the outside.

Other Ropes

- <u>Rescue Ropes</u>
  Groups will sometimes carry a short rescue rope, usually about 6–15m (20–50ft) in length. It's useful for scouting edges, rigging traverse lines, assisting rappellers on a difficult start, short-roping injured team members, etc. Shorter rope lengths are often coiled and carried in a pack or stuffed on top of the primary rope in a rope bag.

- <u>Throw Ropes</u>
  In swiftwater canyons, groups might carry one or more throw ropes for water rescue. These ropes are short, brightly-colored, and float. They're intended to be thrown to a swimmer, who can then be pulled to safety. They're not rated for rappelling. We'll talk more about them in Chapter 19.

- <u>Pull Cords</u>
  Some canyon techniques permit the use of a thin pull cord instead of a rope. The standard seems to be 5–6mm static cord. Pull cords are attractively compact/lightweight, but are far less versatile than a rope. They're used infrequently in aquatic canyons for a number of reasons. We'll discuss their pros and cons in Chapter 10.

Rope Bags

Rope bags are the standard in canyoning for the efficient deployment and transportation of ropes. They come in a variety of sizes. The bag keeps the rope from become snagged when bushwhacking, rappelling, or swimming. Inside the bag, the rope is flaked and ready for immediate use. (See Appendix III for more information on stowing ropes.)

- Some rope bags have built-in flotation to keep the rope from sinking in deep water.

Technical Gear

Helmet
Always wear a helmet. Losing your footing and banging your head on a boulder is just as bad as getting struck by rockfall from above. Other potential falling objects would include ropes, rope bags, and dropped gear. A helmet can also protect your head on a nasty pendulum swing. Many canyon accidents could have been prevented by wearing a helmet. Climbing helmets are the standard, although some canyoneers prefer kayaking helmets in aquatic canyons.

Harness
Almost any harness will work as long as it's comfortable to wear for extended periods. Harnesses are put on right over the wetsuit. It's going to get wet; it's fine.

- Your wetsuit will provide some additional padding.

- A number of companies make specialized canyon harnesses. They're quite burly, come with an integrated PVC seat, and have other special features. They usually have a horizontal belay loop or attachment point.[16]

- Beware hanging heavy items, such as rope bags and packs, from your gear loops. Some gear loops are only rated to hold about 5kg (~10–12lbs). Another option is to clip a carabiner around the waist belt of your harness. This creates a convenient place to hang the bag.

Minimizing Gear

Unlike climbing, try to minimize how much gear racked on your harness. Avoid being the *chandelier of gear* and stow anything you don't need/use regularly inside your pack. The more gear racked on your harness, the greater the odds of getting snagged when bushwhacking, rappelling, and swimming. In high flow, this becomes critical as getting caught on an underwater snag could be life-threatening.

- Tuck in any dangling loops/straps from your harness and pack. Anything hanging below about mid-thigh or in the working area of your harness should be secured. Slings and prusiks can be wound up into tight bundles. Tethers can be wrapped around you or tucked into your harness.

- Small items, such as carabiners, should be racked on your brake side to avoid interfering with the rappel. Everything else goes on your non-brake side.

- Anchor material is generally kept in your pack. Needing to build an anchor on the fly is a rare event when canyoning.

Carabiners
Locking carabiners are the standard; it's a good to carry 3–4 working carabiners on your harness. Large locking HMS carabiners (aka pear-abiners) are preferred as they're more versatile.

- Screw-lock carabiners are cheaper than the auto-locking variety. Both can be opened with one hand with a little practice.[17] Keylock style, with no notch near the gate, makes for easier clipping.

- Round-stock carabiners are preferred with some types of rigging (ex: munter hitch, carabiner block).

- Tip: Using different-colored carabiners makes it easier/faster to find your gear.

---

[16] Most modern descenders are designed for use on a harness with a horizontal attachment point. They can be used on alpine harnesses with a vertical belay loop, but this causes the descender to tilt out of alignment. One way to fix this problem is to use a short *rappel extension*. (See Appendix IV for more information.)

[17] Desert Southwest: Auto-locking carabiners can become jammed with grit and impossible to open.

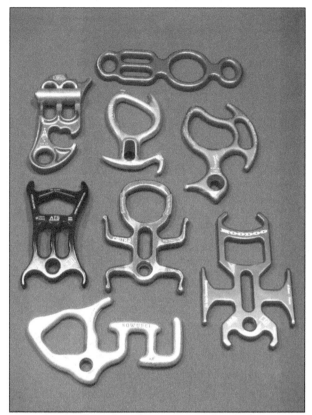

A selection of modern canyon descenders.

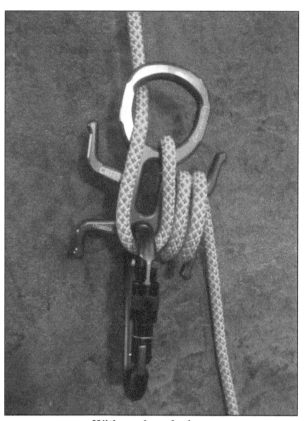

**With modern devices,
it's easy to add the friction on the fly.**

Descender (Rappel Device)

Canyoning has given rise to a wide variety of specialized descenders. Many are modifications of the classic figure-8 rappel device. These new designs have a number of advantages:

- On single-strand rappels, the friction settings are easily changed on the fly. This allows the rappeller to go as fast or slow as desired and accommodates a wide variety of ropes under different conditions.

- It's much easier to lock off and go hands-free with modern descenders.

- Most modern devices don't need to be removed from your harness when disconnecting from the rappel. This makes them harder to lose when exiting into deep water (e.g., too deep to stand).

- Figure-8 style devices tend to be more tolerant of twisted ropes. You may be able to rappel right past an obstruction that would stop a narrow-aperture device such as an ATC.

We'll take a closer look at two modern descenders: the *Pirana* and the *Critr* in Appendices IV and V respectively.

<u>Other Notes</u>

- Rappel devices that auto-lock or require a complex disconnect (ex: bar racks, bobbins, gri-gris) aren't recommended in aquatic canyons. The rappeller must be able to quickly disconnect from the rope.

- Always practice with unfamiliar devices and become fully proficient before using them in the field. If possible, try rappelling on a variety of ropes to get a feel for the friction settings required.

- All figure-8 style devices will introduce some amount of twisting into the rope. If the rope length has been set, this generally isn't a big deal. (See "Setting the Length" in Chapter 8.)

Air Traffic Controller (ATC)

While fine for rappelling dry pitches, an ATC is, at heart, a belay device. They're not recommended in aquatic canyons for a number of reasons:

- An ATC may not provide adequate friction on skinny ropes. This has been a factor in several accidents.[18]

- It's possible to add friction while rappelling, but it's cumbersome compared to modern devices. Locking off an ATC to go hands-free (ex: mule-overhand) is similarly awkward.

- An ATC must be removed from your harness when disconnecting from the rope. This creates a risk of losing the device when exiting a rappel into deep water.

- Two-strand rappels: If the rope strands below you become sufficiently tangled around each other (ex: moving water or a new rope), it can create an obstacle that a narrow-aperture device cannot pass.

ATCs are not recommended in aquatic canyons.

In the Desert Southwest, dirty ropes will quickly wear out ATCs and cause them to develop sharp edges. Use caution when rappelling on skinny ropes that are not as cut-resistant.

---

[18] The *ATC Guide* is rated for 9–11mm ropes on single-strand rappels; 7-11mm on double strand. Note that single-strand rappels are fairly common when canyoning. Experienced teams may be using ropes in the 8mm range.

Rigging a classic figure-8 device.   **"Vertaco" – one way to increase the friction.**

Classic Figure-8 Descender

Figure-8 descenders come in many shapes and sizes. They're still widely used in Europe and New Zealand, but are not as popular in the United States. They can be rigged in a number of ways with more or less friction. The classic figure-8 is better than the ATC for use in aquatic canyons, but still has some disadvantages and things to watch out for:

- Like the ATC, adding friction on the fly is cumbersome.

- When preparing to rappel, make sure that the descender is not cross-loading its dedicated carabiner.

- The photo above-left shows the standard way to rig a classic figure-8. If the rope is loaded into the device in the opposite direction, it opens the door to a potential problem. If the rope passing around the device's collar were to get dragged up over the body, it can snap up to become a girth hitch. This can happen when the device is scraped over the rock on a difficult rappel start.

- In standard mode, the descender must be removed from your harness in order to disconnect. This create a risk of losing the figure-8 in deep water.

While the classic figure-8 might not be your first choice for rappelling, you might carry one anyway as it has other applications in rigging. It also makes a great backup rappel device.

Ascenders

Every canyoneer should carry some means of climbing a rope and be ready to do so at any time. Typically, ascending requires a pair of *rope grabs*: either mechanical ascenders, friction hitches, or some combination thereof. These should always be available on your harness. We'll talk more about ascending systems in Chapter 17.

- Side-loading ascenders are preferred in aquatic canyons as they're fast to install on the rope. Imagine trying to tie a prusik on the rope while underneath a waterfall.

Safety Tethers (Leashes, Lanyards)

Be aware: the more loops and extra strands in your tether, the greater the potential it has to get caught on things. In aquatic canyons, a more streamlined system is generally preferred (i.e., a short section of dynamic rope with no loops at all). Avoid using chain-link style tethers, daisy chains, and Purcell prusiks. Long tethers will hang down, get in the way, and take more time to deploy and stow.

- All tethers should be sized to the individual for best efficiency.

- Avoid tethers made of low-stretch material, such as Dyneema or spectra.

- In canyoning, the ability to adjust the length of your tethers is nice, but isn't essential.

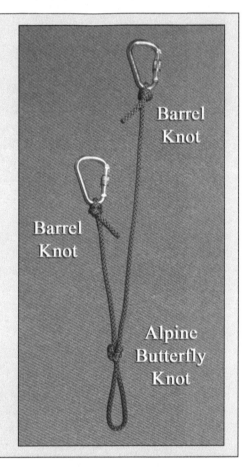

Cowstails

Many canyoneers use a pair of single-strand tethers known as *cowstails*. They are of different length (one long and one short) to facilitate the use of mechanical ascenders. They're also used for traversing safety lines, pack management, rappel extension, etc. Both tethers are made from a single piece of rope with no extra loops to get caught or snagged.

Making your own cowstails requires a 2.5m (~8ft) length of 9–10mm dynamic rope. To begin: tie a barrel knot on each end to house a locking carabiner. Next, tie an alpine butterfly knot in the middle. The butterfly knot can be clipped (or girth hitched) to your harness.[19] Once in place, the length of each tether can be adjusted.

- Short Tether
  Your short tether should be about as long as the crook of your elbow to the palm of your hand. When sized properly, the carabiner at the end of the tether should just reach your chin.

- Long Tether
  Install a hand ascender on a fixed rope and clip the long tether to it. Slide the device up as high as you can. When hanging completely from the tether, you should just be able to just touch the top of the ascender with your fingertips.

Foot Loop

For ascending, you'll also need a foot loop. Foot loops don't need to be life-safety rated, but should still be durable. A foot loop might be made for one or both feet, using cord, slings, or webbing. Commercial versions are also available. The exact size required will depend on your height and preferred ascension system. We'll talk more about proper sizing in Chapter 17.

- For best efficiency, foot loops should be made from low-stretch material. A quick and dirty solution is to use a nylon or Dyneema sling.

- Again, the ability to adjust the length of your foot loop is nice, but isn't required.

---

[19] If your harness has a "soft" attachment point, consider using a 10mm quick link to attach your cowstail. Soft fabric goods rubbing against each other will abrade more readily. Tighten down the gate with a pair of pliers.

Other Technical Gear

- Knives

  Knives are used to cut anchor material or free yourself in an emergency (ex: rope entanglement). The best knives are serrated and have a blunt tip. Knives should be easy to access, but also secured so that they cannot accidentally come open / get loose. Use caution as sharp blades and ropes don't mix well.

  Some canyoneers carry a folding blade that can be opened one-handed. The knife is locked in the closed position and clipped to a carabiner. Con: They can be difficult to open with gloves or while swimming.

  In canyons with more water, you'll probably want a fixed-blade water rescue knife. They're usually kept in on a sheath attached to your harness. Consider connecting the knife with a short breakaway cord or retractable tether to keep it from becoming lost.[20]

- VT Prusik

  A VT prusik is a short length of accessory cord with two small loops sewn or tied at either end. They come in a variety of sizes. The standard seems to be about 7–8mm in diameter and 70–80cm (~30in) long. The VT prusik has many uses in ropework. (For more information, see Appendix I.)

- Rescue Pulley

  Pulleys are useful for increasing the efficiency of mechanical advantage systems. They might be used to lift or haul during a rescue. Some canyoneers will carry specialized carabiners with a built-in pulley (ex: Petzl Rollclip). Progress capture pulleys (i.e. a pulley and cam in one) are also useful.

Marking Your Gear

It's a good idea to mark your gear so it can find its way back to you. Unfortunately, most marking methods don't last for long in aquatic canyons. Paint and nail polish wear off. Marking tape, stickers, and labels get wet and dissolve. It may be better to memorize the gear you carry (or keep a list back at the car). Get in the habit of performing a harness/pack check upon arriving back at the trailhead.

Anchor Material

The team, collectively, should bring enough material to rebuild every anchor in the canyon. This includes a good supply of webbing, plus a selection of quick links / rappel rings. On a first descent, an experienced team might also carry a bolt kit for additional security.

Webbing

It depends on the canyon, but team members should typically bring about 5–10m (20–30ft) of 14–26mm (9/16 to 1in) tubular webbing. Cut off what you need when building anchors.

- Use natural-colored webbing that will blend in with the environment. Greens and browns work well in the Pacific Northwest. When in doubt, go with black; the color of shadow. It can be used anywhere.

- Thinner varieties of tubular webbing have similar strength, but are lighter and less bulky. Con: It's also less abrasion and cut-resistant. Wider webbing is a better solution for long-term use.

- Use caution with flat webbing (i.e., non-tubular) as some varieties are stiff and difficult to tie. Again, tubular webbing may be a better solution for anchor longevity.

- Tip: It's not a bad idea to carry an extra sling or two on your harness. They can be used to connect unlinked bolts, as a backup foot loop, for rappel extension, to create a temporary clip-in point, or a quick anchor on the fly (i.e., a girth hitch on a tree).

---

[20] A quick test for aquatic canyons: can you access your knife one-handed with your eyes closed?

Typical 7mm quick link.

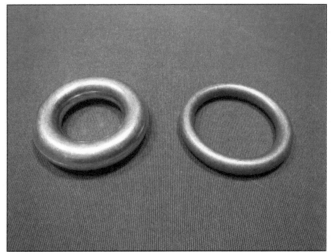

Solid-cast rappel ring (left) vs. hollow aluminum (right).

Quick Links[21]

Quick links are manufactured at many different levels of quality. The best ones are climb-rated, but are more expensive. Decent ones are usually stamped with a strength rating (ex: "SWL" or Safe Working Load). Beware unmarked knock-offs. Some unmarked ones are okay, but others are best used for hanging houseplants. It can be difficult to tell the good from the bad.

- Steel 6–8mm quick links are the standard in canyoning. They're reasonably lightweight and large enough to accommodate most ropes.

- Avoid very small quick links as large diameter ropes won't fit through them. If the rope has a tight fit, it'll be a harder pull from the bottom of the pitch.

- Avoid very large quick links. They're overkill for anchoring and can complicate the use of rope blocks. (We'll discuss this issue in Chapter 10.)

- Tip #1: Need to tighten down (or open) a quick link on the anchor? You might be able to use another quick link as an improvised wrench.

- Tip #2: Hang your quick links on an old non-locking carabiner. If you run out of quick links, the carabiner can be sacrificed to build an anchor.

Rappel Rings

Rappel rings can be used in lieu of quick links, although the good ones are of comparable price. The best rappel rings are solid-cast aluminum or titanium.

Avoid thin aluminum rings. Occasionally, you'll find them in pairs at rappel stations, but they're not a great solution for long-term use. The ring is a hollow shell of 1mm aluminum and it can fail quite suddenly upon wearing through. If you encounter such rings in popular canyons, consider replacing them as a public service.

> **Bolt Kits**
> Carrying a bolt kit might seem like a good idea for an extra margin of safety. This is true, provided you know how to set bolts. Don't expect to learn bolting on the fly, however. There's a lot to know about bolt placement and it's easy to do a poor job of it. We'll talk more about bolting ethics in Chapter 6.

---

[21] *Quick links* are also known as rapides, rapid links, screw links, C-links, maillons, etc. We'll refer to them as quick links throughout this manual.

Communication

Rushing water can make it difficult to hear verbal commands. Hand signals, whistles, and radios generally work better in aquatic canyons. (See also "Communication" in Chapter 7.)

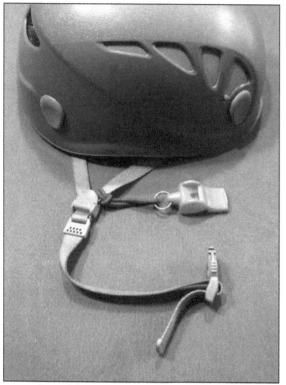

Attaching a whistle to your helmet.

Whistles

Everyone should carry a loud, reliable signal whistle; ideally one with no moving parts (pealess). Attach the whistle to your helmet with a thin elastic cord; stretchy hair ties work well. Hikers often attach a whistle to their pack, but this isn't a great solution for canyoning as the packs are sometimes sent down the pitch separately. If the whistle is on your helmet, then it's always with you.

- If the whistle's batting you in the face, attach a piece of Velcro to it and another to the side of your helmet. It can then be stowed up when not in use.

Radios

Handheld radios can be useful, but are expensive and aren't always reliable. In aquatic canyons, water protection will likely be required. One solution is to keep the radio in a thin waterproof pouch that's clipped to your harness. Ideally, the radio can be operated inside the pouch without ever opening it.

If using radios, make sure they're fully charged pre-trip and that everyone knows how to use them. Before entering the canyon, make sure all radios are working and on the same channel. It's a good idea to give them a quick test before committing to the canyon.

First Aid Kit

While you might carry a small personal first aid kit as part of the *Ten Essentials*, the team should also carry a more comprehensive kit for emergencies. It's good to be prepared for common injuries and environmental concerns. Are you prepared to deal with a broken ankle or spend a night in the canyon? We'll talk more about canyon first aid in Chapter 25.

While not a complete list, here are some items to consider carrying:

- General: pain relief medication, sterile gauze pads, antiseptic wipes, band-aids, waterproof dressings, medical tape, roll of gauze, adhesive wrap, steri-strips, butterfly bandages, tweezers, and protective gloves.

- Splinting: SAM splint, wrap bandages, and plastic zip ties. Duct tape is also useful for repairs.

- Environmental: emergency space blanket (or bivysack), emergency candle, lighter, spare headlamp & batteries (ideally waterproof), extra TP, and water purification tablets.

- A Wilderness First Aid reference card and accident forms.[22] Round out the group kit with a waterproof notepad and pencil (ex: Rite-in-the-Rain).

---

[22] A SOAP note (Subjective, Objective, Assessment & Plan) is a widely-used method of documenting injuries and illness. Using an accident form makes it easier to monitor the patient's condition and hand off care.

Personal Flotation Device (PFD)

Wetsuits will provide some innate buoyancy, but weaker swimmers still should consider wearing a personal flotation device (PFD) if long stretches of swimming are anticipated. Check on local regulations too. PFDs are required by law when running canyons in some parts of the world. Guides will sometimes require their clients to wear them. You might also wear a PFD purely for buoyancy if it's a hot day and you're not wearing a wetsuit.

It's a good idea to test out PFD flotation in shallow water ahead of time. A PFD should have a snug fit and not ride up when floating in a pool. If it's too restrictive or is getting in your way, then it's not a good choice. How does it perform when swimming?

Advantages	Disadvantages
o PFDs can save lives.	o Can restrict movement and limit agility.
o Increased buoyancy. Saves energy.	o Awkward/uncomfortable to wear with a pack.
o Extra insulation in cold water.	o Can obstruct visibility of the working area of your harness.
o Acts like body armor.	o Exterior straps can get snagged.
o Pockets and places to attach gear.	o Can be problematic on jumps.
o Often brightly-colored for visibility.	o Can get in the way when ascending.
	o Buoyancy. Limits your ability to dive.[23]

There are many PFDs on the market. The two varieties most suitable for canyoning would probably include:

- Type III (ex: whitewater kayaking vest)
  This type of PFD is a little bulky, but comfortable. Newer designs provide better mobility for swimming while retaining sufficient buoyancy.

- Type V (special use)
  Specialized rescue PFDs are equipped with a quick-release belt to instantly separate you from a rope in swiftwater. Their use requires training and practice.

Some canyoneers will wear an impact vest. These provide some extra buoyancy and are less bulky, but are not rated as a safety flotation device. These are probably best for strong swimmers comfortable in fast-moving water.

Miscellaneous Gear

- Keep your snacks where they're easy to access. If your food is buried deep in your pack, you're less likely to stop and get it out. It's good to keep snacking throughout the canyon to keep your energy level up.

- Water bottles work better than bladders. Bladders may be prone to rupture on a hard impact (ex: a pack getting tossed down a short drop), and a dangling hose can get caught on things.

- A small folding saw is useful for clearing brush around rappel stations. By clearing away fallen branches in the creek, you can encourage future groups to stay in the watercourse.

- Trekking poles can be handy on the approach, exit, and for balance within the creek. However, they can be annoying on rappels. You'll need to find a way to stow them and keep them out of the way. Folding poles that break down into segments and can be stuffed into a pack may work well here.

---

[23] Many expert canyoneers feel that wearing a PFD can be problematic in swiftwater canyons as it'll prevent you from diving deep to escape a hydraulic. We'll talk more about the use of PFDs in Chapter 19.

- Tip: Keep a copy of the map/beta on a waterproof phone or camera. You can then access the information at any time. Multiple team members should have copies of the beta.

- Some canyoneers will hide their car keys on or near the vehicles. This removes any possibility of keys becoming lost mid-canyon. It also provides options if the group should get separated in an emergency.

- Wristwatches, rings, and jewelry are easily scratched/damaged. It's best to remove them prior to starting the canyon, or leave them at home.

Adjusting Your Kit

Your personal gear should change with the season, current conditions, group size, and the canyons you plan to run.

- Summer
  Most canyons in the Pacific Northwest flow year-round, so there's no need to bring lots of extra water. Bring a water filter or purification tablets instead. When you need water, take a break and tank up. Be sure to stay well hydrated. In hot weather, a thin wetsuit may be preferred.

- Winter
  A thick wetsuit, extra layers, and neoprene booties are the way to go. (Or a drysuit?) A thermos with a hot drink or soup is a nice way to warm up. An emergency or unplanned bivy during the winter is a much more serious affair. Consider carrying a bivysack, a warm hat and gloves, synthetic down jacket, extra dry clothes, and small backpacking stove.

Back at the Car

Always leave a full change of dry clothes and footwear back at the car, or carry them with you if it's a long hike out. Don't drive home soggy!

- Tip #1: Once back at the vehicles, do a quick check of all packs and harnesses. Make sure any wandering gear gets back to its rightful owner.

- Tip #2: Bring a tarp to lay out on the ground and change on top of it. This will keep your wetsuit and other gear cleaner.

Post-Trip

Here are a couple tips for drying things out post-canyon:

Neoprene

Decaying vegetation and bacteria cause neoprene to emit offensive odors. At a minimum, thoroughly rinse your wetsuit and other neoprene items before hanging them up to dry in a place with good ventilation. Check with the manufacturer on the preferred cleaning method. A quick soak in a gentle detergent can help get rid of the funk.

Neoprene is not breathable, so exterior surfaces will dry much faster. Give your wetsuit and socks a day or so to dry, then turn them inside out. If running back-to-back canyons, dry the inside first.

Ropes

Ropes should be hung up to dry in a well-ventilated place out of direct sunlight. Once dry, the rope can be stuffed back into its bag. This is a good opportunity to inspect it for damage. While bagging, run your hand over the entire length of the rope and look for abrasion and abnormalities.

Kendra Kallevig rappelling Kitchen Falls, Wash.
(Photo: Kevin Clark)

Chapter 4: Anchors

This manual assumes the reader is already largely familiar with the building and evaluation of anchors. If not, taking an anchor-building class is highly recommended. The ability to construct anchors that you'd trust your life to is a critical part of canyoning. While this chapter touches on many aspects of anchoring, it's really an overview of a much larger topic.

Pre-Existing Anchors

WARNING! *All pre-existing anchors are guilty until proven innocent!* Any anchors found in a canyon should be thoroughly inspected prior to use. Don't assume that whoever built them knew what they were doing. They may have made poor choices, tied mystery knots, or used inappropriate materials (ex: cheap quick links that are not life-safety rated). The group might have run the canyon successfully, but perhaps they just got lucky.

A one-year old anchor in the Pacific Northwest.

Don't like the anchor? Cut it and replace.

How old is this anchor?

Prolonged exposure to moisture and sunlight causes webbing to deteriorate. Being sampled by local wildlife or getting left underwater will also take a toll. Take your time and check every part of the webbing, including the knots. Look for discoloration, fraying, stiffness, and moss. Would you trust your life to this anchor? Rappelling on shoddy anchors and old webbing has led to fatal accidents.

The inspection should also include the anchor's *master point*.[24] If you don't like it for any reason, replace it. If no metal connection is found, the previous party may have run their rope directly through the webbing. In this case, extra scrutiny is warranted as the webbing may have incurred friction damage when they pulled their rope.

---

[24] The master point is usually a metal connection (often a quick link or rappel ring) that the rope is threaded through. A metal connection is preferred to facilitate rope recovery from the bottom of the pitch.

Does it make sense to use this anchor?

Finding an anchor does not obligate you to use it. The anchor might be safe, but perhaps you don't want to use it for other reasons. Consider the following situations:

- An anchor is found right at the top of a waterfall. This might be a fun rappel in late summer, but using it could be dangerous in high flow.

- An anchor is found well outside of the watercourse. It might have been placed by a party who ran the canyon when the flow was high, or beginners who were eager to stay out of the water.

A good question to ask: *given today's conditions, does it make sense to use this anchor?* If the answer is *no*, consider moving the anchor or building another in a better location.

Summary

If you don't like, don't understand, or lack confidence in an anchor, don't hesitate to back it up or re-rig. If you have any doubts, it's better to err on the side of safety. The cost of some webbing and a quick link is much less than a hospital bill. What's your life worth?

Rappel Station Etiquette

- Don't let gobs of webbing accumulate at rappel stations. If the anchor's becoming a rat's nest, cut any excess and replace it with your own. Always leave a tidy anchor that's easy to inspect. Pack out any old webbing.

- If you're not going to use a pre-existing anchor because it's sketchy or has other problems, please remove it as a public service.

- Canyons see their fair share of beginners, so it's good to leave textbook anchors. If beginners see enough bad anchors, they may come to believe that's how it's done.

Building Anchors

If no anchors are found, you'll probably need to build one. Building an anchor is something of an art and requires good judgement, skill, and sufficient material. There are a number of factors to consider.

Choosing a Rappel Line

Upon arriving at a vertical drop in the canyon, usually the first step is an assessment. What does the pitch look like? Are there any hazards below? Where's the best place to rappel? A clean line down the pitch is generally preferred to one cluttered with brush or other obstacles. A brushy rappel might be preferred, however, if the clean line has some problem or hazard associated with it. Possible hazards include sharp edges, loose rocks, or if the rappel would exit into a dangerous water feature.

Another aspect to consider: do we want to rappel in or out of the water? In light to moderate flow, rappelling down the waterfall might be fun. In high flow, it may be safer to rappel off to one side or out of the water entirely.

Once you've located a suitable line of descent, take a look around the top of the pitch. Are there any natural anchors present that would allow you to use this rappel line? In places where natural anchors are limited, you might be able to construct one. (See "Constructed Anchors" later in the chapter.)

- ➤ If you can see down the pitch from above, it's easy to locate a suitable anchor.

- ➤ If your view down the pitch is obstructed, consider rigging a quick safety line. A scout can be sent out to the edge gather more information. (See "Edge Lines" in Chapter 14.)

Anchor Placement

The perfect anchor is one that's easy to access, is located right at the top of the pitch, and allows use of your preferred rappel line. Nature, however, doesn't always cooperate, so you may have to settle for one that's less than ideal in some respects. Here are some things to think about when building anchors:

- Access
  Is it easy to reach the anchor? If the anchor's in an exposed location, a traverse line could be rigged to protect the approach. (See "Safety Lines" in Chapter 14.)

- Avoiding abrasive rock
  Anchors right at the edge are often preferred to help minimize the rope's contact with sharp edges and abrasive rock. If sharp edges are unavoidable, you may need to take special steps to protect your rope. (See "Protecting the Rope" later in this chapter.)

- Getting on rappel
  Ideally, anchors should be placed so as to make it easy to get on rappel. Generally, this means a high placement, such as up in a tree or on the canyon wall. It may be harder to get on rappel from a low-placed anchor or one that's in an inconvenient location.

- Conducting rescues
  How far down the pitch can you see? Is there room at the anchor to lower or haul? It may be harder to conduct rescues from a low-placed anchor. A low-placed anchor may also increase the edge friction.

- Pulling the rope
  The ideal anchor is one that can be seen from the bottom of the pitch. A clear line of sight makes for an easier pull. An anchor set well back from the top will make the rope pull harder.[25]

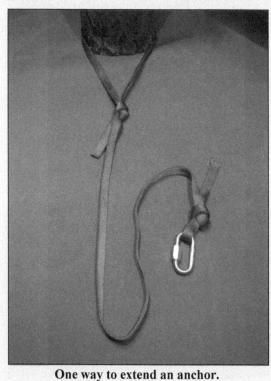

One way to extend an anchor.

Extending the Anchor

If the only options for anchoring are well back from the top of the pitch, the anchor could be extended. Essentially, this means rigging so that the anchor's master point is situated closer to (or hanging right out over) the edge. Extending the anchor might be done in order to:

- Make the rope pull easier.

- Keeps the rope away from sharp edges and rope-eating cracks.

- To prevent rope grooving in sandstone environments.

Disadvantages
- A master point hanging over the edge will make it harder to get on rappel.

- It may be difficult to belay / conduct rescues from an extended anchor.

---

[25] Desert Southwest: An anchor that's situated too far back is another cause of rope grooving in sandstone.

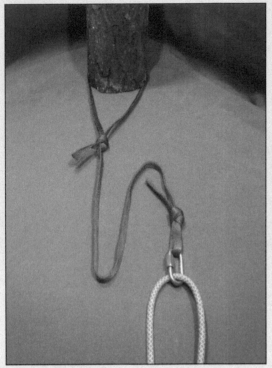
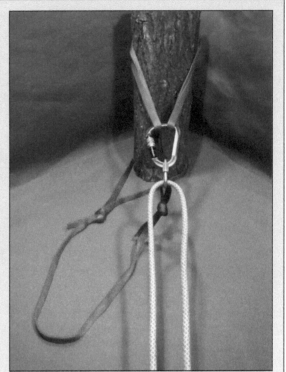

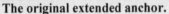

The original extended anchor. **The same anchor rigged for courtesy.**

Courtesy Rigging

<u>Scenario</u>: We've arrived at a drop in the canyon. There's a bombproof tree for an anchor here, located some distance back from the edge. The top of the pitch, however, is riddled with rope-eating cracks. If the anchor's master point is above the lip, the rope will probably get stuck during the pull. If the master point is below the lip, getting on rappel will be difficult. What to do?

Instead of making everyone to perform an awkward/difficult rappel start, you can rig for courtesy. A *courtesy anchor* is a temporary anchor established in a place that's more conducive to getting on rappel. There are many ways to rig for courtesy. Here's one method:

1) Build an extended anchor with the master point hanging over the lip.

2) Next, build the courtesy anchor. Using another sling, set a basket hitch high up in the tree with a carabiner at the master point. (Ref: blue sling in the photo above.)

3) The quick link at the end of the original anchor is pulled up and clipped into the carabiner.

4) If necessary, adjust the rope length. (The rope may have been pulled up too.)

The rigging is complete, and the rappel station is open for business. Making it easier to get on rappel increases group safety and speed.

<u>Cleaning</u>

The last rappeller unclips the quick link and returns the anchor to its original extended position. Next, the courtesy anchor is cleaned. The last person is the only one who needs to perform the difficult start. Once everyone is safely at the bottom, it's easy to pull the rope.

Assessing Anchors

Okay, having identified a possible anchor, the next step is to give it a thorough assessment. Is this anchor strong enough for our purposes? We'll need to classify it as one of the following:

Bombproof	The anchor it is deemed solid and capable of holding the required load, plus a wide margin for additional safety.
Marginal	The anchor is questionable. It probably can support the required load, but we don't know for certain. There may be little-to-no margin of error.

Being marginal doesn't mean the anchor's unusable, only that additional steps must be taken for safety. One option: back up the anchor until trust has been established. Alternatively, two or more marginal anchors can be linked together to create an anchor of sufficient strength. (See "Strategies for Marginal Anchors" later in this chapter.) |

While making the assessment, here are some other things to keep in mind:

- <u>What's the expected load?</u>
  A typical rappel anchor should be able to support, at minimum, a three-bodyweight load. A stronger anchor may be required if large loads are anticipated.

  - Is the anchor in an exposed location? If so, multiple team members may need to be clipped into it and/or hanging on it at once.

  - Will more than one person be rappelling at the same time? A two-person load on the anchor is sometimes referred to as a *rescue load* (i.e., a patient and attendant).

Edge Friction

When rappelling, the maximum force on the anchor usually occurs just as the rappeller is passing over the edge atop the pitch. Once below the edge, the load will be reduced by the friction generated where the rope runs over the lip. The more contact the rope has, the greater the friction. There are a number of factors involved, but testing has shown that when a rope runs over the edge at a 45-degree angle, load on the anchor can be reduced by as much as 50%. If passing over the edge at a 90-degree angle, the load reduction can be as high as 66%.[26] Be aware: if the edge is wet or submerged, the amount of friction produced will be much less.

- <u>Is this rigging a force multiplier?</u>
  Be aware: some rigging systems (ex: ground anchors, guided rappels, traverse lines, and some types of hauling) act as *force multipliers*. The nature of the rigging causes the anchor to experience forces greater than the actual load. We'll talk more about these systems as we introduce them later on.

- <u>High flow</u>
  Rappelling in high flow can increase the load on the anchor (i.e., the force of the water striking the rappeller and pushing them downwards).

- <u>How experienced is your team?</u>
  Jumping, bouncing, and sudden stops mid-rappel will place additional stress on the anchor. Beginners are more likely to have poor rappel technique.

<u>Summary</u>
Always be aware of the load you're placing on the anchor. This is particularly important with marginal anchors.

---

[26] Black, David. *Canyoneering: A Guide to Techniques in Wet and Dry Canyons – 2ⁿᵈ Edition*. Falcon Guides, 2013.

Natural Anchors

A *natural anchor* is any natural feature that a rigging can be attached to. Some examples would include trees, fallen logs, boulders, chockstones, rock horns, and contact points. As part of your assessment, give the anchor a good shake, kick, or otherwise try to dislodge it as a stability test. If you can't move it, that's a good sign.

- Trees
  Ideally, trees should be living, well-rooted, and at least 12cm (~5in) in diameter. Beware trees near cliff edges that may have shallow root structures. For maximum strength, the anchor should be placed around the base of the tree. Setting the anchor higher makes it easier to get on rappel, but may subject the tree to a leveraging force. *Cinching wraps* work well for high placements; the friction in the wrap keeps the anchor from sliding down the trunk. (See Appendix II for more information.)

- Fallen Logs & Root Balls
  Assess dead wood anchors carefully to make sure they're not hollow, rotten, or brittle. Cinching wraps can be used to keep the anchor from moving when placed under load.

- Rocks & Boulders
  A good rule of thumb: look for a boulder at least the size of a crouching person that won't shift under load. The ideal boulder is one that's situated directly on the ground with plenty of contact. A large rock supported by a number of smaller ones might not be safe. Some other things to look for: sharp edges and if the webbing can slip up over the top when placed under load. Con: Big rocks require a lot of webbing.

Constructed Anchors

If natural anchors are lacking, here are a few other options to consider. Bolting, of course, is another solution that we'll talk about in Chapter 6.

- Cairns
  Tie an overhand on a bight at the end of a piece of webbing and girth hitch it around a large rock (or thick branch).[27] Bury it under a pile of others to keep it from moving. The end of the webbing should emerge from the bottom of the pile. Run this out to the edge and tie a second overhand on a bight. Add a quick link to complete the anchor. Cairns are very secure when built properly, but should be regarded as marginal and backed up until trust has been established. Build the cairn far enough back so that any rocks that are accidentally dislodged cannot fall on rappellers. Con: Cairns must be completely disassembled in order to perform a full inspection of the webbing. They may need to be rebuilt after every flood.

- Chocks
  Girth hitch a large rock (or thick branch) and place it behind a natural constriction. It must be impossible for the object to pull through or work its way free. When loaded, the chock is pulled into a more secure position. In some cases, additional rocks can be piled on top for greater security. Like cairns, chocks are marginal and should be backed up until validated.

  Another type of chock can be created by placing a small rock (or carabiner) deep in a tapering crack in the canyon wall. These can be quite secure when built properly.

- Gear Anchors
  Some canyoneers will carry a small set of rock protection (e.g., nuts, tri-cams, or pitons) for use when natural anchors are lacking. Fixed protection is usually a measure of last resort as it's expensive and will be left behind. While a single good placement might be sufficient for a rappel, three is best for redundancy. A gear anchor of less than three placements should be regarded as marginal.

---

[27] If a girth hitch won't hold securely, try a parcel knot (i.e. tie the rock up like a package).

Human Anchor (Meat Anchor)

Let's detour away from fixed anchors for a moment to discuss a temporary anchoring solution. The concept is simple: it's using one or more of your teammates as an anchor. Human anchors are generally used to descend short drops when natural anchors are lacking, or as a way to speed up progression. Alpine climbers will recognize this technique as a close cousin of the sitting hip belay. The last person (i.e., the person serving as the anchor) will downclimb, jump, or find another way to descend.

- This technique is somewhat terrain-dependent. Some drops lend themselves to its use better than others.

- Consider the use of *sequencing* with human anchors.

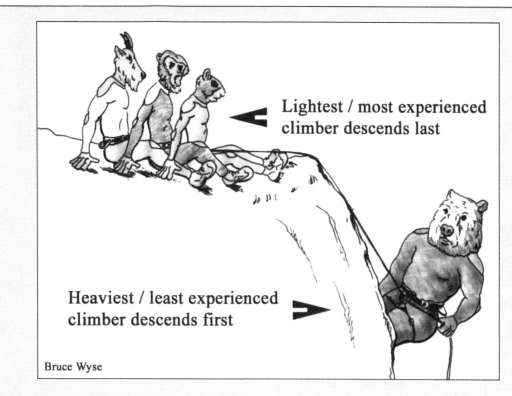

Lightest / most experienced climber descends last

Heaviest / least experienced climber descends first

Bruce Wyse

FAQ: "What is *sequencing*?"
Sequencing is the process of sending team members down a rappel in a particular order. This is usually done to increase team safety. Here are two examples:

- Rappelling a short drop
  The lightest and best climber on the team is called upon to be a human anchor. The team is then sent down in sequence. The largest and least experienced team members rappel first, followed by progressively lighter and more experienced individuals. Anyone who is not rappelling can help back up the anchor. In this way, even the heaviest members of the team can rappel safely. The last person will downclimb or jump, while spotted from below.

- Backing up a marginal anchor
  If a given anchor doesn't inspire confidence (ex: single bolt, cairn, or a tree that's a little too close to the edge), it can be backed up with a human anchor. The largest individuals on the team will rappel first, and, simply by rappelling, will test the anchor for everyone else. The last person, being the smallest and most experienced, is the only one who rappels without a backup.

Running the rope over a natural feature helps reduce load on the anchor.

Being a Human Anchor

<u>Scenario:</u> The team arrives at a short drop in the canyon. Downclimbing is feasible, but there are a couple of moves that would be difficult for beginners. To speed things up, the team decides to use a human anchor.

1) Who will be the anchor? The duty usually falls to the lightest and best climber on the team. Let's refer to them as *the belayer*.

2) The belayer deploys enough rope (single-strand) to reach the bottom. The rope bag and extra rope will be kept atop the pitch.

3) The belayer finds a good place, well back from the edge, and sits down in a secure position, maximizing their contact with the ground and facing the direction of pull. The ideal location is behind some sort of natural feature, such as a large boulder or log that they can brace against.

   o If possible, the rappel rope should run over the top of this natural feature. The more contact the rope has, the greater the friction produced. Edge friction will help reduce load on the anchor.

4) Next, the belayer attaches the rope to their harness. A simple figure-8 knot clipped to the harness is okay, but a better solution is to run the rope through the descender and lock it off.[28]

5) (Optional) Any team members not rappelling can help back up the anchor. If there's nothing present to brace against (or large loads are anticipated), the belayer should definitely get a backup.

When the belayer is ready, the rappel station is open for business. Team members are sent down in *sequence* with the largest and most inexperienced going first.

---

[28] Using the descender provides an advantage. If the belayer finds the load is too much, releasing rope might keep them from getting pulled out of position. We'll talk about other benefits of releasable rigging in Chapter 11.

<u>Cleaning</u>
Once the rest of the team is down, the belayer disconnects from the rope. For best efficiency, the rope is dropped to the team below. The team can get to work packing the rope away while the belayer downclimbs. Team members who are not stowing the rope can help spot the belayer.

<u>Other Notes</u>

- A human anchor should not be used if there's potential for a high-factor fall.

- Quite often, the belayer cannot see the rappeller, so good communication is key. If the rappel rope goes slack, the rappeller might be at the bottom, but could also be on a ledge partway down. Never release the belay until the rappeller signals.

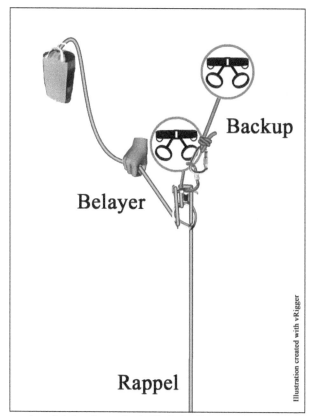

A quick backup: just clip into the master point.

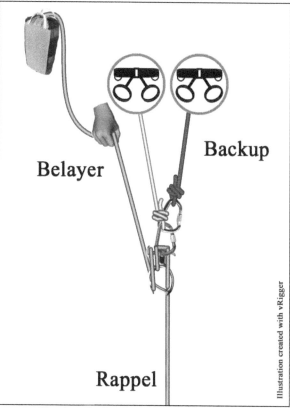

Sharing the load as a two-point anchor.

Backing up a Human Anchor
The easiest way to back up a human anchor is to clip a tether into the master point of the belayer's descender. The backup then sits down in a good braced position, also facing the direction of pull. Adjust your position and/or length of your tether until it becomes taut. If your tether isn't long enough, it could be extended.

Another option is for the belayer to extend the master point. This can be done by rigging the descender at the end of a short tether.[29] This allows the belayer and backup to sit comfortably side-by-side. Pay attention to the *critical angle* created between the legs of the anchor. As with any other multi-point anchor, the angle should be kept to 90-degrees or less. (We'll talk more about this issue in a moment.)

- Anyone joining the anchor should be seated where they won't interfere with the belayer's ability to release rope. Backups should not tie into the rope or run it through their own descender.

---

[29] Make sure the descender stays within reach. If the belayer can't reach the descender, it may be impossible to release rope in an emergency.

Rappelling from Human Anchors

Be nice to your anchor when rappelling. While it might be possible to start the rappel from a standing position, doing so actually inflicts maximum leverage/discomfort on the belayer. Not recommended. Instead, rappellers should get as low as possible and perform a *soft start*. The more contact the rope has with rock surfaces, the greater the load reduction on the anchor. (See also "Rappelling Softly" in Chapter 15.)

- Before weighting the rope, ask the belayer: "Is the anchor ready?"

Other Uses for Human Anchors

- Scouting
  A human anchor could be used to belay a scout out to the edge. A scout could also be belayed while downclimbing. (See "Belaying a Scout" in Chapter 9.)

- Assisting Beginners
  The team arrives at a drop in the canyon. Jumping is feasible, but a several team members are nervous about it. A quick human anchor allows them to rappel.

- Anchor a Safety Line
  If the risk of falling is low, a human anchor could be used to secure one end of a traverse line.

- Speeding up Progression
  The team arrives at a significant drop in the canyon. A couple of individuals get to work building an anchor on a nearby tree. If the terrain permits, two other team members with a second rope can become a human anchor. With multiple rappel lines open, the team can get down the pitch even faster. In this situation, the belayer will ultimately rappel from the tree anchor.

Human anchors are an efficient way to get the team down a short drop.

Strategies for Marginal Anchors

Rappelling from dubious anchors is, of course, not recommended. Before committing to significant risk, be sure you've considered all the options. Are there any ways to improve your situation? Here are some strategies:

- Find another anchor
  Don't get fixated on using a particular anchor. Take your time and look around. Are there any better options available? The safe anchor may not be the ideal one.

Human anchor sharing the load with a cairn.

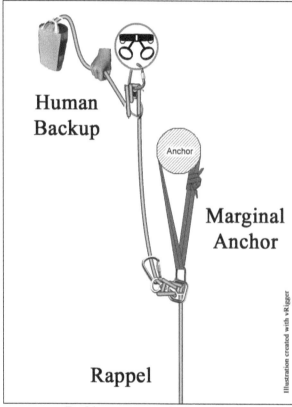
Backing up a marginal anchor.

- Use a temporary backup
  One way to increase security and build confidence is to add a temporary backup. The lightest and most experienced person on the team runs the reserve rope out and becomes a human anchor. The belayer sits down in line with the main anchor with just a touch of slack in the rope. If the main anchor shifts under load, the backup comes into play immediately. When the belayer is ready, the team is sent down in sequence with the largest individuals going first.[30] Each person rappelling helps test the anchor. Assuming the anchor passes muster, the belayer is the only person who will rappel without a backup.

- Bounce testing
  Another confidence-building measure is to apply a *bounce test* to the anchor. This is usually performed by the first rappeller while backed up with a temporary anchor (or a separate belay). To perform the test: set up your descender normally, then lean back to weight the anchor. If it holds, try a gentle bounce. If it continues to look good, try again with more enthusiasm. The goal is to simulate a standard rappel load before fully committing to the anchor.

---

[30] If there are concerns about the main anchor having a weight limit, heavier individuals could rappel entirely on the backup.

- Improve the anchor
  Sometimes, two or more marginal anchors can be linked to form an anchor of sufficient strength. Ideally, each anchor point will experience a fraction of the total load on the system.

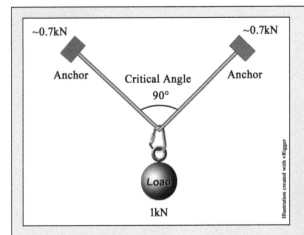

Critical Angle	Approximate Load on Each Anchor Point
0°	50%
30°	53%
60°	60%
90°	70%
120°	100%
150°	190%
170°	570%

If two marginal anchors are supporting a 1kN load with a critical angle of 90-degrees, then each anchor will experience about 0.7kN.

The Critical Angle
When building multi-point anchors, be aware of the *critical angle* formed between the legs of the anchor. The wider the angle, the greater the force exerted on each anchor point. Why is this happening? When loaded, the anchors are also pulling in opposition to one another. Best practice in anchor-building is to keep the critical angle to 90-degrees or less.

The same principle applies to simple anchors, such as a single loop of webbing tied tightly around a bombproof tree. A very wide angle at the master point (i.e., a quick link situated too close to the tree) will increase the force exerted on each strand of webbing and the knot.[31]

- Stay out of the water
  Strong flow striking the rappeller will increase the load on the anchor. If you only have marginal anchors to work with, it may be safer to rappel outside the watercourse.

- Be nice to your anchor
  When rappelling from marginal anchors, it's good to default to a *soft start*. Get as low as you can and carefully slide over the edge. The goal is to maximize the edge friction and reduce the load on the anchor. (See "Rappelling Softly" in Chapter 15.)

Protecting the Rope
Sharp edges, abrasive rock, and rope-eating cracks are all best avoided. You may need to take steps on occasion to protect your rope and/or prevent it from becoming snagged when it comes time to pull.

Sharp Edges & Abrasive Rock
The act of rappelling (and ascending) causes tiny back-and-forth movements in the tensioned rope. This repeated sawing motion across any rough surfaces or sharp edges can result in abrasion and damage.[32] There may be multiple sharp edges present on any rappel; those at the top of the pitch are easiest to detect. In aquatic canyons, sharp edges can also be hidden under the water.

---

[31] CMC Rescue. *Rope Rescue Manual – 5th Edition.* CMC Rescue, Inc., 2017.
[32] A place where the rope has been damaged enough to expose the core is known as a *core shot*. Core shots should be tied off (or otherwise isolated) to ensure they are no longer loaded or rappelled on.

Here are some strategies for protecting your rope:

- Find a better anchor
  Don't rappel over sharp edges if you can avoid it. Are there any better anchors nearby?

- Edge protection
  An easy way to protect your rope is to run it over a rope bag or pack. Whatever item is used, the station manager should take precautions to keep it from becoming lost. Sometimes, the item can be connected to an anchor with a short sling or section of rope. Edge protection is easiest to apply atop the pitch. Commercial rope protectors are also available; these might be used when training.

- Change the rope's position
  By shifting the rope's position between every few rappellers, you can change the wear points along the course of the rappel. This practice helps spread any abrasion over a wider area. Alternatively, a belayer at the anchor can provide an extremely slow lower as team members rappel. This is known as *rope creeping*. We'll talk more about this technique in Chapter 11.

- Avoid very long rappels
  The longer the rappel, the greater the rope stretch. More stretch means more rope movement and increased odds of damage. If possible, consider a series of shorter rappels instead of a single long one.

- Practice good rappel technique
  Avoid jumping, bouncing, and sudden stops when on rappel. Situational awareness is also important as ropes can be easily damaged by an inadvertent pendulum swing. Beginners with poor rappel technique are more likely to damage ropes.

What ropes are you using?
Not all ropes are created equal. Skinny ropes (i.e., those in the 8mm range) are attractively lightweight, but require greater care and management. More attention must be paid to rope protection and rigging. Skinny ropes are better for experienced canyoneers seeking to cut back on pack weight. Larger diameter ropes are heavier, but more durable and cut resistant.

- Dynamic ropes may be more prone to damage due to their inherent stretch.

Cracks & Constrictions
Beware cracks, notches, grooves, and pinches along the course of the rappel that could catch a rope during the pull. It doesn't take much; even a tiny pinch can stick a rope and render it unrecoverable. Rope blocks and knots can also get caught. In aquatic canyons, constrictions can also be hidden under the water.

- Beware anything on the ends of your rope (e.g., knots, labels, tape, or plastic caps) that could get caught in a crack during the pull.

- If a chockstone (i.e., a large rock or boulder wedged between the canyon walls) forms the top of the rappel, check the sides for rope-eating cracks.

- Sometimes, you may be able to jam a convenient rock or branch into (or across) a crack to keep the rope out of it. Be sure the blocking object is wedged firmly in position and cannot accidentally come loose to fall on anyone.

- Desert Southwest: Deep grooves in sandstone can trap ropes during the pull (i.e., one strand pinching the other). One way to avoid this problem is to extend the anchor so that the master point is hanging over the lip. A courtesy anchor could be used to avoid the difficult rappel start.

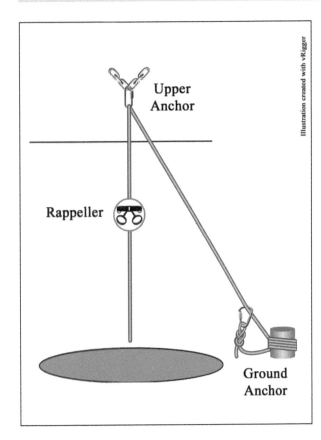

Upper Anchor

Rappeller

Ground Anchor

Illustration created with vRigger

Ground Anchors

While we're discussing anchors, let's introduce one in an unusual place: namely at the bottom of the pitch. Ground anchors have a number of applications; we'll talk more about them in later chapters.

A ground anchor is similar in concept to the "slingshot belay" used in rock climbing. Rope travels from the ground anchor up through the master point of the anchor atop the pitch and then back down to the ground again.

This technique is dependent on local terrain and the availability of anchors at the bottom of the pitch.

Advantage
- A ground anchor can be dismantled as soon as the last rappeller is down. There's no need to leave anything behind.

Disadvantages
- This rigging is a force multiplier. When someone is rappelling, the force on the upper anchor can be up to twice that of the actual load. The anchor atop the pitch must be bombproof.

- Rappellers should double-check that they're setting up on the correct rope strand.

Ground anchors can be rigged in a number of ways:

- A tensionless hitch (or bowline) could be used to secure the rope to any convenient natural feature at the bottom of the pitch.

- If natural anchors are lacking, a human anchor could be used. As usual, the individual(s) providing the anchor should sit down, facing the direction of pull. Standing is not recommended as you could get pulled off your feet when the system is loaded. The rope could be run around corners or other obstacles to reduce the load on the anchor.[33]

Anchors of Last Resort
Ideally, the rope should be run through a metal connection (ex: quick link) at the master point. If you're out of quick links, a carabiner could be used. If you're completely out of gear, the rope could be run directly through the webbing. Be aware, however, that the friction generated during the pull may damage the anchor for future parties.

- A dry bag, pack, or rope bag could be filled with sand/gravel and buried as a deadman anchor.

- If you're running low on webbing, a retrievable system might be an option. (See Chapter 13 for more information.) In a worst-case scenario, consider cutting the material you need off the end of the rope.

---

[33] A floating human anchor (i.e. one or more team members linked together and floating in a pool) is unlikely to be effective. Not recommended.

Chapter 5: Redundancy in Anchors

Deep in the canyon, it's common to run across simple anchors that are nothing more than a single piece of webbing (with an accompanying quick link) tied around a sturdy tree or boulder. An alpine climber might raise an eyebrow here. "Hey, wait a minute; that anchor's not redundant!" True, but does it need to be?

What is Redundancy?

Redundancy is a core principle of anchor building. If any component of the anchor were to fail, a backup comes into play immediately. A redundant anchor generally has a higher margin of safety.

Redundancy comes in many forms. A simple way to make our tree anchor redundant would be to tie another sling around the tree and run it through the same quick link. If we had more webbing available, we could replace the single wrap with a basket hitch with an overhand above the master point. If the tree didn't appear trustworthy, we could rig a multi-point anchor to distribute the load.

Should this anchor be redundant?

Climbing vs. Rappel Anchors

A distinction should be drawn between climbing anchors and anchors that will be used exclusively for rappelling.

- Climbing Anchors
  Anchors used in rock climbing must be extremely strong. They need to be capable of withstanding major shock loads in the event of a fall.[34] Sometimes, climbing anchors also need to be multi-directional. A given anchor might need to protect someone above the anchor, below it, or, occasionally, both. It's almost always a good idea to build such anchors with redundancy. In the climbing world, an anchor that is not redundant is generally regarded as inadequate or unsafe.

- Rappel Anchors
  The load placed on a rappel anchor is usually a static one, which, barring unusual circumstances, will never exceed three times that of a single bodyweight. Rappel anchors are seldom shock loaded and only need to provide support in one direction (i.e., below the anchor). Craig Connally, author of *The Mountaineering Handbook*, writes:

  > "[A rappel anchor] does not, however, need to be particularly strong, because the possible peak forces are somewhere south of 1.5kN (337lbf), something a loop of burly shoelace might hold."[35]

  Does a rappel anchor require redundancy? Redundancy isn't a hard-and-fast rule, but it's often a good idea. Redundancy is especially important if there's any question as to the strength of the anchor, or if the anchor could fail in some other way. Some other methods of failure would include poorly-tied knots, rockfall, or if the webbing is passing over a sharp edge.

---

[34] In basic testing, *Petzl* found that a fall factor of 0.3 could place as much as 4kN on the anchor. (Petzl. "Forces at Work in a Real Fall". *Tech Tips*. https://www.petzl.com/US/en/Sport/Forces-at-work-in-a-real-fall)
[35] Connally, Craig. *The Mountaineering Handbook*. Ragged Mountain Press, 2005.

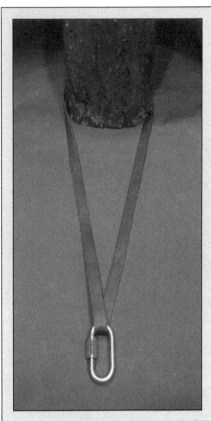

FAQ: "Is a single wrap anchor strong enough?"
As always, we want an anchor that's stronger than the maximum force it will ever encounter. A typical rappel anchor must be able to support the expected load, plus a wide margin for safety. Does a single wrap meet these requirements?

- Let's start with a single strand of 2.5cm (1in) tubular webbing. Checking with the manufacturer, we find the tensile strength is 18kN (4046lbf). This is the breaking strength of a free-hanging piece of webbing with no knots.

- Next, the webbing is tied around a tree. Testing has shown that a water knot decreases the anchor's strength by about 30–40%, so now we're now down to 10.8kN (~2400lbf).[36]

- Let's imagine our rappeller weighs 80kg (175lbs). To make the math easy, we'll assume the static load is 1kN (225lbf).

- The *static safety factor* of an anchor is defined as the minimum breaking strength divided by the static load. In our case, that's 10.8kN divided by 1kN for a safety factor of about 10:1. The world's worst rappeller (who is jumping, bouncing, and deliberately yanking on the rope) might be able to generate as much as 2–3kN, but this still falls within the anchor's margin of safety.

Is Redundancy Necessary?

Even though the math checks out, the skeptical climber might remain dubious. "Okay, it's strong enough, but wouldn't it still be safer to add redundancy?" The answer is situationally dependent. Every part of the anchor should be thoroughly inspected (including the knots), and a judgement call made. What's the likelihood that this anchor could fail?

- If the anchor is not trustworthy for some reason, it's definitely a good idea to add redundancy, back it up, or cut it and re-rig. Bolts are inherently difficult to inspect, so redundancy is always a good plan. If you're on the fence about redundancy, it's better to err on the side of safety.

- If planning to rappel on a non-redundant anchor, failure must be impossible or exceedingly unlikely.

A non-redundant anchor might be acceptable if:
- o A bombproof natural feature is available.
- o The webbing / other materials are new.
- o You built the anchor yourself.
- o Only one person is rappelling at a time.
- o No force multipliers are in play.
- o All parts of the anchor have been carefully inspected and are not suspect.

Consider adding redundancy if:
- o Only marginal anchors are available.
- o Large loads are anticipated (ex: rescues).
- o Rigging will act as a force multiplier.
- o Rappel passes through high flow.
- o Rappelling from bolts (i.e., hard to inspect).
- o Anchor is subject to rockfall.
- o The webbing would pass over a sharp edge or other abrasive surface.

---

[36] Why does tying a knot reduce the anchor's strength? The knot creates several sharp turns in the webbing. As the internal strands are being compressed and no longer loaded equally, this creates a point of weakness.

> **Temporary Redundancy**
>
> Adding redundancy or going without may not be your only options. In some cases, a compromise might be possible in the form of a temporary backup. Adding a backup is easy: just establish a secondary anchor (possibly a human anchor) and link it to the primary with a touch of slack. If the main anchor shifts under load, the backup comes into play immediately. (See "Strategies for Marginal Anchors" in Chapter 4.)

Other Considerations

- Is redundancy being applied consistently?

  A great deal of attention is paid to redundancy in anchors, but what about the rest of the rappel system? Big bombproof natural anchors usually get a pass, but on most rappels there's only one rope, one harness, one rappel device, and one quick link on the anchor. The argument here is that these are manufactured goods and are, hopefully, designed to some standard, but all of them can be subject to failure too. Is that a climb-rated quick link or a cheap knock-off? Is your descender rigged correctly? Rockfall can sever ropes, and canyons will slowly destroy your harness and hardware. The failure of any component in your rappel system can be catastrophic.

- How much webbing do we have?

  The team, collectively, should bring enough material to rebuild every anchor in the canyon. In canyons that are run frequently, you probably won't use much if the anchors are in good shape. In a canyon that sees a handful of visitors per year, you might need to rebuild every anchor. Often, you won't know how much webbing is required, so it's prudent not to overdo it when it comes to building anchors. Making every anchor redundant will burn through your supply a lot faster.

- Leave No Trace

  In popular canyons, old webbing will (hopefully) be cut and packed out. In canyons that see fewer visitors, excess webbing ultimately becomes excess trash. One day, it'll wash into the creek. Safety always comes first, but try to avoid leaving more material than you need to.

Summary

Rappellers should develop the ability to critically assess anchors and make good decisions as to whether or not redundancy is called for. Redundancy should certainly be applied when appropriate. When in doubt, improve the anchor, re-rig, or use a temporary backup. The goal is always to rappel from an anchor that inspires confidence.

Chapter 6: Bolts

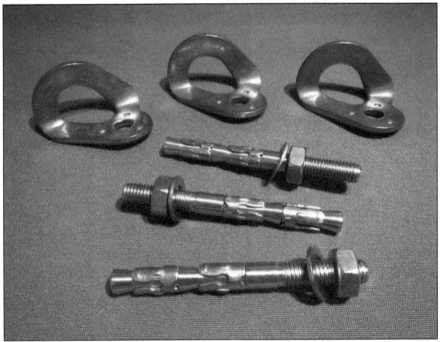

A set of stainless steel hangers and expansion bolts.

Bolts are another type of anchor that really merit their own chapter. As they're difficult to inspect, they're usually found in pairs for redundancy. Bolts are often, but not always, linked with webbing, chains, or accessory cord. There are many different types of bolts.

To Bolt ... or Not to Bolt?

Bolting ethics will vary considerably depending on where you are in the world. In the American Southwest, canyons tend to be dry and often have a wealth of natural anchors. In places where anchors are lacking, you can often get by with some clever problem-solving. Bolts are generally regarded as unnecessary, so this has led to a strong anti-bolting ethic throughout the region. Canyons in Arizona and Utah have even been the site of "bolt wars." Numerous canyons were bolted up, only to have those same bolts subsequently removed by other groups wishing to maintain a wilderness aesthetic.

In Europe, however, bolting is considered standard practice. Why such a difference in perspective? One big reason: European canyons have a lot more water. With high flow, solid rock, and large numbers of visitors, bolting is deemed a better solution for safety and long-term use. Attempting to run a European canyon entirely on natural anchors might be impractical or downright dangerous.

New Zealand falls somewhere between these two perspectives on the spectrum of bolting. Their canyons vary widely in terms of flow. Some can be descended entirely on natural anchors, whereas others require bolts for a safe descent. Local canyoneers try to strike a balance on the question of bolting. The New Zealand Canyoning Association (NZCA) puts it this way:

> "Well-placed, quality bolts are generally considered acceptable in most circumstances by the canyoning community, but inferior, unsafe or excessive bolting is not."[37]

---

[37] Fraser, Shanan. *NZCA Bolting Code of Practice v1.9*. New Zealand Canyoning Association, 2017.

How Much Water is Present?

Canyons throughout the world are very diverse, so it makes sense that rigging systems, techniques, and best practices will also be different. While some differences are due to geology or local culture, how much water is present in the canyon also plays a big role.

Dry Canyons
- There tends to be a greater emphasis on building anchors and problem-solving.

- In sandstone environments, abrasive rock may be less of a concern, so anchors can be established well back from the top of the pitch. Rope grooving can be avoided by extending anchors, edge protection, and using special techniques.

- Marginal anchors and retrievable systems are more acceptable.

- If someone were to get stuck mid-rappel, self-rescue is more likely. If the team needs to take action, it's usually less urgent. Anchor placement is not as critical for rescues.

Aquatic Canyons
- A greater focus is placed on identifying an optimal rappel line for safety or fun.

- Sharp edges may be more of a concern in basalt and granite canyons. An anchor right at the edge is ideal for minimizing the rope's contact with abrasive rock.

- Marginal anchors tend to be less acceptable. As the water level increases, retrievable systems are used less frequently.

- Getting stuck under a waterfall can be life-threatening. As verbal commands and whistle blasts may not be heard, it's important for those atop the pitch to be able to see what's going on. Self-rescue is less likely in high flow. In an emergency, the team may need to respond immediately. Poorly-situated anchors may delay or complicate a rescue.

Arguments in favor of bolting

- Increased safety
  Natural anchors are not always well-situated for a safe rappel. Suppose we have a convenient tree for an anchor, but using it would cause rappellers to enter a high flow waterfall. Canyoneers will gravitate towards pre-existing anchors, so the presence of a bolt station would encourage rappellers to take a safer line. Bolts can be also be placed to encourage the use of traverse lines, redirects, and guided rappels.

  A well-placed bolt station at the edge can help keep the rope away from abrasive rock and allows the team to keep an eye on rappellers. Rescues can be conducted from a better location.

- Reduced environmental impact
  Bolts can be placed to encourage canyoneers to remain on durable surfaces. If our tree anchor is located 3m (~10ft) up a vegetated embankment, a user trail will quickly get worn in by people climbing up and down. The best anchor is one that doesn't require leaving the watercourse or lead to erosion. In the Desert Southwest, well-placed bolts can reduce rope grooving in sandstone.

  Bolts can also help reduce the amount of webbing and other material that's left behind in the canyon.[38] Large natural features (ex: boulders) and anchors set well back from the top of the pitch will require more webbing to rig. If a cairn anchor is destroyed in a flood, its associated webbing will become trash in the watercourse.

---

[38] Unlinked bolt stations require no webbing at all. We'll talk about them at the end of the chapter.

- An option when natural anchors are lacking
  Some canyons in the Pacific Northwest have a wealth of natural anchors to choose from. In others, natural protection is sparse to non-existent. Canyons in this latter category are often tight gorges or narrow slots that experience high flow. Sometimes, there's just nothing to work with.

  In dry canyons, cairn anchors can be built almost anywhere, but building cairns may not be possible/safe in an aquatic environment with deep pools and fast-moving water.[39]

Arguments against placing bolts

- Bolts are difficult to inspect
  The Cascade Range is renowned for friable rock, and it's hard to say from inspection if a given bolt was installed poorly or is nearing the point of failure. Bolts can be bad for many reasons. All bolts have a life expectancy.

- Increased visitation
  Bolting lowers the technical bar and opens the canyon to less experienced canyoneers. Once word gets out, a perception is created that the canyon is now, somehow, safer. Ironically, bolting can lead to more visitation, greater environmental impact, and an increased likelihood of accidents.

- The change you make is permanent
  Bolt placement permanently changes the canyon. Bolts can be chopped/removed and the damage hidden, but it's always there. (See also "Anchors & Minimizing Impact" in Chapter 2.)

Summary
There are good arguments both for and against the practice of bolting. Bolts are not all good, nor all bad.

Of the three perspectives on bolting, the New Zealand model seems like the best match for the Pacific Northwest. Canyons in this part of the world vary widely in terms of flow and the availability of anchors. While some canyons can be descended entirely on natural anchors, others cannot. There are clear cases where bolting appears to be the right solution, whether for safety, a lack of natural anchors, or, in popular canyons, for environmental reasons. Does every rappel need to be bolted? Definitely not. Any bolt placement should be well-considered and done with good reason. Bolt when necessary and appropriate. Don't overdo it.

Placing Bolts

Bolt placement is another big topic that is beyond the scope of this manual. If you're interested in learning, seek out a suitable class or mentor. Some good rules of thumb:

- Before placing any hardware, check with local land managers to become acquainted with area regulations. Bolting is illegal in some parts of the United States. Power drills are not permitted in Wilderness areas.

- Check in with the local canyon community before doing any bolting. Get some second opinions.

- If you're going to bolt, do so responsibly and do it right. Only place bolts if you have the knowledge, experience, and tools to set them. No one wants to rappel on shoddy bolts placed by beginners.

The Future of Bolting?
Certain types of sleeve bolts (ex: Fixe Triplex) are designed to be removable. This allows them to be pulled and inspected, or replaced when they eventually wear out. The replacements can be installed in the same holes with no additional drilling required. Removable bolts could be used in places prone to flooding or that can be accessed by the general public.

---

[39] The use of underwater anchors is not recommended.

Inspecting Bolts

> "The combination of non-stainless bolts, climate, rock type, and well-meaning but sometimes counterproductive installation techniques means that, today, the quality and safety of fixed hardware ranges from very good to abysmal."[40]

Don't assume bolts are always bombproof and reliable. Whoever installed them may not have known what they were doing. Bolts should be treated just like any other anchor and inspected thoroughly.

Are the bolts well-placed?

- Does the location of this anchor make sense? Ideally, bolts should be placed where it's easy to get on rappel and where the rope has a clean line of pull from the bottom of the pitch. Bolts should also be set high enough so that they won't be affected by flood events.

- Bolts should be spaced a good handspan apart; at least 20–30cm (7–12in). If the bolts are too close together, the station may be unsafe.

- When the anchor is weighted, what is the direction of pull? Bolts are strongest when loaded in the *shear* direction (i.e., 90-degrees from their direction of placement). If loading would result in a *tensile* force (i.e., pulling the bolt directly out of its hole) then the station is poorly situated.

- How sound is the rock around the bolts? Beware loose flakes and cracks radiating from installation. Bolts set too close to an edge can also be dangerous.

What condition are the bolts/hangers in?

- How old are the bolts? Ancient bolts with homemade hangers are a definite red flag.

Shear vs. tensile forces.

- Are the bolts rusty, corroded, or damaged? Look for rust streaks on the rock surface below the bolts. Some older bolts may look fine, but can be completely rusted through. Mixed metals between a bolt and its hanger (ex: stainless steel vs. zinc-coated) can result in galvanic corrosion.

- Bolts should be placed perpendicular to the rock surface so the hanger can sit flush. If placed at an angle, the hanger may eventually lever the bolt out of its hole.

- Does the bolt wiggle in place? Sometimes, a bolt can be tightened, but beware over-tightening expansion bolts. If, upon tightening, you feel no increasing resistance, the bolt may be unsafe. A hanger that spins is probably okay as long as the bolt is solid.

Is the load being shared?
Any material linking the bolts (e.g., webbing, chains, or accessory cord) should undergo the same thorough inspection. Is the anchor equalized in the direction of pull? Also, check the angle formed between the legs of the anchor. Is the load being shared when weighted? (See "The Critical Angle" in Chapter 4.)

---

[40] Snider, L. & Haas, J. "Too Important to Fail: The Problem of Aging Bolts." *Vertical Times—The National Publication of the Access Fund—Vol 104.* (2015): 8–10.

FAQ: "Is it safe to run webbing directly through a hanger?"
Some canyoneers express concern about threading webbing directly through a standard clip hanger. Is a point of weakness being created where the webbing passes over the thin band of metal inside the hanger? (Ref: upper-right bolt.)

Testing has shown there's some truth here, although it may be more of a concern with thinner varieties of webbing.[41] Webbing weakened by exposure to the elements and long-term use may also present a risk. When inspecting the anchor, pay special attention to the webbing where it runs through the hanger. Are there any signs of abrasion or wear? Run a finger around the inside of the hanger, looking for sharp edges and abnormalities.[42] Antique hangers are a definite red flag. When in doubt, replace the webbing with your own.

Another solution is to attach a separate quick link to each hanger and run the webbing through them. (Ref: upper-left bolt.) This provides a rounded surface for the webbing to pass over. This is a good strategy for long-term use in canyons that see large numbers of visitors.

FAQ: "Can I run the rope directly through a hanger?"
Don't do it! Running the rappel rope directly through a standard clip hanger is a recipe for damage and making your rope unrecoverable. Ropes should only be run through rappel hangers or another smooth-sided metal connection (ex: quick links, rappel rings, or chains).

- If you encounter standard hangers with no webbing, inspect the bolts carefully. It's possible this station is intended to be an *unlinked anchor* (we'll introduce these shortly), or perhaps the webbing was removed to indicate the bolts are unsafe. In a perfect world, bad bolts should be removed to keep anyone from rappelling on them.

---

[41] Prattley, Grant. "Webbing in Hangers." *Over the Edge Rescue Blog.*
https://overtheedgerescue.com/canyoning/webbing-in-hangers
[42] Rappel hangers with nice rounded surfaces are unlikely to have this problem.

Just your typical five-bolt rappel station with bright red webbing.

An in-line bolt station. It's redundant, but not load-sharing.

Other Bolt Stations

Single Bolts

On rare occasions, you may encounter a lone wolf out there. A single well-placed bolt is strong enough to rappel on, but two is best for redundancy as bolts are inherently difficult to inspect. For this reason, a single bolt should be regarded as marginal and backed up until trust has been established. Single bolts might be installed for other reasons, however. Some examples would include:

- An anchor for a short drop (or low-angle ramp) when the risk/consequences of failure are low.
- An anchor for a *redirect* (i.e., a means of changing the rappel line in the middle of the pitch).
- An intermediate anchor along a traverse line (ex: protecting an exposed approach to a forward anchor).

Single bolts might also be set in emergencies and on first descents. Installing bolts takes time and if you're placing two bolts at every drop in a canyon with ten rappels … well, you're going to be there awhile. If single bolts are placed during a first descent (and the odds are high that this canyon will see lots of future visitors), it's good form to return at a later date and upgrade them to full rappel stations.

In-Line Bolts

Occasionally, you'll find bolts placed vertically, one above the other. In this case, the anchor is redundant, but not load-sharing; one bolt merely provides a backup to the other. Any material linking the bolts (ex: webbing, accessory cord, or chains) should have a minimum of slack to avoid shock-loading if the primary bolt should fail. In-line bolts are sometimes installed as they require less webbing than the traditional "Y-configuration." Con: If the connecting material is removed, in-line bolts can be mistaken for unlinked anchors.

Bolt Gardens

On rare occasions, you may run across bolt gardens where new bolts were installed because the old ones were untrustworthy. So, which is which? Should we sling them all and hope for the best?

One type of unlinked anchor.

Another form of unlinked anchor.

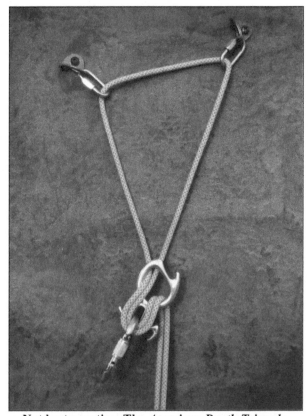

Not best practice: The *American Death Triangle*.

Unlinked Anchors

In aquatic canyons, bolts should ideally be situated above the high-water mark where they won't be affected by flood events. An anchor that's too low may be subject to damage by rocks and boulders getting flushed through. Additionally, any material connecting the bolts will be prone to catching logs and other flood debris. The relentless force of the water leveraged against the bolts can weaken, damage, or even destroy the anchor.

If placement above the high-water mark is not possible, an *unlinked anchor* is a better long-term solution. In this case, the bolts are independent and only become redundant when connected by a rope or rigging. There are several types of unlinked anchor stations:

- Rappel hangers require no connecting material. The rope is threaded through them directly.

- Some hangers come with an integrated rappel ring. For standard clip hangers, you can add a quick link to each bolt for the rope.

- Sometimes, a short section of chain is attached to each bolt (i.e., they are not connected). When the rope is run through both segments, the anchor becomes load-sharing and redundant.

An old bolt damaged by flooding.

Unlinked anchors are common in European canyons, and are starting to appear with greater frequency in the Pacific Northwest. It's good to know how to rig them. Upon arriving at such an anchor, the team's first action is usually to link them with a sling (or quickdraw) for temporary redundancy. The leader can then clip in, inspect the station, deploy the rope, etc. without trusting their life to a single bolt. Redundancy should be maintained as long as the station is in use. The sling is cleaned by the last rappeller.

Advantage
- There's no webbing to inspect or replace. Some canyoneers suggest unlinked anchors should become the standard for all canyon bolt stations.

Disadvantages
- Rigging an unlinked station requires a few extra steps.

- Groups unfamiliar with unlinked bolts may be prone to add webbing and leave it behind. This increases the odds of the station becoming damaged in future flood events.

- Groups unfamiliar with single rope technique (SRT) may be prone to rig an *American Death Triangle*.

The American Death Triangle
Scenario: The team has found a horizontal unlinked anchor atop the pitch.

It might be tempting to run the rope through both bolts to create a two-strand rappel as shown in the photo opposite. This is an *American Death Triangle*: a rigging method infamous as a force multiplier. Assuming the bolts are good and only one person is rappelling at a time, the anchor isn't likely to fail, but it's still not best practice. The American Death Triangle is probably more of a concern when rappelling on antique bolts and other marginal anchors.

Big Creek. One of the best canyons in Washington State.
(Photo: Wade Hewitt)

Chapter 7: Progression

Canyons with deep pools and flowing water are quite different from their dry counterparts. Expect everything underfoot to be loose, uneven, and slippery. As the water level increases, swimming and rope management become increasingly important. Some aquatic canyons offer new options for progression: slides and jumps.

Preparing for Immersion

It's usually time to stop and garb for battle upon reaching the first significant water in the canyon. If wetsuits are required, they're usually put on at this point. Systematically go through your gear and make sure everything is prepared for immersion. The creek is a slippery place and an accidental dunk in a pool gets you and your gear just as wet as a pre-planned swim. Don't be in a hurry; make sure everything is secured and stowed away. Close kegs, seal all dry bags, and batten down the hatches. If not already wearing it, put on your helmet.

- Tip: If you need to use the restroom, do so *before* putting on the wetsuit.

- Generally, harnesses are put on at the same time or upon reaching the first technical obstacle. If you have a harness with a PVC seat, you might put it on to protect your wetsuit.

- Wearing a helmet is always a good idea in a slippery aquatic environment.

Moving Along the Creek

Newcomers to aquatic canyons are frequently surprised at how loose and slippery the creekbed can be. Even with the best footwear available, it can still feel like being at the ice rink. It takes time and practice to get the rhythm of how to move efficiently.

Balance

One solution for balance is to keep your hands free. This allows you to put your arms out to either side for stability and steady yourself against any nearby boulders or logs. Trekking poles are another option for balance. If you don't have one, look around and see if you can find yourself a nice branch or wizard's staff. A walking stick is also handy when crossing strong current and checking the depth. Con: They're annoying to have on a rappel.

Here are some other pointers for traveling in aquatic canyons:

- Look downstream to determine the easiest way forward. The easy route is not always the shortest one.

- Try to keep the team reasonably close together and keep an eye on one another. If you're too spread out, you may not hear a call for help over the noise of the rushing water.

- Avoid aquaphobia. It's often easier/safer to wade or swim through a pool, rather than wasting time and energy trying to keep your feet dry by scrambling around it.

- When hiking along the creek, it's always easier to move in shallow water. In places where the creek passes through a series of bends, you'll find yourself crisscrossing from side to side to remain in the shallows.

- Wading is tricky when you can't see where you're stepping. Feel about with your feet to find secure positions under the water. Keep your center of gravity low and take small steps.

- Avoid rock hopping and jumping down off things. An uneven or slippery landing is a recipe for a twisted ankle. (Jumping into deep pools is a different story; more on that in a moment.)

- Make sure to take adequate breaks. Long stretches of creek-walking can be strenuous.

Downclimbing

Use caution when downclimbing in aquatic canyons. Even trivial drops can be slippery. Setting up a hand line or rappel might take an extra minute, but you'll lose more time dealing with a broken ankle. Also, consider the group's skill level. An experienced climber might find downclimbing a breeze, but a beginner might appreciate the security of a rope. Taller individuals have the advantage of a greater reach and step.

- Climbing is generally easier without a pack. (See "Pack Management" in Chapter 15.)

- If there's a tricky move or two, it may be helpful to have an experienced climber go first and show the team how it's done. This is known as *modeling*.

- When in doubt, don't hesitate to request partner assistance or a rope. It's better to err on the side of caution. Nobody wins with a broken ankle.

- Sometimes, you may need to climb up and over a mid-canyon obstacle (ex: logjam or boulder pile).

Spotting & Assists

On short drops, it's good form to assist the next person down. The spotter's job is to stand at the ready, arms raised with elbows slightly bent. If the climber should slip and come off the wall, the spotter's job is not to catch them, but merely stabilize their center of gravity and slow them down. The goal is to guide the climber down to a safe landing and prevent them from tripping/stumbling on uneven terrain at the bottom. Sometimes, multiple spotters are a good idea for safety. Good communication is key.

- Consider sequencing. Don't make the smallest person on the team spot the largest.

- If the climber's facing in, it can be difficult for them to locate footholds. In this case, the spotter can guide the climber's feet to good positions and push them into the rock for stability.

- If holds are lacking, the spotter could provide a temporary hand or foothold (i.e., a shoulder or knee) for the climber's use. A belay loop on the climber's harness makes a good handle for providing support. Another option: multiple team members could work together to perform a capture.

Jumps

If there's a deep pool below, you may be tempted to jump. Jumping is fun and an efficient way to speed progress down the canyon. There's one caveat: *look before you leap!*

Jumping is a leading cause of canyon injury (i.e., broken ankles and legs). If you're going to jump, always scout it first. Even if you've run the canyon a dozen times before and the guidebook says this is a great jump, scout it anyway. Canyons are very dynamic and that great jump might now be full of rocks, or, perhaps, there's a submerged log right in the middle of the landing zone. Never jump into aerated water without checking it first. Pools can also look deep, but be surprisingly shallow. How does the scout get down? A human anchor is one option.

- Jumps should never be mandatory. Always leave a rope at the top in case it's needed.

- Ideally, jumps should be uncomplicated with a large safe landing area. It's best to err on the side of caution as even minor mistakes can lead to injury. Jumps become more comfortable with practice.

Scouting the Pool

A dive mask (or pair of swim goggles) is useful for checking the depth. If goggles are lacking or the water's too aerated, the scout should swim around and push down vertically to see if they can touch the bottom. A duck dive from the surface is another option; can you physically reach the bottom? Some questions to answer:

- Is the landing zone clear of submerged rocks, ledges, and impaling logs?
- Is the pool deep enough for a safe landing?
- What does the bottom of the pool look like? [43]
- Are there any dangerous water features?

---

[43] Sand, silt, and pebbles make for a softer landing than cobbles and large rocks.

Once the pool has been assessed, the scout makes the call as whether or not it's safe to jump. If it's good, the scout can signal the jumpers (e.g., indicating the safe landing area and how deep the water is). A quick flash of four fingers might mean the water is 4m (~12ft) deep. The scout should remain nearby in case a jumper needs assistance.

> **FAQ: "How deep does it need to be for a safe jump?"**
> The answer depends on the height of the jump and the experience of the jumper. Body size is also a factor. For jumps of up to 5m (~15ft), a safe depth is the jumper's height with their arms extended fully above their head.[44] The *V7 Academy* recommends a pool at least 3m (~10ft) deep for jumps of up to 6m (~20ft). Jumps into shallow water require more skill.

The Launch Platform

Before you jump, take a look at the launch platform. Where is the landing area? Do you need to clear any obstacles to reach the target? The launch platform might be dry initially, but can become increasingly slick as more team members climb up out of the water to jump. Use particular caution on a sloped or slippery platform. When in doubt, find an alternate way to descend.

Technical Jumps

Depending on the height of the jump, different techniques should be used:

- Short Jumps (up to 1m or 3ft)
  One shallow entry technique is to jump out and pull your legs up into an L-position before hitting the water. The idea is to create a large surface area on contact which keeps you from going deep. This method should only be used on very short jumps.

- Moderate Jumps (1–6m or 4–20ft)
  The majority of jumps will fall in this category. It might be okay to wear a pack on short drops, but they should be removed for higher jumps or if the landing area is small. Packs are often removed for comfort. There are two forms of take-off:

  - A simple step off the edge is all you need for a direct vertical drop.

  - If you need some forward momentum, start with one foot in front of the other. Push off, while swinging your arms forward in one continuous motion.

  Once airborne, tuck your arms across your chest in "mummy position" and bend your knees slightly. Should you hit an underwater obstacle, your knees can flex and absorb some of the impact.

  To avoid going deep, you can abruptly pull your legs up into a seated position after entering the water. Splaying your arms and legs out at the same time helps slow you down. It's good to default to this form of shallow-entry technique unless you're confident about the depth.

- High Jumps (over 6m or 20ft)
  WARNING! The higher the jump, the greater the risk. Packs should definitely be removed. On impact with the water, a buoyant pack can jerk upwards and smack you in the back of the head. An ill-fitting PFD can cause similar problems. On even higher jumps, helmets should be removed.

  On high jumps, you'll have more in-flight time. Proper position after take-off is to lean forward slightly with your arms out to either side for stability. Bend your knees. Before entering the water, bring your arms in and adopt the moderate-height jump position. Cross your hands just in front of you to protect your face.

Upon resurfacing after a jump, signal you're okay by tapping your helmet twice (i.e., "I'm good!"). We'll talk more about hand signals at the end of the chapter.

---

[44] Prattley, G. & Clearwater, D. (2020). *Canyoning Technical Manual*. Maxim Print.

A fun slide in Dingford Creek, Wash.

A short slide in Mineral Creek, Wash.

Swimming across a deep pool in Cussed Hollow, Wash.

Slides

When the terrain permits, sliding is another fun option for fast progression. Like jumps, slides should be scouted in advance. The scout can rappel along the line of descent (or adjacent to it), looking for holes and snags. Getting caught on something mid-slide could be dangerous. Similarly, getting a foot caught in a hole could lead to a twisted or broken ankle. A person dropping into a larger hole may risk getting pitched forward suddenly as a result of their own momentum. The pool at the bottom of the slide should be also checked, looking for all the same things as a jump. Is there a large landing area? Are there any submerged obstacles or hazards?

- Like jumps, slides should never be mandatory. (See also "Controlled Slides" in Chapter 15.)

- Slides can be damaging to your harness and wetsuit. A harness with a PVC seat is recommended.

- Before sliding, cinch down your harness and tuck in anything that might be subject to getting caught.

- Packs are not recommended on long, fast slides. If you should accidentally roll over to one side, the pack can throw off your trajectory. It's often better to send them down separately.

- Use caution when getting in position for a slide. Don't get swept before you're ready.

Proper slide position is feet first, seated or lying on your back. Keep your legs together, with knees slightly bent and toes pointed. Arms should be forward with your hands crossed in your lap (or pulled up across your chest in "mummy position"). This keeps your elbows from banging into things. Lean back and fully commit.

Upon re-surfacing, signal that you're okay by tapping your helmet twice.

Swimming

The ability to swim is crucial in aquatic canyons. The more water that's present, the more important it becomes.

In calm pools, you can use your pack as a flotation device (i.e., taking advantage of the trapped air inside your kegs and dry bags). Before entering the pool, cinch down your pack's waist and sternum straps. Gently enter the water, lean back, and start to back-paddle. Your pack will remain centered underneath you, providing support. You should be able to stay afloat and bob about with minimal effort. Backstroke with your arms and kick to move. Con: You may need to turn occasionally to see where you're going.

Swimming face down works too, but is awkward/uncomfortable with a pack. A buoyant pack can ride up and push you down into the water. If you don't want to back-paddle, a better strategy is to remove the pack and hold it to your chest like a kickboard. In calm water, you could also tow your pack along behind you with a foot or a tether.

- Swimming techniques change in higher flow. (See "Swimming in Swiftwater" in Chapter 19.)

Flotation

If an object doesn't float, it'll eventually sink. It's good to test out your flotation and water protection systems at home before relying on them to protect expensive equipment (ex: cameras) in the field.

- A wetsuit alone will provide some extra buoyancy.

- If your pack has insufficient flotation, consider adding an extra keg or some empty water bottles.

- A personal flotation device (PFD) might be a good idea for weaker swimmers, or the entire team if lots of swimming is expected. (See Chapters 3 & 19 for more information on PFDs.)

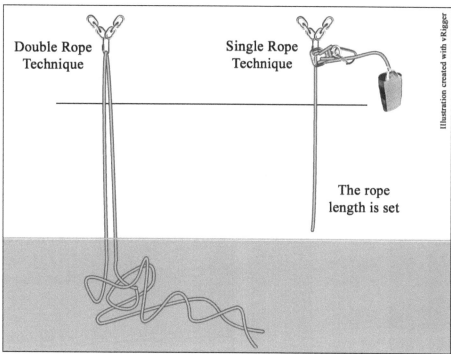

Double Rope
Technique

Single Rope
Technique

The rope
length is set

DRT vs. SRT when rappelling into deep water.

Rappelling into Deep Water

Two-strand rappels are the standard in alpine climbing and mountaineering. Ropes are thrown down the pitch without much concern about excess being present at the bottom. This is known as *Double Rope Technique* (DRT). In aquatic canyons, however, excess rope in a deep pool can become an entanglement hazard. Getting tangled in a calm pool might be annoying, but it can be dangerous in fast-moving or turbulent water. Getting tangled has led to fatal accidents. Disconnecting from the rappel can also be a challenge when it's too deep to stand, or you're getting bombarded under a waterfall.

Another problem with DRT is potential for the two lines to tangle around each other. This can be a particular issue with new ropes (often highly twisted after being pulled off the spool) or due to conditions (ex: ropes hanging in moving water). Minor tangles can make it difficult to pull the rope. An extreme tangle can become an obstacle that a rappeller cannot pass.[45] Getting stuck under a waterfall can be a life-threatening situation.

To avoid these problems, canyoneers often rappel on a single rope strand. This is known as *Single Rope Technique* (SRT). If the rappel exits into deep water, the best practice is to pay out just enough rope to reach the bottom and no more. This is called *setting the length*. The tail of the rope hangs at, or slightly above, the surface of the water. Setting the rope length has a number of advantages:

- No excess rope at the bottom
  With the length set, there's no rope in the pool. All the extra rope is kept in reserve atop the pitch, where it's available for other uses (ex: rescues).

- No tangling
  With only one rope hanging down the pitch, there are no other lines to tangle with.

- Fast exit from the rappel
  There's no need to manually disconnect. Instead, rappellers deliberately slide off the end of the rope and swim away. This eliminates the possibility of getting stuck, struggling to disconnect while floating or treading water. The rappeller moves effortlessly from rappelling to swimming.

---

[45] This is a particular issue for ATCs and other narrow-aperture descenders.

Performing a floating disconnect in a calm pool.

Excess Rope in a Calm Pool
In calm water, rope entanglement is probably more of an annoyance than a threat. It's still good to avoid, however. If you're rappelling into a calm pool, here are a few strategies:

- If other team members are already at the bottom, ask them to secure the rope. The rope can be pulled out of the water, or otherwise kept out of the rappeller's way.

- If there's a convenient ledge above the water, stop and disconnect there. You can lower yourself in or jump out past the rope to avoid entanglement.

- Floating Disconnect
  Upon reaching the pool, gently lower yourself in, and allow your pack flotation to come into play. While floating on your back (sea otter style), pull slack through your descender and disconnect.[46] Carefully swim away, staying near the surface to avoid entanglement.

  o Tip #1: Just before reaching the water, unlock your descender's carabiner. This makes it faster to disconnect.

  o Tip #2: If underneath a waterfall, pull some slack through your descender and swim a few strokes away. Once clear of the waterfall, it'll be easier to disconnect.

Once in a safe place, consider signaling the team above to pull up some rope and set the length. There's no need for anyone else to risk entanglement. Rappelling off the end of the rope and swimming away is faster than requiring everyone to perform a floating disconnect.

Excess Rope in Swiftwater
WARNING! *A free rope in a turbulent water is extremely dangerous!* The rope is pretty much guaranteed to tangle around everything in the vicinity including the rappeller, underwater obstacles, and itself. You may find knots getting tied in the rope purely by action of the churning water. Always set the length when rappelling into swiftwater and use good rope management.

---

[46] If your descender must be removed from your harness (ex: ATC or classic figure-8 device), use caution to avoid losing it. If dropped in a deep pool, you might not get it back.

Setting the Length

<u>Scenario</u>: We've arrived atop a vertical pitch with a deep pool at the bottom. Our plan is to set the length, so everyone can slide off the end of the rope and swim away.

If you can see the bottom …
Setting the length is easy. Pay out rope until the tail reaches the water. Adjust the length as needed.

If you can't see the bottom …
Setting the length is a little trickier. Here are some options:

➢ <u>Measure the rope</u>
If you know the height of the pitch (from the beta), you can measure out pretty close to the right amount of rope by counting arm lengths. It depends on the person, but if you stretch your arms out fully to either side and run the rope between them, it's probably close to 1.5m (~5ft). It's a good idea to measure your own "wingspan" ahead of time. So, if we have a 15m rappel, that'd be about ten arm-lengths of rope. A middle-mark on the rope is useful when setting the length on a long pitch.

➢ <u>Send out a scout</u>
Send someone out along the rim to one side or the other to find a place where the bottom is visible. Alternatively, a safety line could be rigged to permit a safe approach to the edge. (See "Edge Lines" in Chapter 14.) The scout can direct the team to set the rope length appropriately.

➢ <u>Set the rope short</u> (aka *Exploratory Rappel*)
A releasable system could be used to set the length. We haven't introduced these yet, but, essentially, it's a rigging technique that allows rope to be paid out even when the system is fully under load.

Here's how it works. The rope length is deliberately set a bit short. The leader starts down the rappel normally, but stops in a good location where they have a clear view down the pitch. With the tail in sight, the leader signals for rope. A dedicated belayer at the anchor releases, lowering both the rope and rappeller together. As soon as the tail reaches the water (or is deemed "good enough"), the leader signals again for a halt. The leader finishes the rappel, dropping off into the water and swimming away. The rope length is now set perfectly for the rest of the team.

We'll talk more about releasable rigging and exploratory rappels later in Chapter 11.

➢ <u>Set the rope long</u>
If landing in a calm pool (and odds of entanglement are low), the rope could deliberately be set a bit long. The leader, being one of the most experienced on the team, commits to this small additional risk. The leader rappels and performs a floating disconnect upon reaching the water. Once in a safe place, the leader signals the belayer above to pull up some rope and set the length for the rest of the team.[47]

Illustration created with vRigger

Exploratory Rappels: the rope is deliberately set a bit short.

---

[47] FAQ: "Do we really need to set the length in this case?" It depends on your situation. A large experienced team might opt to set the length purely for efficiency. Dropping off the rope into the water is faster than requiring everyone to perform a floating disconnect. No one else risks becoming tangled.

Communication

In aquatic canyons, it's often difficult to communicate between the top and bottom of the pitch. The team needs to be able to signal one another in an emergency, when setting the length, and to indicate when the rappel line is available for the next person. Be aware: there's no universal standard for signals. Preferred signals will vary depending on where you are in the world and who you're with. It's good for the team to agree on a set of signals at the beginning of the day and review them periodically. The best signals are ones that are easy to remember.

- It's a good to have multiple options for communication. Verbal commands and whistle blasts might not be heard, hand signals require a direct line of sight, whistles can get lost, radios can go dead, etc.

- Communication is easier on shorter pitches. On a rappel composed of multiple tiers, you might consider stationing someone in the middle to relay signals.

- Keep messages short, distinct, and non-ambiguous. Confusion and misunderstanding can lead to accidents.

Verbal Commands

Verbal commands generally work well in dry canyons, although acoustics and echoes can sometimes throw you off. Rushing water and weather (e.g., wind and rain) can make it difficult to hear commands. If you're shouting yourself hoarse, other options may be preferred. Also, consider the etiquette angle if non-canyoneers are about. Hand signals are quiet and professional.

- For best clarity, direct your voice towards the person you're addressing.

BruceWyse

Off rappel! All clear!   Take up some rope!   Give me rope!   Stop!

Hand Signals

The illustrations above show a set of hand signals for common messages. Signals that can be given one-handed may be preferred as they can also be used while on rappel. Exaggerated motions can sometimes help with visibility at a distance. The recipient should repeat the same signal back to confirm receipt of message.

Other Hand Signals	
Strong Flow	Put your arms up over your head as if you're a strong-man lifting weights. For "very strong flow," pump your arms vigorously up and down.
Slippery	Hold one hand out, palm down. Rotate your wrist/arm in an exaggerated motion from side to side as if your palm were slipping on an imaginary surface.
Hazard	Make an upward-pointing triangle with both hands.
Sharp Edge	Hold one hand out, palm up. Make cutting motions across your arm with the other hand.
Deep water	To communicate the depth: give a count on your fingers. A flash of five fingers, for example, might mean it's 5m (~15ft) deep.
Pack	Using both hands, with index fingers extended: sketch a square in the air.
Rope Bag	Using both hands, with index fingers extended: sketch a circle in the air.
Guided Rappel or Zip Line	Hold one arm out to your side at a 45-degree angle and run your other hand up and down along it.

When setting the length on a multi-tier drop, the leader can signal how much rope is required with both hands. For example, two fingers on one hand and five on the other might indicate 25m.

Whistle Blasts
Whistles are one of the best options for communication in aquatic canyons. Again, there's no universal code, so the team should agree on a set of signals to use at the beginning of the day. Whistle codes are easy to forget, so it's good to review them periodically, especially when entering a difficult or dangerous area. Upon hearing a whistle blast, it's good to repeat it back as an acknowledgement (i.e., "I heard the following …").

- Attach your whistle to your helmet with a short breakaway cord. Wearing a whistle around your neck is not recommended as the cord can get tangled in pack straps, caught on things, etc. Similarly, whistles should not be attached to your pack. If it's on your helmet, then it's always with you.

- If the rappel passes through a dangerous area, keep the whistle at the ready in your mouth. This removes any need to go fumbling for it in an emergency.

- Face the person you're signaling and use loud blasts. Tiny peeps are unlikely to be heard. To avoid confusion, leave a distinct pause between each blast of the whistle.

Here's a code that correlates the number of whistle blasts to word count:

- 1 blast   *Stop! / Attention!*
- 2 blasts   *All clear! / Off rappel! / I'm okay!*
- 3 blasts   *Give me rope!*   -   release rope (or lower)
- 4 blasts   *Take up some rope!*   -   pull the rope up (or haul)
- 5 blasts   *Find another way to descend!*   -   possible core shot in the rope
- Continuous blast   *Emergency!*   -   keep blowing your whistle

Radios
Radios can be useful, particularly on first descents, long rappels, and in rescues. Con: They're expensive and aren't always reliable. A radio may become useless if it gets wet or the batteries go dead.

Before running the canyon, make sure that the batteries are fully charged and that all radios are on the same channel. Anyone carrying a radio should know how to operate it. Always test them prior to entering the canyon.

The author descending the big drop in Davis Creek, Wash.
(Photo: Wade Hewitt)

Chapter 8: Basic Rigging

When setting up a rappel, one of the big questions is: *what rigging should we use?* The answer is situationally dependent. There are many variables to consider, such as the height of the pitch, how much water is present, the availability of anchors, the presence of hazards, and experience level of the team. Every form of rigging has its own pros and cons; no single technique will work in every situation. Instead of memorizing a complex set of rules, it's better to acquire a broad understanding of rigging systems. Think of every technique as a tool in your toolbox. It's important to understand when that tool is appropriate for use, and when it's not.

- "We always do it this way" is not a good answer to why you're using a particular rigging system.

- Some forms of canyon rigging may seem simple at first glance, but there are many easily-missed subtleties.

Rigging Classification

Rappel rigging usually takes one of three forms:

DRT	Double Rope Technique. Method of rappelling on two rope strands.
SRT	Single Rope Technique. Method of rappelling on a single rope strand.
Twin System	A DRT rigging with a strand isolation applied to create two independent SRT systems. Twin systems can be rappelled SRT or DRT.

The above systems can be further subdivided into two categories:

Releasable	The rigging has the capacity to pay out rope when under load. If the rappeller needs more rope for any reason, it's easily provided. Releasable rigging is often used when rappelling in flow, or if the bottom of the pitch cannot be seen from above. It provides more options in an emergency and can be used to help protect the rope from abrasive rock.
Static	The rigging does not have the ability to pay out rope when under load. Static rigging is generally best for experienced teams (who can self-rescue) in little-to-no flow and on pitches where no abrasion hazards are present.

Some rigging systems are also:

Retrievable[48]	The anchor and/or rigging can be retrieved from the bottom of the pitch. In most cases, nothing is left behind. Retrievables are an advanced form of *ghosting*.

It's good to understand how various rigging systems are related, and how to convert one type of rigging into another. This is most often done to take advantage, or avoid a specific disadvantage, of a given system. It's fairly common to start a rappel with one technique, then convert it to another for the last person.

---

[48] The term *retrievable* is sometimes confused with *releasable*, although they describe different properties of the rigging. Some rigging systems are both releasable and retrievable.

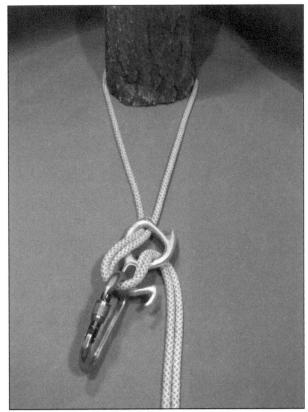

DRT rigged on a fixed anchor.   **DRT tree wrap**

Double Rope Technique (DRT)

Rappelling on two strands is the standard in alpine climbing. It's often referred to as "rappelling double strand" or "Toss and Go." DRT is a form of static rigging.[49]

Advantages

- Fast to rig, especially with a rope bag.

- Each strand bears half the rappeller's weight, so the rope is less likely to suffer damage when passing over abrasive rock. DRT may be a good choice when multiple sharp edges are present.

- DRT may be a good choice on brushy or obstacle-strewn rappels as there are no knots or other obstructions to get stuck when pulling the rope. (Exception: a knot will be present when two ropes are tied together.)

Disadvantages

- The entire rope is committed to the rappel.

- Both ends must reach the ground. DRT can be dangerous if the rope strands are of uneven length and one side does not reach. If the shorter end were to slip through the rappeller's descender, the result could be catastrophic. Rappelling off the end of the rope is a common form of rappel accident.

- Both rope strands must be loaded into the rappeller's descender. Accidentally loading only one strand is a common beginner mistake. If not detected, the rigging will fall apart when weighted.

---

[49] Releasable DRT systems exist, but they're a form of advanced rigging and are beyond the scope of this manual.

- The rope strands can become tangled around one another.[50] Minor tangles will make it harder to pull the rope. They can be difficult to spot from below (particularly on long rappels), and much time can be lost trying to sort them out. Extreme tangles are rare, but can create an obstacle in the middle of the pitch that a rappeller cannot pass. This is a particular issue for narrow-aperture descenders, such as an ATC.

- Rescues are more complicated. There's no easy way to lower a stuck rappeller.

DRT in Aquatic Canyons
WARNING! DRT can be dangerous in high flow or when exiting into a turbulent pool. Here's why:

- If the rope strands hanging down the pitch become sufficiently tangled around each other, they can create an obstacle that a rappeller cannot pass. This can be a life-threatening situation if the rappeller is stuck under a waterfall.

- If the rappel exits into deep water, the excess rope at the bottom can become an entanglement hazard. Entanglement has been the cause of fatal accidents in churning whitewater.

- Excess rope at the bottom also means rappellers will need to perform a floating disconnect. The odds of entanglement increase if the rappeller is struggling to get off the rope in turbulent water, strong current, or while being bombarded under a waterfall.

- Devices that need to be removed from your harness (ex: ATC or classic figure-8) are easily lost.

- When rigging DRT, the rope is not attached to the anchor. High flow and strong current have potential to move the rope. If the rope moves far enough relative to the anchor, it can produce a strand that no longer reaches the bottom. In a worst-case scenario, the rope could be lost.

FAQ: "Yikes! So, DRT should never be used in aquatic canyons, right?"
Not exactly. It depends on your situation. If you have a short uncomplicated rappel that doesn't pass through a waterfall and the landing area is dry or shallow, DRT might be a fine technique to use.

Sometimes, the team will start with a releasable SRT system (ex: munter hitch), then convert it to DRT for the last rappeller. The last person commits the additional risk of rappelling on a static system.

Rigging
DRT requires twice the height of the pitch in rope. The exact steps will vary, but here's the general sequence for rigging a pitch with a clear line of sight to the bottom:

Short Rappels	With a single rope, we can rappel up to half its length. With a 60m (200ft) rope, we can rappel a maximum of about 30m (100ft). Rigging Thread one end of the rope through the anchor. Continue pulling rope through, coiling as you go, until you have enough for the pitch. While holding the rope near the anchor (to avoid losing it), throw the coil. Next, deploy the rope on the other side. Make a note of which side the rope bag is on. That's the rope strand which will be used for retrieval.

---

[50] Tangling might be the result of poorly deployed ropes, outside forces (ex: water movement), or highly twisted ropes (ex: a new rope that was recently pulled off the spool).

Long Rappels	If the pitch is more than half the rope length, a second rope will be required. With two 60m ropes tied together, we can rappel up to a maximum of about 60m. Rigging Thread the end of one rope through the anchor, then tie the ropes together with a stacked overhand. (See Appendix I for more information.) Both ropes are deployed, one after the other, on either side of the anchor. Before departing, make a note of which side of the anchor the knot is on. That's the rope which will be used for the pull.

Tree Wrap (DRT)

Another DRT method is to wrap the rope directly around a tree, log, or other smooth-sided natural feature. This is a quick and dirty technique that requires no webbing or other gear. Ideal use case: getting down a short dry pitch when it's not worth the time it'd take to build an anchor.

- Trees
  Using a living tree for an anchor works, but, arguably, is poor form. When it's time to pull, half the rope will be dragged around the back of the tree causing friction damage. If this happens a couple times, it's not a big deal, but if done too many times by too many people, the bark will become girdled and the tree will die. Additionally, your rope may be subject to abrasion and sap. Leaving a fixed anchor is kinder to the tree and a better solution if future visitors are anticipated.

- Fallen Logs
  Tree wraps work great on logs, but still subject your rope to abrasion during the pull.

- Rocks & Boulders
  Wrapping the rope directly around large rocks generally isn't a good idea. If the rope passes through any cracks or pinches, the friction produced can make retrieval impossible.[51] In most cases, you're probably better off leaving a fixed anchor.

Beware using tree wraps on long pitches. The larger the object, the more contact the rope will have and the greater the friction produced. This friction must be overcome in order to pull the rope from below. On longer pitches, the pull can be very difficult. When in doubt, try a test pull before the last rappeller comes down.

Best Practices

In aquatic canyons, DRT should be used sparingly. It's best on short, dry pitches when no other hazards are present, or as a static system for the last rappeller. Also consider also the experience level of your team.

DRT might be appropriate:
- Short, uncomplicated pitches.
- Dry pitch or low flow.
- Landing is dry or shallow water.
- Pitch is full brush/obstacles.
- Multiple sharp edges are present.
- For beginners unfamiliar with SRT.[52]

DRT is not recommended:
- Long pitches (hard to discern rope tangles).
- Rappel exits into deep/turbulent water.
- Rappel passes through a waterfall.
- Complex rappel or other hazards present.
- Rappellers don't know how to self-rescue.[53]

---

[51] Desert Southwest: Wrapping the rope around sandstone features (including natural arches) is a bad idea as you'll etch out permanent grooves when it's time to pull the rope. *Don't do it!*

[52] A better solution: make sure everyone has adequate training before entering the canyon.

[53] A releasable SRT system may be a better choice if any team members don't know how to self-rescue.

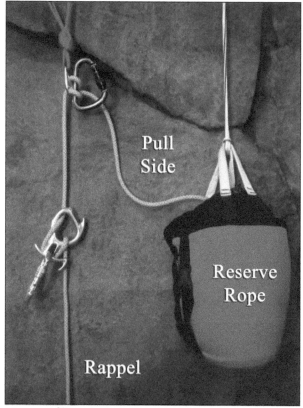 

SRT static system: carabiner block.   SRT releasable system: compact figure-8 block.

Single Rope Technique (SRT)

Single-strand rappels are the standard in canyoning and technical caving. There are many ways to rig for SRT, both static and releasable. We'll talk about the general properties of SRT systems here, then look at some specific techniques in later chapters. We'll introduce rope blocks in Chapter 10 and releasable systems in Chapter 11.

Advantages

- SRT makes very efficient use of the rope, especially when setting the length.

- With only one rope hanging down the pitch, there are no other lines to tangle with.

- The reserve rope atop the pitch can be used for other purposes. It could be used to protect an exposed approach to the anchor, as an edge line, or as a means of backing up a marginal anchor. In an emergency, the reserve rope could be used to lower a rappeller, set up a haul system, rappel down to the victim, etc.

- Ascending is easier on a single rope strand.

Disadvantages

- SRT rigging is a little more complicated than DRT. There are more things to watch out for and increased odds of getting a rope stuck during the pull.

- A single rope must support the entire load. This makes the rope more prone to damage when passing over sharp edges and abrasive rock. Abrasion management techniques may be required. (See "Protecting the Rope" in Chapter 4.)

- Rappellers will require more friction on single-strand rappels. (See "Setting the Friction" in Chapter 15.)

Rigging

There are certain exceptions, but SRT usually requires about twice the height of the pitch in rope. One line is used to rappel, while the other side is used for the pull. Unlike DRT, the two lines are deployed separately. The pull side is usually kept atop the pitch and is not deployed until the very end (i.e., by the last rappeller). By keeping the excess rope in reserve, it's available for use in an emergency.

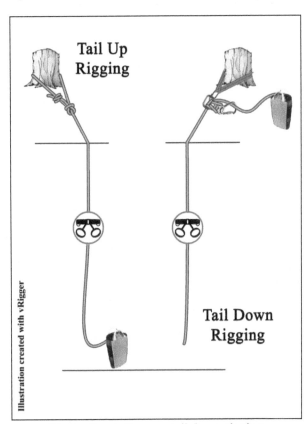

Illustration created with vRigger

Illustrating tail up vs. tail down rigging.

SRT rigging varies slightly depending on the height of the pitch:

- <u>Short Rappels</u>
  With a single rope, we can rappel up to half its length. For example, with a 60m (200ft) rope, we can rappel up to about 30m (100ft).

- <u>Long Rappels</u>
  If the pitch is more than half the rope length, the pull side will need to be extended. This is generally done with another rope.

Classifying SRT

SRT systems can usually be classified as either *tail up* or *tail down*. These terms describe how the system is rigged (i.e., what is done with the tail of the rope when it's pulled out of the rope bag atop the pitch).

- <u>Tail Up</u>
  If the tail will remain atop the pitch, it's referred to as a tail up system. In the example opposite, the rope is tied off to the tree stump with a bowline. (Yes, it's a fixed rope.) In this case, all the excess rope will be at the bottom of the pitch.

- <u>Tail Down</u>
  If the tail of the rope will be lowered down the pitch (as might be done to set the length), then it's a tail down system. In the example above, a fixed anchor was built on the tree stump and we are using a releasable figure-8 block. All the excess rope is kept at the top.

This classification might seem like a trivial distinction at first, but it has definite consequences for the rigging.

Tail Up	Advantage • Tail up systems are generally a little faster to rig and get people rappelling. Disadvantages • All the excess rope is at the bottom of the pitch and is not available for other uses. This means the length cannot be set. • If the rappel exits into a deep pool, everyone will need to perform a floating disconnect. This is less efficient than setting the length. • Pulling the rope tends to be very slow. In some cases, the entire rappel rope must be pulled up through the anchor.
Tail Down	Advantages • *Setting the length* is a form of tail down rigging that is frequently used when rappelling into deep water. There are many advantages. Rope is paid out until the tail hangs at (or slightly above) the surface of the water. • The reserve rope atop the pitch can be put to other uses. • Retrieving the rope is faster / more efficient than a tail up system. Disadvantage • If the length is set and the tail is well above the water, you won't be able to reach it. Re-ascending the rope may not be possible.[54]

Setting the Length

Setting the length is not just for aquatic canyons. In a dry canyon, it might be used to keep the rope out of the mud or a stagnant pool. Setting the length also has an advantage in that it's faster to exit the rappel. When out with a big group, you might consider setting the length for efficiency. Upon reaching the bottom, rappellers can pull the short remaining tail through their descender and walk away. There's no need to manually disconnect.

When rappelling into a deep pool, the end of the rope should hang at (or slightly above) the surface of the water. This doesn't need to be an exact science, however. If it's within about 0.5m (~1–2ft) in either direction, it's probably fine. Even static ropes will stretch a little under load.

- In a calm pool, it's okay if the rope is a trifle long. A rappeller landing in the water can pull the remaining tail through their descender. There's not enough rope present to get tangled in. If the rappel exits into dangerous water feature, you'll probably better off keeping the rope on the shorter side.

- On long rappels, it can be difficult to tell if the length is set properly from above. If you can't tell, rappel a bit further and check again. It's perfectly okay to stop, lock off your descender, and pull the rope up to confirm. Brightly-colored ropes are good for visibility.

- Beware of anything that might interfere with your ability to slide off the end of the rope. Some examples would include autoblocks, stopper knots, a gob of tape affixed to the end of the rope, plastic caps, slippage of the rope sheath, a frayed rope end, etc.

- If the length is set, the tail of the rope will hang free and can spin. Any twists present in the rope, such as those imparted by a figure-8 style descender, can come out of their own accord.

---

[54] A team might need to go back up the rope to fix a problem, retrieve a pack that was inadvertently left behind, etc.

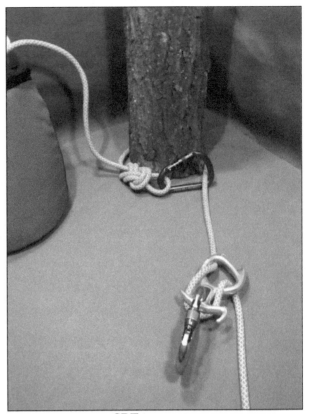

Fixed SRT tied with a bowline. **SRT tree wrap**

Fixed Ropes

Tying the rope directly to a bombproof anchor is, perhaps, the simplest form of static SRT rigging. However, an astute observer might ask: "What good is a rope that can't be retrieved?" Consider the following:

- Suppose there's a 60m rappel at the start of the canyon where you park the car. All the other rappels are 10m or less. Instead of hauling the big rope all the way through the canyon, you can take a short rope instead. The big rope will be fixed in place and left in place to be reclaimed upon your return.

- Fixed ropes are useful on scouting missions. You can rappel into the canyon to look around, then ascend the same rope to get back out. *Rim ropes* might also be left in place to provide an emergency escape route if the team needs to bail during a first descent.

- In rare cases, the plan might be to rappel, then either re-ascend, or hike back up to the top post-canyon. In this case, rigging the rope to be pulled from below might be a waste of time.

As a fixed rope will not be retrieved, we can rappel its entire length. Fixed ropes can be rigged tail up or tail down. It's also possible to set the length. No webbing or other gear is required.

Tree Wrap (SRT)

The photo above-right shows a single-strand version of the tree wrap. This is another form of static rigging and is best used in a tail down configuration. Best use: descending a short dry (or low flow) pitch into a calm pool. To rig: pay out sufficient rope for the rappel, then run the rope around a tree, log, or other smooth-sided natural feature. Tie a figure-8 knot (or alpine butterfly) and clip it to the rappel strand with a locking carabiner. Cinch the resulting loop tightly around the anchor. The rappel station is open for business.

To clean: the last rappeller deploys the pull side. The rope is then recovered from below.

<u>Advantages</u>
- Unlike the DRT tree wrap, it's possible to set the length.

- If the pull side isn't long enough, it can be extended. Beware tree wraps on long rappels, however.

<u>Disadvantages</u>
- This technique has all the same disadvantages of the DRT tree wrap (i.e., friction damage to the tree and subjecting your rope to abrasion and sap).

- A closed loop is pulled down the pitch during recovery, which has higher odds of getting snagged. Note that any obstructions between the rappel and pull lines could render the rope unrecoverable.[55]

Best Practices

SRT provides some major benefits. Single-strand rappels can be of any length, wet or dry. The landing zone can be dry, deep water, or a turbulent pool. The use of releasable SRT systems is quite common in aquatic canyons.

<u>SRT is appropriate:</u>
- Pitches of any height. Can be wet or dry.
- Rappel passes through a waterfall.
- Rappel exits into deep/turbulent water.
- Complex rappel or other hazards are present.
- Rappellers who don't know how to self-rescue (i.e., can be lowered with a releasable system).

<u>SRT might not be recommended:</u>
- Pitch is full of snag hazards.
- Multiple sharp edges are present.
- For beginners familiar only with DRT.

---

[55] One way to avoid this problem: the last person cleans the knot and rappels DRT.

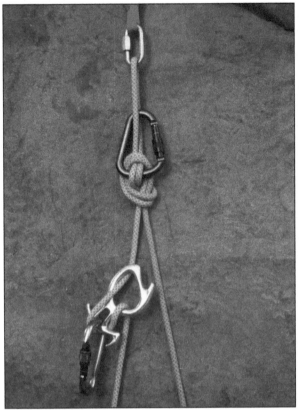

| Static twin system: Stone Knot. | Releasable twin system: Joker. |

Twin Rope Systems

Twin systems are something of a cross between DRT and SRT. They start life as a DRT rigging, but then a strand isolation is applied to create two independent SRT systems. Twins can be rigged in many different ways, both static and releasable. We'll review their general properties here, then look at some selected systems in Chapter 12.

Advantages
- Twin systems can speed up progression with a team of four or more. As the lines are independent, one person can be rappelling (SRT), while the next is setting up and running through their safety checks. As soon as the first person is off the rappel, the next can go immediately.[56] This is an efficient way to move a large group through technical terrain.

- As the two lines are independent, they can be used for different purposes. For example: one line could be used for rappelling, while the other provides a top belay.

- Twin systems can be rappelled DRT or SRT. Rappelling DRT provides some redundancy. For example: if the strand lengths are uneven (or if one side was severed by rockfall), the system will not fall apart when the shorter end slips through the rappeller's descender.

Disadvantages
- Effectively, the rope is fixed to the anchor and is not recoverable. The rigging must be converted to either DRT or SRT to pull the rope.

- The rope strands may be more prone to abrasion/damage when rappelling SRT.

---

[56] We are still sending down rappellers one at a time, so the anchor only needs to support a single-person load.

- As with DRT, the lines have potential to tangle around each other. Tangles are easier to deal with on shorter pitches. It can be avoided if one is being careful.

Twin Systems in Aquatic Canyons

Twin systems are not recommended if the rappel passes through high flow or exits into a deep, turbulent pool. Twin systems have almost all the same disadvantages as DRT.

- With a classic twin system, the length can only be set on one side. It's possible to set the length on both sides (using either end of the rope), but this is an advanced rigging technique.

- Excess rope in the pool can present an entanglement hazard. Some rappellers may be required to perform a floating disconnect.

- If the rope strands are hanging in fast-moving water, they have the potential to tangle.

Rigging

Rigging a twin system is essentially identical to DRT with the extra step of applying a strand isolation. Always check that both sides reach the bottom. We'll introduce several methods of strand isolation in Chapter 12.

Best Practices

Twin systems are best used on short/moderate dry pitches when unconcerned about excess rope being present at the bottom (i.e., a dry or shallow landing). They may be a good choice when out with a big group.

A twin system is appropriate:
- Large groups (i.e., four or more).
- Short or moderate-length pitch.
- Pitch is dry or low flow.
- Landing is dry or shallow water.
- Training beginners.

A twin system might not be recommended:
- Small groups (not very efficient).
- Long drops (hard to discern rope tangles).
- Rappel exits into deep/turbulent water.
- Rappel passes through a waterfall.
- Complex rappel or other hazards are present.
- Multiple sharp edges are present.

Putting It All Together

To wrap up the chapter, here's a table to help categorize the various types of rigging systems. Don't worry if you haven't seen some of these yet; they're coming in later chapters.

	Static	Releasable
DRT	○ Toss & Go ○ tree wrap (DRT)	○ *releasable DRT (advanced)*
SRT	○ static blocks ○ fixed rope ○ tree wrap (SRT)	○ munter hitch ○ figure-8 blocks (compact, EMO)
Twin Systems	○ stone knot ○ double alpine butterfly ○ *... and many more.*	○ Joker ○ Jester
Retrievables	○ retrievable sling ○ toggles	○ retrievable sling

Be aware: this is not a comprehensive list of all possible rigging systems. It's a set of frequently-used ones, plus a few others that are good to be aware of.

Daniel Elson in the depths of Big Creek, Wash.
(Photo: Wade Hewitt)

Chapter 9: Pitch Management

Every technical obstacle encountered in the canyon must be assessed and a plan made to get the team safely through. In the case of a vertical pitch, quite often the solution will be: "set up a rappel." In doing so, we walk through the same general sequence:

Step I	Gather information and make a plan.
Step II	Establish an anchor and rigging.
Step III	Deploy the rope.
Step IV	The team descends. (The first and last rappellers have some special duties.)
Step V	Pulling the rope.

There's a lot going on here, so let's unpack this sequence and walk through each of the steps in turn.

Step I: Gather Information & Make a Plan

Upon reaching an obstacle in the canyon (such as a vertical drop), the first step is to determine the best way forward. This is easy when the entire pitch can be seen from above. If the view is obstructed, you may need to send out a scout. A scout could move along the rim to one side or the other to obtain a better vantage. Another option would be to set up a safety line out to the edge. The scout could then downclimb or rappel a short distance to get a better view. The goal is to find out what you're dealing with.

- Keep in mind: rigging rappels takes time. It may be worth looking for more efficient options if anticipating a long day out or when daylight is waning. Could the drop be downclimbed or bypassed? If there's a deep pool below, jumping or sliding might be an option. A human anchor or safety line could be used on short drops and ramps. There's still some rigging here, but it's faster than setting up a full rappel.

- In some cases, you might not want to rappel, but it's the safe choice. "We could downclimb here, but an accidental slip might break an ankle." The team needs to weigh the risks and possible consequences.

> **Belaying a Scout**
> Scenario: This drop might be downclimbable, but it's difficult to tell from above.
>
> One solution is to set up a human anchor and have a scout downclimb on belay. If the climbing proves difficult, the scout can be lowered. If the pitch is anything other than an easy downclimb, a rappel can be rigged for the rest of the team. Advantage: The rope length is already set.

Step II: Establish an Anchor & Rigging

Okay, having assessed this drop, we've decided that rappelling is our best option. The next step is to establish an anchor and select an appropriate rigging system.

What anchors are available?

All pre-existing anchors should be thoroughly inspected prior to use. If you don't like, don't understand, or lack confidence in an anchor, it should be backed up or replaced. If no anchors are found, you'll likely need to build one. In this case, what are your options? If we were to build an anchor on this tree, what would the rappel be like? What about that boulder over there? Can natural anchors be used, or will bolts be required for a safe descent? The goal is always to rappel from an anchor that inspires confidence. (See Chapter 4–6 for a discussion of anchors.)

- When building anchors, take your time and get it right. Rushing is usually counterproductive. No one wants to rappel on shoddy anchors.

- Don't build anchors by committee. If you have a large group, it's better to assign a couple of experienced team members to the job. Everyone else takes a break.

- Try to clear away any loose rocks or branches atop the pitch that could fall on rappellers or snag the rope during the pull.

Temporary Clip-in Point

When arriving at an anchor, you'll sometimes find there's limited real estate to clip things in.[57] You might need to connect a traverse line, find a place hang the rope bag, and need still more room for rappellers to clip in while they set up to rappel. One way to reduce clutter at the anchor is to add a temporary clip-in point. Here are some options:

➢ Clip a large locking HMS carabiner (or rigging plate) to the anchor. The carabiner is usually clipped near the top of the anchor where it's easy to reach.

➢ A short sling could be clipped or girth hitched to the anchor. An overhand knot or two creates multiple places to clip in. The sling will protect rappellers while they set up on the rope.

This temporary clip-in will be cleaned by the last rappeller.

What rigging should we use?

The team should select a rigging system that best fits the situation at hand. In aquatic canyons, releasable rigging is an excellent go-to. If the rappel exits into a deep pool, you'll likely want to rappel SRT and set the length. If you have a large team, a twin system might be a good choice for speed. On a short pitch into a deep pool, perhaps a human anchor could be used.[58] (See Chapter 8 for more information on basic rigging systems.)

Some variables to consider:

- How tall is the pitch? Do we have enough rope to lower a stuck rappeller?
- Does the rappel pass through a waterfall?
- What does the landing area look like? Should the rope length be set?
- Do we need to manage the rope for abrasion?
- How large is the team?
- How experienced is the team? Can everyone self-rescue?

Choosing a rigging system is a matter of judgement, and good judgement comes from training, practice, and experience. Often, there will be multiple ways to achieve the goal.

Rigging for Rescue

When rigging a rappel, it's good to be thinking several steps ahead. "If someone were to get into trouble on this rappel, how would we rescue them?" This is particularly important in aquatic canyons as getting stuck on the rope in high flow could be life-threatening. An immediate response may be required. In a dry canyon, there may be less urgency to act, but the team will still need to respond if the rappeller doesn't know how, or is unable, to self-rescue.

Releasable rigging is often a good idea because it provides options. Rope can be paid out even when the system is fully under load. If the rappeller needs rope for any reason, it's easily provided.

---

[57] This is a particular issue with some types of bolt stations (ex: unlinked bolts, singles, and in-line anchors).
[58] This would allow inexperienced team members to rappel, while everyone else jumps or downclimbs.

Step III: Deploy the Rope

Once the anchor and rigging have been established, the rope needs to be deployed. There are many ways to deploy the rope; each with its own pros and cons. The method you choose will depend on the current conditions, nature of the drop, the rigging system in use, and whether or not there are people in the landing zone.

How many ropes need to be deployed?

We often talk about deploying the rope as if it were a single action. For most rappels, however, there are actually two lines that need to be deployed.

- **DRT & Twin Systems**
  The rope on one side of the anchor is deployed, followed immediately by the rope on the opposite side.

- **SRT**
  Single-strand rappels also have two deployments: the rappel rope and a second line that is used for the pull. The pull side is generally kept atop the pitch and deployed by the last rappeller. This practice avoids tangles and allows the reserve rope to be used for other purposes.

- With fixed ropes (SRT), there's only one line to deploy.

- A *retrievable sling* usually requires three deployments. We'll introduce this technique in Chapter 13.

Pull

Rappel

Situating the pull strand on the outside of the quick link makes the rope pull easier.

FAQ: "Does it matter which way the rope is threaded through the anchor?"
In some cases, yes. The anchor should always be rigged for best odds of a clean pull.

Some things to think about:

- If the master point of the anchor is lying flat against the rockface (as shown in the photo opposite), the pull strand should be situated on the outside. If the pull strand was on the inside, the quick link could pinch the rappel strand against the canyon wall, making retrieval harder.[59]

- SRT: Try to visualize ahead of time where the pull strand will be located. The goal is to avoid situations where the pull side would cross and pinch the rappel rope.

- DRT: If ropes of different diameter are joined for the rappel, the thicker one should be threaded through the anchor. This will keep the rope from creeping slowly through the anchor as team members rappel.[60]

---

[59] One way to make the pull easier is to attach a second quick link to the anchor. This will reorient the master point (i.e., making it perpendicular to the rockface).

[60] DRT rope slippage has potential to create a dangerous situation. Imagine the case where the rope moves enough so that one side no longer reaches the ground.

Method #1: Throw the Rope

Throwing a coil of rope down the pitch is a classic method of deployment. It works best on uncomplicated, vertical pitches.

1) Thread the rope through the anchor. Continue pulling rope through, creating a butterfly coil as you go, until you have enough for the pitch.

2) Before throwing, signal to alert anyone in the landing zone and give them a moment to clear the area.[61] In some cases (ex: a tight slot with rapid-fire rappels), it may not be possible to get out of the way. If you can't confirm the landing zone is clear, you'll need to use a different method of deployment.

3) While holding the rope near the anchor (i.e., to avoid losing it), throw the coil. Be aggressive and try to throw the coil clear of any snags/obstructions.

Disadvantages

- If the rope gets caught or tangled partway down the pitch, it may take some time to sort out. Try giving the rope a good shake. If that doesn't work, you may need to pull it back up and re-deploy. Alternatively, the first person down the rappel gets the job of cleaning any tangles. Sorting out tangles can be problematic in significant flow or underneath a waterfall. Consider using a different method of deployment.

- Throwing a loose coil may not be a good idea in a number of situations:

  - Pitch is full of snag hazards or brush.
  - Pitch is less than vertical.
  - Windy conditions; ropes are being blown around.
  - Rappel passes through high flow.
  - People are in the landing zone.

> **Variation: Pay Out the Rope**
> Instead of throwing the entire coil at once, start with a small coil (perhaps with rope for half the pitch). This provides some initial weight. After that, you can slowly pay out rope until the end reaches the bottom. This is one way to avoid hitting anyone in the landing zone.
>
> - This technique can also be used on uncomplicated waterfalls and slides. Toss a small coil of rope into the water and allow the current to carry it downwards.

Method #2: Throw the Rope Bag

If you have a clear line of sight to the bottom and know where it will land, throwing the rope bag might be an option. With the rope stacked in the bag, it'll deploy automatically as the bag falls. Canyon rope bags are burly and designed to take a good bit of abuse. Some varieties are equipped with flotation, which keeps any excess rope in the bag from sinking in a deep pool.

1) Before throwing:

   - Make sure the end of the rope is tied securely to the bag. Otherwise, you'll risk losing the bag during deployment. (See Appendix III for more information on packing rope bags.)

---

[61] Yelling "ROPE!" is traditional, but don't count on anyone being able to hear you in an aquatic canyon. A single whistle blast for attention may be more effective.

o Verify the rope emerges cleanly from the bag and does not pass through any loops, handles, or straps. Twists or snarls in the rope can get caught and interfere with deployment.

o The bag should be open about halfway. If the opening's too small, loops and twists can get stuck. If the bag's fully open, large amounts of rope can emerge all at once. This can be a problem if the bag is overstuffed (i.e., the rope is jammed into a bag that's too small for it).

2) Before throwing, signal to alert anyone in the landing zone.

3) While holding the rope with one hand (to avoid losing it), throw the bag with the other.

Throwing rope bags blindly is not recommended. Bags can get caught on obstacles, stuck in trees, brush, etc. Listening for a thud or splash might mean the bag reached the bottom, but it could also mean the bag landed on a ledge or pool partway down the pitch. If your view down the pitch is obstructed, a better option is for the leader to take the bag with them on rappel. As soon as there's a clear line of fire to the bottom, the bag can be jettisoned.

Rope Bags & Swiftwater
WARNING! Never throw a rope bag into strong current or turbulent water. Free ropes in swiftwater are extremely dangerous.

- In recirculating water, the odds are high that the rope will come out of the bag and tangle around everything in the vicinity. Entanglement has led to fatal accidents.

- If the bag lands in strong current and gets swept downstream, the rappeller might receive an unwanted bottom belay. If this happens at the wrong time (ex: in the middle of a waterfall, or during a floating disconnect), it could be life-threatening.

- A bag in moving water may exert a pull force on the rope. If the rope is not attached to the anchor (ex: DRT) or otherwise weighted, it can start moving. If the rope moves enough, it could result in uneven strand lengths. In a worst-case scenario, the rope could be lost.

A rope bag should always be tossed down into a safe place (i.e., an area of calm water, dry ground, or other location where it can be easily retrieved).

Jettisoning a rope bag in the middle of the pitch.

Deploying an unweighted pull rope.

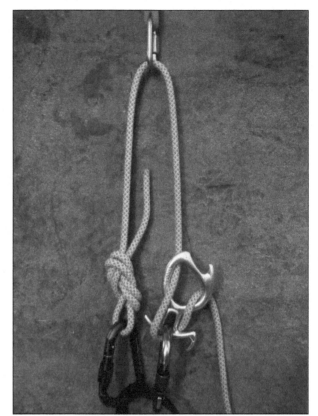

One method of self-lowering.

Method #3: Deploying While on Rappel

A third way to deploy the rope is to take it with you (i.e., deploying it as you rappel). You might be rappelling on the same rope that you're deploying, or you might be paying out an unweighted pull line (ex: pull side of an SRT system). Simply clip the rope bag to your harness and rappel.[62] Another option is to hang the bag by your side or below you on a tether. (See "Pack Management" in Chapter 15.)

> ➢ If you're rappelling on the same rope that you're deploying, hang the bag on your brake side.[63]

> ➢ If you're deploying an unweighted line, hang the bag on your non-brake side.

Advantage
- This method of deployment maintains full control of the rope while descending. This may be a good option in situations where the pitch is full of snag hazards.

Disadvantages
- Increases the complexity of the rappel. The rope bag is one more thing to manage.

- Sometimes, rope bags can get in the way or become snagged (ex: on a difficult rappel start). If the bag's annoying you, consider jettisoning it when you have a clear line of fire to the bottom.

- Rappelling with a rope bag can be problematic in high flow. It makes you a bigger target. (See "Rappelling Through Waterfalls" in Chapter 15.)

---

[62] Be aware: not all harness gear loops are load-bearing; check with the manufacturer. For heavy ropes, it may be better to clip a carabiner around the waist belt of your harness and hang the bag on that. Some canyon harnesses and packs have special attachment points for rope bags.
[63] If the rope is tied off securely inside the bag, you have an automatic stopper knot.

- Use caution while rappelling as twists in the rope can emerge from the bag and get caught in your descender. This is a particular issue with new ropes. One strategy for avoidance: pull 3m (~10ft) of rope out of the bag, rappel a short distance, and repeat.

- If rappelling on the same rope that you're deploying, keep an eye on how much rope you have left. Is there enough to reach the bottom? An unweighted rope may need to be extended.

Variation #1: Backpack Method
Deep in the canyon, your pack will be pretty much empty as you're wearing everything, so why not use it as a rope bag? The pack could be worn on your back or clipped to your harness.

- Instead of throwing a loose coil down the pitch, the rope could be stacked in the leader's pack. This method maintains full control of the rope during deployment.

- Con: It can be difficult to tell how much rope is remaining in your pack. Consider tying a stopper knot for extra security.

Variation #2: Self Lower
Here's a clever method for deploying two rope strands while rappelling:

1) Thread one end of the rope through the anchor and tie a figure-8 knot.

2) Clip the knot to the load-bearing point of your harness. (Alternatively, the knot could be clipped to the end of a tether or the large opening of your descender.)

3) Next, rig your descender for an SRT rappel on the other rope strand. The rope bag can be clipped to your harness or tossed down the pitch.

As you rappel, both lines are deployed simultaneously. Once at the bottom, disconnect, and you have a DRT system ready to go. If a twin system is desired, a partner at the anchor can apply a strand isolation.

- Rappelling feels a little strange as you're moving at half-speed. Additional friction is also generated where the rope moves through the anchor.

- Self-lowering is not a good idea in high flow or if the rappel exits into turbulent water.

- Desert Southwest: Edge protection will be required in sandstone canyons as the moving rope stands will quickly groove out any rock surfaces they come in contact with.

Method #4: Lower the Leader
Another way to deploy the rope is to lower the leader. Here are two variations:

➤ The rope is deployed most of the way down the pitch. The leader rappels to a point where they have an unobstructed view to the bottom. The leader is then lowered a short distance to set the length.

➤ On rare occasions, the leader is lowered all the way to the bottom.[64]

Both options require a belayer, good communication, and a releasable system at the anchor. We'll cover both of these techniques in more detail when we introduce releasable SRT systems in Chapter 11.

---

[64] Lowering someone the full extent of the pitch is not recommended in significant flow or if the rappel would exit into a dangerous water feature.

<u>Advantage</u>
- The rope length is set perfectly for the rest of the team.

<u>Disadvantages</u>
- Rappelling is generally preferred to being lowered a significant distance.

- Edge protection may be required in sandstone environments to prevent groove formation.

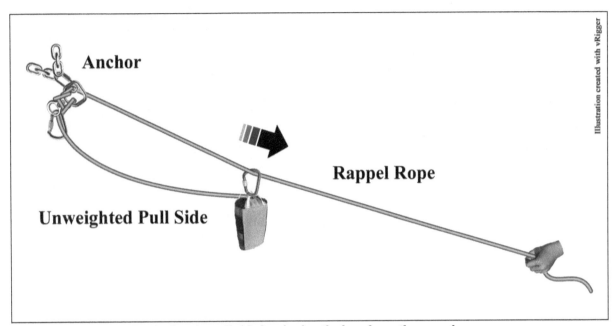

Deploying the pull side by zipping the bag down the rappel rope.

Method #5: Zipline
Once a rope has been successfully deployed, it can be used as a zipline for future deployments. For example, the rappel rope could be used to deliver the pull side of an SRT system directly to the team below. This technique requires a partner at the bottom to tension the rope.

Before sending the bag down, make sure the rope emerges cleanly from the top and does not pass through any loops or handles. It should be open about halfway. Also, make sure your partner is ready to receive it. Use a single whistle blast to get their attention.

When ready, clip the bag to the zipline with a carabiner and send it down. The speed of the bag's descent is controlled by introducing slack at the bottom. By creating a droop in the rope, the bag can be steered in to a gentle landing.

<u>Advantages</u>
- The rope bag is kept away from snags/hazards in the middle of the pitch and the landing zone. In the Desert Southwest, a zipline could be used to keep the bag out of a stagnant pool or pothole.

- Ziplines can also be used for transporting packs. (See "Pack Management" in Chapter 15.)

<u>Disadvantages</u>
- Ziplines require an unobstructed line of travel between the top and bottom of the pitch. They may not work as well on complex drops, low-angle ramps, or brushy rappels.

- On long vertical pitches the rope bags / packs may come in too fast to control and can cause injury.

Step IV: The Team Descends

With the rope deployed, the rappel station is open for business. The first and last rappellers should be among the most experienced on the team as they have some special duties to perform. Less experienced team members will rappel in the middle.[65]

The Leader (First Rappeller)

- Does the rope reach the bottom?
  WARNING! While we deliberately rappel off the end of the rope when the length is set, doing so when the rope is too short could be catastrophic. *Don't do it!*

  As the leader, your most important job is to verify the rope is long enough. As soon as you have an unobstructed view down the pitch, stop and check. If you can't tell, go a little further and look again. Sometimes, it can be difficult to tell (ex: top of a long rappel, or if the rope passes through a waterfall).[66] It's good to know as soon as possible if there's a problem.

- Survey the pitch
  Sometimes, the leader is also a scout. Once in a good position, take a quick look down the pitch. Are there any hazards, obstacles, or special challenges that were not visible from above? Ideally, this information can be communicated to the rest of the team while still within earshot. If you decide the rappel is too dangerous, you should be prepared to re-ascend.

Tips for the Leader

- Always know where you are with respect to the end of the rope.

- Keep your ascenders at the ready in case you need to transition and go back up.

- In rare cases, a rappel backup might be desired for extra insurance. Consider using a backup on long rappels, multi-pitch rappels, or when visibility is limited (ex: rappelling in the dark). We'll discuss the pros and cons of rappel backups in Chapter 16.

- Clean the pitch
  The leader should watch for potential hazards along the course of the rappel. If feasible, try to clear away any debris (i.e., rocks and branches) that could come loose and fall on rappellers. Also keep an eye out for cracks or pinches that could trap the rope when it comes time to pull.

- Cleaning tangles
  If the rope became tangled or snagged during deployment, the leader will need to stop and fix it. Always clean tangles from above. Don't rappel on by and hope to pull the rope down from below; this can get you into trouble. If you need to, lock off and go hands-free. (See "Rappel Lock-offs" in Chapter 15.)

  Once safely at the bottom, the leader might also need to clean up the landing zone. Signal the team above to pull up some rope and set the length. Alternatively, coil or bag up any excess rope and get it out of the way. Don't leave rope lying around where it can get stepped on, become a trip hazard, or get struck by falling rocks. If there's sufficient rope, a bottom belay could be provided.

Depending on the situation, the leader may have other duties as well. Examples include scouting a pool for a jump, building a ground anchor, or setting up a guided rappel.

---

[65] This another example of *sequencing*. The team rappels in a particular order to promote safety.
[66] Brightly-colored ropes are best for visibility.

The Last Rappeller
The last person to rappel also has some special duties. They should be one of the most experienced members of the team as there's no one else present to inspect their handiwork. Check and double-check everything. And, above all, don't lose the rope!

- Reconfigure the rigging
  Some rigging systems (ex: munter hitch, twin systems) must be reconfigured in order to recover the rope.

  o Some techniques make use of an optional safety system that secures the rope to the anchor. If a safety is being used, the last person must remember to clean it.

  o Other systems may need to be cleaned too. Examples would include a temporary backup, a traverse line used to approach the anchor, a courtesy anchor, a temporary clip-in point, etc.

- Deploy the pull side
  For SRT systems: the pull side will need to be deployed. The pull rope is usually kept atop the pitch until the very end for several reasons:

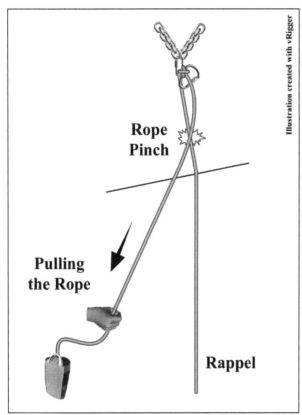

Rope Pinch

Pulling the Rope

Rappel

Illustration created with vRigger

o With only one rope hanging down the pitch, there's no confusion about which one should be used for rappelling.

o There are no other ropes to tangle with.

o The reserve rope is available for use in an emergency.

Depending on the situation, the last person could rappel with the pull bag, toss the bag down from above, or zip it to the team below. Regardless of the method used, special care should be taken to keep the two lines from becoming crossed or tangled.

Beware situations where the pull side could cross and pinch the rappel rope. Ideally, both lines should be kept in parallel. If the two must cross, they should be situated so that the pull side is underneath the rappel rope. It's worth taking a few extra moments to ensure the pull will be as easy as possible.

Before departing, ask yourself: "Can the rope be recovered from below?" When in doubt, call upon the team to do a test pull.

The last person should take care to keep the rappel and pull lines from becoming crossed or tangled.

Performing a Test Pull
It's easier to sort out any pull issues while someone is still at the anchor. If the test is unsuccessful, the last person can direct the team to try again from a different location.

- In a worst-case scenario, the last person might need to pull up the rope and find a better anchor.

- Some rigging systems don't lend themselves to a test pull prior to retrieval.

Deploying the Pull Side
A couple of notes for the last rappeller:

- SRT: Consider rigging your descender on the rappel rope *before* deploying the pull side. This precaution eliminates any possibility of accidentally setting up on the wrong rope. (See "The Problem with Rope Blocks" in Chapter 10.)

- If the situation calls for it, the last person can work with a partner at the bottom to move the pull line into a better position. This might be done to avoid rope-eating cracks or to keep it out of the last person's way. One trick is to flip the rope up onto one or more projections along the canyon wall. Alternatively, a partner below can apply a little tension to the pull side (i.e., just enough to hold it up and out of the rappeller's way).

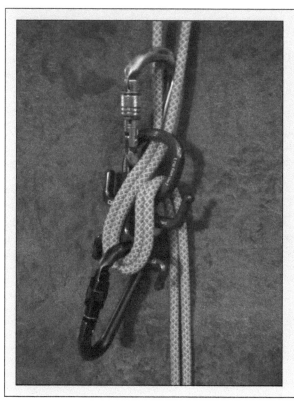

Clever Tricks: Strand Separation (DRT)
Scenario: The last person is rappelling DRT with a figure-8 style descender.

Most modern descenders tend to be forgiving of minor twists and tangles in the rope. These can often pass right through the device while rappelling. One method of removing them, and thereby increasing the odds of a clean pull, is to force the rope strands to take separate paths upon exiting the device. Here are some options:

- ➢ Clip a carabiner into the large opening of the device and around one of the rope strands above the descender as shown.

- ➢ Clip a tether to one of the rope strands above your descender.

Note that strand separation will increase the friction while you're rappelling. This technique may not help with extreme tangles.

- Final sweep
  Take a last look around the rappel station before departing. It's easy to get excited and jump on a rappel, while forgetting about packs, rope bags, gloves, etc. Leave no gear behind!

Step V: Pulling the Rope
Once the team is safely at the bottom, the final step is to recover the rope.

- In canyons with rapid-fire rappels, don't pull the rope until you've found the next anchor. Sometimes, rappels are *chained*, meaning that a single anchor is used to rappel multiple drops.

- Before pulling the rope, make sure the rappel and pull lines are not crossed anywhere between you and the anchor. If the ropes are tangled, it's worth taking a few extra moments to sort them out. Tangles can be difficult to spot on long rappels.

- Make sure the landing zone is clear before beginning the pull. Starting the pull immediately could trigger rockfall on the last rappeller.

Efficiency Tips

Quite often, it's possible to get ready for the pull while other team members are still coming down the pitch.

- Preparing for Retrieval
  Any of the following actions can happen at any time:

    o If any stopper knots were tied, they can be untied.
    o If necessary, remove and untie the rappel rope from its rope bag.
    o Any excess rope at the bottom of the pitch can be flaked out into a neat pile before the pull commences.

- Pull Teams
  A team of two works quite well for pulling a rope. One person pulls, while the other packs the rope away. Alternatively, several team members can work together to pull and bag the rope. (See Appendix III for more information.)

FAQ: "Where should I pull from?"

Ideally, the pull should take place in a safe location (i.e., not too close to an edge) with a clear line of sight to the anchor above. If you can't see the anchor, try moving back or finding higher ground. Moving back even a short distance can help reduce edge friction and may allow any obstructions (ex: knots, rope blocks) to clear the lip. Sometimes, the pull side can be extended, allowing you to move back even further.

The Rule of Recovery

When pulling the rope, your most important job is to pay attention! Pull slowly and carefully, while watching the rope going up the wall.[67] Make sure no knots, tangles, or snarls get pulled out of reach. If you see a problem, stop immediately and fix it. If a knot is pulled out of reach, it could lodge in the anchor (or get stuck in cracks along the way), making rope recovery impossible.

Other Notes

- Giving the rope a sharp tug at it comes free of the anchor will cause it to fall out away from the rockface and, hopefully, keep it from getting snagged on any terrain features. On an obstacle-strewn pitch, a slow pull may be preferred to keep the rope from flying out and becoming tangled.

- In canyons with high flow, don't allow rope to accumulate in the landing zone. A rope caught in the current will get swept downstream and tangle around anything in the vicinity. Instead, pull the rope slowly and give the person packing the bag time to catch up. When the tail comes down, reel it in with a fast butterfly coil. Other team members can be called on to assist here.

- What happens if the rope gets stuck? This is a problem worthy of additional discussion. Take a look at the "Stuck Rope" scenario in Chapter 24.

- Desert Southwest: In sandstone environments, you can extend the lifespan of your gear by keeping the rope clean. Silt worked into the sheath can do an impressive amount of damage to your descender in a single day of rappelling. If feasible, try to pull the rope right back down into its bag. If the rope goes into a pool, pull it directly up out of the water. Try to avoid dragging a wet rope through dirt, sand, or mud.

---

[67] Alternatively, another team member could be assigned to watch the rope.

Rigging Teams

Many alpine climbers will be familiar with the catch-phrase: "He who throws, goes." The idea is that the person who built the anchor and deployed the rope will also be first to rappel. Requiring the anchor's architect to go first creates a strong personal incentive to make sure everything is rigged correctly.

For more complex rappel systems, however, it's safer and more efficient if the architect rappels last. The architect is always the person who understands the rigging best. Relying upon others to figure out how to clean the safety and backup systems is not a good plan. Even if well-explained, there's still room for human error to creep in, especially if multiple steps are involved. If the architect is present at the anchor, a further advantage is gained: they can direct other team members where to set up and be an extra pair of eyes on safety. In this model, the architect is responsible for running the rappel station from beginning to end. We'll refer to them hereafter as the *station manager*.

Typically, the station manager partners with another experienced team member, who will be first to rappel. Taking charge of a rope, both individuals become a *rigging team*. Upon arriving at a drop in the canyon, their job is to manage the pitch from start to finish. The rigging team determines the best means of descent, builds the anchor, and deploys the rope. One member of the team rappels first, while the station manager remains atop the pitch. Once everyone else is down, the station manager reconfigures the rigging (if required) and rappels last. Reunited at the bottom of the pitch, the rigging team pulls their rope and continues down the canyon.

FAQ: "When should we use rigging teams?"

The rigging team methodology is a good one to use with large groups or any time something unusual is going on at the rappel station. Some examples:

- A retrievable traverse line is rigged protect an exposed approach to the anchor.
- A courtesy rigging or ground anchor is being used.
- A releasable system that is being manned by a belayer.
- A retrievable system.
- A redirect must be passed while on rappel.
- A guided rappel is being used to avoid some obstacle or hazard below.

Other Notes

- The rigging team should establish a flight plan before separating. Keep the plan simple. Plans with lots of steps are easy to forget.

- If someone gets into trouble mid-rappel, the station manager will usually conduct the rescue.

- Group members who are not part of a rigging team can still help by carrying ropes, assisting with the pull, stuffing rope bags, acting as an extra pair of eyes on safety, etc.

Speeding up Progression

If you have sufficient leadership, multiple rigging teams can really speed things up.[68]

Speed Tip #1: Multiple Rappel Stations

If the terrain permits, consider opening multiple rappel stations at a given drop. Each rigging team will run their own station. With more rappel stations available, more team members can be rappelling at once. You could even set ropes at different skill levels: a dry pitch for beginners and one right down the waterfall for the more experienced.

---

[68] For best efficiency, each rigging team should have their own set of ropes, gear, and anchor material.

Speed Tip #2: Leapfrogging

Another speed increase can be realized by sending a rigging team ahead to set up the next rappel. The next anchor can be built and the rope deployed while team members are still coming down the previous one. It takes some coordination and discipline to pull off, but rigging teams can leapfrog one another to make rapid progress down the canyon.

- Leapfrogging works best when rappels are in close proximity. If the team is too spread out, they won't be able to help each other in an emergency.

- Don't send a rope forward unless you're certain it's no longer required. Once a rope is sent forward, it's usually difficult to get it back.

- The forward team may have the anchor built and rope deployed, but you may want hold off on sending anyone down until there's a confirmed retrieval at the previous rappel. Again, this helps keep the group from getting too spread out.

Efficient Teamwork

Canyoning is very much a team sport and working together efficiently makes a huge difference in speed, especially on a long day out. If you find yourself standing around, ask yourself: "Is there anything useful I could be doing?" Quite often, the answer is: yes. Be pro-active: jump in and help out if you see something that needs doing. Even small things can help speed the group's progression down the canyon. Here are some examples:

- Safety is everyone's responsibility. If something doesn't look right, say something.

- At the rappel station: be ready to go as soon as the rope is available. Have your pack on and descender at the ready. Make sure the working area of your harness is clear.

- If you're waiting around at the top or bottom of a rappel, that's a good time to put on a layer, have quick snack, drink of water, adjust your pack, etc.

- If feasible, each rappeller should provide a bottom belay for the next. (See "Bottom Belay" in Chapter 16.)

- When the time comes, jump in and help pull the rope. It may be possible to get ready for retrieval while team members are still coming down the pitch.

- When the rope pull is underway, watch carefully to ensure that no knots or snarls get pulled up out of reach. You can be monitoring the rope even if you're not part of the pull team.

- Open your pack and get ready to receive the rope bag as soon as the rope is packed away.

- If the team stops for any length of time (ex: rappels, having lunch, restroom break, changing in or out of wetsuits), take a look around before you depart. Try to avoid leaving any gear behind.

Henline Falls, Ore.
(Photo: Wade Hewitt)

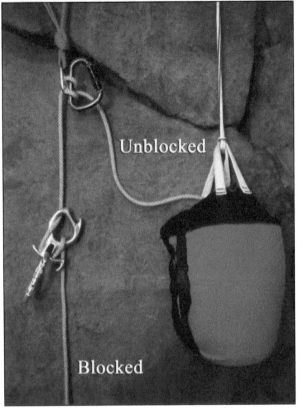

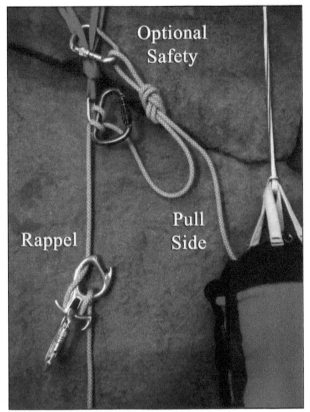

Blocked vs. unblocked strands.   **A rope block with optional safety.**

Rappelling single strand (SRT) has many benefits, but how do you rig for it? The system must be safe to rappel on, but we also need to recover the rope from below. A first glance, these requirements might seem contradictory. One solution is to use a *rope block*. This is a form of rigging that allows rope to move through the anchor in one direction, but not in the other. This is accomplished by creating an obstruction on the rope, known as a block. It could be a large knot or another object that's attached to the rope. The block is simply too big to pass through the anchor. The photos above show a *carabiner block*; a form of static rigging. Blocks are an efficient way to rig for SRT, particularly when used in concert with a rope bag.

The Golden Rule of Blocks
It must be physically impossible for a block to pass through the anchor.

A couple of definitions:

Unblocked	The rope on the same side of the anchor as the block can move freely. The unblocked side will be used to pull the rope from the bottom of the pitch.
Blocked	The rope on the opposite side of the anchor from the block cannot move when placed under load. Rappelling always takes place on the blocked side of the anchor.[69]

---

[69] There are rare exceptions to this rule. (See "Guided Rappels" in Chapter 20.)

The Problem with Rope Blocks

So, what happens if someone attempts to rappel on the wrong (unblocked) side of the anchor? As the rope can move freely in that direction, rappelling on that side could be catastrophic. This mistake has led to fatal accidents. Here are some things you can do to keep this from happening:

- Don't deploy the pull side until the very end. With only one rope hanging down the pitch, there's no confusion about which strand should be rappelled on.

- The station manager should remain at the anchor and rappel last. Their job is to direct other team members where to set up and be an extra pair of eyes on safety.

- Before rappelling, visually check that you're on the correct side.[70]

- The last person can rig their descender on the rappel rope prior to deploying the pull side. This eliminates any confusion about which strand is which.

(Optional) Using a Safety

Another way to safeguard against accidents is to tie a figure-8 knot in the pull side and clip it to the anchor. This knot is referred to as *the safety*. Once clipped to the anchor, both strands become isolated and the rope cannot move in either direction. Now, if someone attempts to rappel on the wrong side, they'll still be safe when the rope is weighted.

- Con: With the safety in play, the rope cannot be recovered from below. Some canyoneers dislike using a safety because the last person must remember to clean it.

Other Notes

- A safety might be a good idea if you have any concerns about the block. It's also an insurance policy against rigging mistakes. It will protect you from:

  - A block that was rigged on the wrong (i.e., rappel side) of the anchor.
  - A block that's able to pass through the anchor.
  - An incorrectly rigged block.[71]
  - Rope slippage through the block.[72]

  When setting a safety, leave some slack between the knot and the block. This allows the block to be tested by simply rappelling on it.

- With the safety in use, the rigging is now a static twin system. Isolating both sides can also be useful in situations where you want to use the reserve rope for another task without interfering with the rappel system. Some examples:

  - Rigging an *edge line* to keep an eye on rappellers. (See Chapter 14 for more information.)

  - Providing a top belay or assisting someone on a difficult rappel start. (See "Top Belay" in Chapter 16.)

  - Emergencies. The reserve rope could be used to rappel to an injured rappeller or haul them back to the top. (See Chapter 23.)

---

[70] Don't rely on pulling the rope strands to tell you which side is blocked. (You might be tempted to do this if the anchor is some distance away.) If the rappel side was caught in a crack, you could get a false positive.

[71] Carabiner Block: Tying a munter instead of a clove hitch has been the cause of several accidents.

[72] Slippage can be an issue with stiff ropes; we'll talk more about this problem in a moment.

Classifying Blocks

Rope blocks can be divided into two categories:

- Releasable

  Blocks in this category are a form of releasable rigging (SRT). A belayer at the anchor can pay out rope even when the system is fully under load. (Releasable blocks will be introduced in Chapter 11.)

- Static

  With a static block, rope cannot be paid out while the system is under load. In an emergency, the team cannot lower and some other means of rescue will need to be devised. Static blocks are best used by experienced teams on dry (or low flow) pitches. Static blocks are occasionally used by the last rappeller.

Carabiner Block

Knot Block

Carabiner Block

A carabiner block is a form of static rigging. The concept is simple: it's a large locking carabiner, or pear-abiner, attached to the rope with a clove hitch. A carabiner with a thick round spine is preferred to maximize surface area inside the hitch. Note that the carabiner is not clipped to anything other than through the hitch; its job is purely to function as a block. Make sure the carabiner is locked and that the hitch is cinched down securely. Don't rely on the weight of the first person rappelling to tighten it.

- It must be physically impossible for the carabiner to pass through the anchor.

- Test the clove hitch by pulling on both strands. If the hitch flips through the carabiner, you probably tied a munter hitch in error.

> **Clove Hitches & Stiff Ropes**
> **WARNING!** A clove hitch tied with stiff rope can loosen up and wander. This might happen as the result of cyclically loading and unloading the anchor as team members rappel. If the clove hitch isn't binding well, the rope can slip. If this happens and the unblocked side isn't secured, the outcome could be catastrophic. If you're using a stiff rope, a triple clove hitch or constrictor knot is a better solution. Alternatively, use a knot block or hybrid block instead.

Knot block with optional safety applied.

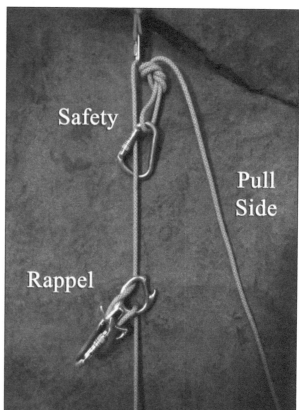

Knot block with a safety for the last person.

Knot Block

This static block is a big knot (such as a figure-8 on a bight) that's incapable of passing through the anchor. If a safety is desired, the knot can be clipped to the anchor with a locking carabiner. Knot blocks are simple, but have a few issues to be aware of:

- After being loaded by a series of rappellers, the knot can be difficult to untie.

- Knot blocks can be dangerous when tied on skinny ropes with large quick links at the anchor. If the knot tightens under load, it could jam in in the anchor or slip through. A jammed knot could make the rope pull difficult. If the knot were to slip through while someone was on rappel, the result could be catastrophic. Here some ways to keep this from happening:

  - Replace the quick link on the anchor with a smaller one. Alternatively, tie a bigger knot.

  - Use a *hybrid block*. This is a knot block with the carabiner clipped through it. It makes the block larger and ensures the knot remains easy to untie. Con: The hybrid is slightly bigger and has greater odds of getting snagged.

A hybrid block.

o   Use a safety. When it's time for the last person to rappel, the safety carabiner could be unclipped from the anchor and re-attached it to the rappel line. Now, if the knot were to slip through the anchor, the rope would be unrecoverable, but the rappeller would still be safe.[73]

Rigging Blocks

The exact steps for rigging a block will vary depending on the height of the pitch. A *short rappel* is any rappel up to half the length of the rope. If it's more than half a rope length, then it's a *long rappel*. Long rappels come in two flavors: tail down and tail up. In a moment, we'll present all three scenarios. The examples depict the use of static blocks, but the steps are pretty much the same for releasables.

Is the pull side long enough?

Suppose we're at the top of a 45m pitch with a single 60m rope. If we set the length, that means there's only 15m of rope remaining. To recover the rope from the bottom of the pitch, we'll need to extend the pull side. We could use a second rope to make up the difference, but we don't have to. As all rappels are performed on the blocked side, the pull line will never be weighted. This means a rappel-rated rope is not strictly necessary for retrieval. Here are some options:

➢   Use another rope to extend the pull side.

➢   Use a lightweight pull cord.

➢   If the pull side's just a little short, any excess webbing, cord, carabiners, shoelaces, packs, etc. can be used to make up the difference.

Extension Tips

- Tip #1: If you see the rope's middle mark go through the anchor, the pull side must be extended.

- Tip #2: Keep tabs on where your ropes are. If you need a second rope for the pull, make sure it doesn't accidentally go down the rappel in someone's pack. It may be difficult to get it back.

- Tip #3: Suppose the pull side is long enough, but there's a large deep pool at the bottom of the pitch. You might consider extending the pull side anyway. This would allow the team to retrieve the rope from the far side of the pool, thereby avoiding a potentially awkward pull while treading water or swimming.

- Tip #4: The pull side could also be extended from the bottom of the pitch. As we've discussed, this allows the team to move back further for a better pull. (See "Pulling the Rope" in Chapter 9.)

Ropes vs. Pull Cords

Are pull cords are appropriate for use when canyoning? This is a question that has stirred much internet debate. Let's take a look at the arguments.

<u>Arguments in favor of pull cords</u>
- Reduced pack weight. Suppose, in our canyon, there's one 60m drop and all the rest are 20m or less. Instead of carrying two 60m ropes all the way through the canyon, we could bring one 60m rope and an equivalent length pull cord. This allows you to shed ~1.5kg (~3–4lbs) from the group gear. Both the rope and pull cord will be used to rig the big drop, while the rope alone will be used to rig the shorter pitches.

---

[73] Note that clipping the carabiner to the rappel strand creates a closed loop. If there are any obstacles between the rappel and pull strands, the rope might be unrecoverable.

Ropes vs. Pull Cords (continued)

- Pull cords lend themselves well to use with some retrievable systems. (See Chapter 13.)

<u>Arguments against the use of pull cords</u>
- It's better to be prepared for rescues and bring a real rope. Using a pull cord to lower could be dangerous. Pull cords are not rated for rappelling or ascending. They're not as durable and have less cut resistance. A rope will provide more options in an emergency.

- Pack weight generally isn't much of a concern on a day outing with a decent-sized group. If you have a small group, consider inviting some others along to help carry the gear.

- Retrievable systems are used less frequently in canyons with significant water.

It should be noted that pull cords aren't your only option. One compromise is to bring two ropes: a 9mm for rappelling and a lighter 8mm for the pull.[74] This reduces the pack weight a little, but provides a greater margin of safety. Another solution would be to regard the pull cord as an optional extra. Bring all the ropes you normally would, plus a pull cord for additional rigging options.

<u>Summary</u>
In aquatic canyons, it's better to bring another rope. The use of pull cords is probably more appropriate for dry environments, where self-rescue is more likely. Even in a dry canyon, however, additional rope may be required in an emergency. If someone were to get into trouble on this rappel, how would you rescue them?

FAQ: "Does it matter which side of the anchor the block is situated on?"

The block should be placed on the side of the anchor that offers the best odds of a clean pull from below. The local terrain, type of anchor, and location of the master point will all play a role.

If the anchor's master point is hanging in space, it probably doesn't matter which side the block is on. If the master point is lying flat against a rock surface, the block should be positioned on the outside to allow a clean pull away from the anchor. (It would also be difficult to operate a releasable block trapped between the quick link and the canyon wall.)

For unlinked anchors, the block is usually situated on the higher of the two bolts. This makes it easier for the block to clear the edge atop the pitch.[75] (For more information, see "Unlinked Anchors" in Chapter 6.)

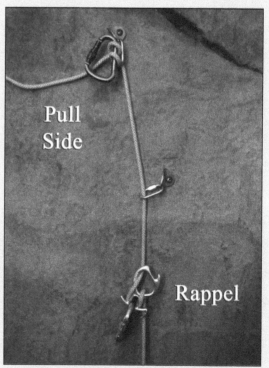

A block rigged on an unlinked anchor.

---

[74] FAQ: "Why not bring two 8mm ropes?" You could, but the 9mm will have greater durability and cut resistance.
[75] If the block was placed on the lower bolt, a force multiplier would be created on the upper one (i.e., doubling the load). If the bolts are good, it's probably safe, but it's not best practice.

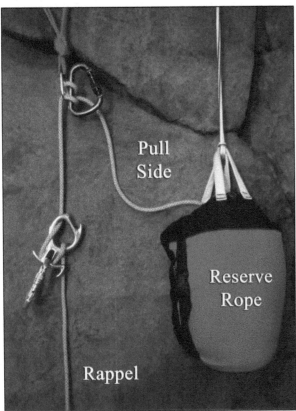

Setting the length on a short rappel.

Short Rappel

Scenario: The team has arrived at the top of a 15m pitch into a deep pool. We have a single 60m rope. The entire pitch can be seen from above.

As the height of the pitch is less than half the rope, this is a short rappel. Short rappels lend themselves well to a tail down rigging. When setting the length, exactly the right amount of rope is paid out for the drop.

Advantages

- The reserve rope is kept atop the pitch, where it's available for other uses. It's even more useful when a releasable system is in use.

- Rope recovery is speedy and efficient. The rope is pulled right back down into its bag.

Rigging

1) Set the length. Thread the tail through the anchor, and continue pulling rope until you have enough for the pitch. Once deployed, the end of the rope should hang just at or slightly above the surface of the water. This will be the rappel line.

2) Block the rope. Install a block on the pull side and snug it up tight against the anchor.

3) (Optional) Set a safety. For a carabiner block, tie a figure-8 in the pull side and clip it to the anchor with a locking carabiner. Leave some slack between the block and safety. This allows the block to be tested.

4) The bag with the reserve rope should be clipped to the anchor or stashed somewhere nearby where it can't accidentally get knocked down.

Voilà! The rappel station is open for business. The team rappels on the blocked side of the anchor. At the bottom, rappellers deliberately slide off the end and swim away.

Retrieval

Once everyone else is down, the last person sets up to rappel and deploys the pull side. The exact method of deployment will be situationally dependent. The last person could rappel with the rope bag, toss it down, or zip it to the team below. They should take special care to ensure the rappel and pull lines do not become crossed or tangled.

The last rappeller has several other duties as outlined in Chapter 9:

- If a safety was set, it must be cleaned.

- The last person should perform a final check of the rigging before departure. Can the rope be recovered from below? If there's any doubt, call upon the team to do a test pull.

Once safely at the bottom, the pull side is used to recover both the rope and the block.

Long Rappel: Tail Down Method

<u>Scenario</u>: The team is atop of a 45m pitch that drops into a deep pool. We have two 60m ropes. The entire pitch can be seen from above.

As the pitch height is more than half the rope length, this is a long rappel. The rigging here is identical to that of a short rappel, except that this time we'll use another rope to extend the pull side (shown in green). In this case, the rappel rope (yellow) has been removed/untied from its rope bag atop the pitch. The ropes are then tied together with a *stacked overhand*.[76]

<u>Advantage</u>
- This method can be used to set the length.

<u>Disadvantages</u>
- As the pull side needs to be extended, the system takes a little longer to rig.

- Rope recovery is also a little slower. The entire rappel rope will need to be packed away, plus some portion of the extension.

- If a releasable block is in play and you need to lower, you may be faced with the prospect of moving the knot past the anchor.

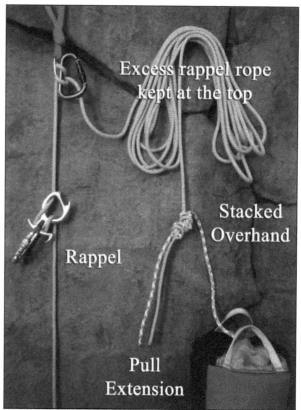

Setting the length on a long rappel. The excess rappel rope is kept atop the pitch.

FAQ: "How do we manage the excess rope?"
If feasible, the extra rope atop the pitch can be stuffed into the top of the pull rope bag. The last rappeller should make sure the pull bag is open wide enough to allow the knot to exit. The empty rope bag (from the rappel rope) is sent down the pitch in someone's pack.

If there isn't room in the pull bag, here are two other options:

➢ On a vertical pitch with a clear line of fire to the bottom, the pull bag could be tossed or zipped to the team below. The last person can then feed out the extra rope from above.

➢ If the rappel line is full of obstacles/brush, the second-to-last person could deploy with the pull side (i.e., taking the bag with them on rappel). The last person can then feed out the excess rope. Once exhausted, the pull line will deploy normally out of the bag.

<u>Retrieval</u>
The last person to rappel sets up on the blocked side of the anchor. They perform a final check of the rigging, and, if required, clean the safety. Once everyone has rappelled, the pull side is used to recover both ropes and the block.

---

[76] FAQ: "Couldn't a European Death Knot (EDK) be used to connect an unweighted pull rope?" Yes, although it's good to get in the habit of using a stronger knot when joining ropes. It might matter during a rescue. (For more information on the use of the EDK, see Appendix I.)

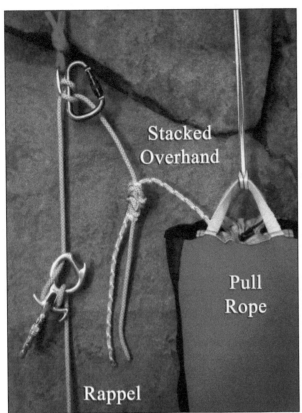

**A long rappel rigged tail up.
The excess rappel rope (not shown) is at the
bottom of the pitch.**

Long Rappel: Tail Up Method

Scenario: The team is atop a 45m drop into a calm pool. We have two 60m ropes. This time the pitch is full of obstacles or brush. Any ropes thrown down are going to get caught or snagged.

This is another way to rig a long rappel.

Advantages
- It's relatively quick to rig and get the team rappelling.

- Both ropes are contained. The leader does not need to stop to sort out any snags or tangles.

Disadvantages
- As the entire rappel rope is committed, the length cannot be set. All rappellers will need to perform a floating disconnect.

- For a releasable system, the knot joining the ropes should be pre-positioned on the rappel side. Any lowering will be done using the pull rope. (See "Pre-Rigging" in Chapter 22 for more information.)

- This method of rigging has the slowest recovery. The entire rappel rope (used or not) must be pulled up through the anchor.

Rigging
1) Thread the tail of the rappel rope through the anchor and pull about 0.5m (1–2ft) through. The ropes are tied together with a stacked overhand.

2) (Optional) Set a safety. Pull more rope through the master point. Tie a figure-8 and clip it to the anchor.

3) Block the rope. Pull a little more rope through the anchor and set the block. As always, it must be physically impossible for the block to pass through the anchor.

4) The pull rope bag can be clipped to the anchor or stashed somewhere nearby.

5) The leader rappels on the blocked side of the anchor, taking the rappel rope bag with them. The rope is deployed automatically as they rappel.

Once the leader is down, the rappel station is ready for other team members to descend.

Retrieval
Once everyone else has rappelled, the last rappeller sets up on the blocked side of the anchor. They perform a final check of the rigging, and, if required, clean the safety. The last person then rappels, taking the pull bag with them. Once at the bottom, the pull side is used to recover both ropes and the block.

Efficiency Tip
The rappel rope (yellow) must be removed and untied from its rope bag at the bottom of the pitch before the pull commences. This can happen at any time, even while other team members are still rappelling. Coil up the excess rope and flake it out into a neat pile where it's ready to go.

Retrieving a Blocked Rope

Rope blocks work great when there's a clear line of pull between the anchor and bottom of the pitch. Blocks can be problematic, however, if the pitch is full of brush or other obstacles. Gaps, pinches, and cracks can also catch blocks. On long rappels, there's also a knot to get stuck. Here are some tips for avoiding problems:

- High-placed anchors are nice as they make it easier for blocks and knots to clear the edge. Alternatively, consider extending the anchor's master point. (A courtesy anchor could be used to avoid a difficult start.)

- Try to clear away any branches or debris atop the pitch that could catch the block.

- If the block gets stuck and the rappel side is still within reach, you might be able to return it to the anchor by pulling down on the rappel strand. Once the block is back at the anchor, try the pull again from a different direction.

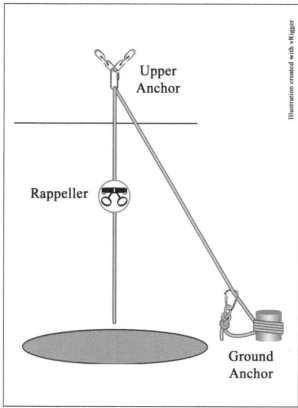

A ground anchor is rigged using the pull side. This allows the last person to remove the block.

Other Options

If you have special concerns about a block getting stuck, here are some other strategies:

➤ Rappel DRT
The last person removes the block and rappels DRT. This should be done sparingly in aquatic canyons. (See "DRT in Aquatic Canyons" in Chapter 8.) The last person should be one of the most experienced members of the team.

➤ Use a Ground Anchor
The last person deploys the pull side and signals the team below to rig a ground anchor. Once accomplished, the block can be removed. The last person then rappels SRT, anchored from below. If natural anchors are lacking, a human anchor might suffice. (For more information, see "Ground Anchors" in Chapter 4.)

  ○ A releasable system could also be rigged on a ground anchor. We'll talk about ground contingencies in the next chapter.

  ○ Con: This method of rigging may double the load on the upper anchor. The upper anchor should be bombproof.

Chapter 11: Releasable Rigging

A releasable system is one that has the capacity to pay out rope at any point, even when fully under load. This property of the rigging has a number of applications. Let's look at one example:

Need More Rope!

Scenario: Suppose you're the first person down an SRT rappel. Midway down, you realize the rope doesn't reach the bottom. *Too short!* At this point, you have several options. If the terrain permits, you might be able to downclimb or find a place to build an intermediate anchor. You could switch to ascending and go back up. Or … you could signal the team above for more rope.

The team's ability to provide rope depends on the rigging used up at the anchor:

- Static
  With a static system, rope cannot be paid out while under load. The rappel rope must be unweighted first. This is easy if the rappeller can find a safe, convenient ledge to stand up on. Otherwise, the team will need to convert the rigging to a releasable system. (We'll talk more about *conversions* in Chapter 22.)

- Releasable
  If a releasable system is being used, a belayer at the anchor can pay out rope immediately. This can happen even when the rappeller is hanging on it. Both the rope and rappeller are lowered together. The rope is lowered until the tail reaches the bottom.

The big advantage of releasable rigging is that it provides options. If you need to pay out rope for any reason at all, it's easy to do. Releasables are sometimes referred to as contingency systems.

FAQ: "Why Rig Releasable?"

Prepared for Rescue

Being prepared for emergencies is the number one reason to rig releasable. If someone were to get stuck in the middle of a rappel, the team has the option to lower.[77] Getting stuck might be annoying on a dry pitch, but could be life-threatening under a waterfall. A rappeller stuck in serious flow might not be able to self-rescue, so the team needs to act immediately. This is why releasable rigging is used more frequently in aquatic canyons.

- Be aware: lowering can sometimes create more problems than it solves. (See "Lowering" in Chapter 23.)

- How experienced is your team? Anyone can get stuck mid-rappel, but it's more likely to happen to inexperienced rappellers.

Rope is Easily Provided

Scenario: The bottom of the pitch can't be seen from above and we're not sure how much rope is required.

If we have good beta, we can measure out close to the right amount of rope. Otherwise, the team might opt for an *exploratory rappel*. Start by paying out the rope you think you need for the pitch. The leader starts down the rappel, stopping at a good place where they can see the bottom. If the rope's too short, the leader signals for a lower. A belayer at the anchor releases rope until the leader signals again to stop. The rope length is now set perfectly for the rest of the team.

---

[77] There are many ways to get stuck on the rope. One of the most common is a jammed descender (i.e., long hair, beard, pack strap, loose clothing, autoblock, or vegetative scunge on the rope getting sucked into the rappel device).

Some other reasons to pay out rope:

- The beta was wrong or out-of-date.
- The person measuring out the rope did a poor job of it, or the pitch was taller than we expected.
- The team used a different anchor that requires more rope.
- When packing for the trip, someone grabbed the wrong rope (ex: the 45m rope, thinking it was a 60m).
- Belaying a scout who is downclimbing.
- Multi-tier rappels. The length is set for the first pitch. The leader goes down and, from a safe place, requests additional rope to set the next pitch.
- Lowering a beginner or an injured party member who can't manage the rappel on their own.

Protecting the Rope

Releasable systems can be used to protect the rope from abrasive rock and sharp edges. As team members rappel, a belayer provides an extremely slow lower. It's so slow that the rappeller isn't even aware it's happening. The slow release of rope continually changes the wear points, spreading any abrasion over a wider area. This technique is known as *rope creeping*; we'll talk more about it later in the chapter.

Prerequisites

All releasable systems have a common set of requirements:

Quick Conversion

Releasable systems always have two modes: *locked* and *unlocked*. The belayer must be able to quickly convert the rigging from one mode to the other.

Locked	The rope cannot move through the rigging. When locked, the system is safe to rappel on. A belayer is not required.
Unlocked	Rope can move through the rigging. The rope can be rappelled on, but must be managed by an active belayer.

Sufficient Rope

In order to lower, there must be enough rope atop the pitch. This might sound obvious, but it can become an issue on a long rappel (i.e. when the height of the pitch is more than half the rope length).

- Scenario #1
  We're at the top of a 20m pitch with a 30m rope and a pull cord of equal length. With 20m of the rope committed to the rappel, there's only 10m of reserve to lower with. If a rappeller were to get stuck right at the top of the pitch, we don't have sufficient rope to lower them to the bottom. (Lowering someone on a pull cord is not a good idea as they have less cut resistance.)

- Scenario #2
  We're back atop the same pitch, but this time we have two 30m ropes. By tying them together, we now have sufficient rope to lower … but now there's a new problem: there's a knot that will need to be moved past the anchor. We'll discuss this problem further when we introduce *conversions*. (See "Moving a Knot Past the Anchor" in Chapter 22.)

Always keep tabs on where your ropes are at. For efficiency, ropes are sometimes sent ahead to start rigging the next rappel (i.e., leap-frogging). This should only be done, however, if absolutely certain the rope is no longer required. If a given rope is being held in reserve (i.e., just in case we need to lower), then it's not available to be sent forward. Once a rope has been sent forward, it's generally difficult to get it back.

Summary

If you don't have sufficient rope to lower with (or there's no one present at the anchor to lower), a releasable system may not make sense.

Eyes on the Rappeller

Communication can be difficult in aquatic canyons. If the belayer can't see what's going on, another team member should be stationed at the edge to watch the rappeller. The observer can relay signals and direct the belayer accordingly. If the rappel passes through high flow, it's even more important to have eyes on the rappeller. This is another reason why anchors right on the edge are preferred in aquatic canyons.

Anchor Placement

Releasable systems require adequate space in which to perform the belay. If the anchor's in an awkward location, it may be difficult to release rope in a timely manner. A courtesy anchor might allow belaying to take place in a better location. (See also "Courtesy Rigging" in Chapter 4.)

Using Releasables

Releasables can be used in several different ways depending on the situation:

> ➢ If you can see the bottom of the pitch from above, you can set the rope length and lock the rigging. If anyone gets into trouble, you retain the ability to unlock and lower.

> ➢ If you can't see the bottom, the leader gets a belay. Once the leader is safely at the bottom and the length is confirmed, the rigging can be locked.

> ➢ If some hazard is present/suspected (ex: the rappel passes through high flow), everyone gets a belay. This allows the belayer to respond instantly in an emergency. No time is lost getting in position and unlocking the rigging.[78] If the hazard is serious enough that the last rappeller also wants a belay, the team could rig a *ground contingency*. We'll talk about these at the end of the chapter.

> ➢ If sharp edges are present/suspected, the belayer can creep the rope for the rest of the team.

The Belayer

When a rappeller signals for rope, the belayer should release and keep releasing until told to stop. Lowering should be slow and steady. The rappeller may need to make course corrections and negotiate obstacles en route down the pitch. Try not to scare the person you're lowering.

- Don't release the belay until signaled. A slack rope may not mean the rappeller is at the bottom. They might have landed on a ledge and unweighted the rope temporarily.

- If you lower someone in an emergency, be sure to pull the rope back up afterwards and reset the length.

- Beware situations where the end of the reserve rope is free and could slip through the belayer's system. If the end of the rope is tied securely to a rope bag, this might serve as an emergency backstop.

The Rappeller

Everyone on the team should know how to request a lower. It's a good idea to review signals periodically as they're easy to forget. (See "Communication" in Chapter 7.)

- Practice good situational awareness. Always know where you are with respect to the end of the rope.

- Signal for rope before you need it. If you're rappelling on a locked rigging, it can take a few moments for the belayer to get in position and unlock the system.

- The rappeller can request the belayer to speed up or stop the lower at any time. This can be done with hand signals to an observer atop the pitch.

---

[78] Rather than taking turns belaying, it's more efficient if one person remains on belay duty for the entire team. This job usually falls to the *station manager*.

Releasable SRT Systems

There are many releasable systems out there and a variety of ways to rig them. We'll look at several SRT systems in this chapter, and then some releasable twin systems in Chapter 12.

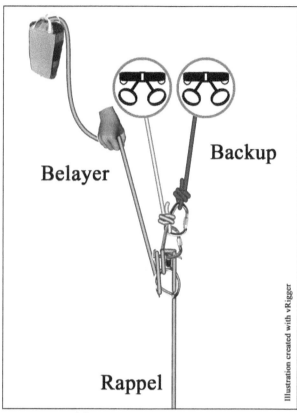

A human releasable system.

Human Anchors

We've already covered the simplest SRT releasable: it's the *human anchor*. The rappel rope is run through the belayer's own descender and locked off. If additional rope is required, the belayer unlocks and lowers. This technique is best used on short pitches. (See also "Human Anchors" in Chapter 4.)

This technique could also be used to belay a scout who is downclimbing.

If the belayer finds the load is too much, lowering might prevent them from getting pulled out of position.

Advantages
- Fast to rig.

- The belayer is an integral part of the system and can respond immediately.

Disadvantages
- Human anchors are somewhat terrain dependent.

- Escaping the belay may not be possible without outside help.

- The belayer must find another way to descend.

Rigging	1) Deploy the rope for the pitch. If desired, the length can be set. 2) The belayer runs the rope through their descender and sits down in a braced tripod position. If necessary, the belayer can be backed up by a partner. 3) The belayer might use a hard or soft lock depending on the likelihood of needing to lower the rappeller. The brake must be maintained with a soft lock, but the belayer can respond faster. Backing up a Human Anchor: Anyone backing up a human anchor should not tie into the rope or run it through their own descender. This would interfere with the belayer's ability to release rope. A backup can help, however, by holding onto the free end of the rope.
Release	The belayer unlocks and releases rope to the rappeller.
Final Configuration	The belayer disconnects their descender and drops the rope to the team below. The belayer then downclimbs, jumps, or finds another way to descend.

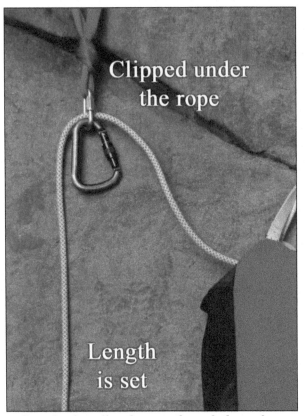

Clipped under the rope

Length is set

Start by threading the rope through the anchor.

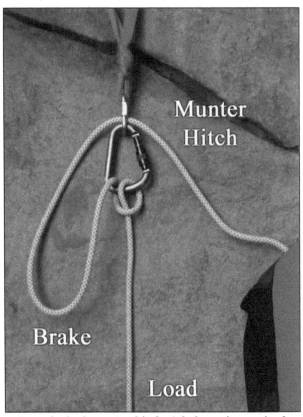

Munter Hitch

Brake

Load

An unlocked munter hitch. A belayer is required.

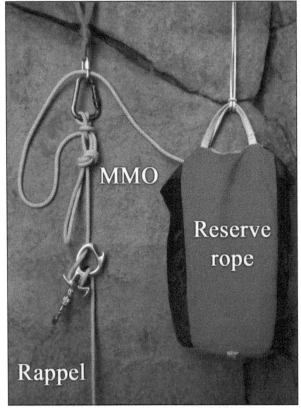

MMO

Reserve rope

Rappel

A locked munter hitch (MMO).

The Munter Hitch

Another simple SRT releasable is the munter hitch. It's rigged directly on the anchor. To lock the rigging: use the brake strand to tie a mule hitch and cinch it tightly up underneath the munter. The mule alone is not secure, so it must be backed up. One way to do this is to tie off the remaining bight with an overhand knot. This creates a munter-mule-overhand (MMO).

The munter hitch requires sufficient space in which to perform the belay. A high-placed anchor generally works well.

<u>Advantages</u>
- Simplicity. All you need is the rope and a single locking pear-abiner.

- The rope length is easily adjusted. (See "Fast Release" later in the chapter.)

- A munter hitch can also be used for belaying. The belay can even be reversed with no change to the rigging. A scout could be belayed out to the edge, then right back to the anchor.

- Lowering introduces twists into the rope. To minimize this effect, try to keep the brake and load strands in parallel as much as possible. Another strategy is to hold the rope firmly and feed it into the anchor while lowering. This forces the twists out onto the rappel side. If the length is set and the end can spin freely, the twists will then come out of their own accord when the rope is unweighted.

- The munter must be re-rigged in order to retrieve the rope. As usual, the last person should be one of the most experienced members of the team as there's no one present to check their handiwork.

Rigging	1) Begin by threading the rope through the anchor.[79] 2) Deploy the rope for the pitch. If desired, the length can be set. 3) Clip a pear-abiner to the anchor. If clipped into the master point, it should be positioned underneath the rappel rope to avoid pinching. (A spacer could also be employed to position the munter further away from the anchor.) 4) Tie a munter hitch on the pear-abiner in the correct orientation for the load.[80] Make sure the pear-abiner is locked. 5) Lock the rigging with a mule-overhand. This creates an MMO. (See "Mule Hitch" in Appendix I for more information.) Voilà! The rappel station is open for business.
Release	The belayer unties the overhand and performs a controlled release of the mule. Pull the bight slowly, taking care that it doesn't get twisted up on itself. Once the bight is as small as you can make it, pull the brake strand hard and fast to remove all slack from the system without dropping the rappeller. The rappeller is then lowered directly from the anchor. Backing up a Lower The munter hitch will provide plenty of friction, but you might consider a backup when lowering a real person. Here are some options: ➢ Quick and dirty solution: get a partner to help hold the rope. ➢ Run the brake strand through your own descender.
Final Configuration	The MMO is not retrievable (and we don't want to leave a carabiner behind), so the last person must clean the system and re-rig. It's common for the last person to rappel on a static system.[81] Some options: ➢ Clean the munter and rappel DRT. ➢ If SRT is desired, the last person could rig a static block on the pull side while the second-to-last is rappelling. Once the rappel line is clear, the munter is cleaned, and the last person shifts the rope's position to set the block.

[79] FAQ: "Why do we thread the rope through the anchor first?" It saves the last person a little time and helps prevent an accidental loss of the rope.

[80] If you need to lower, you don't want the hitch to immediately flip through the anchor.

[81] Note that a releasable system provides no benefit if there's no one available to lower.

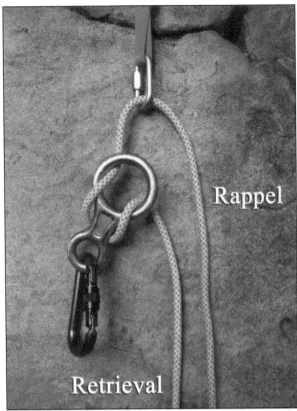

Start as if rigging the figure-8 for an SRT rappel.

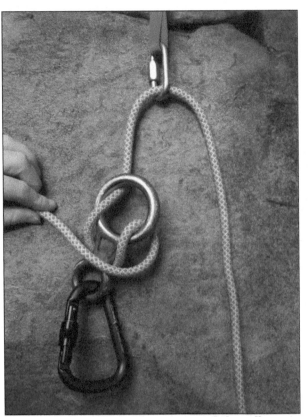

Wrap the pull strand once around the collar.

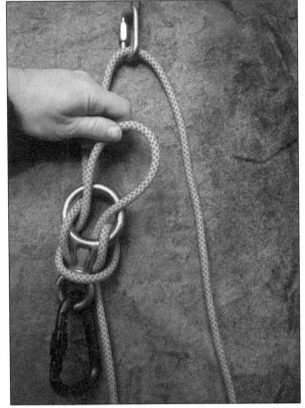

Pull a bight of rope up through the large opening and over both the carabiner & head of the device.

Clip the carabiner to the pull strand and lock it. The rigging is now locked.

Compact Figure-8 Block

Another common releasable is the compact figure-8 block. It's a rope block and releasable system in one.

The block is rigged by wrapping the rope around a classic figure-8 descender. This *friction wrap* is the locking mechanism. When under load, the individual strands pinch one another, preventing rope from moving through the block. To release rope: the belayer removes the wrap, and lowers through both the figure-8 and the anchor.[82]

- There are at least a half-dozen variations of the friction wrap. The method presented here was chosen because it's straightforward and relatively easy to inspect. There are no half-twists to remember. It works best with a long-necked figure-8 device.

- Classic figure-8 descenders come in many shapes and sizes. Some friction wraps work better with certain types of descenders. The diameter of the rope is also a factor.

See Chapter 10 for more information on the use of rope blocks.

Rigging	1) Thread the rope through the anchor and deploy it. If desired, the length can be set.
	
	2) Clip a locking carabiner into the small opening of the figure-8.
	
	3) Rig a compact figure-8 block on the pull side of the anchor:
	
	    ○ Pull a bight of rope up through the large opening and cinch down over both the carabiner and head of the figure-8 device. We'll call this the "first bight." At this point, it looks like you're setting up for an SRT rappel. (See the first photo in the sequence on the previous page.)
	
	    ○ Pass the free end of the rope around the collar of the figure-8.
	
	    ○ Using the same strand, push a second bight of rope through the large opening in the same direction as the first. Pull the bight up and over both the carabiner and head of the device. Cinch it down firmly into place.
	
	4) Clip the locking carabiner to the free end of the pull side and lock it. The carabiner keeps the rope from accidentally popping up over the head of the device.
	
	5) (Optional) Set a safety. There are several variations; we'll talk about them shortly
	
	The releasable system is locked and ready for action.
	
	<u>Common Mistakes</u>
	- The rope should always enter at the top of the figure-8 device. If the rope enters at the bottom, the quick link may be able to enter the block and cause problems. To correct this problem, try rotating the block 180-degrees.
	
	- The friction wrap should always be created with the free end of the pull side. Never use the rappel strand, or the rope between the figure-8 and the anchor.
	
	- The block's carabiner is clipped to the free end of the pull side. Clipping it to the rappel side is safe, but doing so creates a closed loop. This loop can be problematic when it comes time to pull the rope. If there are any obstacles between the rappel and pull strands, the rope may become unrecoverable.

---

[82] A friction wrap is one type of locking mechanism, but there are others. We'll introduce the Eight-Mule-Overhand (EMO) shortly.

Release	1) If there's a safety in use, it must be cleaned before you can lower. 2) Unclip the figure-8's locking carabiner from the pull strand, but leave it in place. 3) Pull the second bight of rope up over the head of the figure-8 and the carabiner. While keeping a careful hold on the pull side (now brake strand), pull the bight free and unwrap the collar. 4) (Optional) If there's concern about the rope popping over the head of the figure-8 while lowering, the carabiner can be clipped back to brake strand. 5) The belayer releases rope through both the block and anchor. Backing up a Lower The figure-8 will provide plenty of friction, but you might consider a backup when lowering a real person. Here are some options: ➢ Quick and dirty solution: get a partner to help hold the rope. ➢ Run the brake strand through your own descender.
Final Configuration	The last rappeller checks to ensure that the rigging is locked.[83] If there's a safety in play, it will need to be cleaned. The pull side is deployed, and the last person rappels on the blocked side of the anchor.

Advantage
- Little-to-no reconfiguration is required by the last person.

Disadvantages
- A classic figure-8 descender (or similar device) is required.

- Friction wraps can be tricky to inspect. There are many variations.

- Be aware: rope slippage has been reported in rare cases with the compact figure-8. Slippage might be due to a poorly-rigged block, or some combination of heavy loads, skinny ropes, certain types of friction wraps, and certain types of figure-8 devices. The belayer should use a backup and/or keep a firm grip on the pull side until it's clear that the friction wrap is holding.

- It's difficult to release rope efficiently through a figure-8 block when it's not under load. If a belay is not required, you may be better off cleaning the block first. (See also "Fast Release" later in the chapter.)

- The compact figure-8 block can be difficult to unlock. The rope can also become pinched when lowering. We'll talk more about these issues in a moment.

- The figure-8 block is somewhat larger than a carabiner block and will have slightly higher odds of getting snagged when it's time to pull the rope. (See "Retrieving a Blocked Rope" in Chapter 10.)

---

[83] **WARNING!** An unlocked compact figure-8 will not function as a block.

Don't Rappel on the Pull Side!

As always, the biggest concern with rope blocks is someone who attempts to rappel on the wrong (unblocked) side of the anchor. As we discussed in the previous chapter, there are a number of ways to keep this from happening. One of the simplest: don't deploy the pull side until the very end. With only one rope hanging down the pitch, there's no confusion about which one is the rappel line. The station manager (aka belayer) can also show rappellers where to set up. (See "The Problem with Rope Blocks" in Chapter 10.)

Securing a releasable block with a safety.

(Optional) Using a Safety

There are several ways one can rig a safety with a figure-8 block. One method is to tie a figure-8 knot in the pull side and clip it to the anchor with a locking carabiner.

Advantages
- The safety will protect anyone who attempts to rappel on the wrong side of the anchor.

- A safety will also protect rappellers from incorrectly-rigged blocks and rope slippage.

Disadvantages
- With this safety in play, lowering is not possible. It will take slightly longer for the belayer to respond in an emergency.

- The last person must remember to clean the safety or the rope cannot be recovered.

Using a safety is not a good idea if hazards are present or suspected. In this case, the station should be unlocked and manned by a belayer.

| Avoid clipping the block to the anchor. | Securing the block with a quickdraw. |

FAQ: "Can't I just clip the block directly to the anchor?"

Don't do it! Clipping the block to the anchor looks like a good way to protect someone from setting up on the wrong side. If you need to lower, however, you may find there's a problem. With both the block and anchor weighted, it may be impossible to unclip the carabiner. If you can't unclip the block, the system cannot be unlocked which defeats the purpose of the rigging.

FAQ: "What about connecting the figure-8 to the anchor with a quickdraw?"

Some canyoneers use a locking quickdraw, alpine quickdraw, or short sling to connect the block to the anchor. The extra slack avoids the problem described above. This is another form of safety system.

<u>Advantage</u>
- Once the belayer has unlocked the figure-8, the quickdraw can be reconnected. This makes it impossible for the rope to pop up over the head of the device while lowering.

<u>Disadvantages</u>
- Note that a quickdraw won't protect you from rope slippage. If rope can slip through the block, then both sides may be unsafe to rappel on. In this sense, a quickdraw is only a partial safety.

- If a safety was set, the last person must remember to clean it. Once removed from the anchor, the quickdraw could be clipped back to the pull side. If there are concerns about the block getting snagged, here are some other options:

  o Replace the quickdraw with a locking carabiner clipped to the pull side.
  o Replace the figure-8 block with a smaller static block.
  o Clean the block and rappel DRT.
  o The team below rigs a ground anchor using the pull side. Clean the block and rappel SRT.

Rope Pinching

One disadvantage of the compact figure-8 is that the friction wrap can sometimes become pinched between the descender and the anchor, or between the anchor and the canyon wall. This makes it difficult to unlock the system and can delay the belayer's response. Some factors that can lead to pinching include: the local terrain, location of the anchor, orientation of the block, size/shape of the figure-8 device, and diameter of the rope in use.

If the rope becomes pinched, here are two options:

> Try pulling the carabiner in different directions. You may be able to release the pinch by reorienting the block relative to the anchor.

> If that doesn't work, clip a short tether into the large opening of the figure-8. You may be able to release the pinch by leaning back and using your bodyweight to pull the block away from the anchor. Often, it only needs to be moved a matter of centimeters or inches.[84]

Pinching can also happen while lowering. If the belayer isn't paying attention, accumulating slack at the anchor could pop up and over the head of the figure-8. In a worst-case scenario, this could lead to a rigging failure. Here are some ways to address this problem:

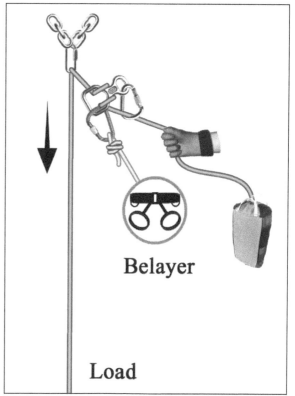

Releasing a pinch by leaning back and pulling the block away from the anchor.

○ Clip the block's associated carabiner around the brake strand.
○ Connect the block back to the anchor with a quickdraw.
○ Use a backup when lowering (i.e., run the brake strand through your own descender).

---

[84] **WARNING!** If pulling towards an edge, make sure you're clipped into an anchor. If the rope were to suddenly become unweighted, you may be at risk of falling.

The Eight-Mule-Overhand (EMO)

Here's another figure-8 block that uses a half hitch as a locking mechanism.[85] The EMO has two main advantages: rope slippage becomes impossible, and rope pinching is less likely. It requires a large figure-8 device.

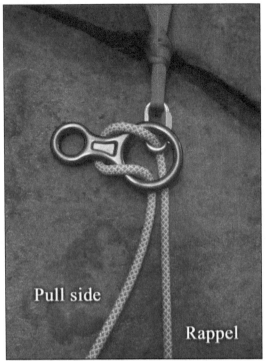

Start as if rigging the figure-8 for an SRT rappel.

Push a second bight through the large opening.

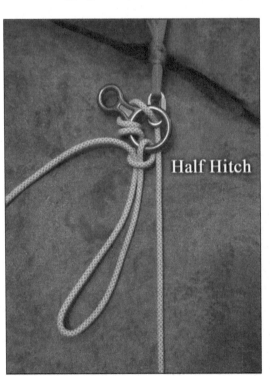

Push a third bight through the second to create a half hitch.

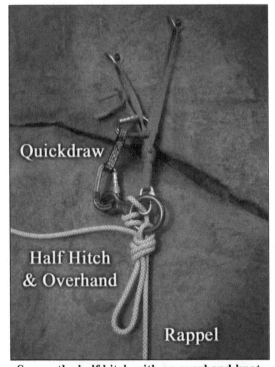

Secure the half hitch with an overhand knot. A quickdraw connects the block to the anchor.

---

[85] Possibly this rigging should be called an *EHHO* (Eight-Half-Hitch-Overhand)?

Rigging	1) Thread the rope through the anchor and deploy it. If desired, the length can be set.
	
	2) Rig the EMO on the pull side of the anchor:
	
	    ○ Pull a bight of rope up through the large opening and cinch down over the head of the device. At this point, it looks like you're setting up for an SRT rappel. (See the first photo in the sequence on the previous page.)
	
	    ○ Using the free end, push a second bight of rope through the large opening in the opposite direction of the first. Keep this second bight relatively small.
	
	    ○ Create a third bight in the free end and pass it through the second to form a half hitch. Cinch the hitch tightly up against the descender.
	
	    ○ The half hitch can slip, so must be backed up. Pull some additional slack through to enlarge the third bight, then tie it off to the pull strand with an overhand knot. Tie the overhand immediately underneath the half hitch.
	
	3) (Optional) Set a safety. Use a quickdraw or short sling to connect the small opening of the figure-8 to the anchor.[86]
	
	The rigging is locked and ready for rappellers.

Release	The belayer unties the overhand and performs a controlled release of the half hitch. Pull the bight slowly, taking care that it doesn't get twisted up on itself. Once the bight is as small as you can make it, pull the brake strand hard and fast to remove all the slack without dropping the rappeller. Rope can then be released through the block and anchor.
	
	Backing up a Lower
	The figure-8 provides plenty of friction, but consider using a backup when lowering a real person. Here are some options:
	
	    ➢ Quick and dirty solution: get a partner to help you hold the rope.
	
	    ➢ Run the brake strand through your own descender.

Final Configuration	The last rappeller checks to ensure that the rigging is locked. If there's a safety is in play, it will need to be cleaned. The pull side is deployed, and the last person rappels on the blocked side of the anchor.

Advantages
- The EMO is easy to rig and inspect.

- The locking mechanism makes rope slippage impossible.

- If you need to lower, it's easy to unlock the system. Rope pinching is less likely.

- The quickdraw version of the safety doesn't need to be unclipped in order to lower. This allows the belayer to respond a little faster. The quickdraw also prevents the rope from popping over the head of the figure-8.

---

[86] Another option for a safety: clip the overhand knot's bight back to the anchor. (Con: The bight must be unclipped in order to lower.)

<u>Disadvantages</u>

- Tying a half hitch may be difficult on smaller figure-8 devices.

- Like all figure-8 blocks, it's difficult to release rope when the system is not under load.

- The EMO is larger than the compact figure-8, so may have slightly higher odds of getting snagged.

Exploratory Rappels

If you can't see the bottom of the pitch and aren't sure how much rope is required, one option is to perform an *exploratory rappel*. Here's how it works:

During deployment, the rope is deliberately set short. Ideally, the end should be about two-thirds to three-quarters of the way down the pitch. The leader starts down the rappel and finds a place with an unobstructed view to the bottom. With the tail of the rope in sight, the leader locks off the rappel (or stays on the brake), and signals for rope. The belayer releases, lowering both the rope and rappeller together. If enough rope was fed out initially, the actual lower should be fairly short. As soon as the tail reaches the bottom (or is deemed "good enough"), the leader signals again to halt. Once accomplished, the leader completes the rappel, dropping off the end of the rope and swimming away. The rope length is now set perfectly for the rest of the team.

Once the leader is off the rope, the belayer can lock the rigging. The team retains the ability to unlock and lower if anyone gets into trouble.[87]

- The leader should be one of the most experienced members of the team.

- Sometimes, the leader can indicate how much rope is required. Holding up two fingers could mean: "Give me 2m (~6ft) of rope!"

- <u>Desert Southwest</u>: Edge protection may be required to prevent groove formation in sandstone.

Variation #1: Is there a safe place to stop?
If there's a convenient ledge (or other safe place) partway down the pitch, the leader could stop there and use it as a staging area to set the length. The leader may not even need to disconnect from the rope. Instead, the leader stays put and pulls slack rope through their descender.

This is a good technique to use when multiple tiers will be rappelled from the same anchor.

Variation #2: Lower & Release
If the pitch is dry or low flow, another way to set the length is to lower the leader all the way to the bottom. On a dry pitch, the leader could tie a figure-8 knot and clip it to their harness. If the rappel exits into deep water, a quick-release system should be used. The easiest method is to run the tail of the rope through the leader's descender and lock it off. Upon reaching the bottom, the leader signals the belayer to stop. The leader then unlocks and drops off the end of the rope to swim away.

- Unless the pitch is short, rappelling may be preferred to being lowered.

---

[87] If any hazards are present or suspected, the belayer should remain on duty for the rest of the team. If a rappeller gets into trouble, the belayer can respond immediately.

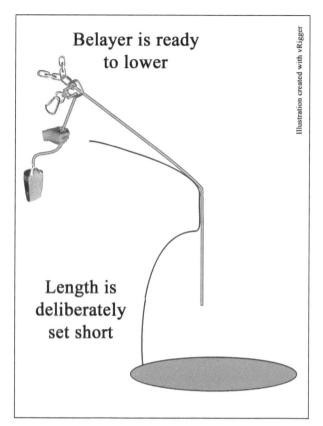

Belayer is ready
to lower

Length is
deliberately
set short

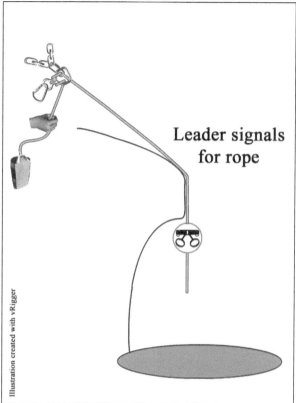

Leader signals
for rope

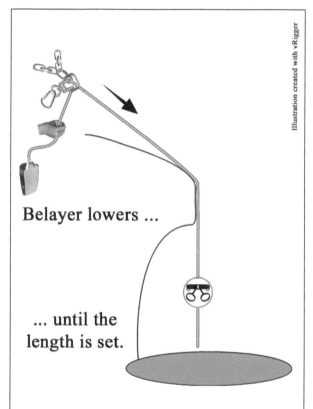

Belayer lowers ...

... until the
length is set.

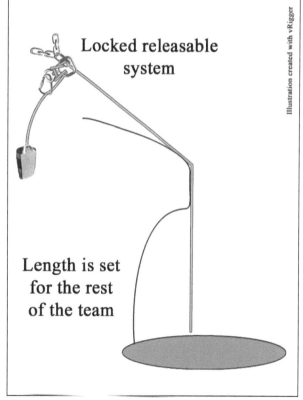

Locked releasable
system

Length is set
for the rest
of the team

Sequence for an exploratory rappel.

Fast Release

Usually, the belayer releases rope at a slow, steady pace. Occasions will arise, however, where you need to pay out a lot of rope all at once. Some examples include:

- An exploratory rappel on a multi-tier drop. The leader has rappelled the first pitch and, from a safe place, requests additional rope to set the length on the second. In this case, the leader is not being lowered, but might need 20m of rope all at once.

- Setting up a guided rappel. The leader reaches the bottom and must swim across a pool (potentially through turbulent water), while taking the end of the rope with them. The belayer must feed out rope quickly.

- A rappeller reaches the bottom and becomes stuck, struggling to perform a floating disconnect, under a waterfall. If the belayer can provide some slack, this would allow the rappeller to swim a few strokes away, making the disconnect easier.

In all three of these examples, the rope is not weighted and the rappeller no longer requires a belay.

Munter Hitch

If you anticipate the need to feed out a lot of rope at once, the munter is a good rigging choice. It's easy to pay out rope when the system is unweighted. The rigging does not need to be modified or changed.

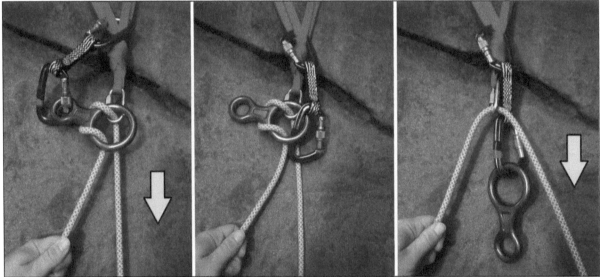

The figure-8 block is removed to release rope quickly.

Figure-8 Block

Releasing rope through a figure-8 block is difficult when the rope is not under tension. Here's a nifty trick that requires a quickdraw (or short sling), perhaps the same one that's being used to connect the block to the anchor.

1) As soon as the rappel rope is unweighted (or the leader's in a safe place and signals for rope), unclip the quickdraw and reconnect it to the large opening of the figure-8.

2) Pop the brake strand up and over the head of the figure-8 device. The descender will fall away as the rope comes free. The quickdraw keeps the figure-8 from becoming lost.

The belayer can now pull rope directly through the anchor's master point without impediment. Once sufficient rope has been paid out, the block can be re-established.

Rope creeping in action.

Slow Release (Rope Creeping)

During a rappel, there's always a risk of damage when the rope passes over rough surfaces or a sharp edge. Padding the edge and changing the rope's position between rappellers are two strategies for combating this problem. Another option is a continuous release system. As team members rappel, the belayer performs an extremely slow lower. This is known as *creeping the rope*. The idea is to continually change the wear points and spread any abrasion out over a wider area. Ideally, the lower is so slow that the rappeller isn't even aware it's happening.

The belayer should vary the speed of release with the perceived level of threat. A common rule of thumb is to count to five, then slowly release 1cm (~0.25in) of rope. If sharp edges are known to exist, you might reduce the count to three.

- The rappeller can signal a halt to the lower at any time. They might be needed to negotiate an obstacle, clean a tangle, make a tricky balance move, etc.

- If excess rope is accumulating at the bottom of the pitch, the length will need to be reset. A partner below can direct the belayer appropriately.[88]

FAQ: "Do we need to creep the rope?"

It likely depends on your situation. There are a number of factors to consider:

- Anchor location. An anchor that's out on the edge is generally kinder to your rope. The rope will have less contact with rock surfaces and will be less likely to get damaged.

- Are sharp edges present? Certain types of rock are more abrasive than others. In sandstone canyons, sharp edges may present less of a threat.

- Not all ropes are created equal. Creeping is a good idea with skinny ropes (i.e., those in the 8mm range) as they have less cut-resistance.

- Creeping may be a good idea on long rappels (i.e., over 60m (~200ft)). The increased rope stretch means more bouncing as team members rappel.

- How experienced is your team? Beginners are more likely to have poor rappel technique and greater odds of damaging ropes.

While rope creeping doesn't provide perfect protection, some protection is better than none. Creeping will definitely increase the lifespan of your ropes.

---

[88] Alternatively, a marker knot (ex: alpine butterfly) could be tied in the rappel side to indicate when the length is set. After creeping the rope for each rappeller, the belayer simply pulls the marker knot back up to the anchor.

Ground Contingencies

One weakness of the releasable systems presented so far is that they cannot be used to lower the last person. If the situation is so severe that the last rappeller wants a belay, one solution is a *ground contingency*. This is a releasable system that's rigged on a ground anchor. Once established, a belayer at the bottom of the pitch can release rope. It's similar to lowering a climber off a route at the rock gym. If the threat of sharp edges is severe, the belayer can creep the rope for the last person. (See also "Ground Anchors" in Chapter 4.)

Note that some reconfiguration atop the pitch is necessary in order to lower. For example, if a block was set on the pull side, it will need to be removed.

Advantage
- It's easier for a belayer on the ground to keep an eye on the rappeller.

Disadvantages
- Ground anchors are terrain-dependent. If there's a deep pool at the bottom of the pitch, a ground anchor may not be feasible.

- A ground anchor is a force multiplier and may double the load on the upper anchor. The upper anchor must be bombproof.

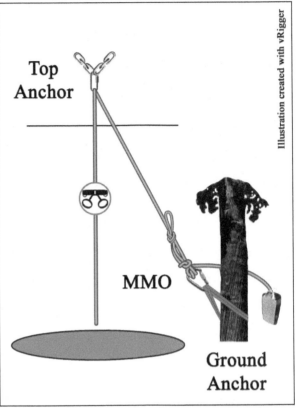

A releasable system rigged on a ground anchor.

- In order to lower the last person fully to the ground, you'll need at least three times the height of the pitch in rope. For example: if the height of the pitch is 30m, you'll need 30m for the rappel and 30m for pull. If the last rappeller gets stuck at right at the top, you'd need another 30m of rope to lower them.[89]

Other Options

If a ground anchor isn't feasible (or the upper anchor is marginal), here are two other possibilities. Both of these may not be good choices if the rappel passes through high flow or exits into turbulent water. The last person should be one of the most experienced members of the team as they may be committing to significant additional risk.

➢ The last person converts the system to DRT. A two-strand rappel has an advantage in that each strand bears only half the rappeller's weight. This reduces the odds of rope damage.

➢ The last rappeller performs a *self lower*. With both strands in motion, the wear points are constantly changing. Effectively, it's a way to creep the rope for yourself. (See also "Self Lower" in Chapter 9.)

---

[89] Tip: If extra rope is lacking, one trick that might work is to tie the ends of the rappel and pull sides together. We can then lower the rappeller using the excess rope that's accumulating at the bottom of the pitch. This reduces the amount of rope required to about twice the height of the pitch. Con: Depending on the rigging, you may need to move a knot past the ground anchor while lowering.

Chapter 12: Twin Systems

There are a great many ways to rig twin systems, so we'll narrow the focus of this chapter to a few particularly interesting ones. As discussed previously, twin systems can be a good way to speed up progression with a large group. (See "Twin Rope Systems" in Chapter 8.)

- Twin systems can be rappelled either SRT or DRT.

- The last rappeller must reconfigure the rigging as the rope cannot be pulled from below.

Static Twin Systems

All of the following systems are static, meaning that rope cannot be paid out while the rigging is under load.

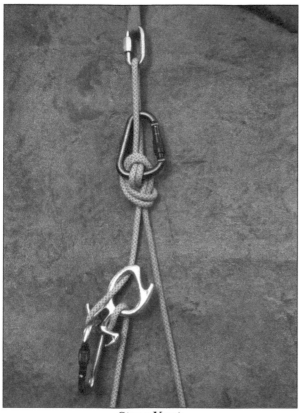

Stone Knot

Double Alpine Butterfly

Stone Knot

A stone knot is a classic strand isolation technique. The knot can be tied any distance from the anchor. To clean the rigging, the last person removes the carabiner and it becomes a DRT system. (See Appendix I for more information on how to tie the stone knot.)

Double Butterfly

Rig as if for a DRT rappel, then tie a *double butterfly* (i.e., an alpine butterfly knot using two rope strands as one). This has the effect of isolating both strands below the knot. The double butterfly can be tied any distance from the anchor and requires no gear other than the rope itself. The knot is easy to untie after being loaded. The bight makes a convenient clip-in point, or it could be used as the master point for a top belay.

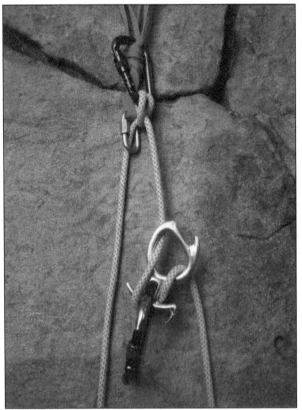

Clip & Block with both strands isolated.

Clip & Block for the last person (SRT).

Stone Eight: start as if rigging for a DRT rappel.

The completed Stone Eight.

Clip & Block

Start by rigging as if for a DRT rappel. The strands are then isolated by tying a clove hitch on a locking carabiner and clipping it to the anchor. Once the rest of the team has rappelled, the last person unclips the carabiner from the anchor. The clove hitch is then repositioned to the carabiner's spine. Snug the carabiner up against the anchor, and, suddenly, you have an SRT carabiner block. Even the pull side has already been deployed. The last person rappels on the blocked side of the anchor.

Stone Eight

This static twin system requires a classic figure-8 descender or a similar device (ex: Petzl Pirana). It can be rigged any distance from the anchor.

Start by rigging the figure-8 as if for a DRT rappel. Once in place, rotate the device 180-degrees to create a loop of rope around the device's collar. Next, attach a locking carabiner to the small opening of the descender, and clip it around both rope strands. The carabiner is clipped to both ropes either above or below the device. Its purpose is to keep the figure-8 from rotating back into its original position. The weight of a rappeller causes the rope strands to pinch one another, creating the strand isolation.

The last rappeller unclips the carabiner and rotates the descender back into its original alignment. The figure-8 is then clipped to their harness for a DRT rappel.

Releasable Twin Systems

A smaller number of twin systems are releasable. If a rappeller were to get stuck in the middle of the pitch, they can be lowered using the rope strand that's not in use. Twin releasables must meet all the same requirements as SRT releasable rigging. (See "Prerequisites" and "Using Releasables" in Chapter 11.)

We'll take a look at two releasable twins in the remainder of this chapter: the Joker and the Jester.

- Be aware: the strand isolation for both of these systems is created by friction. Some combinations of heavy loads, skinny ropes, and certain rappeller movements (ex: significant bouncing while on rappel) could lead to rope slippage. To keep this from happening, the station manager should keep a firm grip on the rope strand that's not in use until the next rappeller starts setting up.

- Limitations
  Rope cannot be released if rappelling DRT, or if multiple individuals are rappelling at the same time. This defeats the purpose of the rigging.

The Joker

This releasable twin requires two classic figure-8 descenders (or a single device such as a Totem). If using a pair of figure-8 devices, they should be about the same size.

Rigging
1) Start by rigging as if for a DRT rappel.   2) Clip a locking pear-abiner into the master point of the anchor with the gate facing out. The rope should pass through both the anchor's quick link and the pear-abiner. (Alternatively, a spacer could be employed to move the rigging further away from the anchor.)   3) Clip the large opening of both figure-8 devices into the pear-abiner.   4) Rig one side. Pull a bight of one rope up through the large opening of both devices. Pass it up over the head of the figure-8 on the same side of the anchor and cinch it down.   5) Rig the other side. Push a bight from the other rope strand through the large opening of both devices in the opposite direction of the first. Pass it over the head of the remaining figure-8 and cinch it down.[90]   6) Connect the small opening of both devices with a quickdraw (or short sling). This prevents the rope from accidentally popping up over the head of either figure-8.   The rappel station is ready for action.

Joker using a VT prusik in lieu of a quickdraw.

Release	To release rope: clear the other line of rappellers. Unclip the quickdraw on the unweighted side and pull the corresponding bight of rope up over the head of the figure-8. Keep a firm grip on the rope as it comes free. The belayer can now release rope and lower the rappeller through the rigging. There should be plenty of friction, but, as always, you might consider using a backup when lowering.
Final Configuration	Clean the entire rigging. The last person rappels DRT, or blocks one side for SRT.

Disadvantages
- The Joker is fairly gear-intensive.
- This rigging is slow to build and clean.

---

[90] Loading the bights in opposite directions reportedly helps hold the rigging together a little better. This may be more of a concern when the Joker is resting up against a rock surface.

The Jester

Here's another releasable twin that uses a descender with a twin-aperture sticht plate (such as an ATS). With a minor adjustment, the same rigging can be used as a releasable SRT system.

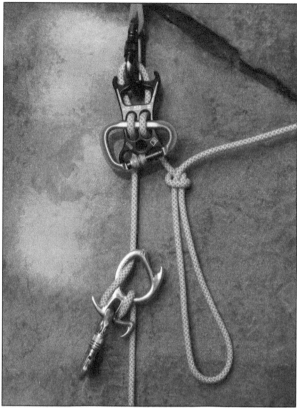

Jester rigged as an SRT releasable.

Rigging
1) Start as if rigging for a DRT rappel.
2) Clip a locking pear-abiner into the master point of the anchor with the gate facing out. The rope should pass through the anchor's quick link and the pear-abiner. (Alternatively, use a spacer to move the rigging further away from the anchor.)
3) Clip the descender into the locking pear-abiner so that both strands hang down behind it.
4) Pull a bight of rope from each strand through the device's sticht plate and secure them in place with a second locking carabiner (shown in orange). Both ropes should run over the spine. Make sure the carabiner is locked.
5) **SRT version** Tie a half hitch in the unused rope where it exits the descender. The bight can be secured with an overhand knot.[91]
The rappel station is open for business.

Release	If the belayer needs to release rope: ➢ If the Jester is rigged as a twin system, clear the other line of rappellers. ➢ If rigged for SRT, release the slip knot. Pull slack from the unused rope up through the sticht plate to enlarge the bight on that side. While holding the bight firmly, release rope by feeding it into the rigging. There should be plenty of friction, but consider an additional backup when lowering.
Final Configuration	Unclip the descender from the rigging, and rotate the sticht plate carabiner (shown in orange above) so that both rope strands run through the wide end. Clip the narrow end to your harness. Finally, clean the pear-abiner on the anchor. Once accomplished, the last person uses the descender's sticht plate to rappel DRT. • If rappelling into deep water, clip a tether to the descender to avoid losing it.

Disadvantages
- This technique requires a specialized descender.

- There's a lot of friction when lowering through the Jester. Slack rope on the unweighted side must continually be pulled up through the sticht plate.

---

[91] A half hitch is recommended as it's easy to untie even if pulled up into the sticht plate.

Simultaneous Rappels

While we're discussing twin systems, let's look at one special case: the *simultaneous rappel* (simul-rap). Up until this point, we've been assuming that only one person will be rappelling at a time. With a simul-rap, two individuals will be rappelling at the same time from the same anchor on different rope strands.[92] Surely, sending rappellers down two at a time is even faster, right? Or is it?

Special considerations:

- o The anchor must be bombproof and capable of supporting a two-person load.
- o Both rappellers should remain in close proximity to avoid knocking rocks on one another.
- o How would you rescue a rappeller in an emergency?

Simultaneous rappels come in two flavors: *counterbalanced* and *fixed*.

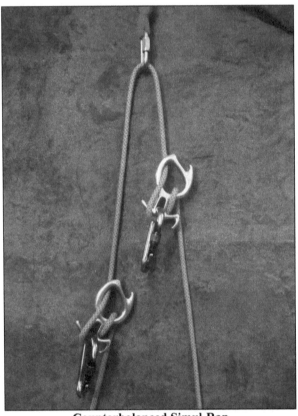

Counterbalanced Simul-Rap

Fixed Simul-Rap (using a stone knot)

Counterbalanced Simul-Rap

The rigging for a counterbalanced simul-rap is identical to DRT. The rope usually run through a fixed anchor or is wrapped around a natural feature such as a tree or rock horn. It could also be used to rappel off either side of an arch or tower. Each person rappels SRT on either side of the anchor, counterweighting one another.

WARNING! This technique enjoys a certain amount of popularity in the alpine climbing world, but be aware: it's significantly more dangerous than your average rappel. Rappelling is risky enough by itself, but now you can do everything 100% correctly and still be injured or killed if your partner screws up. Use of this technique has led to a number of fatal accidents. It's inappropriate for beginners.

---

[92] A simul-rap should not to be confused with a *tandem rappel*, where two individuals are rappelling at the same time using a single descender. (See "Tandem Rappels" in Chapter 15.)

Some issues to consider:

- How experienced is your partner?

- Good communication is key. When starting the rappel, both individuals should weight the rope simultaneously.

- If either rappeller loses control, the result may be catastrophic for both. A backup system, such as an autoblock, is recommended for both rappellers.

- Stopper knots are a good idea unless you can see that both ends are clearly on the ground. If the rope strands are of uneven length, rappelling off the short end could cause both individuals to fall.

- Don't unweight the rope until both individuals are at the bottom. Note that it's very instinctive, upon finishing a rappel, to stand up and give yourself a bunch of slack to disconnect. Unfortunately, this will have the effect of dropping your partner. (Similarly, if one person encounters a ledge partway down the pitch and unweights the rope, the other person could get dropped.) Getting dropped could lead to a loss of control.

Summary

The counterbalanced simul-rap adds considerable risk in an effort to speed up progression. These risks can be mitigated by adding various backup systems, but safety usually comes at the expense of the speed one was hoping to achieve. Planning a simul-rap in waterfall? You're just asking for trouble.

Variation: The Fixed Simul-Rap

By isolating both rope strands (i.e., creating a twin system), almost all of the risks associated with the counterbalanced simul-rap go away. Now, if one rappeller were to lose control or unweight the rope, they will not endanger their partner. This technique is still not appropriate on every rappel.

Advantage
- Assuming the anchor is strong enough, a twin system is a relatively safe way for two experienced team members to rappel simultaneously.

Disadvantages
- Knocking rocks on one another while rappelling is still a danger.

- Rescues are more complicated when both lines are in use.

- As with any twin system, the rope cannot be recovered from below. The last person will need to convert the rigging to DRT or SRT.

Chapter 13: Retrievable Systems

The term *retrievable* describes a class of anchors and rigging systems that can be recovered from the bottom of the pitch.[93] Why rig retrievable? The primary benefit is to conserve anchor material and reduce environmental impact. While this sounds great, these systems are often riskier, and require a greater degree of judgement and experience to use. Some retrievable systems require specialized gear. (See also "Ghosting" in Chapter 2.)

Retrievables in an Aquatic Canyon?

Retrievable systems are popular in the Desert Southwest, but may not always be the best choice in aquatic canyons due to their complexity and inherent risk. As the amount of water in the canyon increases, the more you should look to alternate rigging systems. This doesn't mean that retrievables have no place in the Pacific Northwest, only that their use is more limited in scope.

- Retrievables are best used on dry pitches or in light flow, where the landing is dry, shallow, or a calm pool.

- Retrievables work best when rigged on smooth-sided natural anchors and snag-free pitches. If the pitch is brushy or strewn with obstacles, you may be better off with a different rigging system.

Here are a few situations where retrievables might prove useful:

- In places visible or easily accessed by the general public. The presence of anchors may encourage the unprepared to try to follow you.

- First descents. There's no need to leave an anchor to get down a short nuisance rappel.

- The team is running low or has run out of anchor material.

Summary:
Retrievables are just another tool in the toolbox. Use when appropriate.[94]

Last Person at Risk

Retrievable systems are usually locked down (or otherwise backed up) for everyone except the last person. In their locked state, rappelling is quite safe. As team members rappel, the system is tested and trust established. Only the last person commits to the risk of rappelling on an unlocked system.

We'll look at two retrievables in the remainder of this chapter, but there are many others out there. Be aware: some retrievables are better and safer than others. You'll find many on the internet that are obsolete, overly-complicated, sketchy, or all of the above.

> **Beware flying objects from above!**
> Many retrievable systems involve various objects falling down the pitch along with the rope. Make sure the landing zone is clear before beginning the pull.
>
> - Carabiners and quick links do not microfracture on impact. This is a myth stemming from ceramic components in turbines. While microfracturing isn't an issue, hardware should still be inspected occasionally for damage. A quick link accidentally opening may be a bigger issue.

---

[93] See also "Rigging Classification" in Chapter 8.
[94] Retrievables are also worth knowing about for your next trip to the Desert Southwest.

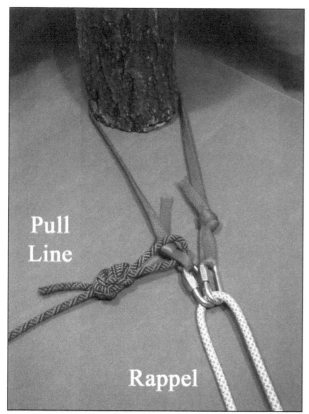

A retrievable sling rigged for DRT.
(Safety not shown for clarity.)

Figure-8 block rigged on a retrievable sling.
(The silver carabiner is the safety.)

Retrievable Sling (Two Ring Sling)

One of the simplest retrievable systems is the *retrievable sling*. This is an anchor that can be recovered from the bottom of the pitch. Retrievable slings are relatively safe and easy to use.

Advantages
- A retrievable sling can be used in concert with any other type of rigging (e.g., SRT, DRT, or a twin system). The rigging could be releasable or static.[95]

- A retrievable sling is easily made on the fly with gear you're already carrying.

> **Making Your Own**
> The classic retrievable sling is a single piece of webbing, perhaps 1.5–2.5m (~5–8ft) long, with a loop tied at either end (i.e., an overhand on a bight). Install a quick link in each loop.
>
> - Another option: use a *rabbit runner* (i.e., a single piece of webbing with a sewn loop at either end). With less material in the anchor, it's a little less likely to get snagged.
>
> - In some cases (ex: rappelling DRT), locking carabiners could be used in lieu of quick links.

---

[95] A figure-8 block rigged on a retrievable sling is both *releasable* and *retrievable*. If the rappel passes through a waterfall, we can rig releasable, set the length, and lower in an emergency. Once everyone is safely at the bottom, we can recover both the rope and the anchor.

- The classic retrievable sling requires three times the height of the pitch in rope (or cord). When rappelling SRT: one line is used to rappel, a second line to pull the rappel rope, and a third to recover the anchor. This means they're slow to deploy and stow.

- A retrievable sling alone is not safe to clip into. An additional safety mechanism is required to fully secure the anchor. With the safety in use, the anchor is not recoverable.

Using a Retrievable Sling
Rigging a retrievable sling is relatively quick:

1) Locate a suitable smooth-sided natural anchor, such as a tree or fallen log. During retrieval, the sling must pull cleanly around the anchor and all the way down the pitch. Beware any debris, cracks, or pinches that it could get caught in.

2) Build the anchor. Create a *basket hitch* by wrapping the sling around the tree.

3) Set the safety. The easiest method is to clip a locking carabiner through both loops above the quick links. Make sure it's locked.

   o If using an SRT block technique, safety systems can be combined. Clip the block's own safety through both loops of the sling.

4) Select an appropriate rigging. Note that the rope is threaded through both quick links at the master point.

5) Finally, attach the anchor's pull line.[96] The line should be attached to the end of the sling that provides the best odds of a clean pull from below. Clip the pull line's rope bag to the anchor or stash it somewhere nearby where it can't accidentally get knocked down.

The rappel station is open for business.

Recovery
There are a few extra steps when the time comes to retrieve the rigging:

- The last person also needs to deploy the pull line for the anchor. The team should take extra precautions to keep the various lines from becoming crossed or tangled.[97]

- With a safety in use, the last rappeller must remember to clean it.

Once everyone is safely at the bottom, the rappel rope is pulled first, which releases the anchor. Next, the anchor is retrieved. Pull slowly and carefully as the sling comes free. On an uncomplicated pitch, the sling could be pulled into the water to assist recovery.

- Efficiency Tip: If you're planning to use the retrievable sling on multiple rappels, you can just leave it tied to the anchor's pull line. The sling can be tucked right into the top of the pull rope bag where it's ready to go upon arrival at the next anchor.

---

[96] As the pull line will never be weighted, a lightweight pull cord, cordelette, or webbing could be used.
[97] Try to avoid deploying multiple lines simultaneously while on rappel; it's a lot to manage. It may be better to have the second-to-last rappeller deploy one line, while you deploy the other.

Variation #1: Using a Rope

Here's way to rig a retrievable sling … without the sling. The pull rope is also the anchor.

To rig: locate a suitable natural anchor and run the end of the pull rope around it. Tie a figure-8 knot (or barrel knot) in the tail. Once the knot is situated where you want it, tie a second figure-8 (or alpine butterfly) on the opposite side. The knots will house the quick links. The remainder of the rope will be used to recover the anchor.

Advantage

- Allows you to create a "retrievable sling" of any size. This allows use of very large anchors or ones that, otherwise, would be out of reach. For example, a fallen log 4m (~15ft) above the creek could be used by throwing the end of the rope over it.

Disadvantages

- This version takes longer to rig and has slightly higher odds of getting snagged.

The pull rope is also the anchor.

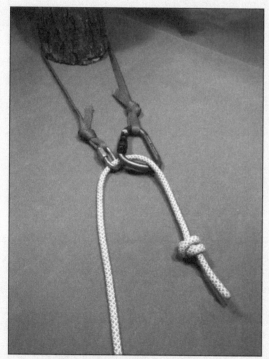

Retrieving a Friction Saver

Variation #2: The Friction Saver

Here's a version of the retrievable sling that only requires twice the height of the pitch in rope.

Replace one of the quick links with a locking pear-abiner. Before you pull the rope, tie a barrel knot in the tail on the same side of the anchor as the pear-abiner. The knot must be small enough to pass through the pear-abiner, but incapable of passing through the quick link. The tail below the knot should be short; no more than 5–7cm (2–3in).

When the knot reaches the anchor, give it a quick tug to pop it through the carabiner. As you continue to pull, the knot will jam in the quick link and bring the anchor down.

Advantage

- A separate pull line is not required.

Disadvantage

- The Friction Saver has slightly higher odds of becoming snagged.

Be aware: the rope strand emerging from the quick link will be the pull side. This has some ramifications for the rigging. If using an SRT block technique, for example, the block must be situated on the outside of the quick link. For DRT, the team must remember which side to pull.

Retrievable Toggle

A toggle is an advanced anchoring tool designed to be used in conjunction with a stone knot. Like all hitches, the stone knot (aka marlinspike hitch) requires an object to bind around. Without such an object, the hitch will fall apart.

Let's assume the tail of our rope is wrapped around a tree and secured with a stone knot. This time, however, we'll insert a narrow rod into the knot to keep it from collapsing. If the rod could be extracted from the bottom of the pitch (using a separate pull line), the stone knot would fall apart and the rope would be released from the anchor.

Introducing the *FiddleStick*: the original toggle developed by Imlay Canyon Gear in 2011 and released to the public in 2013. Today, a variety of toggles are available commercially. Toggles are usually made from a polycarbonate Lexan (an extremely tough transparent plastic).

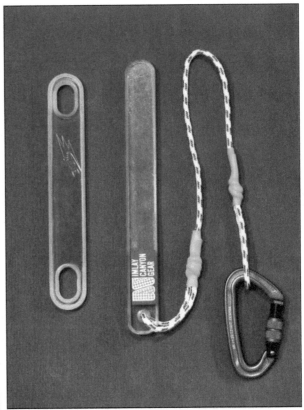

Two retrievable toggles.
Left: Smooth Operator. Right: FiddleStick.

> **WARNING!**
> Toggles come with significant disclaimers and risks. These should be read carefully and thoroughly understood. Check with the manufacturer on their usage and best practices.

Advantages
- Increased options for anchoring. Anchors can be used that are well back from the top of the pitch.

- Fast to rig and get the team rappelling. Toggles require about twice the height of the pitch in rope (or cord).

- Toggles can help protect trees from rope abrasion and reduce grooving in sandstone environments. In most cases, only a short length of rope is pulled around the anchor during retrieval.

Disadvantages
- Terrain and flow dependent. Toggles are not appropriate on every rappel.

- Toggles are a form of static rigging. Usually, they're rigged tail up, meaning all the excess rope will be at the bottom of the pitch.[98] If a rappeller gets into trouble, an alternate means of rescue will need to be devised. What would you do to assist the rappeller in an emergency?

- Reportedly, very supple ropes can bind so tightly around the toggle that it cannot be pulled free. If the toggle can't be removed from the stone knot, this defeats the purpose of the rigging.

Avoid using toggles in significant flow, even if you can set the length. The danger of an accidental release is much higher, and your options for rescue are limited.

---

[98] It's possible to set the length with a toggle, but the rigging is a little more complicated.

Pull Line for the Toggle

The toggle's pull line is positioned out of the water on a short rappel.

Avoiding Accidental Release

WARNING! If a toggle were to accidentally release while someone was rappelling, the result could be catastrophic. For this reason, a safety mechanism is used to secure the toggle for everyone except the last rappeller. The last person is the only one who takes the risk of rappelling on an unlocked system.

When it's time for the last person to rappel, the stone knot will be tightly cinched around the toggle. With the rappel rope fully weighted, it would take a good deal of force to pull it free. It's difficult, but not impossible. Here are some situations that could trigger an accidental release:

- The toggle's pull line is hanging in moving water (i.e., current or a waterfall).

- The pull line is being blown around (ex: high winds on a long rappel).

- The pull line's bag lands in the current and is swept downstream.

- The last person trips or gets caught on the pull line. The pull line should always be kept well away from the rappel rope.

<u>Summary</u>
Study the pitch before rappelling and determine where the toggle's pull line will be situated. If the pull line cannot be kept away from outside forces … or if the pull and rappel lines would share the same space (ex: a tight slot), then this is not a good place to use a toggle.

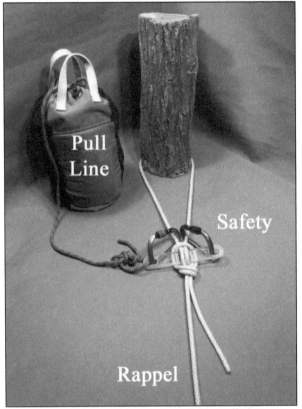

Smooth Operator with safety applied.

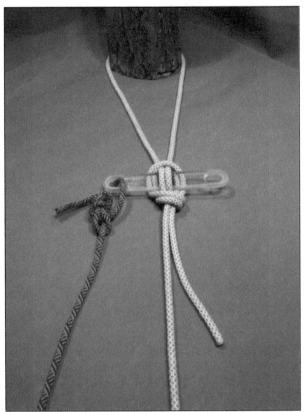

Final configuration: The pull line has been deployed and the safety cleaned.

Rigging a Toggle

We'll use a *Smooth Operator* in this example, but the steps are similar for most toggles.

1) Locate a suitable smooth-sided natural anchor, such as a tree, log, or rock horn. During retrieval, the end of the rappel rope must pull cleanly around the anchor and all the way down the pitch. Beware any cracks or pinches along the way that could snag the rope.

2) Take look over the edge and determine where the toggle's pull line will be situated. If the pull line could be affected by outside forces ... or if the pull and rappel lines would share the same space, then a toggle is not an appropriate technique for the pitch.

3) Set the toggle. Run the tail of the rope around the anchor and tie a stone knot.[99] Insert the toggle and cinch the knot firmly around it.

   o When dressing the knot, try to keep the two central strands flat. The outer strands of the stone knot should do all the bending around the toggle. This stacks the deck in favor of a clean pull.

   o Ideally, the toggle should be situated so it hangs in space where it cannot interact with any other objects or terrain features.

4) Set the safety. A carabiner is clipped to each end of the toggle, then around one of the rope strands above the stone knot. With the safety in place, it's impossible for the toggle to release accidentally.[100]

---

[99] Testing has shown that an *upward overhand* stone releases most reliably. (Galyan, Luke. "Stone Knot - aka Stein Knot." http://www.bluugnome.com/cyn_how-to/gear/smooth-operator/smooth-operator_stoneknot.aspx)

[100] Alternatively: connect both ends of the toggle with a quickdraw or short sling.

5) Attach the pull line to the toggle. The line should be tied to the end which has the best odds of a clean pull. The manufacturer recommends using a bowline as it has a narrower profile than a rewoven figure-8 knot. Clip the pull line's rope bag to the anchor, or stash it in a safe place nearby.

6) Deploy the rappel rope. Depending on the situation, the rope bag might be tossed down the pitch, or the leader could rappel with it.

7) As the leader descends, the station manager should watch the toggle to see how it behaves. The rope can sometimes move unexpectedly, causing the toggle to change position or orientation. If the toggle starts bumping into things, it'll need to be repositioned. Once the leader is safely at the bottom, the station manager can make any adjustments.

Once satisfied with the toggle's placement, the rappel station is open for business.

Final Configuration
The last person deploys the pull line and moves the rigging into its final configuration state.

1) Deploy the pull line. If you have a snag-free pitch, the last person could toss down the pull bag or zip it to the team below. If the pitch is low angle, brushy, or full of obstacles, the second-to-last person can deploy the pull line while the safety is still in place.

2) Once deployed, the last person can work with a partner below to position the pull line. In some cases, the line could be flipped up onto projections along the canyon wall to keep it out of the way. Alternatively, a partner below could provide a slight amount of tension (i.e., enough to keep the pull out of the water and away from the last rappeller). This technique works best on shorter pitches.

3) The last person sets up to rappel.

4) Clean the safety. Remove the carabiners (or quickdraw), while taking care to keep the rope tightly cinched around the toggle. At this point, the weight of the pull line may shift onto the toggle.

   o **WARNING!** Once the safety is removed, the last person should have no interaction with the pull line. If you need to fix something, put the safety back on.

5) After a final check of the rigging, the last person rappels. Try to keep the rope weighted to ensure the stone knot remains cinched. If the rope is unweighted for any reason (ex: crossing a horizontal ledge mid-rappel), move carefully and try to avoid significant rope movement at the anchor.

Once the last person is down, the pull line is used to extract the toggle from the stone knot. Pull slowly until the toggle pops free. The rope often falls down the pitch of its own accord. It's like a magic trick.

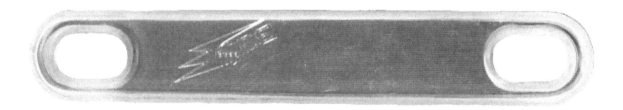

Retrievable Toggles: Additional Notes

Placement

Ideally, toggles should be suspended in space where they cannot bump into any objects or terrain features. It's okay for a toggle to lie flat on the ground, provided it's not moving around. If you don't like the placement, re-rig or find a better anchor.

- Tip: If the toggle is in a vertical alignment with one end is bumping into the ground, try twisting the rappel rope above the descender with your free hand. By twisting the rope one way or the other, you might be able to re-orient the toggle to lie flat. Once you're over the edge, friction will hold the toggle in place.

> **Toggle Placement**
>
> Imagine we have an anchor (ex: a stout tree) that's located 3m (~10ft) back from the top of the pitch:
>
> - A toggle set close to the tree will make the rope pull easier; this means less rope needs to be pulled around the trunk during retrieval. The toggle will have increased odds of getting snagged, however, when it's dragged across the ground over to the edge.
>
> - A toggle situated right at the top of the pitch has the best odds for a clean pull, but now there's more rope that must be pulled around the tree.

Load on the Toggle

Once the safety has been removed, the full weight of the pull line may shift onto the toggle. Testing has shown that load on the toggle should be kept to 3.5kg (~8lbs) or less in order to avoid an accidental release.[101] Some recommendations:

Pitch Height	Notes
Up to 30m (100ft)	A standard rope can be used to pull the toggle.
From 30–60m (100–200ft)	A pull cord should be used (ex: static 6mm).
More than 60m	An ultra-lightweight pull cord should be used (ex: 3mm Dyneema).

Things that can increase load on the toggle:
- Sand, mud, or water adhering to the pull line.
- Long rappels (the taller the pitch, the greater the weight of the pull line).
- Pull line is hanging in moving water.

Things that will reduce load on the toggle:
- Edge friction.
- Creating slack in the pull line (ex: flipping it up onto the canyon wall).
- Using an intermediate pull point.

> **Tip: Using an Intermediate Pull Point**
>
> If concerned that too much weight would transfer onto the toggle, you might use an intermediate pull point. For example, the last rappeller could tie a clove hitch around a thin branch or stick atop the pitch. Leave some slack between the branch and the toggle. The idea is to have the branch fully supporting the weight of the pull line. When it's time to retrieve the rigging, the team below pulls hard enough to break the branch.
>
> - Another option: place a small rock or two atop the pull line to hold it in place. The rocks should be set far enough back so that they can't fall on anyone when the toggle is pulled free.

---

[101] Galyan, Luke. "Smooth Operator Pull Cord and Release Considerations." *BluuGnome.* http://www.bluugnome.com/cyn_how-to/gear/smooth-operator/smooth-operator_pull-consider.aspx

Chapter 14: Safety Lines

Approaching a forward anchor atop a waterfall.

Safety lines are another class of rigging used to protect team members on less technical, but exposed terrain. Their use can save a lot of time in situations where, otherwise, you might need to belay everyone on the team. There are many ways to rig safety lines; some methods have more overhead than others.

Safety lines are used more frequently in aquatic canyons as everything underfoot is loose and slippery. They're an extra insurance policy when approaching or working near an edge. In popular canyons, you'll sometimes find anchors set to encourage their use.

Some common uses:

- To protect anyone working near an edge.

- Protecting an exposed approach to a forward anchor or side anchor.[102]

- Providing some security on short drop or low-angle ramps.

Some canyon teams will carry a short 6–15m (20–50ft) length of rope for rigging traverse lines.

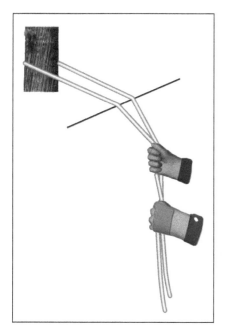

Hand Lines

If the risk and consequences of a fall are low, a quick and dirty hand line might suffice. In this case, the rope is just something to hang onto. A hand line might be anchored at one or both ends. It could be used on a traverse, or to protect a short drop when you want a little security, but it's not worth the time it'd take to set up a rappel. A hand line could be rigged with rope, cordelette, or webbing.

Scenario
The team arrives at a short drop in the canyon. It's possible to downclimb, but it's slippery. Rather than risk anyone going for a tumble, a short rope is wrapped around a tree with both ends thrown down. To descend: hang on both strands and lean back to weight the anchor. Carefully downclimb, while moving hand-over-hand. Once everyone is safely at the bottom, the rope is pulled from below.

This method requires about twice the height of the drop in rope.

---

[102] Safety lines are often rigged from an anchor in a less ideal, but safe, location to a better one out on the edge.

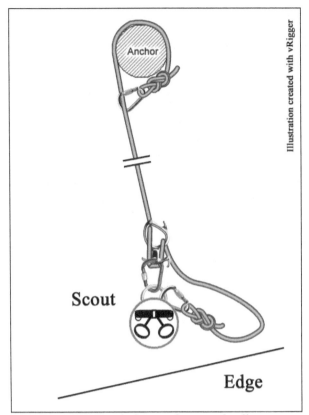

A short rope being used as an edge line.

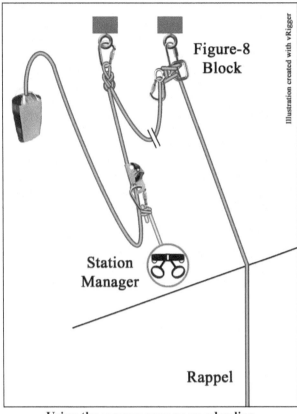

Using the reserve rope as an edge line.
(The anchor is set some distance back.)

Using an edge line to scout the pitch.

Edge Lines

Here's a quick way to protect an approach to the edge. Edge lines are typically used to scout the pitch, keep an eye on rappellers, or as a way to get some great photos.

Rigging an edge line requires a single anchor (it could be a human anchor) and short length of rope. The scout deploys the rope and rappels or self-belays to the edge. If extra security is desired, tie a stopper knot or clip the other end of the rope to your harness. When finished, the scout returns to the anchor.

- If rappelling, the scout can lock off upon obtaining a good vantage point. To return, the scout could use the rope as a handline, or install an ascender and climb back up to the anchor.

- The reserve rope atop the pitch can also be used to provide an edge line. If the other end of the rope isn't available, tie a figure-8 knot in the pull side and clip it to the anchor. With both strands isolated, the remaining rope can now be used as an edge line.

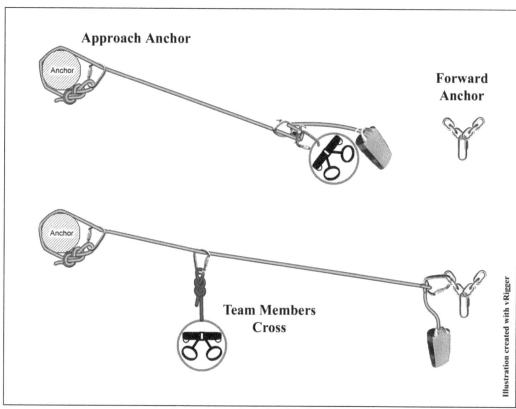

One way to rig a fixed safety line.

Fixed Safety Lines

Another type of safety line is one that links two anchors. The variation shown above is a fixed line. This technique is generally used on easier, low-risk terrain.

Fixed lines can be rigged in a number of different ways. The method you choose will depend on the local terrain, angle of incline, the availability of anchors, and what you're trying to accomplish. Fixed lines require a length of rope that's about equal to the distance between the anchors.

Let's suppose we want to protect the approach to a forward anchor. Here's the general sequence:

1) If required, build an *approach anchor*. When rigging a fixed line, the approach anchor is often temporary, so a quick and dirty one will do. A simple method is to wrap the rope around a convenient natural anchor (ex: tree) and clip it back to itself. If natural anchors are lacking, a human anchor might suffice.

2) Deploy the rope. Fixed lines can be rigged *tail up* or *tail down*.

   o Tail Down
     If you can see your destination, it's easy to pay out the right amount of rope. Once the near end has been secured, the leader can rappel or self-belay to the forward anchor.[103]

   o Tail Up
     If unsure how much rope is required (i.e., the forward anchor is not in sight), the leader could rig tail up and take the rope bag with them.[104]

---

[103] If additional security is wanted, the leader could tie a stopper knot or clip the free end to their harness.
[104] Once the safety line is established, any remaining rope could be used to rig the rappel.

3) Upon reaching the forward anchor, the leader performs a careful inspection. If no anchor exists, they'll need to lock off and build one.

4) Once satisfied, the leader clips into the anchor and secures the forward end of the safety line. The line may need to be tensioned to remove slack.

   o Be aware: clipping the line directly to the forward anchor is not always desirable. If someone were to take a fall on the safety line while another person was rappelling, the anchor could experience cross-loading. In some cases, it may be safer to use two independent anchors.

   o If using the same rope for both the traverse line and rappel, the two systems should be isolated from one another. Using the same rope for both is efficient, but can complicate rescues.

The fixed line is open for business. The rest of the team can now cross to the forward anchor.

Cleaning
The last person cleans the approach anchor, then self-belays across with a rope grab.

> **Traverse Lines**
> If a safety line is more horizontal than vertical (ex: traversing along the canyon wall), there are a couple of other things to keep in mind:
>
> • The anchors on both ends of a traverse should be bombproof. A horizontal traverse line can be thought of as a giant two-point anchor with a *critical angle* at close to 180-degrees. If someone were to fall while crossing, both anchors would experience forces far in excess of the actual load on the system. Traverse lines should be rigged with a minimum of slack, but should not be taut either. (See "The Critical Angle" in Chapter 4.)
>
> • On a long traverse (or if the safety line changes direction), the leader might install additional intermediate anchors for safety. The rope is threaded through these intermediate points. Team members who follow should know how to pass these secondary points of protection while remaining attached to the traverse line (or an anchor) at all times. Typically, the last person across will clean the intermediate protection.

Retrievable Safety Lines
Here are two more options for establishing a safety line between anchors. These are generally used on more exposed or difficult terrain. Both of these techniques require a length of rope that's about twice the distance between the anchors. The approach anchor is generally left behind.[105]

• Both of these techniques can be used to reach a forward anchor that's not in sight. There's no need to measure out any rope in advance.

• Again, use caution to avoid cross-loading the forward anchor. You may want to use separate anchors, or rig so that the two systems are isolated from one another.

• Another advantage: the last person gets to use the safety line too.

---

[105] A *Friction Saver* might be one way to avoid leaving an approach anchor. (See Chapter 13 for more information.)

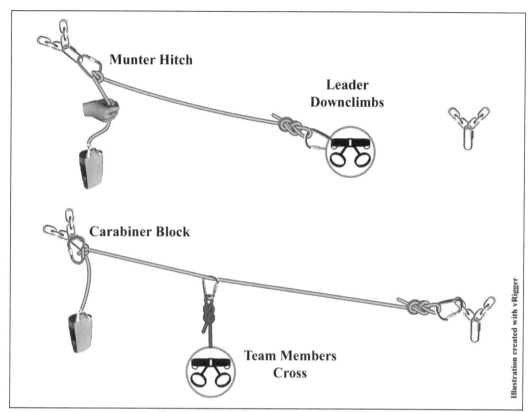

Retrievable Safety Line: Belay & Block

Illustration created with vRigger

Belay & Block

Here's a way to rig a safety line to a forward or side anchor. It requires an active belayer. One major advantage: the leader's hands are free for climbing. If necessary, the leader can also be lowered.

1) Tie a figure-8 knot in the end of the rope and clip it to the leader's harness.[106]

2) Rig a munter hitch on the approach anchor and belay the leader out. (See "Top Belay" in Chapter 16.)

3) Upon reaching the forward anchor, the leader performs a careful inspection. If no anchor exists, they'll need to build one.

4) Once satisfied, the leader clips into the anchor with a tether. Next, the figure-8 knot is transferred from their harness to the anchor. Upon completion, the leader signals the team above.

5) The belayer cleans the munter hitch and, if not already done, passes the rope through the quick link on the anchor. Tension the rope and secure it with a static block. Clip the rope bag to the anchor or stash it somewhere nearby where it can't accidentally get knocked down.

The safety line is open for business. Team members can now cross to the forward anchor. The last person will bring the rope bag across.[107]

Cleaning
Untie the figure-8 knot and retrieve the rope via the pull side. The carabiner on the forward anchor can be used as a high point for stuffing the rope back into its bag.

---

[106] Clipping is preferred to tying in. This makes it easier to transfer the rope to the forward anchor upon arrival.
[107] If the rope bag is brought over early, the pull side should also be secured to the forward anchor. If left free, this creates a potentially unsafe situation (i.e., only one rope strand at the approach anchor is safe to clip into).

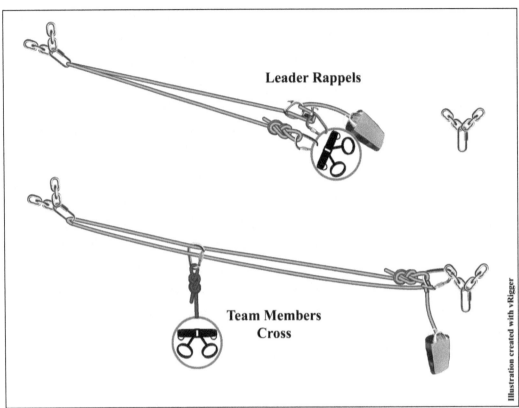

Retrievable Safety Line: Self-Lowering

Self-Lowering

Another way to establish a safety line to a forward anchor is by self-lowering. In this case, the leader is rappelling, so this technique may not work as well for reaching a side anchor.

1) The leader *self-lowers* from the approach anchor, taking the rope bag with them on the descent. Both rope strands are deployed simultaneously. (See "Self Lower" in Chapter 9.)

2) Upon arriving at the forward anchor, the leader performs an inspection. If no anchor exists, they'll need to lock off and build one.[108] Once satisfied, the leader clips into the anchor with a tether.

3) The leader continues rappelling until their weight shifts onto the tether. The figure-8 knot can then be removed from their harness and transferred to the anchor.

4) Next, disconnect from the descender. While being careful not to lose the rope, tie a clove hitch and clip it into the same carabiner with the figure-8 knot. (Make sure the two lines linking the anchors are not crossed or tangled.) The rope bag can be clipped to the anchor or stashed somewhere nearby.

5) Adjust the clove hitch to tension the safety line. Once accomplished, signal the team above.

The safety line is ready. Team members can now cross to the forward anchor. If using a single tether, it should be attached to both rope strands.

Cleaning

Untie the figure-8 knot at the forward anchor. The clove hitch can then be removed and the rope retrieved. The carabiner on the forward anchor can be used as a high point for stuffing the rope back into its bag.

---

[108] A belay can also be provided at the approach anchor by pinching the two rope strands together.

A traverse line being used to reach an anchor in an exposed location.

Crossing a Safety Line

On easy, low-risk terrain, a safety line might serve as a bannister or just something to hang onto. It's more common, however, to clip into the line with a tether or self-belay with an ascender.

- On steep/exposed terrain, it's best to cross one a time. This ensures that someone falling does not pull anyone else off.

- Avoid climbing above a safety line as this could lead to a high-factor fall.

Using a Tether

If the risk of falling is low, team members can attach themselves to the safety line with a tether. Be sure to you're your carabiner. The tether provides a measure of security and allows team members to cross quickly.

- Tethers should be clipped with carabiner's gate facing outward (i.e., away from the rock surface). This prevents the carabiner from getting scraped over the rock and accidentally opening.

- When crossing a traverse, try to keep your tether under a little tension. If you slip, this will limit how far you can fall.

- Passing an intermediate anchor is easy with a pair of cowstails. All you need to do is clip past with the tether that's not in use.[109]

---

[109] If you only have one tether, consider adding a second before crossing. A quick and dirty solution: girth hitch an extra sling to your harness and add a carabiner. A VT prusik could also be used in a pinch.

Self-Belaying
When the terrain gets steeper, self-belaying with a rope grab is a safer way to go.

Ascenders
Canyoneers will frequently use a hand ascender at the end of a tether to self-belay. Side-loading ascenders are nice as they're fast to install and remove from the rope. Make sure the device is installed in the correct orientation for your direction of travel.

- To pass intermediate protection: clip into the anchor temporarily, then move the ascender.

| Beware loading a Petzl Basic at an angle. | Device rigged correctly for a traverse line. |

Using a Petzl Basic on a Traverse Line
A Petzl Basic is designed to be loaded in a direction parallel to that of the rope. If loaded at an angle (something that could happen while crossing a horizontal traverse line), the device will torque out of alignment with the rope. If the cam isn't fully engaged, there's a risk that the device could accidentally come off the rope. To keep this from happening:

1) Rotate the ascender 180-degrees until the spine of the device is underneath the traverse line. This will help keep the cam in its proper position.

2) The carabiner at the end of your tether should be clipped around the rope. This will keep you connected to the traverse line even if the ascender were to pop off the rope.

Friction Hitches
A prusik or other friction hitch could also be used to self-belay. In the event of a fall, the hitch cinches down tightly around the rope. This might be required in the event of a lost ascender. Friction hitches are slow to install and clean.

- Prusiks should always be pushed along the rope. Grabbing or holding the hitch may prevent it from engaging. (See "The Problem with Friction Hitches" in Chapter 16.)

- Passing intermediate anchors is also slow. One option is to clip into the anchor with a tether, then move the hitch. Or, with two prusiks, leave one in place while the next is installed past the anchor.

Wade Hewitt and Deb Hill at Gnat Creek, Ore.
(Photo: Kevin Clark)

Interlude: Common Rappel Accidents

According to *Accidents in North American Mountaineering*, there were more than 300 rappel accidents in the United States between 1951 and 2012. The vast majority of these accidents were attributable to human error. A separate study reviewed the incidents taking place between 2000 to 2012 and identified three primary causes.[110]

I. Rappelling Off the End of the Rope

The rope was too short for the pitch and the subject rappelled off the end.[111] This is a common rappel accident that has led to numerous fatalities. To keep this from happening:

- o Don't assume the rope length is good. Look down and confirm the length for yourself.
- o Pay attention to what you're doing. Always know where you are with respect to the end of the rope.
- o Try to minimize the number of systems requiring active management while rappelling.
- o If appropriate, consider the use of stopper knots.

II. Anchor Failure

Anchors can fail in many different ways. Pre-existing anchors (including bolts) should always be regarded with suspicion and thoroughly inspected prior to use. Questionable anchors should be backed up, made redundant, or rebuilt. Also, what is the expected load on the anchor? If the anchor is intended for one person at a time, it may not be able to support larger loads. Some rigging systems, by their nature, are *force multipliers* and will cause anchors to experience forces great than the actual load. Ideally, any anchor should be able to support the expected load, plus a wide margin for additional safety.

- o *All pre-existing anchors are guilty until proven innocent.*
- o Just because someone left an anchor does not obligate you to use it.
- o Always be aware of the load you're placing on the anchor.
- o Once an anchor is built, get another experienced team member to check your handiwork.

III. Inadequate Rappel Backup (Loss of Control)

There are many ways to lose control while rappelling. Some examples would include: an incorrectly-rigged descender (or one rigged with inadequate friction), rockfall, pendulum swings, distractions, fatigue, or a beginner letting go of the brake. If appropriate and feasible, consider the use of a rappel backup. For example: if sufficient rope is present at the bottom of the pitch, a bottom belay could be provided.

Be aware: all rappel backups have their pros and cons. No backup system is completely reliable in every situation. In aquatic canyons, some backups will actually put the rappeller at increased risk.

Backups are great when you can use them, but preventative measures to avoid losing control are even better. Some examples would include:

- o Ensuring everyone has adequate training before entering the canyon.
- o Developing full proficiency with your chosen descender.
- o Performing safety checks prior to every rappel.
- o Maintaining situational awareness while rappelling (i.e., actively looking around).
- o Focus on what you're doing. Pay attention and avoid becoming distracted.
- o Practice good rappel technique.

---

[110] Hess, Robb. "Know the Ropes: Rappelling – Fundamentals to Save Your Life." *Accidents in North American Mountaineering.* (December 2012)

[111] DRT can also be dangerous if the rope strands are of uneven length and one side does not reach the bottom.

Chapter 15: Rappelling Revisited

The ability to rappel safely is another a critical part of canyoning. They're performed so frequently that they start to become routine. Don't let yourself get complacent, however. Rappels must be set up correctly every single time. Try to avoid taking shortcuts and instead develop good habits to promote safety for both you and your team. The vast majority of rappel accidents are due to human error.

Preparing to Rappel

At the Rappel Station

The party line says everyone should be clipped into an anchor, safety line, or otherwise belayed when close to an edge where a fall could cause injury. Aquatic canyons are notoriously slippery, so a greater margin of caution may be called for. Minor slips can have big consequences.

- Tip: Not enough room for everyone at the anchor? You can create more space to clip in by adding a short-term attachment point. (See "Temporary Clip-in Point" in Chapter 9.)

Safety Checks

Always perform safety checks prior to rappelling. It's even better when a partner is present, but don't rely on them unduly. Saying "Check me!" to your partner is not adequate. You know your own kit better than anyone else. Your partner may not be familiar with your harness, descender, ascending system, etc. It's much better to work sequentially through all your systems and demonstrate that everything is set up correctly.

There are a number of mnemonics or safety checklists that can be used when setting up to rappel. You can often catch problems by running through the checklist. *BARK* is one that may be familiar to alpine climbers.

B	Belt/Buckles	Is your harness set up correctly? Are you wearing a helmet?
A	Anchor	A reminder to thoroughly inspect the anchor and rigging.
R	Rappel Device	Is your descender set up correctly? Is it rigged with sufficient friction? Are all carabiners locked?
K	Knots	A reminder to look down and verify that the rope reaches the bottom of the pitch. If you can't tell, consider the use of stopper knots.

- As part of your preparation: tie back long hair, tuck in any loose straps or clothing, and secure anything in your working area that has the potential to get caught in your descender.

- In high flow canyons, it's good practice to reduce the gear that's racked on your harness. Carry only what you use regularly and stow the rest in your pack. (See "Minimizing Gear" in Chapter 3.)

Other Tips

- Take a last look around before departing. It's easy to get excited and jump on a rappel while forgetting important things like packs, rope bags, gloves, etc.

- Before passing over an edge, remove all slack between your descender and the anchor.

- Once safely at the bottom, disconnect promptly, but don't signal "Off Rappel!" until clear of the landing zone. Signaling prematurely means it's okay for the next person to go and you may be at risk of getting hit by rockfall, rope bags, etc.

- If the terrain cooperates and there's sufficient rope at the foot of the pitch, it's good form to provide a bottom belay for the next rappeller. (See "Bottom Belay" in Chapter 16.)

Testing the Rappel
Not confident in your rappel system? While still clipped to the anchor (and with a decent amount of slack in your tether), lean back to weight the system and try a quick mini-rappel. This is a good way to identify any problems while still connected to the anchor.

Setting the Friction

When setting up to rappel, there are two things that need to happen:

- The rope must be loaded correctly into your descender.
- The descender must be rigged with adequate friction.

If there's too much friction, moving down the rope will be jerky and awkward. If there's not enough friction, you may experience an unpleasantly fast trip to the bottom with potential rope burns. For a smooth, controlled descent, the friction needs to be set just right. How much friction is required? It depends on your situation. There are a number of factors:

Load on the System	The larger the load, the more friction will be required. The load includes the rappeller, plus any passengers and cargo. Additional passengers might be present in an assist or a rescue. Cargo includes packs and rope bags.
Rigging	More friction will be required for SRT; less for DRT.
Rope Diameter	Skinny ropes will require more friction than those with a larger diameter.
Age of the Rope	New ropes can be slippery due to a coat of lubricant adhering to the fibers.
Rope Condition	Wet, dirty, stiff, or icy ropes may require more or less friction.
Descender Condition	A worn-out descender may provide more or less friction than a new one.
Angle of the Rappel	More friction will be required on vertical pitches; less on low-angle terrain.
Rappel Length	On long rappels (i.e., over 30m) less friction will be required at the top due to the weight of the rope. Further down, more friction may be desired.[112]
High Flow	In high flow, additional friction may be necessary due to the force of the water pushing you down the rope.

---

[112] Friction adjustments should be made about every 30m (~100ft), or whenever you feel the need.

Friction settings are device-specific. Some settings are applied when rigging your descender; others can be set on the fly while mid-rappel. Friction is generally increased by adding additional bends that the rope must travel through. The more bends, the greater the friction. Modern rappel devices make it much easier to add and subtract friction. For example, suppose we have a low-angle ramp leading to a vertical drop. You might rig initially for low friction to move down the ramp, then dial it up just as you pass over the edge.

- If you find yourself moving in jerks and starts (or you're needing to push rope into your descender), you probably have too much friction. Try dialing your settings down a notch or two.

- A rope moving through a descender generates a lot of friction. On long, dry rappels, the descender may become too hot to touch.[113] You're not likely to damage the rope, but it's still good to disconnect promptly once you're at the bottom. Overheating generally isn't a problem in aquatic canyons as the ropes are wet.

Developing Proficiency

Every canyoneer should seek to develop full proficiency with their chosen descender. As a competent rappeller, you should be able to:

1) Set up your rappel device with appropriate friction for the pitch and the rigging.

2) Execute the rappel smoothly and in control. You should be able to add or subtract friction on the fly to move at whatever speed the situation calls for. You might want to move quickly through a waterfall or slow down to negotiate obstacles.

3) You should be able to stop at any point and go hands-free.

Practice with your descender in a safe place. If possible, try rappelling on a variety of ropes and rigging systems to get a better feel for the friction settings required. Your goal is to get to the point where you can quickly evaluate the rappel and know exactly what your settings should be.

If you carry a backup rappel device, it's good to develop equal proficiency with it. The classic figure-8 is a good choice as it has other applications in rigging.

---

[113] Gloves can come in handy here.

Locking off a Petzl Pirana to go hands-free.

Using a leg wrap to go hands-free.

Rappel Lock-offs

Every canyoneer should be able to stop in the middle of a rappel and go hands-free. This might be done to clean a tangle in the rope, deal with a jammed descender, switch to ascending, build an intermediate anchor, take a photo, jettison a rope bag, etc. There are a number of ways to lock off mid-rappel:

- Descenders
  Every rappeller should know how to lock off their chosen descender. Check with the manufacturer on the preferred method and best practices. For most modern devices, the rappeller continues to wrap rope around the device, slowly increasing the friction until they can no longer move. As the brake must be maintained, this is known as a *soft lock* (or "static position"). A soft lock is useful if you want to stop and perform some quick action with one hand, such as unclipping from the anchor. To go hands-free, add a quick cleat around the descender for security. This is known as a *hard lock*.

  o A mule-overhand can also be used to lock-off most rappel systems. (For more information, see "Mule Hitch" in Appendix I.)

- Leg Wrap
  Here's a quick and dirty lock-off method. While holding yourself on the brake, pull some slack rope up from below you with your free hand. Wrap the rope 3 to 4 times around your thigh on the brake side. Once accomplished, slowly ease off on the brake; you'll slip down slightly until the rope tightens and holds. Be aware: the wraps can slip off if you're not being careful. If you're planning to stay for awhile, pull up some slack and tie a backup knot for extra security (ex: figure-8 knot clipped to your harness). To continue on your way: remove the backup and re-establish your brake hand before releasing the wrap.

  o Con: You may not be able to rig a leg wrap near the end of the rope.

- Bottom Belay
  Signal a partner below to tension the rope and hold you in place. (See "Bottom Belay" in Chapter 16.)

- Autoblock
  If using an autoblock, ease up on the brake and allow the rope grab to catch. Make sure it's holding before releasing the brake. (See also "Autoblocks" in Chapter 16.)

Situational Awareness

It's very common to go into tunnel vision on rappel and proceed straight down the pitch without any attempt to look around. This is a bad habit and can lead to knocking down rocks, bumping into obstacles, going for pendulum swings, and rappelling off the end of the rope. *Not good!* Instead, get in the habit of slowing down and taking the time to look around. There's nothing wrong with stopping occasionally to get your bearings. The goal is to rappel efficiently, while remaining vigilant.

Get in the habit of looking down.

Looking Down

While rappelling, look down to see where you're going. This helps keep you from running into things and allows you to plan your next move.

- Are there any obstacles or hazards below?

- Does the rappel pass through a waterfall?

- What does the landing area look like? Should you be prepared for a floating disconnect?

- And, most importantly: *Does the rope reach the bottom?*

Even if other team members have rappelled successfully, it's still a good habit to confirm the rope length for yourself. Rare cases have been reported where a rappeller in the middle of the party discovered rope damage (e.g., a core shot, or the rope was severed by rockfall) partway down the pitch.

There may be other reasons why a rope no longer reaches the bottom. Consider a DRT rigging where the rope is not attached to the anchor. Any outside force acting on the rope, such as hanging in moving water, can result in movement. If the rope moves far enough, it could result in uneven strand lengths.

Looking Up

It's also important to look up occasionally while on rappel to ensure you're not straying off the rappel line. Moving off the rappel line can be deliberate (ex: trying to stay out of the water), or it can happen inadvertently due to the shape of the pitch.

A rappeller has some ability to move back and forth, but go too far and you risk a *pendulum swing* back to the center. The farther you go, the greater the swing potential and the more uncomfortable the rappel becomes. Ironically, a rappeller moving off the rappel line in an attempt to stay out of the water (a perceived threat) may actually be putting themselves at increased risk. Pay attention to where you are relative to the anchor and local terrain. Try to avoid setting yourself up for a pendulum.

- If you find yourself significantly off of the rappel line, don't allow any more rope to pass through your descender. Instead, carefully traverse sideways to get back in line with the anchor.

Bruce Wyse

Stray too far off the rappel line and you risk a pendulum swing.

Pendulums

Pendulum swings should be avoided for several reasons:

- A swing into a waterfall, or crash into a rockface, could lead to injury or a loss of control.

- The sudden rope movement above you could trigger rockfall.

- A tensioned rope can be easily damaged if dragged laterally across a sharp edge during a swing. This means ropes can be damaged simply because the rappeller wasn't paying attention. It also means beginners are more likely to damage ropes.

Rappel Technique

There's knowing how to rappel and then there's knowing how to do it well. Here are some technique pointers:

Don't Stress the Anchor

Avoid rodeo starts, jumping, and sudden stops while on rappel.[114] These are bad habits that needlessly stress the anchor and subject your rope to abrasion and damage. Jumping is an especially bad idea when rappelling on skinny ropes and marginal anchors. Instead, try to rappel smoothly and in control. Weight the rope gently and keep a consistent load on the system. (See also "Rappelling Softly" later in the chapter.)

---

[114] A *rodeo start* is leaping backwards off the top of the pitch when starting the rappel. While this looks great in the movies, it's bad form in real life.

Stay on the Brake!

Beginners are directed to keep their brake hand on the rope and never let go. For experienced rappellers, however, the rule relaxes to become: *Always keep one hand on the brake.* Occasionally, situations will arise where it's necessary (or convenient) to switch hands. For example: needing to clean a tangle in the rope, access gear on your harness, or push yourself away from an obstacle. It's fine to switch hands provided the brake is always maintained.

- Tip: Keep your fingers away from your descender. They can have a nasty bite.

FAQ: "What should I do with my free hand?"
Rappellers sometimes have a hard time figuring out what to do with their non-brake hand. Beginners are told to never hold the rope above their descender out of concern that they may come to believe it's a braking technique.

For an experienced rappeller, who would never let go of the brake under any circumstances, lightly holding the tensioned rope above the descender is fine as long as it's for balance only. Holding the rope in this manner really helps on uneven, slippery terrain.

- **WARNING!** Beware holding the rope above your device during a difficult rappel start. You may be at risk of getting your hand pinned under the tensioned rope. (We'll talk more about this issue shortly.)

Using your free hand for balance.

- If you're gripping the rope tightly with your free hand, this likely means your descender has inadequate friction. Your free hand should provide balance only.

Your free hand can also be used to push yourself away from the rockface and other obstacles. On long vertical rappels, another option is to reach under your descender and hold the brake with both hands. This two-handed method is preferred when using an autoblock.

Rappel Stance

Try to sit far back far enough so that your legs are perpendicular to the rockface. On a vertical pitch, your body, ideally, should be in an L-position. Keep your knees slightly bent and your feet about shoulder-width apart. Try to keep the soles of your feet flush with the rock. The direct pressure of your feet provides stability on slippery surfaces and in high flow. Look over your brake-side shoulder to see where you're going.

This is, of course, the ideal stance and rappels in the real world are seldom down nice smooth surfaces. Instead, you'll need to improvise: bending your knees, stemming out with your feet, and working your way past obstacles. Occasionally, you may need to put a hand out for balance. In all cases, try to keep your legs in the ballpark of 90-degrees to the rock surface to maximize stability.

- Footholds are nice on slippery terrain and can help reduce load on the anchor, but, otherwise, they're not really necessary. Rappelling is not downclimbing. Lean back and trust the anchor.

- Inexperienced rappellers frequently don't sit back far enough and try to "tiptoe" their way down the pitch. If your feet are slipping out from under you, try sitting back farther. Don't lean back too far, however, as this might cause you to invert on the rope.

- Watch your foot placement while rappelling. Try to avoid knocking down rocks.

- Beware cracks and grooves where you might be apt to get a foot stuck. Constrictions can sometimes be hidden under the water. Avoidance is generally the best plan, either by stemming over or sliding past the obstacle. (See also the scenario "Vertical Entrapment" in Chapter 24.)

- On a slippery pitch, moving to rappel on your knees may provide greater stability.[115]

- Good technique is particularly important when rappelling outside the watercourse. With a good stance, you can place your feet with precision and avoid trampling the plant life. (See also "Rappelling in the Watercourse" in Chapter 2.)

Terrain-Specific Techniques

Bruce Wyse

One way to start a rappel from a low-placed anchor.

Difficult Rappel Starts

Awkward rappel starts are fairly common in canyoning. If the usual technique of facing the anchor and backing over the edge feels uncomfortable, try getting lower. The more you can reduce the angle between the rope and the rock surface, the more comfortable you'll feel. Negotiating edges gracefully takes practice. Here are some options:

- For particularly awkward starts, consider rigging for courtesy. This will speed up progression as only one person on the team needs to perform the difficult start. (See "Courtesy Rigging" in Chapter 4.)

- Try moving to a kneeling position right on the edge and slowly working your way over. Knee pads make this method more comfortable. Revert to a normal rappel stance when sufficiently below the lip.

- Another option is to start from a seated position. Give yourself enough slack to sit down with your feet hanging over the edge and your brake hand away from the anchor. Give yourself a touch more rope, then lean back and slowly scooch your way over the edge. Use your legs, knees, and free hand to push yourself up, out, and away from the lip. You'll need enough space to allow your descender to clear. Once sufficiently below the edge, revert to a normal rappel stance.

---

[115] Tip: Knee pads make this technique more comfortable and will protect your wetsuit from damage.

- If the anchor's master point is situated over the edge (or in a similarly awkward location), pull up the rappel rope and rig your descender as close as possible to the anchor. Next, lock it off to go hands-free. You can now carefully downclimb until your descender becomes weighted. Once fully supported by the anchor, unlock and rappel.

Don't Get Pinned
WARNING! Avoid holding onto the rope above your descender during a difficult start. You may be at risk of getting a hand, arm, or glove pinned underneath the tensioned rappel rope. Instead, use your free hand to push yourself away from the lip and take it slowly as you pass over the edge. (See also the scenario "Pinned Hand or Arm" in Chapter 24.)

Long Rappels
On long rappels, the weight of the rope can present another source of difficulty. It may be a struggle to pull the rope up and load it into your descender. An easy solution: ask a partner to hold the rope for you. If you're on your own, here are two options:

➢ Pull the rope up and hold it in place by stepping on it. Yes, the party line says "don't step on the rope," but damaging a burly canyon rope is pretty unlikely. It'll be fine.

➢ Alternatively, use a side-loading ascender at the end of a tether as a "third hand." Pull up some slack and clip the ascender on the rope to hold it in place while you rig the rappel.

Rappelling Softly

Occasionally, you'll find yourself rappelling from an anchor that you'd like to avoid stressing. It might be a human anchor, a rock cairn, single bolt, or a tree that's a little too close to the edge. Some strategies:

- Send the packs and rope bags down separately to reduce the load.

- Even if it's easy to get on rappel, treat it like a difficult start. Sit down on the edge and slowly scoot your way off. The goal is to maximize the rope's contact with the rock and create friction. The more friction you can generate, the greater the load reduction on the anchor. You could even press down on the rope with your free hand as you slide over the edge. This is known as a *soft start*.

- When weighting the rope, do so gently. Try to keep a constant load on the system while rappelling and avoid sudden movements. If footholds are present, they can also be used to reduce load on the anchor.

If you're unsure about the anchor, it's always best to default to a soft start. (See also "Strategies for Marginal Anchors" in Chapter 4.)

Rope Positioning

Pay special attention to any edges that you pass over along the course of the rappel. If the rope goes into a crack, it could cause problems during retrieval. A rope passing over a sharp edge could lead to abrasion and damage. If you can find a good stance below the lip, sometimes it's possible to unweight the rope momentarily and "bump" it over onto more favorable terrain. You probably won't be able to move it far, but, sometimes, a few centimeters or inches is enough. You might be able to move the rope out of a crack and onto a smoother rock surface.

- Terrain features can also be used to change the course of the rappel. By popping the rope over a knob or running it behind a tree, you can modify the rappel line. This trick is known as *redirection*. It's often used to avoid a hazard below or keep the rope away from abrasive rock. (We'll talk more about this technique in Chapter 20.)

- If using edge protection, make sure it's back in position once you've rappelled past it. (See also "Protecting the Rope" in Chapter 4.)

A controlled slide.

Controlled Slides

In aquatic canyons, you'll occasionally encounter slippery rappels where it's a struggle to remain on your feet. One option for greater stability is moving to rappel on your knees. Another is a *controlled slide*. This is effectively sitting down and sliding while on rappel. It works best on smooth rock surfaces.

On a vertical pitch, get in as close to the rockface as you can, then flip sideways to put your non-brake hip up against the wall. Continue to rappel, now doing a controlled slide down the face. Continue until you feel comfortable resuming a normal rappel stance.

- Controlled slides can be damaging to your harness and wetsuit.

- This technique can also be used to scout a slide for the rest of the team. (See "Slides" in Chapter 7.)

- Con: Gear, tethers, and packs can get snagged on terrain features.

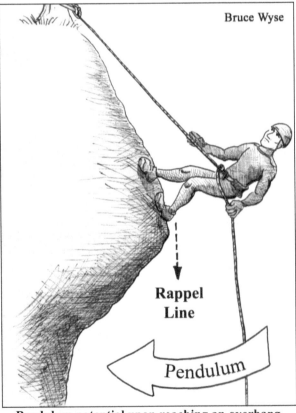

A free-hanging rappel.

Bruce Wyse

Rappel Line

Pendulum

Pendulum potential upon reaching an overhang.

Overhangs

Overhangs present another rappelling challenge. The wall you're descending falls back and the rappel continues on into empty space. When nearing the overhang, you may start to feel uncomfortable as the potential for a new type of pendulum appears (i.e., a swing beneath the roof). In this case, the swing potential is being created by your own feet which are pushing you off the rappel line. To avoid a swing, you need to reduce the angle between the rope and the rock surface above you. Here are some options:

- Try moving to a kneeling position on the lip of the overhang. With the rope closer to the rock, the rappel becomes more comfortable. You can then work your way past the edge.

- Another option is to position your feet on the lip of the overhang. Once situated, give yourself a touch more rope and lower your hips slightly below the level of your feet. Bend your knees to get in close and slowly work your feet down the underside of the roof until the rope above you comes into contact with the rock. Continue to rappel, now free of the wall.

Once you've descended and are back in contact with the wall, revert to a normal rappel stance. Be aware: rappellers will sometimes spin on a free-hang as twists in the rope come out.[116]

Rappelling directly in the flow.

Rappelling Through Waterfalls

Rappelling through a light or moderate waterfall can feel like being hit by a firehose. Higher flows can be dangerous as the force of the water can push you around, threaten to sweep your feet, and flip you on the rope. One way to reduce the force acting on you is to turn sideways to the flow, thereby minimizing your profile. Another option is moving to rappel on your knees for greater stability.[117]

If feasible, try to keep your head up and out of the torrent. If that's not possible, lower your head instead. With your chin tucked, your helmet will deflect the falling water and create an airspace underneath.[118] You may not be able to see anything while surrounded by falling water, but keep rappelling until you pass through and exit the flow. You might even find yourself emerging behind the falls.

- Tip: Next time you're passing through a waterfall, consider pausing for a moment mid-rappel. This is a way to get more comfortable in an extremely noisy and distracting environment.

- If the flow is too high, try to find a rappel line along the edge of the falls or out of the water entirely. Safety always comes before environmental concerns.

- The force of the water striking the rappeller will increase the load on the anchor. This is another reason why marginal anchors are less acceptable in aquatic canyons.

- Rappelling in significant flow makes rescues harder. Is the team prepared to assist in an emergency?

---

[116] In some cases, spinning can be prevented with the application of a very light bottom belay.
[117] Again, knee pads make this technique more comfortable.
[118] Some canyoneers wear a visor or ball cap under their helmet to create a larger air space.

Pack Management

Rope bags and packs are great for transporting ropes and gear, but they can also get in the way and cause problems. Sometimes, wearing a pack can even the rappeller at increased risk. Here are some examples:

- Packs can be a hinderance when squeezing through narrow spaces. They're annoying in tight slots.

- Downclimbing and mid-rope maneuvers are generally easier without a pack.

- Heavy packs can be annoying on long rappels. The weight of the pack is constantly threatening to pull you over backwards.

> **Backpacks in Aquatic Canyons**
> Wearing a pack can be dangerous in high flow as it makes you a bigger target. The force of the water striking the pack can knock you off balance or flip you on the rope.
>
> Generally, the rigging team will make the call as to whether or not packs should be worn on the rappel. A good rule of thumb: "When in doubt, go without!" Even if it's safe to rappel with a pack, make sure the lid is closed and firmly cinched down. Ideally, water striking the top should spill off to either side. Similarly, tighten down any compression straps to minimize the pack's profile.
>
> - Packs with inadequate drainage (ex: a non-canyon backpack) can fill when passing through a waterfall. The sudden increase in weight can flip you on the rope.[119]
>
> - Packs can be problematic on jumps and slides. They should be removed on long fast slides as they can throw off your trajectory. (See "Jumps" and "Slides" in Chapter 7.)
>
> - Packs can be dangerous in swiftwater as they can interfere with your ability to swim. Their buoyancy may also prevent you from diving to escape a hydraulic.

Here are some strategies for managing packs and rope bags:

Bring Fewer Packs
It takes some pre-trip planning and coordination, but the team can minimize the number of packs that are carried.

Partner Pass
On short drops, have a partner downclimb first, then pass the packs one at a time. On a more complex downclimb, you could set up a chain of people, passing packs from one to the next.

Pack Toss
On a short drop into water, you can toss the pack down. On longer pitches, you might rappel most of the way, then toss your pack from a safe height. Packs can also be tossed across water features that you intend to swim.

- Make sure your pack has adequate flotation and any fragile items are well padded. Overstuffed dry bags may be prone to rupture on a hard impact.

- When tossing the pack to a partner, make sure they're ready to receive it. Use a single whistle blast to get their attention.

- Avoid throwing packs blindly. Ideally, packs should be tossed into a safe location where they're easily recovered. If the pack goes into a hydraulic, retrieving it may require considerable effort and risk.

---

[119] A pack can also fill if it has insufficient drainage, or the drainage holes are blocked by the pack's contents.

Pack dangle on a 50m dry pitch.

Using a zipline to move packs over a stagnant pool.

Pack Dangle

Instead of wearing the pack on your back, hang it from your harness. Here are two options:

- In aquatic canyons, the pack can be hung on your non-brake side. It's usually clipped to a gear loop or short tether.[120] Leave the carabiner unlocked. This allows you to quickly jettison the pack if it's annoying or getting in your way.

- On a dry, vertical pitch, a heavy pack could be attached to a tether and lowered down to hang between your legs.[121] It will remain in line with the rappel and shouldn't need much attention unless there are ledges or other obstacles to contend with. Don't hang the pack too far below you as the tether could tangle around the rappel rope. This method is not recommended if the rappel passes through significant flow.

Disadvantages

- A pack hanging on your side will reduce the odds of getting flipped on the rope in high flow. The pack's presence will still make you a bigger target, however.

- Having a rope bag or pack clipped to your harness can be a distraction. It's one more thing to manage, get caught on things, and throw you off-balance. It can be annoying on a difficult rappel start.

- A pack hanging below you can partially obstruct your view down the pitch.

---

[120] Be aware: not all harness gear loops are load-bearing. Check with the manufacturer. Alternatively, you could clip a carabiner around the waist belt of your harness and hang the pack on there.

[121] Alternatively, girth hitch a short sling to the pack's haul loop and clip the other end to the master point of your descender.

Zip the Packs

Another option is to send the packs and rope bags down on a zipline. Clip the packs to the rope and zip them down one at a time. A partner at the bottom can tension the rope initially for speed, then introduce slack (i.e., creating a droop in the rope) to slow them down. Packs can be steered in to a gentle landing or a nearby pool. Ziplines require a clear line of travel and may not work as well if the pitch is cluttered with obstacles.

- Before sending packs down, make sure your partner is ready to receive them. A single whistle blast can be used to get their attention.

- Use caution on steep pitches as the packs will come in fast and could cause injury. In extreme cases, packs could be lowered along the zipline with another rope.

Lower the Packs

On an uncomplicated vertical pitch, the packs could be lowered. Tie a figure-8 knot on the end of the rope and send them down a few at a time. The rope could be run through a descender for more control.

Chest Harness

On long dry rappels, a makeshift chest harness will keep you from getting pulled over backwards by a heavy pack. You can make one ahead of time with a double-length sling. Alternatively, a quick and dirty method is to clip the sternum strap of your pack to the rappel rope with a carabiner.

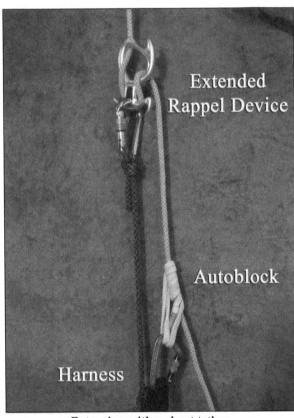

Extension with a short tether.

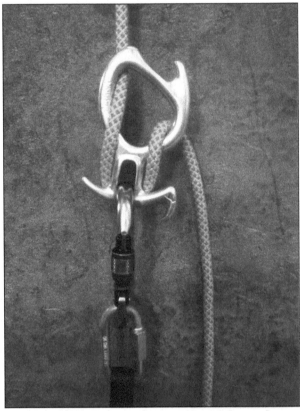

A short extension used to re-orient a descender.

Rappel Extension

A descender is usually attached directly to your harness, but in some situations, it's useful to rig it further away. This is accomplished by means of a tether, short sling, or another type of spacer. Some climbing organizations advocate using extension on every rappel, but, like all rigging systems, extension comes with its own pros and cons.

FAQ: "Why would I want to extend my rappel device?"

- Re-orient a Descender
  Most modern descenders are designed for use on a harness with a horizontal attachment point. If rigged on a climbing harness with a vertical belay loop, the descender still works, but will tilt out of alignment when loaded. Some canyoneers use a very short extension to solve this problem.

- Floating Disconnect
  Some canyoneers like using a short extension as it can make a floating disconnect a little easier.

- Autoblocks
  Rappel extension is a good idea whenever an autoblock is in use. An autoblock coming in contact with a descender is usually a bad thing. To keep this from happening, the rappel device is moved just out of range. (We'll discuss the pros and cons of autoblocks in Chapter 16.)

- Assisted or Tandem Rappel
  A *tandem rappel* is when two individuals are rappelling at the same time using a single descender. We'll talk more about this technique in just a moment.

Methods of Extension

- Short Extension
  A 10mm climb-rated quick link or small locking carabiner can be used to re-orient a descender.

- Cowstails
  A short tether can be used for extension. The goal is to keep the descender within reach.

Lacking cowstails, extension can be rigged with whatever materials you have available: webbing, runners, accessory cord, a locking quickdraw, VT prusik, etc. There are many ways it can be done.[122] One simple method is to use a short sling (either tied or sewn). Girth hitch one end to the load-bearing point of your harness and attach the descender to the other.

Advantages
- Braking is easier with an extended device. It's also easy to switch hands on the brake. If control of the rappel is lost, beginners are more likely to grab the brake strand.

- It's harder for clothing, pack straps, and autoblocks to get sucked into your descender and jam. It's easier to see what's going on in the working area of your harness.

Disadvantages
- Extension increases the complexity of the rappel; it's one more thing to check and manage. It also creates another potential point of failure in your rappel system.

  o Short extension: beware cross-loading carabiners. Quick links can accidentally come open.
  o A moving rope coming into contact with a sling or tether can result in friction damage.

- Extension makes difficult rappel starts harder. The longer the extension, the greater the odds of scraping the device over the rock and getting it stuck. The same problem can happen when passing over any edge (or overhang) along the course of the rappel.

- A longer extension moves the descender closer to your head. This increases the odds of getting long hair and beards caught. Whistles and helmet chin straps can also get snagged.

---

[122] There are even some fancy ways to rig a combined tether and rappel extension in one.

- A descender at the edge of your reach will make it harder to change friction settings, go hands-free, or transition to ascending (i.e., self-rescue).

Summary

Extension is just another tool in your toolbox. Use when appropriate. Don't extend more than you need to.

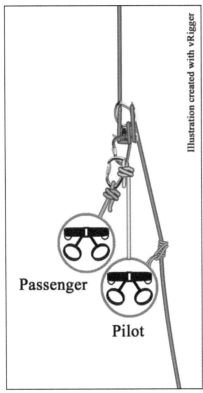

Illustration created with vRigger

Tandem Rappel

Tandem Rappels

A *tandem rappel* is when two individuals are rappelling at the same time on a single descender. This technique is most often used to assist nervous beginners or rescue an incapacitated rappeller. In a tandem rappel, one person controls the rappel (the pilot), while the other is along for the ride (the passenger). Ideally, the passenger should be situated on the pilot's non-brake side. Tandem rappels can be performed SRT or DRT.

The rigging for a tandem rappel is relatively straightforward. The pilot uses rappel extension (shown in grey) to move the descender away from their harness. A short tether is used to keep the descender within reach. The passenger then clips into the master point with a separate tether (shown in blue). The passenger's tether might be longer or shorter depending on the situation:

- If the passenger is injured, a short tether might be preferred. This will place the passenger in front of the pilot. The pilot can then use their free hand to help support the patient during the descent.

- If the passenger's tether is longer, both individuals will rappel side-by-side and will have a greater range of movement. This might be a better choice when assisting an inexperienced rappeller.

Other Notes

- The anchor must be capable of supporting a two-person load. If there's a releasable system in use, it should be rigged for a rescue load.

- The pilot's descender should also be rigged with friction for a two-person load.

- There's a lot going on in a tandem rappel. This may be a good time to employ a rappel backup, such as a bottom belay or autoblock, for extra security.

- If starting the rappel from atop the pitch, both individuals should weight the system simultaneously. Be aware: if there's a significant height discrepancy, there may be potential for injury. If one person were to suddenly weight the descender, the other could be pulled off-balance.

- Movement and coordination can be awkward while rappelling; take it nice and slow. Use caution when passing edges. Good communication is key.

Wade Hewitt rappelling Hopkins Creek Falls, Wash.
(Photo: Annalisha Cox)

Chapter 16: Rappel Backups

Many climbing organizations lay down the law: "When rappelling, thou shalt always use a backup." A rappel backup is an extra insurance policy in case control is lost during the descent. A backup system could be self-administered (ex: a friction hitch connecting you to the rope), or it might be provided by a partner. Other backups are passive, such as a stopper knot tied in the end of the rope.

While backups can increase safety, every method has its own pros and cons. No backup system is completely reliable in every situation; there are always ways that it can be ineffective or fail.

- Be aware: in aquatic canyons, some backup systems can actually put the rappeller at increased risk. As backups are used infrequently, a greater emphasis is placed on managing rappels and ensuring that everyone has adequate training before entering the canyon. Canyoneers should learn to judge for themselves whether or not a given backup is appropriate for the pitch.

Autoblocks

An *autoblock* is a term used to describe any self-belay system that's used while on rappel. If the rappeller loses control, the autoblock functions as a deadman switch; it seizes up on the rope and prevents a fall. An autoblock is usually a type of friction hitch, although some mechanical devices can serve the same purpose (ex: Petzl Shunt). Autoblocks can be rigged either above or below the descender. Rigging below is more common.

- An autoblock should always be tested to ensure it grips and releases properly.

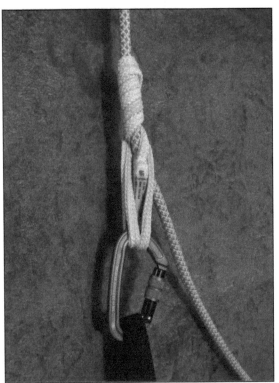

French Prusik (descender omitted for clarity)

Rigging Below the Descender

One of the most common autoblocks is the *French Prusik*.[123] It's rigged below the descender and requires a short sling (usually about 35cm or 15in long). Commercial versions are available or you can make your own.

Start by clipping a small locking carabiner to the load-bearing point of your harness.[124] Clip the sling into the carabiner, then wrap it in a tight uniform spiral around the brake strand. The number of wraps required will depend on the load, the rope diameter, condition of the rope, etc. (See "Setting the Friction" in Chapter 15.) Once you have a sufficient number of wraps, clip the sling back into the same carabiner and lock it. The knot (or sewn area of the sling) should be kept outside the friction wrap.

- Tip: Try starting with three wraps. If the hitch doesn't grip well, add more. If it's too tight and doesn't release easily, remove a wrap or two.

- An autoblock below the descender only needs to support a fraction of the rappeller's weight. The descender will support the rest.

---

[123] It's sometimes referred to as an "autoblock hitch."

[124] Autoblocks are sometimes rigged on a leg loop, although this may not be appropriate for all harnesses. Check with the manufacturer. Most harness leg loops are not intended to be a suspension point.

> **The Problem with Friction Hitches**
> A friction hitch will only cinch down on the rope if it's weighted and allowed to stretch out to its full length. If the hitch cannot stretch out fully (i.e., it's blocked from doing so by the rappeller or a descender), it may not engage and the autoblock will fail.
>
> - When rappelling, the autoblock should always be pushed down the rope. Grabbing or holding the hitch may prevent it from engaging on the rope.
>
> - Beware an autoblock coming into contact with your descender. The hitch could get minded, or it may enter the device and jam. Rappel extension is often used to solve this problem. Adjust the length of the extension and/or autoblock until the descender is out of range. Note that rappel extension comes with its own pros and cons. (See "Rappel Extension" in Chapter 15.)

Rigging Above the Descender

An autoblock can also be rigged above your descender, although some friction hitches work better than others in this capacity. A standard prusik, for example, would be a poor choice. If it were to engage on the rope, it would keep the rappeller from falling, but might be very difficult to release after being weighted. A self-rescue might be necessary to get moving again.

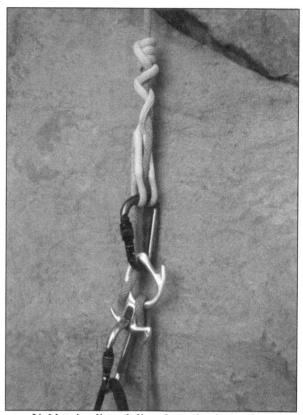

A better choice is a releasable hitch such as the *Valdotain Tresse* (VT).[125] When tied properly, it only takes a light touch to release. (For more information, see "Valdotain Tresse" in Appendix I.)

Advantages
- There's no danger of the autoblock coming into contact with your descender.

- The autoblock must be able to support the full weight of the rappeller. This has an indirect benefit of making it easier to pass knots while rappelling. (We'll talk more about passing knots in Chapter 18.)

Disadvantages
- An autoblock above the descender is not beginner-friendly. If control of the rappel is lost, an inexperienced rappeller may instinctively grab

Valdotain clipped directly to the descender.

the rope above their descender. The odds of this happening are even higher if they have one hand up there already to tend the autoblock. Grabbing or blocking the hitch may cause the autoblock to fail. Non-intuitively, the safest course of action is to completely let go.

- An extended autoblock can be problematic when passing edges along the course of the rappel. The rappeller may need to pull the hitch closer to their descender to keep it from getting dragged over the rock or stuck.

---

[125] The Valdotain Tresse is usually attached to the end of a short tether or is clipped directly to the large opening of your descender. (Clipping to the descender will complicate knot-passing.)

Pros & Cons

<u>Advantages</u>

- If control of the rappel is lost, an autoblock might save the day.

- A rappeller can stop at any point and immediately go hands-free.

<u>Disadvantages</u>

- Using an autoblock increases the rappel's complexity. It's one more thing to check and manage.

- Autoblocks are not fail-proof. If rigged incorrectly or with insufficient friction, they may not function. Conversely, if rigged with too much friction, they can be difficult to release.

- Rigging, testing, and cleaning an autoblock is slow. Progression will be slowed significantly if everyone on the team is using an autoblock on every rappel.[126]

- Autoblocks may cause beginners to become complacent. They may come to believe it's okay to let go of the brake at any time.

Autoblocks in Aquatic Canyons

While autoblocks can increase safety, they can also lead to a rappeller getting stuck on the rope. For this reason, they're used infrequently in aquatic canyons. Getting stuck in high flow or under a waterfall could be a life-threatening situation. Here are some ways to get stuck:

- The autoblock is rigged with too much friction. If it engages, it may be impossible to release.

- The autoblock enters your descender and jams.

- An obstruction (ex: frayed rope end, gob of tape, or plastic cap) prevents you from pushing the autoblock off the end of the rope when the length is set.

- Unable to remove the autoblock from the rope during a floating disconnect.

FAQ: "So ... autoblocks should never be used in aquatic canyons, right?"

Not exactly. While these are significant disadvantages, a compromise might be possible in some cases. Consider a long, dry pitch that exits into deep water. An autoblock could be used as a backup while descending the pitch. The rappeller stops above the water, locks off, and removes it.

<u>Some reasons to use an autoblock:</u>
- Protect the leader (no bottom belay).
- Need to stop frequently mid-rappel.
- Exhausted or injured rappeller.
- Cold, rainy, windy, icy ropes.
- Long or complex rappel.
- Multi-pitch rappel or passing knots.
- Rappelling in the dark.
- Rescue situations (ex: tandem rappel).

<u>You might not want an autoblock if:</u>
- Bottom belay is available.
- Setting the length.
- Rappelling through high flow or waterfall.
- Drop is short and straightforward.
- Experienced rappeller.
- The team is in a hurry (ex: approaching thunderstorm).

<u>Summary</u>

Autoblocks are not all good, or all bad. In aquatic canyons, you might look at it this way:

- If the risk of falling is greater than the risk of drowning, consider using an autoblock.
- If the risk of drowning is greater, then go without.

---

[126] A more efficient solution: send the leader down on an autoblock. Everyone else gets a bottom belay.

Providing a bottom belay.

Belaying: attentive, standing in a braced position, ready to pull down immediately.

Bottom Belay (Firefighter's Belay)

The bottom belay is a common rappel backup. If control of the rappel is lost, a partner at the bottom of the pitch pulls down hard and fast on the rope. The tensioned rope can no longer slip through the rappeller's descender, bringing them to a halt. Effectively, the belayer becomes the rappeller's brake hand.

If local terrain cooperates and there's sufficient rope is at the bottom of the pitch, it's good form to provide a belay. Each person rappelling can belay the next.

- This technique is not just for beginners. Rappels in aquatic canyons can be extremely slippery.

- The greater the rope length between the belayer and rappeller, the harder it will be to sufficiently tension the rope. It can be difficult to provide a good belay on rappels greater than 30m (~100ft).[127]

- It may be harder to tension semi-static and dynamic ropes due to their inherent stretch.

- DRT: The belay must be provided to both rope strands.

FAQ: "Where should I belay from?"

The place with the least amount of slack in the rope is right at the foot of the pitch (i.e., directly underneath the rappeller). Belaying from this location is not a good idea, however, as it puts the belayer at risk of getting hit by rocks, rope bags, dropped gear, etc. Ideally, the belay should be provided a short distance away and out of the line of fire. Avoid standing too far away as that means even more rope must be tensioned in order to arrest a fall.

---

[127] Kovach, Jim. (2004). "The Effectiveness of a Bottom Belay on Long Drops." *Nylon Highway #49.*

Upon arriving at the bottom of the pitch, look around and find a good place to belay from. The ideal location is a nice level area, free of trip hazards, where the belayer can get a good stance. Avoid belaying near edges or from an unstable/precarious position. Ideally, the belayer should have a clear line of sight to the rappeller.

- If the belayer's safety cannot be guaranteed (ex: high risk of rockfall), this may not be a good technique to use. In some situations (ex: the bottom of a tight slot), it may not be possible to get out of the line of fire.

- Avoid aquaphobia. Belaying in shallow water is fine as long as you can get a good stance.

Bottom Belay Technique

Testing has shown that the belayer's reaction time is important, particularly on long rappels. The faster the belayer responds, the more likely they'll be able to stop a fall.[128] Keep a close eye on the rappeller, especially when negotiating edges/obstacles and passing through significant flow.

To provide an effective belay: take an active stance by keeping one hand high on the rope, and be ready to pull down in an instant. Some canyoneers like to wrap the rope around their wrist for added control. Standing is better than sitting as the belayer can drop their center of mass immediately to help tension the rope. Moving quickly backwards works too, but watch out for trip hazards.

Pros & Cons

Advantages
- A belayer responding immediately can protect a rappeller who has lost control.

- Fast to implement. The belay requires no gear or additional rigging.

- The belay requires no active management on the part of the rappeller.

- In some cases, the belay can be used like a tag line. By tensioning the rope, the belayer can slow down or prevent a pendulum swing.

Disadvantages
- A bottom belay cannot be provided for the leader.

- Terrain dependent. If there's a deep pool at the bottom of the pitch, it may not be possible to provide a belay.[129]

- The belay won't work if the rappeller's device is rigged incorrectly or with insufficient friction.

- Belaying is difficult when the rappeller is not in sight. The rappeller might be hidden behind a waterfall, around a corner, or out of sight on a multi-tier rappel. Even if visible, it can be hard to tell if someone's in trouble at the top of a long rappel.

Common Mistakes
- If you're not ready to arrest a fall, then you're not belaying. Be attentive while on belay duty. Don't get distracted by chitchat, taking photos, etc. Your job is to protect the rappeller.

- Beginners often hold the rope too tightly. Don't tension the rope unless the rappeller's in trouble.

- Similarly, don't permit an excess of slack in the rope. A big loop of rope hanging below the rappeller is a sign of a poor belay. A good belayer will take in or pay out rope as the rappeller descends. Try to keep a minimum of slack in the rope, while still allowing the rappeller to move.

---

[128] Kovach, Jim. (2004). "The Effectiveness of a Bottom Belay on Long Drops." *Nylon Highway #49*.
[129] A floating belay is unlikely to be effective. Not recommended.

The Bottom Belay in Aquatic Canyons

Belaying from the bottom of the pitch works great in aquatic canyons, but isn't always feasible.

- A belay cannot be provided if the rope length is set.

- If the rappel exits into a calm pool, the rope could deliberately be set long. The leader commits to a small additional risk of entanglement but, once down and in a safe place, the excess rope could be used to belay the rest of the team. Con: Everyone will need to perform a floating disconnect which will slow progression.

Lowering with a Bottom Belay

On a snag-free vertical pitch, it might be possible to lower the rappeller. Lowering someone with a bottom belay is a delicate technique and takes a little practice. Carefully ease up on the belay until rope starts to slip through the rappeller's descender. Note that this method of lowering is not a true contingency technique. If the rappeller has a jammed descender or is using an autoblock, you won't be able to lower them.

Stopper Knots

In the world of alpine climbing, it's standard practice to tie knots in the ends of your rope prior to deployment. The idea is to prevent anyone from rappelling off the end should the rope prove too short for the drop. As rappelling off the end is a common rappel accident, it's drilled into climbers to use stopper knots on every rappel.

In the canyon world, stopper knots are used infrequently. If you can see down the pitch and the end of the rope is clearly at the bottom, there's no need for them. If you can't see the bottom, the team might perform an *exploratory rappel*. In this case, the leader already knows with certainty that the rope is too short. The leader's job is to go down and set the length. (See "Exploratory Rappels" in Chapter 11.) Stopper knots are more likely to be used when something unusual is taking place, such as multi-pitch rappels, rappelling in the dark, or anytime that there's an increased risk of distraction (ex: rescues).

Don't rappel off the end!

WARNING! If the rope's too short, rappelling off the end could be catastrophic. *Don't do it!* Rappellers should get in the habit of looking down and confirming the rope length. Never rappel blindly. A stopper knot is only an emergency backstop. Ideally, you should know long before reaching the knot that the rope's too short. (See "Situational Awareness" in Chapter 15.)

- In theory, the stopper knot will jam in the rappeller's descender and prevent them from going off the end. It's more likely, however, that the knot will function as an early warning system (i.e., the rappeller will first encounter the knot with their hand).

- Always know where the end of the rope is, and what you're going to do when you get there.

FAQ: "What type of knot should I use?"

The answer depends on what ropes and descenders are in use. A simple overhand or barrel knot might suffice for a narrow-aperture device (such as an ATC), but smaller knots can pass right through a modern figure-8 style descender. If more security is wanted, tie a bigger knot.

- The *Big Fat Knot* (BFK) is a good choice for modern descenders. Create a bight (about 2m or ~6ft long) at the end of the rope, then double it up again. Tie off all four strands as a gigantic overhand knot. The knot's size makes it impossible to pass through a descender. The BFK uses a lot of rope, but having plenty of extra rope to work with may not be a bad thing in an emergency.

- If you're rappelling on a rope that you're deploying out of a rope bag, you get an automatic stopper knot (i.e., where the rope is tied securely into the bag).

Pros & Cons

<u>Advantages</u>
- A good stopper knot will prevent an inattentive rappeller from going off the end of the rope.

- Stopper knots require no active management on the part of the rappeller.

<u>Disadvantages</u>
- Knots can cause problems during rope deployment (i.e., getting caught in cracks and brush). In windy conditions, the rope could get blown sidewise around a corner and become stuck.

- Knots can also cause problems during recovery. If the team forgets to untie the knot, it can get pulled up out of reach. If the knot jams in the anchor (or gets stuck in a crack), the rope may not be recoverable.

- Stopper knots are not intended to protect a rappeller who's lost control. Falling a significant distance onto a knot tied in a static rope could lead to injury.

The Rule of Recovery

A number of solutions have been proposed to ensure stopper knots will always be untied:

- <u>Attach the tail to your harness</u>
  Prior to rappelling, tie a figure-8 knot in the end of the rope and clip it to your harness. This forces the leader to untie the knot in order to disconnect.

- <u>DRT:</u>
  If both rope ends are tied together, the team will be forced to untie them in order to pull the rope. Con: Throwing a rope coil down the pitch with both ends tied together has a high likelihood of becoming a tangled mess. Not recommended.

A better solution is to *pay attention* when it's time to pull the rope. If you're pulling the rope, part of your job is to make sure that no knots, snarls, or tangles get pulled up and out of reach. If you see a problem, stop immediately and fix it. (See also "Pulling the Rope" in Chapter 9.)

Stopper Knots in Aquatic Canyons

Stopper knots are used even less frequently in aquatic canyons. If the rappel exits into deep water, the knot can actually put rappellers at increased risk. Getting stuck under a waterfall or in a turbulent pool could be life-threatening.

- If the rope length is set, tying a stopper knot does not make sense. The goal is to deliberately rappel off the end of the rope and swim away, so a knot would defeat the purpose of the rigging.

- Beware anything on the end of the rope that could function as a stopper knot, such as a frayed end, gob of tape, or a plastic cap. This may be a particular problem for narrow aperture devices.

- In theory, a stopper knot could be used on an exploratory rappel to protect the leader. It will need to be untied again as soon as the length is set, however. As the leader is one of the most experienced members of the team and is already aware that the rope was set short, tying a stopper knot should be unnecessary.

<table>
<tr><td>Some reasons to use stopper knots:</td><td>You might not want to use stopper knots if:</td></tr>
</table>

Some reasons to use stopper knots:
o   Multi-pitch rappels.
o   Deploying the rappel rope out of a pack (i.e., can't tell how much rope is left).
o   Rappelling in the dark.
o   Cold, exhausted, injured rappellers.
o   Inexperienced team.
o   Rescue situations.

You might not want to use stopper knots if:
o   You can clearly see the bottom.
o   Setting the length.
o   Releasable system is in play.
o   Rappel passes through a waterfall.
o   Pitch is full of snag hazards.
o   Windy conditions.
o   Experienced team.

Summary
While stopper knots are used infrequently, they're neither all good, nor all bad. Use when appropriate.

Top Belay

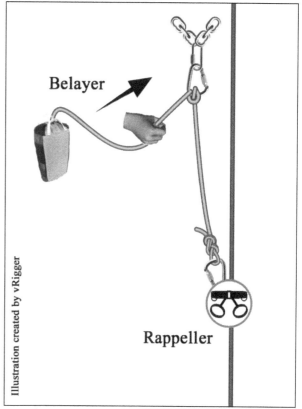

Here's another backup method: a belayer atop the pitch uses a separate rope to protect the rappeller. If the rappeller loses control, the belayer immediately applies a stopping force to prevent a fall. A top belay could also be used to assist rappellers on a difficult start or as a backup during a rescue. Canyon guides will often belay their clients. It's the highest level of safety, but takes the longest to rig.

Other Uses

•   The same rigging (minus the rappel rope) can be used to belay a scout out to the edge, or protect the leader on an exposed approach to a forward anchor. (See "Safety Lines" in Chapter 14.)

•   A top belay could also be used to protect someone who is climbing. Examples would include escaping the canyon or getting up and over a mid-canyon obstacle (ex: pothole).

Belayer

Rappeller

Illustration created by vRigger

Providing a top belay with a separate rope.

Rigging
A top belay requires an anchor and a lowering system. If there's sufficient reserve rope atop the pitch, it could be used to provide the belay.[130] Otherwise, you'll need another rope. A top belay could be rigged on the same anchor or another anchor close by. If the belay anchor is too far away and the rappeller loses control, they could go for a pendulum swing.

•   Top belays must meet all the same requirements as releasable rigging. (See "Prerequisites" in Chapter 11.)

•   Clipping the belay rope to the rappeller's harness is preferred to tying in. This makes it faster to disconnect at the bottom. The rope and carabiner are pulled up for the next rappeller.

•   When belaying, leave a little slack in the rope. The belay should only come into play if the rappeller gets into trouble.

---

[130] A twin system is an efficient way to rig both a rappel and a belay using a single rope. The two systems must be isolated from one another.

Here are two common top belay systems:

Human Anchor	A human anchor could be used to belay a scout out to an edge. A scout could also be belayed when downclimbing. (See "Belaying a Scout" in Chapter 9.)
Munter Hitch	Clip a locking pear-abiner to the anchor and tie a munter hitch on it.[131]

Pros & Cons

Advantages
- A belayer responding immediately can protect a rappeller who has lost control.

- A top belay requires no active management on the part of the rappeller. The belayed individual is free to concentrate on rappelling or climbing.

- Redundancy. A top belay provides a separate rope and braking system. In some cases, there might even be two anchors.

Disadvantages
- Setting up a top belay is time-consuming. Even lowering team members one at a time might be faster than belaying everyone. Rigging for courtesy might be more efficient than belaying on a difficult start.

- If the belay line gets pinched under the rappel rope, the rappeller could get stuck in the middle of the pitch. A similar problem can happen if the two lines become tangled (ex: spinning around on a free-hang).

- Beware the knot and carabiner becoming snagged when pulling the rope up for the next rappeller.

Top Belaying in Aquatic Canyons
If the rappel passes through significant flow or exits into a turbulent pool, a top belay is risky. If the rappeller gets stuck on the rope, it could be a life-threatening situation.

- A top belay adds complexity, as the rappeller now has two ropes to disconnect from.[132]

- When setting the length, the goal is to slide off the end of the rope and swim away without impediment, so a top belay might not be a great idea if exiting into deep water. A compromise is possible in some cases. Consider a dry pitch that exits into a deep pool. The rappeller is belayed the length of the pitch, then stops just above the water to disconnect the belay.

---

[131] Before pulling the rope back up for the next person, it may be helpful to remove the munter hitch. This will help keep twists from accumulating in the rope.
[132] If the rappel exits into deep water, consider connecting the belay line to a tether instead of the rappeller's harness. This makes it easier to unclip while floating.

Rodney Rodriguez entering Olallie Creek's slanted corridor.
(Photo: Wade Hewitt)

Canyoning is mostly about descending, but, occasionally, situations will arise when you'll need to climb a rope. The process is easy on low-angle terrain, but more complicated and strenuous on vertical pitches. Aquatic canyons can increase both the difficulty and the risk — imagine climbing straight up through a waterfall. Every rappeller should have some means of ascending a rope racked on their harness and be ready to do so at any time.

> **FAQ: "Why would I need to climb a rope?"**
>
> - The rope gets stuck during the pull and someone has to go back up to fix it.[133]
>
> - Important gear was left atop the pitch (ex: rope, pack, car keys).
>
> - To get up and over a mid-canyon obstacle (ex: escaping a pothole), or to reach an anchor station high up on the canyon wall.
>
> - Mid-canyon escape. The team might need to ascend a previously-set *rim rope*. Alternatively, the best climber on the team climbs out while trailing a rope. Once secured to an anchor, the rope becomes a fixed line for everyone else to follow.
>
> - Rescue situations. If the last rappeller gets into trouble, the team may need to send someone up the rope to assist.

---

[133] **WARNING!** Ascending stuck ropes can be extremely dangerous and has led to fatal accidents. Whether or not a rope is safe to ascend depends on the conditions and rigging above. *When in doubt, don't do it!*

> **Ascending in Aquatic Canyons**
> If at all possible, try to avoid ascending in flow. Getting bombarded by even a small amount of water makes everything harder. You may not be able to see what you're doing. Rope grabs may be difficult to move. Foot loops can slip off your feet. Getting stuck on the rope could be life-threatening.

FAQ: "What ascending system should I use?"

Ascending is usually performed with a pair of *rope grabs* (i.e., a set of mechanical ascenders or friction hitches). These rope grabs are usually attached to the end of a tether or clipped directly to your harness.

Your chosen system should reflect how much ascending you plan to do. In technical caving, it's common to go back up your own ropes, so ascending is expected and part of the plan. Cavers spend lots of time ascending, so it makes sense to have very efficient systems. In canyoning, however, ascending is usually infrequent, unplanned, and rarely performed by more than one person. A pair of ascenders or friction hitches is probably all you'll need.

- In an aquatic environment, side-loading ascenders are preferred as they're fast to install and remove from the rope. Imagine trying to tie a prusik on the rope while underneath a waterfall.

- For efficiency, tethers and foot loops should be sized to the individual. It's good to work out proper sizing prior to entering the canyon. (See "Safety Tethers" in Chapter 3.)

> **Foot Loops**
> A foot loop might be made for one or both feet. The best foot loops are made from low-stretch, non-absorbent material. A very simple foot loop is a Dyneema sling.
>
> - Tip #1: Use a separate carabiner to attach your foot loop to the rope grab. This makes it easier to deploy and stow. A separate foot loop is also be handy in other circumstances (ex: needing a place to step up in order to unclip from a hanging rappel station).
>
> - Tip #2: If your foot loop's too long, tie a knot to shorten it, or wrap it around your foot a couple of times. A girth hitch could also be tied around your foot to hold it in place.

Transitions

Another important skill to master is the ability to change directions on the rope (i.e., moving from rappelling to ascending. or vice versa). This mid-rope maneuver is known as a *transition* or *change-over*.

> **FAQ: "Why would I need to switch directions mid-rappel?"**
>
> - The leader might need to go back up if:
>   - The rope doesn't reach the bottom and the rigging isn't releasable.[134]
>   - The leader discovers some hazard below that wasn't visible from atop the pitch.
>   - An inattentive leader rappels past a rope tangle and is unable to pull it down from below.
>   - Multi-pitch: the leader inadvertently rappels past the next anchor station.
>
> - An inexperienced rappeller discovers a core shot in the rope. Going back up might be safer than attempting to pass the knot.
>
> - Self rescue (ex: jammed descender or vertical entrapment).

---

[134] Alternatively, it was rigged releasable, but the leader is unable to communicate with the team above.

Practicing with asymmetric prusiks.

Friction Hitches

Everyone should have (or be able to rig) some means of ascending a rope that is not a mechanical device. Prusiks are traditional, but there are many hitches out there that can do the job.[135]

A friction hitch needs to grip the rope securely under load, but should also release easily. If the hitch doesn't grip, it may be poorly dressed or requires additional wraps. Conversely, a friction hitch with too many wraps can be difficult to release.

How many wraps are required? Three is a good place to start, but the answer is situationally dependent. Some factors include the load on the system, diameter of the rope, the rope's condition, type of hitch in use, etc. (See also "Setting the Friction" in Chapter 15.)

A friction hitch should always be pushed along the rope in the direction of travel. Avoid grabbing the hitch as this could interfere with its ability to cinch down when it comes under load. (See also "The Problem with Friction Hitches" in Chapter 16.)

Advantages
- Cheap. Standard prusik loops and webbing slings are easy to make. A VT prusik costs a bit more, but is still cheaper than a mechanical ascender.

- Lightweight, compact, and multi-use. A friction hitch could be used as an autoblock, to self-belay along a traverse line, or as a rope grab in a haul system. A sling could be pressed into service as an extra tether, as an alpine quickdraw, or to create a quick place to clip in (ex: girth hitch around a tree).

- Friction hitches can be used to ascend both SRT and DRT.

- A friction hitch might slip, but cannot accidentally come off the rope.

Disadvantages
- Friction hitches are very slow to install and clean.

- Ascending is slow and strenuous.

- A friction hitch that's been weighted can be difficult to release. This is another reason to avoid the use of friction hitches when ascending in flow.

Even if you use mechanical ascenders regularly, it's still a good idea to practice with friction hitches on occasion. If you were to lose one or both devices mid-canyon, could you still climb a rope?

---

[135] Examples would include the klemheist, bachmann, and asymmetric prusik. A klemheist might also be a good choice as the team usually has an ample supply of webbing.

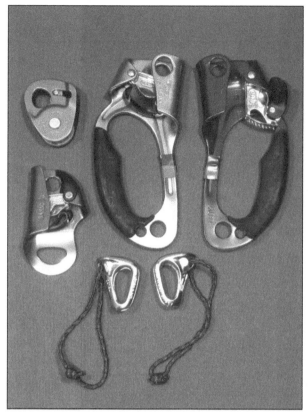
A selection of mechanical ascenders.

Going back up to repeat a jump.

Mechanical Ascenders

Mechanical ascenders are the fastest and most efficient way to climb a rope, particularly on long pitches. The ideal canyon ascender is small, lightweight, and multi-use. Ascenders must be installed on the rope in the correct orientation for your direction of travel.

<u>Advantage</u>
- Climbing with mechanical ascenders is more efficient than using friction hitches.

- Some ascenders can be used to self-belay along a traverse line, or as a rope grab in a haul system. A few can be used as an autoblock when rappelling (ex: Petzl Shunt).

<u>Disadvantages</u>
- Mechanical devices are more expensive.

- Most ascenders (with a few exceptions) are designed for SRT only.

- Toothed ascenders must be unweighted and pushed upward just slightly (i.e., usually about 1cm (0.5in)) to disengage the teeth. The device can then be removed from the rope. If the device can't be moved upward (i.e., it's right up against an anchor or another obstruction), removing it from the rope can be tricky.

FAQ: "Will ascenders damage the rope?"
Toothed ascenders, when used properly, don't place that much extra wear on the rope. Ascenders can damage the rope, however, if used incorrectly or if the device becomes weighted when the cam isn't fully engaged. Overloading and shock loading can also lead to rope damage.

Types of Ascenders

There are many types of ascenders on the market; each with their own pros and cons.

- Petzl Tibloc
  Tiblocs might seem like the perfect choice for a canyon ascender as they're tiny and lightweight. While some canyoneers like them, they may not be the best choice in aquatic canyons as they're fiddly to install and easily lost. They still might be useful, however, as a backup ascending system or a rope grab when hauling. Be aware: Tiblocs can easily damage a rope if you're not careful.

- Side-Loading Ascenders
  Side-loading devices are preferred in aquatic canyons as they're fast to install and efficient for climbing. It's good to practice installing and removing the device from the rope with one hand. A device at the end of a tether can also be used as a convenient "third hand" to hold the rope for you.

> **The Problem with Side-Loading Ascenders**
> It's rare, but there's always a risk that a side-loading device could accidentally come off the rope while climbing. An accidental disconnect could happen if:
>
> - The ascender wasn't installed on the rope properly.
> - The device is being torqued out of alignment with the rope (ex: crossing a traverse line).
> - The cam is blocked by a foreign object (ex: plant debris, mud, or a pack strap).
>
> An accidental disconnect could be catastrophic, so it's critical to maintain (at least) two points of contact with the rope at all times. We'll talk more about this in a moment.
>
> Additionally, side-loading ascenders should always be attached to your harness: either clipped in directly or at the end of a tether. This will keep the device from becoming lost should it accidentally come off the rope.

- Compact vs. Handled Ascenders
  Handled ascenders are nice on long ascents and make it easier to move past edges, but they're large and bulky. Compact hand ascenders are smaller and lighter, but not as efficient in movement.

- Progress Capture Pulleys
  Some mechanical devices, such as the Edelrid Spoc or Petzl Micro Traxion, function as a pulley and cam in one. These devices can used as a progress capture, simple pulley, or as an ascender. While not ideal for ascending in aquatic canyons (i.e., not side-loading), they're still very useful as a part of a rescue kit.

Two Points of Contact

An oft-quoted principle says: "When suspended well above the ground, thou shalt always be connected to the rope in a minimum of two places." Multiple points of contact means redundancy. If one of your connections should fail for any reason, you're still attached to the rope. In practice, the number of contact points you need is situationally dependent. When rappelling, for instance, a descender (i.e., a single connection) is usually considered adequate. A single point of contact might also be fine when ascending low-angle terrain when the risk of a fall is low.

- Two points of contact is a definite minimum if there's any risk of an accidental disconnect (ex: using side-loading devices).

- Consider adding a point of contact whenever something unusual is going on. It's not a bad idea to add one when performing mid-rope maneuvers (ex: transitions or knot-passing) or moving past edges. It's an insurance policy against rigging mistakes and gear failure.

Before Leaving the Ground

Always perform safety checks before leaving the ground. It's even better when a partner is present to act as an extra pair of eyes on safety.

- Double-check the working area of your harness. Make sure your tethers and foot loop are positioned to avoid tangles and maximize efficiency. Stow anything that might be apt get in your way.

- Test your rope grabs to ensure they grip and release properly. Double-check that any mechanical devices are installed in the correct orientation.

- Ascending is easier without a pack. If you need to bring it with you, consider hanging it below you on a tether (ex: pack dangle). Alternatively, tie it to the end of the rope and haul it up once you're at the top.

Ascending Technique

Climbing a rope is a series of load transfers (i.e., shifting your weight back and forth between the rope grabs). With one grab weighted, the other can be moved upwards. Repeat the process until you're at the top.

- Rope grabs are easier to move when the rope is under a little tension. If you're close to the ground, you might ask a partner hold the rope. Once you're a short distance up, the weight of the rope should suffice. Suspending your pack from the end of the rope is another option.

- Ascending is strenuous. The amount of energy required depends on the efficiency of your system, your technique, and how far you have to go. While speed might be required in rare circumstances (ex: moving swiftly through a waterfall), trying to rush is usually counterproductive. It'll tire you out. If the situation allows, it's better to climb slowly, prioritizing efficiency over speed. Take breaks as required.

- Try to move smoothly and avoid bouncing. Ascending, like rappelling, causes tiny back-and-forth movements in the tensioned rope above you. If the rope happens to be passing over any rough surfaces or sharp edges, this can result in damage.[137]

- Beware ascending on marginal anchors. Bouncing and poor technique will stress the anchor.

- Situational awareness is not just for rappelling. Watch for obstacles and look up to see where you're going.

- When climbing, try to keep your body close to the rope. Use leg strength as much as possible and avoid pulling yourself up with your arms. When stepping up in the foot loop, try to push downwards, not outwards. If stepping up is too difficult, try moving your rope grabs in smaller increments. Alternatively, the length of your foot loop may need adjusting.

---

[136] Some climbers prefer a clove hitch as it can be adjusted without being removed from your harness. Con: A clove hitch tied with stiff rope could experience slippage when it comes under load.

[137] If you know ahead of time that you'll be ascending, consider setting edge protection.

- If moving a rope grab past an edge proves difficult, it might be possible to disconnect the rope grab and re-install it past the edge. Make sure to set a backup before doing so.

- When ascending, check your carabiners occasionally to make sure they're still locked. Screw-lock carabiners have been known to work their way open on long ascents. Tip: Flipping the carabiners upside-down will help keep them closed (e.g., gravity working in your favor).

Ascending DRT
<u>Scenario</u>: You need to go back up a DRT rappel, but only have SRT ascenders.

- If you have a partner atop the pitch, a strand isolation (ex: stone knot) could be applied. Or, if the rope's under tension, a separate friction hitch can be tied on each strand and clipped to the anchor. (Your partner may not know which rope strand you'll be climbing on.)

- Build a ground anchor using one end of the rope and ascend on the other. Note that this rigging is a force multiplier and will increase the load on the upper anchor.

- Tie both ends of the rope together. Next, tie a clove hitch on one side of the knot and clip a locking carabiner through it. Pull down on the opposite side of the rope to transport the carabiner up to the anchor. You've created a static block and can ascend on the blocked side. It must be impossible for the block to pass through the anchor.

Transitions

Transitions are simple in concept, but can feel surprisingly complicated while hanging on a rope in the middle of the pitch. Don't rely on being able to hear shouted instructions from a partner. It's much better/safer to practice these maneuvers in a safe place and become fully proficient.

A transition is just a different series of load transfers. This time you're shifting your weight from the descender to the rope grabs (or vice versa). The exact steps will depend on your ascending system and how steep the terrain is. Again, a minimum of two points of contact should be maintained throughout the process.

Here's the general sequence for a transition. Switching from rappelling to ascending is easier.

Rappelling to Ascending	Ascending to Rappelling
1) Lock off the descender and go hands-free.	1) Install the descender underneath your rope grabs, but don't lock it off yet.
2) Install your rope grabs (and accompanying foot loop) above the descender.	2) Step up in the foot loop, while simultaneously pulling rope up and through your rappel device. When the descender is as close as possible to the lower rope grab, lock it off.
3) Climb upwards with the rope grabs until the rappel device becomes unweighted.	3) Lower yourself back down to load the descender.
4) Clean the descender and continue climbing.	4) Clean both rope grabs and the foot loop.
	5) Unlock the descender and rappel.

<u>Other Notes</u>:

- Your ascending gear should always be at the ready when rappelling. You never know when you might need it to self-rescue or go back up the rope.

- If you need to turn around in the middle of the pitch, it's better to do so near the top. The further down you go, the greater the distance you'll have to climb back up.

- Be careful not to drop anything during a transition as you might not get it back. If you were to accidentally drop your descender, what's your backup plan for rappelling? [138]

Downclimbing

On rare occasions (ex: knot passing or rescues), you might need to downclimb a rope. When descending, try to move your rope grabs in smaller increments, keeping them about a handspan apart (~10cm (4in)). Don't try for too much distance at once, or you'll run into problems. Downclimbing a rope is slow and strenuous; it takes some practice to get it right.

- If you need to downclimb more than a short distance, you're probably better off transitioning to a rappel. Rappelling may not be possible, however, if the rope is under tension (i.e., the victim is hanging on it).

- Tip: When lowering yourself from a rope grab at the end of a tether, the carabiner makes a good handhold.

- Descending with Ascenders:
  Note that most ascenders will need to be pushed upwards just slightly in order to disengage the teeth. The cam can then be thumbed open and the device moved downwards. Try to keep the device in line with the rope while it's being moved. This will keep the teeth from snagging on the rope sheath. Once in the desired position, release and allow the cam to re-engage.

Other Skills to Practice

- Long Ascents
  Once you've got a handle on ascending, test your mettle by climbing a good 30m (~100ft) pitch. Ascending may get your attention in a new way when there's lots of air underneath you.

- Edges & Overhangs
  Moving past edges can be challenging depending on how much contact the rope has with the rock. Some systems work better than others in this capacity. Also, practice exiting atop the pitch.

---

[138] This is an excellent reason to practice rappelling with a classic figure-8 descender or the munter hitch.

Ascension Methods

In the remainder of the chapter, we'll take a look at several ascending systems commonly employed by canyoneers. The Frog Rig is an excellent go-to in aquatic canyons.

Single Device Technique

If the climbing is easy and the risk of a fall is low, a single rope grab can be used. Essentially, you're climbing a vertical safety line. This might be done on low-angle, slippery terrain.

Steps:

1) Install your hand ascender (at the end of your long tether) on the rope. Slide it up until the tether becomes taut.

2) While holding the rope below your ascender, step up on a convenient foothold.

3) With the ascender unweighted, slide it up again as high as you can.[139]

Repeat the process of stepping up and moving the hand ascender.

Clever Tricks: Quick Foot Loop

If footholds are lacking, a quick and dirty option is to use the rope itself. With the ascender weighted, reach down and pull up some slack rope. Wrap the rope once or twice around one foot, then bring the free end up in parallel with the strand below the ascender (ref: illustration far right). While holding both strands firmly, step up in the makeshift foot loop and quickly push the ascender upwards. Repeat as needed.

 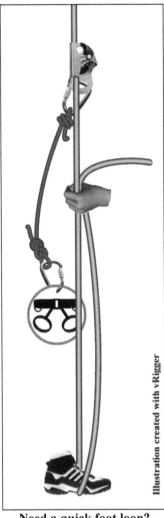

Illustration created with vRigger

Ascending with a single rope grab.

Need a quick foot loop?

Transition: Ascend to Rappel

1) Install your rappel device on the rope below the ascender, but don't lock it off yet.

2) Step up on a foothold, while pulling slack through the rappel device. Lock off the descender, then step back down to weight it.

3) Clean the hand ascender, unlock, and rappel.

---

[139] While climbing, try to keep a minimum of slack in your tether as this will limit how far you can fall.

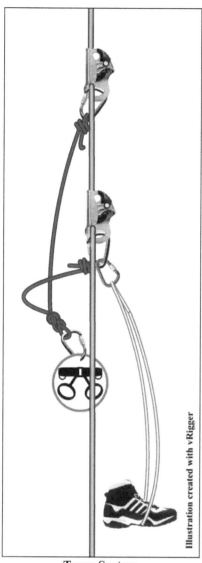

Texas System

Using a pair of ascenders is the classic way to ascend steep vertical terrain. This method, with each rope grab attached to the end of a tether (i.e., a set of cowstails), is called the *Texas System*. The tethers create another point of contact with the rope, and also keep side-loading devices from becoming lost in the event of an accidental disconnect.

Steps
1) Install your bottom ascender (attached to your short tether) on the rope. Add a foot loop and adjust to the appropriate length.[140]

2) Install the top ascender (attached to your long tether) on the rope. Slide it upward until the tether becomes taut.

3) Sit back to load the top ascender. With the bottom device unweighted, you can slide it up the rope.[141]

4) Step up in the foot loop. With the top device unweighted, it can be moved up the rope. Slide it up as high as you can.

5) Repeat the process, moving alternating ascenders as you climb. Continue until you reach the top.

Advantage
• This is a fairly simple system for ascending vertical terrain.

Disadvantages
• Moving past edges can be difficult as the ascenders are situated further away from your harness. To work your way past edges, try moving them upward one at a time in small increments.

• Both of your tethers are in use. Upon arriving at the top of the pitch, you may need to add another point of connection before you can clip into the anchor.

Texas System

Transition: Ascend to Rappel

1) While hanging on your top ascender, slide the bottom one up as high as you can.

2) Next, install your rappel device on the rope below both descenders, but don't lock it off yet.

3) Step up in the foot loop, while simultaneously pulling slack through your rappel device. Try to get it as close as possible to your bottom ascender, then lock it off.

4) Lower yourself back down to weight the rappel device. You'll know immediately you were successful if both tethers have gone slack.

5) Clean both ascenders and the foot loop. Unlock and rappel.

---

[140] Sizing: Hold the bottom device with your elbow bent at a 90-degrees. The foot loop should just reach the ground.
[141] Note that your short tether will limit how far you can move the lower device. In some cases, you may want to add a spacer (i.e., extend the tether) for greater efficiency.

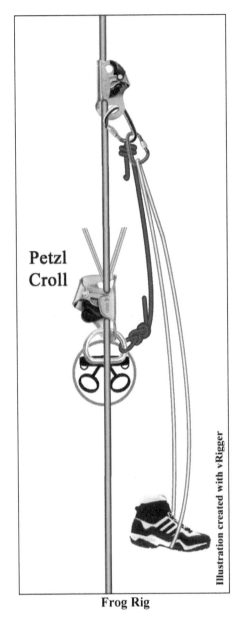

Petzl Croll

Illustration created with vRigger

Frog Rig

Frog Rig

One of the most popular ascending systems used by canyoneers is the Frog. It requires a chest ascender, such as Petzl Croll or Kong Cam Clean.[142] The device is held firmly in place between the climber's harness and a separate chest harness. This provides a major advantage: when the climber steps up in the foot loop, the Croll automatically slides up the rope.

The system gets its name from the motion the climber makes while ascending: a repeated sit-stand cycle that looks like a swimming frog. It was originally developed for use in caving.

Steps
1) Insert the rope into the Croll and tighten down your chest harness to hold the device in place.

2) Install the top ascender (attached to your long tether) on the rope. Add a foot loop and adjust to the appropriate length.[143] Slide the device upward until the tether becomes taut.

3) Step up in the foot loop while keeping your body close to the rope. The Croll will slide upwards automatically.

   o   When leaving the ground, it's helpful if the rope is under a little tension. If you don't have a partner to hold the rope, you can hold the rope below the Croll with one hand as you step up. Some canyoneers will hold the rope between their feet.

4) Sit back to weight to the Croll.

5) Using both hands, push the top ascender up as high as you can. While this is happening, simultaneously lift one or both feet as you prepare to stand up again.

6) Repeat the cycle of standing and sitting to make rapid progress up the rope. Continue until you reach the top.

Advantages
- The Frog Rig is fast to install on the rope and get climbing. Ascending is very efficient on long pitches and free-hanging rappels. It's relatively easy to move past edges.

- Once underway, the Croll requires little-to-no management. This allows the climber to focus on good technique.

Disadvantages
- When wearing a pack, the waist belt should be clipped so as to avoid interfering with the Croll. It may be difficult to wear a chest harness with a PFD.

- The chest harness will need to be removed in order to add/subtract layers mid-canyon.

---

[142] We'll refer to the chest ascender hereafter as a Croll, but there are a number of devices that could be used.
[143] Sizing: Position the top ascender immediately above the Croll. The foot loop should just reach the ground. (Note that climbing will be more efficient if the foot loop can house both feet.)

Transition: Ascend to Rappel

1) While hanging on the Croll, slide the top ascender down until it's a few centimeters/inches away.

2) Install your rappel device on the rope immediately below the Croll and lock it off.

3) Step up in the foot loop and disconnect the Croll from the rope.

4) Lower yourself back down to weight the rappel device.

5) Clean the top ascender and foot loop. Unlock and rappel.

<u>Other Notes</u>

- Consider moving your descender to a gear loop to free up space in your working area.

- Chest ascenders are designed to be used on a harness with a horizontal attachment point (i.e., a canyon or caving harness). Some efficiency will be lost if used on a harness with a vertical belay loop.

- Canyoneers will often set up the Croll at the beginning of the day. The chest harness is worn right over the wetsuit, but can be loosened up for comfort when moving between rappels.

- The chest harness is not designed to be load-bearing. Its only purpose is to hold the Croll in place, so canyoneers will sometimes make their own. Sometimes, a sling is worn over the shoulder like a bandolier or a lanyard worn around the neck. Again, these will lose a little efficiency, but should get the job done.

Chapter 18: Passing Knots

On rare occasions, you may need to pass a knot while rappelling or ascending. These skills are used infrequently, so it's good to practice for the day that you're called to action. Ideally, all canyoneers should be able to pass a knot quickly and efficiently. Knot-passing is a great way to train for mid-rope maneuvers.

- We'll discuss another form of knot-passing (e.g., moving a knot past the anchor during a lower) later in Chapter 22. This is actually a form of rigging conversion, not an on-rope skill.

Passing Knots: While Rappelling

If you need to pass a knot in the middle of a rappel, it's usually a sign that something bigger has gone wrong. Here are a couple of situations in which it could happen:

- Scenario #1
  The team encounters an unexpectedly tall drop in the canyon. Perhaps the beta was wrong, someone brought the wrong rope, or the team underestimated the amount of rope required to run the canyon. Two ropes must be tied together for sufficient length.

- Scenario #2
  Partway down the pitch, a rappeller discovers a core shot in the rope. Continuing to rappel past the damaged section would be risky. Some better options would include:

    o Requesting a lower from the team above.
    o Re-ascending the rope.
    o Finding a place nearby to build an intermediate anchor.
    o Locking off and tying a knot in the rope to isolate the damaged section.[144] Once accomplished, they pass the knot and finish the rappel.

Passing a knot is a fancy *transition*. It's a series of load transfers to move you from one side of the knot to the other. If you can transition between rappelling and ascending, you can pass a knot while on rappel. There are many ways to pass knots; how you go about it will depend on the situation, the gear you have, and personal preference. We'll look at two methods in just a moment.

The Problem with a Knot in the Rappel Rope

Be aware: tying a knot in the rappel rope may cause the rope to become unrecoverable. Why would this happen? Let's imagine there's an SRT block system at the anchor. With a block on one side of the anchor and a knot on the other, the rope cannot be pulled from the bottom. Some form of reconfiguration will need to happen in order to get the rope back. Here are some options:

➢ Re-rig the block so that the damaged side will be used for the pull.

➢ Some retrievable systems, such as toggles, allow rope recovery without needing to pull the rope through an anchor. (See "Retrievable Toggles" in Chapter 13.)

➢ Instead of a quick link, leave a pear-abiner at the anchor's master point. This might allow retrieval in the rare case when there's a knot on both sides of the anchor.

---

[144] An alpine butterfly knot is a good choice. By positioning the core shot inside the knot's bight, this ensures the damaged section will no longer be loaded or rappelled on.

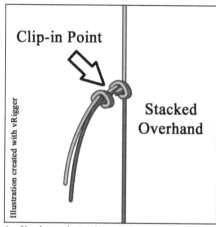

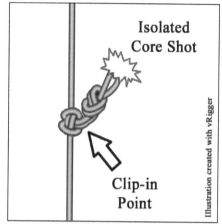

| A clip-in point when joining two ropes. | Creating a safe clip-in for a core shot. |

Two Points of Contact

At least two points of contact should be maintained during mid-rope maneuvers. Here are some options:

➢ Incorporate a loop in the knot that rappellers can clip into with a tether.

  ○ When tying two ropes with a stacked overhand, leave a gap of about 2cm (~1in) between the overhand knots. (Ref: diagram above-left.)

  ○ For a core shot, tie the alpine butterfly with an extra-large bight. A separate overhand can then be tied in the bight to create a safe clip-in. (Ref: diagram above-right.)

➢ Use a *catastrophe knot*. Pull up some slack rope from below the knot. Tie a separate figure-8 and clip it to the load bearing point of your harness.

Using a Frog Rig

Here's a way to pass a knot on rappel using a Frog ascending system. Note that this method of knot passing works on SRT only. Two points of contact are maintained throughout the process.

1) Rappel until the knot is adjacent to your descender and lock off.

2) Install your top ascender (long tether) on the rope above with an accompanying foot loop.

3) Step up in the foot loop and attach your Croll to the rope. Sit back to load it.

4) Remove your descender from the rope and replace it directly below the knot. Lock it off again.

5) Downclimb on your ascenders until you reach the knot.

6) Step up in the foot loop again and disconnect the Croll. Lower yourself back onto the descender.

7) Clean the top ascender and foot loop. Unlock and finish the rappel.

VT Prusik Method

Here's a slick method of knot-passing that requires a VT prusik. A Valdotain Tresse (VT) is used as a temporary autoblock. (See Appendix I for more information.) This method of knot-passing can be used on both SRT and DRT. A backup should be set to maintain two points of contact with the rope.

1) Rappel to the knot, stopping about 0.5m (~2ft) above it. Lock off your descender.

---

2) Tie a Valdotain Tresse above your descender as an autoblock. Clip the hitch to your short tether to keep it within reach.

3) Unlock and rappel until the VT prusik becomes weighted. Verify the hitch is holding before releasing the brake. Note that the Valdotain might slip, but cannot come off the rope.

4) Remove your descender from the rope and replace it immediately below the knot. Lock it off.

5) Slowly release the Valdotain to lower yourself. The goal is to transfer your weight back onto the descender before the friction hitch reaches the knot.

6) Clean the VT hitch, unlock, and finish the rappel.

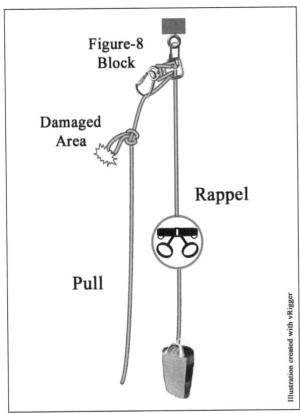

Figure-8 Block

Damaged Area

Rappel

Pull

Illustration created with vRigger

The system has been re-rigged to use the damaged side for the pull.

Rigging for Efficiency

While an experienced canyoneer might be able to pass a knot in a minute or two, less-experienced team members (and those who haven't practiced in awhile) will require more time. Here are some ways to speed things up with a group:

- Lowering
  Let's imagine a core shot is discovered in the middle of a rappel. If the rappeller is inexperienced (or in the middle of a waterfall), lowering might be faster and safer than requiring them to pass a knot. (See also "Lowering" in Chapter 23.)

  Once the rappeller is in a safe place, the team can pull the rope back up and re-rig.

- Move the Block:
  You may be able to avoid knot passing completely by using an SRT block technique. The team re-rigs to use the damaged side for the pull. It might be as easy as moving the block from one side of the anchor to the other. The bag side is deployed and becomes the new rappel rope.

  If you have two ropes and one is damaged, use the damaged one for the pull.

- Position the Knot
  Depending on the local terrain and how much rope is available, you might be able to move the knot to a better location. If there's a safe, convenient ledge partway down the pitch, position the knot there. Upon reaching the ledge, the rappeller stands up, moves their descender, then continues on their way.

  o If you must pass a knot in a waterfall, try to situate the knot out the water or in an area of light flow.

  o Another good strategy is to situate the knot close to the ground. This reduces the consequences of failure and makes it easier to coach less experienced team members.

Passing Knots: While Ascending

On extremely rare occasions, you might need to pass a knot while ascending. Here are two situations in which it could happen:

- Scenario #1:
  Two ropes are tied together in order to have sufficient length to escape the canyon.

- Scenario #2:
  The last rappeller gets into trouble and needs assistance. A rescuer must ascend the rope and pass the rappeller like a human knot. (See also "Rescue from Below" in Chapter 23.)

Again, there are a number of ways to pass knots while ascending. How you go about it will depend on the situation, your preferred ascending system, and the gear you have to work with.

Using a Frog Rig

Passing a knot is relatively easy with a pair of side-loading ascenders. A backup should be set to maintain two points of contact. Note that this system works on SRT only.

1) Climb until your top ascender is a few centimeters/inches below the knot.

2) Step up in the foot loop to move the Croll as close as possible to the top ascender. Sit back to weight it.

3) Disconnect the top ascender and re-attach it above the knot. Push it up as high as you can.

4) Step up in the foot loop again. Disconnect the Croll and re-attach it above the knot.

5) Clean your backup connection and continue the ascent.

Classic Method

If you don't have side-loading ascenders, you'll likely need an extra rope grab to pass the knot. In this example, let's assume the climber has a pair of prusik loops and an extra sling for a klemheist. This method will work on both SRT and DRT. A backup should be set to maintain two points of contact.

1) When your top prusik (chest prusik) is 3–5cm (1–2in) from the knot, sit back to load it.

2) Tie a klemheist on the rope just above the knot. Test it to be sure it's gripping properly.

3) Slide your bottom prusik (foot prusik) up as high as you can, and step up in it.

4) Clip a short tether into the klemheist sling and push it until it becomes taut. Sit back to transfer your weight onto it.

5) Clean both original prusiks and re-install them above the knot.

6) Step up in the foot loop and slide your top prusik up as high as you can (i.e., to a point just below the klemheist). Unclip your tether and sit back to load the top prusik.

7) Clean the klemheist and continue on your way.

Wim Aarts dropping into Big Creek, Wash.
(Photo: Wade Hewitt)

Chapter 19: Introduction to Swiftwater

The more water that is present, the more difficult and dangerous the canyon. With high flow and strong current, it becomes increasingly important to look ahead and identify dangerous areas before reaching them. Any water hazards encountered need to be assessed and a plan made to get the team safely through.

This chapter provides only a high-level introduction to swiftwater. Additional training is recommended if interested in taking on objectives with more water.[145] Consider taking a class in swiftwater canyoning (offered in only a few places in North America), a river rescue course (offered by many whitewater outfitters), or try to go on outings with more experienced canyoneers. Nothing beats hands-on practice in a real environment. The more time you spend in and around fast-moving water, the more comfortable you'll be.

Basic Hydrology

The movement of water might appear chaotic at first, but it's actually following a set of rules that are orderly and predictable. These rules hold true regardless of how much water is present, whether it's a minor creek or a major river. Patterns and disturbances on the surface are clues as to what's going on beneath. By knowing something of water behavior, you can:

- Make better calls as to whether or not it's safe to run a given canyon.

- Determine the best route (or rappel line) for safety and efficient forward progress.

- Identify water hazards before reaching them and judge their level of threat.

The ability to "read the water" is a skill that's developed over time. It comes with training and experience.

Flow Rate

A flowing creek always has some volume of water moving through it. The amount of water passing a given point at a particular moment in time is called the *flow rate* or *discharge*. In the United States, it's usually measured in cubic feet per second (abbreviated cfs).

A creek's flow rate is variable and is determined by many factors, such as the size of the watershed, number of springs in the area, snowmelt, and recent precipitation. The flow rate will also change along the course of the creek. As you travel downstream, the volume will gradually increase as tributaries (both large and small) enter and groundwater seeps into the creek.

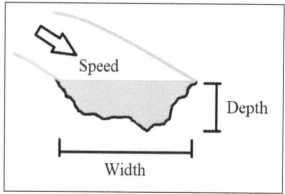

Flow Rate = Depth x Width x Speed

The flow rate will also change from year to year and season to season. Creeks are generally at their highest during spring floods and lowest in late summer. They can change dramatically, however, over the course of a few hours or days due to heavy precipitation, sudden snowmelt, or a dam release. Large bodies of water will rise and fall more slowly than their smaller counterparts. As the amount of water in the system increases, your odds of encountering swiftwater hazards will also increase. A given canyon can be a quite different experience depending on when you run it. (See also "Estimating Water Levels" in Chapter 1.)

- Every creek is on its own cycle. It may take a few trips to determine the best time of year to visit.

---

[145] Canyons rated Class C2+ under the ACA Rating System, or a5+ under the International System.

A curtain-style waterfall on Unicorn Creek, Wash.

The same creek surging down a narrow chute.

Local Terrain

Note that flow rate is a measurement of throughput, not speed. Let's say we take a measurement at a point along the creek and discover the water is moving at a rate of 10 cfs. A cubic foot is about the size of a milk crate, so this means a volume of ten crates is flowing by every second. However, it makes a difference how these crates are arranged. Consider the following:

- If the creek is 10ft wide, the crates can be lined up neatly in a row, with all ten passing by in one second. The water is moving relatively slowly.

- If the creek narrows to a 1ft wide gap, all ten crates must still pass in one second in order to maintain the same throughput. This means the depth and/or speed must increase. If the water is only 1ft deep, this means each crate flashes by in a tenth of a second. The water is moving much faster.

While the flow rate is important, the local terrain and geology also plays a big role. A higher cfs rating might be dangerous in a tight canyon, but could be safe in a wide shallow area. Think of a ford on a river. Where's the safest place to cross?

> **Rappelling Waterfalls**
> When evaluating whether or not it's safe to rappel in the flow, consider the shape of the waterfall.
>
> - On a wide, curtain-style waterfall, the rappellers will experience only a small percentage of the total flow. The total volume of water is being spread out over a wider area.
>
> - If the creek constricts and plunges down a narrow chute, rappellers will be exposed to the full force of the torrent (i.e., the entire volume of the creek at once).

How Strong is the Flow?

Quite often, we talk about how strong or "pushy" the flow is. This is a description of how much force the water exerts on any obstacles (such as canyoneers) in its path. The strength of the water depends on how fast it's moving. The water's speed is governed by three factors:

1) <u>Volume</u>
   The higher the flow rate, the more water is present in the system. Running a canyon during a flood event is much higher risk than the same canyon in low water.

2) <u>Gradient</u>
   The steeper the angle of incline, the faster the water will move. The steepest possible incline is, of course, a vertical waterfall. The taller the falls, the greater the speed. Water passing through a series of short drops or ramps will more slowly compared to a vertical waterfall of the same height.

3) <u>Terrain & Obstacles</u>
   If the channel constricts (or enters a tight canyon), the speed or the depth must increase to maintain the same throughput. Large obstacles in the creek will play a similar role. For example, water passing through a gap between boulders will speed up momentarily.

As the speed increases, so does the creek's strength and power. Note that the force does not increase linearly, but instead increases as a square of the speed. Double the speed and the force exerted on any object in the water's path is quadrupled. Note that this force is continuous and unceasing. It never stops.

- Tip: To get a sense of a creek's strength/power, get a good stance and dip a foot into the water. This is a quick test that can be performed even when on rappel.

Current passing through a series of bends.

Bruce Wyse

Current Vector

The speed of flowing water in a creek is never uniform. There are always places where the water is moving faster or slower than the water around it. Water along the banks and bottom will move more slowly due to friction with the creek bed, shore features, and other obstacles.

- The place where the majority of the water is moving is known as the *current*.

- In straight channels, the water will move fastest near the center, just under the surface.

- In places where the creek turns and changes direction, the water will be moving fastest on the outside of the bend. The current here is eroding the bank, carrying material away and deepening the channel. Conversely, the inside of a bend is often shallow as this is where material from upstream is being deposited. The water here moves more slowly. If caught in a flash flood, the inside of a bend is usually the safer place to be.

Water always follows the path of least resistance. It will continue to flow in that direction until it encounters some new obstacle or is acted on by an outside force.

- Tip: To get an idea of the water's speed and flow pattern, try tossing a stick into the water and watch what happens. In rare situations, a pack could be used for the same purpose.

Bruce Wyse

Eddies

As the amount of water in the canyon increases, swiftwater features will start to appear. Not all such features are dangerous, however. An *eddy* is a relatively calm pocket of water that forms on the downstream side of an obstacle. Water striking the obstacle is diverted around it. As it surges past, a space is created on the backside that is filled in by slower water circling back upstream. Eddies can also form behind shore features. They're usually safe places to stop and rest.

To identify: look for an area of calm water on the downstream side of an obstacle. There may be a noticeable line on the surface, known as the *eddy line*. This denotes the place where the upstream and downstream currents meet. The higher the flow rate, the more apparent the eddy line becomes. In high flow, the eddy line can be a place of instability and may require some effort to pass through.

Wading in Fast-Moving Water

The faster the water is moving, the more force it'll exert on a person who is wading. Even ankle-deep water can sweep someone off their feet if it's moving fast enough. Larger team members will have an advantage here as they have more mass to resist the force of the current.

Before entering the water, it's good to perform a quick assessment:

- Route Planning
  Where are you trying to go? When crossing fast-moving water, look for wide, shallow areas where the water is moving more slowly. Another strategy is to find an area of braided channels where you'll be dealing with a smaller percentage of the total flow. Plan your route to take advantage of eddies and places where you can climb out of the water to rest along the way.

- Look Downstream
  If you were to lose your footing and get swept, where would you go? It's best to cross in an area with a good downstream runout where you can swim to shore. Avoid wading above dangerous areas, such as rapids or waterfalls. If there are concerns about getting swept, consider stationing someone downstream with a throw rope. (See "Throwing a Rope" later in this chapter.)

- Depth
  The deeper the water, the harder it will be to resist the force of the current. Smaller team members will be at a disadvantage here. If the water's too deep, then you'll be swimming.

Movement

When wading in swiftwater, it's critical to move slowly and find good foot placements. Smooth bedrock may be slippery and will provide fewer footholds. If the bottom of the creek is a jumbled field of cobble, footholds may be plentiful, but the rocks underfoot can shift / be unstable. Work about with your feet to find secure positions.

When crossing fast-moving water, face upstream and move at an angle to the current. If you can find one, a thick branch is handy for support. Set it in front of you and brace against it by leaning slightly forward. To maintain stability, move only one leg of the tripod at a time (i.e., shuffling your feet or resetting the branch's position). A branch is useful for probing ahead and placing it into the current to get a feel for the water's strength.

- If you're struggling to stay on your feet, consider crossing as a group or swimming.

- If you get swept in high flow, consider jettisoning your pack. It may interfere with your ability to swim. You may want to unbuckle your waist belt / sternum strap before crossing.

- Additional caution should be used near edges as there may be risk of getting swept by the current.

Crossing as a Group

Another way to increase safety is to cross in the company of others. There are a number of group techniques for crossing fast-moving water: in a line, circle, or a wedge formation. Team members can support one another by holding onto one another's shoulders, packs, or PFDs. Larger team members can also be positioned upstream to create an artificial eddy, making it easier for those downstream to move. Use good communication and don't rush.

Descending a Water-filled Chute
Scenario: The team needs to descend a chute that the entire creek is being funneled through.

Whether downclimbing or rappelling, try to avoid sitting down right in the middle of the chute. If you barricade the flow (i.e., become a one-person dam), the water will build up behind you and the force will increase. If you're not being careful, this can lead to a sudden and uncontrolled ride to the bottom. To minimize getting pushed around, try to keep your body elevated and out of the water. It may be safer to stem or bridge your way over the torrent.

If staying out of the water isn't an option, try to minimize your exposure. Place your feet in shallow water (or on ledges to either side of the torrent). Another option is to turn sideways to the flow. The narrower your profile to the flow, the less force you'll experience.

Rappelling a water-filled chute.

Practicing swimming in a turbulent pool.

Swimming in Swiftwater

Being a strong, efficient swimmer is a critical skill to develop for swiftwater canyoning. It's quite different from swimming in calm water and takes some practice. Being physically fit is extremely important.

- **WARNING #1:** Free ropes in turbulent water are extremely dangerous. When not in use, ropes should be stowed inside a rope bag or backpack. Never hang a coil on the outside of your pack.

- **WARNING #2:** Never tie a rope to a swimmer. Even quick-release knots (ex: mule hitch) can be difficult to release when surrounded by churning whitewater. If you require a rope as a swimmer, it's safer to use a specialized rescue PFD with a quick-release belt.

- Remove unnecessary gear from your harness to reduce the odds of it getting snagged while swimming. Consider locking carabiners on your gear loops.[146] Tuck in loose straps on your harness, and secure anything that might be subject to getting caught. Consider stowing your chest harness if you use a Frog Rig for ascending.

- Packs and rope bags can be an impediment and even dangerous in swiftwater. They make swimming difficult and can get caught on things. In swiftwater canyons, it's good to minimize the number of packs carried by the team. Fewer packs means less management and faster progression.

- Going with the current is always easier than fighting against it.

---

[146] This makes it impossible for anything to accidentally get clipped into them, such as ropes and other swimmers.

Defensive Swimming

If you get swept by the current, move immediately to a defensive swimming posture. Float on your back, while turning your body to face downstream with your legs out in front of you. Bend your knees slightly and arch your back to stay close to the surface. This will help you avoid submerged rocks. Backstroke with your arms to slow down and control your direction of movement.

- The defensive position gives you a chance to rest, get your bearings, and look ahead downstream.

- This technique is best used when there's a good downstream runout with no hazards.

Ferry Angle

By turning your body at a 45-degree angle to the flow (with your head in the direction you want to go), you can get the current to work for you. The water will push you in the desired direction like a sail. This technique is known as a *ferry angle*. It can be used to move towards shore or away from an obstacle. It's even more effective when you backstroke simultaneously to slow your downstream movement.

Active Swimming (Combat Swim)

Occasionally, when swimming, you'll need to put on a short burst of speed. You might need to cross an area of

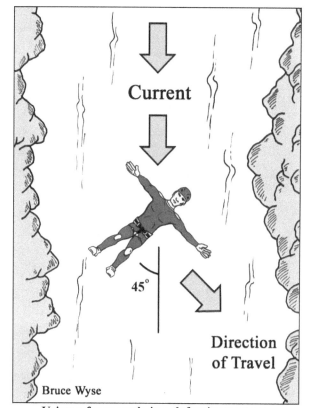

Using a ferry angle in a defensive posture.

strong current, enter an eddy, or move quickly away from an obstacle. Active swimming is strenuous and is performed with a powerful crawl stroke. This technique is different from the one that's taught in swimming classes. While keeping your head out of the water (as much as is feasible) to see where you're going, make deep scooping strokes with your arms and hands with the intent of pulling yourself through the water. You can kick with your feet, but it's not very effective. Active swimming will quickly tire you out; it's not intended for traveling long distances.

- From a defensive position: keep your feet up, roll over, and start swimming.

- When crossing fast-moving water, you can still use the ferry angle by aiming for a point significantly upstream of your actual target. By positioning your body at a 45-degree angle, the current will push you in the desired direction. Starting upstream of your target will also work to your advantage.

- Getting some initial momentum is helpful for crossing fast-moving water. Avoid diving in as submerged rocks may be present. Instead, a flat jump across the surface is a better way to give yourself an initial boost of speed. If you're already in the water, you may be able to use your feet to propel yourself off the canyon wall or nearby obstacles.

Current

Bruce Wyse

Foot Entrapment

Entrapment is a leading cause of swiftwater accidents. It typically happens in knee to waist-deep water when the victim's foot becomes caught (ex: between rocks or underneath a submerged log). The force of the water pushes the victim forward and down, making it difficult to escape. In a worst-case scenario, the victim could be forced underwater. Entrapment in unlikely in very shallow water or when the water is more than chest-deep. In the latter case, you'll probably be swimming.

Avoidance

Move cautiously when you can't see where you're placing your feet. Feel about for secure positions under the water, and try to avoid stepping in holes or constrictions.

- Moving together as a group can increase safety. If someone gets caught, the others are there to assist. If you discover a submerged obstacle, alert the rest of your team.

- Beware dangling your feet from a defensive swimming posture. This may put you at increased risk of entrapment in shallow water. Try to keep your legs close to the surface.

- Entrapment can also happen if a swimmer tries to stand up too soon. Always wait for the water to become slow and shallow before attempting to stand.

Foot Entrapment (continued)

<u>Self-Rescue</u>
If you get a foot caught, try rolling to one side or the other to work it free. Swimming or pulling yourself down (i.e., toward the bottom of the creek) might also provide enough leverage to torque your foot out in some situations. Jettisoning your footwear also might work.

If self-rescue isn't possible, other team members will need to come to your aid. Try to find a position where you can keep your head out of the water without becoming exhausted. You might be able to prop yourself up against nearby rocks, other terrain features, or your knee. Your pack, if available, could be removed and used for flotation.

<u>Team Rescue</u>
If the victim is underwater, an immediate response will be required. Rescue classes teach that the first step is to stabilize the victim. There are a number of methods that can be used, but one low-risk technique is to throw a rope across the creek. Rescuers on both sides can then move the rope upstream. The goal is to give the victim something to hang onto, so they can stay above the water without expending energy. In some cases, the rope itself might provide the necessary leverage to escape.

Once the subject is stable, the team needs to form a plan for rescue. There are a number of cinching techniques that could be used, but these are beyond the scope of this manual.

A recirculation in Dingford Creek.

Swiftwater Hazards

Swiftwater hazards are not fixed features of the canyon, nor do they always present the same level of threat. They will come and go depending on how much water is present. In flood conditions, your odds of encountering them are higher. As water levels subside heading into summer, hazards will slowly diminish and may disappear entirely.

- In tight canyons, even small hazards can be dangerous. Avoidance is often the best plan. Never hesitate to bypass an obstacle if not confident of your ability to overcome it directly.[147]

- Always have a plan for rescue before committing to a serious water hazard. The team may want to station someone downstream (or another convenient location) with a throw rope at the ready. We'll talk more about the use of throw ropes at the end of this chapter.

- In high water, study vertical drops carefully and find a safe line to rappel. Sometimes, safety will dictate rappelling outside the watercourse. If that's not possible, a redirect or guided rappel might be rigged to avoid the hazard. We'll introduce these techniques in Chapter 20.

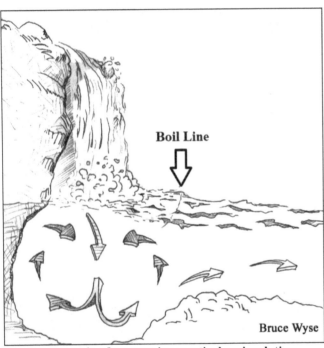

Boil Line

Bruce Wyse

An example of current in a vertical recirculation.

Hydraulics (Recirculations, Holes)

Hydraulics form in places where the creek pours over an obstruction into deep water below. They come in many shapes and sizes, and are often associated with waterfalls. The falling water accelerates downwards, going deep, and creating a void that's filled in by water circulating back on itself. Strong hydraulics can be dangerous as they can trap and hold buoyant objects, such as packs, rope bags, logs, and even swimmers.

Water in a hydraulic is highly aerated, giving it a white foamy appearance. Look for an area of surging or upwelling immediately downstream. This is known as the *boil* or *boil line*. It's a visual marker denoting the boundary between water circling back into the hydraulic and the downstream current. The greater the distance between the waterfall and the boil line, the stronger the hydraulic. The downstream water is often darker and smoother in appearance.

- Highly-aerated water is less dense and provides less support. Buoyancy will not work as well and swimming is less effective. You can literally fall into the "hole" created by a large hydraulic.

- If the waterfall enters the pool at a steep vertical, this may indicate a deep recirculation with more holding power. The taller the falls, the more energy will be present in the hydraulic.

- If the water surges into the pool at a lower angle, it may create a horizontal or surface recirculation. This type of hydraulic won't trap a swimmer underwater, but it can still be strong enough to prevent escape. Buoyant objects will circle endlessly around the pool.

---

[147] One possible strategy: exit the drainage and rappel back in downstream of the hazard.

<u>Avoidance</u>
Landing next to a hydraulic might be safe provided you can stand, but use caution when setting the length and exiting into deep water. Swimmers who are too close may risk getting pulled in. Strong hydraulics are best avoided.

- If a convenient ledge exists above the water, it might be possible to rappel to the ledge, then perform a flat jump out past the boil line.

- Sometimes, it's possible to perform a *rappel jump*. This is an advanced technique where you rappel to a point about 1-3m (3-10ft) above the water, then leap backwards off the end of the rope. The goal is to land out past the boil line. Con: Jumping can be high risk if the pool has not been scouted in advance.

- If you need to enter a hydraulic, don't wear a pack or PFD. Find a way to send the packs and rope bags down separately (ex: zipline).

<u>Self-Rescue</u>
Depending on the shape of the falls and local terrain, hydraulics can have a very different character. Here are two general strategies for escape:

- Swim to one side or the other. The idea is to find a weakness where more water is flowing downstream. This strategy may work better for hydraulics found in larger creeks and rivers.

- Go deep. Try to dive as deep as you can. The idea is to get down underneath the recirculation and catch the exit current. In some cases, tucking into a "cannonball" may increase your odds of going deep and getting flushed out. This is where flotation will work against you.

In a horizontal recirculation: try to avoid fighting the current directly. Instead, swim hard and fast when nearing the exit. If unable to escape, a pack (possibly tossed to you by a teammate) could be used as flotation until help arrives.

Strainers (Sieves)
A strainer is a net-like obstruction such as a logjam, fallen tree, or a narrow gap between boulders. Strainers can also be man-made, such as a section of old fencing that's fallen into the creek. Water will flow right through a strainer, but larger objects swept in may risk getting pinned in place by the force of the current. Another danger is becoming snagged. A root ball under the surface can catch the harness of an unwary canyoneer. Getting snagged could be deadly if a swimmer is stuck underwater.

- Strainers are often found in tight constrictions or along the outside of the bend on the creek.

- Note that strainers are not fixed features of the canyon, but will be created, moved around, and swept out again by flood events. They may be repositioned every year.

<u>Avoidance</u>
Be wary of submerged obstacles. If you spot a strainer ahead, swim aggressively away from it. If avoidance is not possible, swim towards it instead and use your momentum to mantle your way up on top. If you can get your body up and out of the water, you may be able to avoid getting pinned by the current. This maneuver also provides better odds for keeping your head out of the water should you become trapped. Swimming underneath strainers and logs is not recommended due to the risk of getting snagged.

Siphons
A siphon, essentially, is an underwater drain. These can be very difficult to detect and are usually found in creeks strewn with large boulders. Keep an eye out for deep pools where the water entering seems to exceed the outflow. A pool with a siphon might be safe to swim in, except near the exit drain. A strong siphon may be able to trap a foot, leg, or entire canyoneer. Getting stuck in a siphon could be deadly. Avoidance is generally the best plan.

A strainer in low water conditions.

An undercut carved by extreme flooding.

Undercuts

Undercuts are usually found on the outside of a bend where the current has eroded a cave-like space below the waterline. Undercuts can be dangerous if a swimmer gets swept in and trapped (i.e., either pinned by the force of the current or caught on an underwater snag). An undercut combined with a strainer can be deadly.

Watch for places where the water seems to run straight into a cliff face or boulder. Look for an area of upwelling or splashing along the base of the cliff, known as a *pillow* or *cushion wave*. It's formed by the water crashing into the obstacle and changing direction. If no such wave is observed, be on your guard as an undercut is likely to be present.

<u>Avoidance</u>

If swept towards an undercut, try to swim away from it. If that's not feasible, adopt a defensive swimming posture and stay as close to the surface as possible. On contact, try to position your feet against the lip and brace to avoid being swept in. Swim and/or pull yourself along the rockface, moving downstream, until clear of the hazard.

- If you get swept in, diving deep and catching the exit current might be the only option for escape.

Swiftwater Rescue

A deep dive into swiftwater rescue is beyond the scope of this manual, so we'll only look at a few simple techniques that might be used by canyoneers. Again, taking a swiftwater canyoning or river rescue class is highly recommended if planning to take on objectives with more water.

Contact Rescue

WARNING! If someone gets caught in the current, it may be instinctive to swim out in an effort to save them. *Unless you're a strong swimmer and are trained in rescue techniques, don't do it!* A panicked victim may latch onto anyone in the vicinity and can unthinkingly force the would-be rescuer underwater. Contact rescue while swimming is high risk and has led to fatal accidents. The first rule in a rescue: don't create more victims.

Reaching Rescue

In some cases, a rescuer may be able to reach a swimmer either from shore or shallow water. In some cases, a long stick or branch could be extended. The rescuer needs a good stance and should brace against the pull. Other team members can assist by holding onto the rescuer's harness or pack to keep the rescuer from getting pulled in.

Throwing a Rope

In swiftwater canyons, it's not a bad idea to bring one or more *throw ropes* (i.e., a lightweight rescue rope that can be thrown to a swimmer). Once caught, the swimmer can be pulled to safety or, in strong current, swung in towards shore. Some cautions:

- Don't throw a rope unless you need to. If there's a good downstream runout and the swimmer could reach the shore on their own, intervention may not be required.

- In strong current, try to pendulum the swimmer into shallow water or a nearby eddy. If the rope would swing the rappeller into a hazard (ex: an area of rapids), then this is not a good technique to use.

- Beware throwing multiple ropes to a swimmer as this may create an entanglement hazard.

Note that throwing a rope will only work if: 1) you can get it to the swimmer, and 2) the swimmer manages to catch hold of it. Throwing rope with precision takes practice. An underhand throw is usually better for accuracy, whereas an overhand throw is better for range. Beware any obstacles, such as overhanging tree branches that might interfere with your throw.

Throw Ropes

Canyon throw ropes are usually short (about 7–15m (25–50ft)), lightweight, brightly-colored and designed to float in water. They're typically stowed in a small rope bag or pouch that's clipped to your harness.

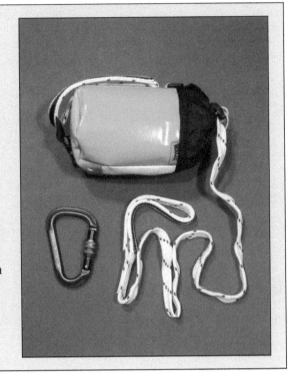

- Throw ropes are intended for water rescues; they're not rated for rappelling. They could be used for other purposes, however, such as extending the pull side of an SRT system, lowering packs, etc.

- Don't have a throw rope? A standard rappel rope will do in a pinch, but the swimmer will have seconds to grab it before it sinks. Most rope bags float, but throwing a large bag with any accuracy is unlikely. Throwing a small coil of rope is a better solution.

Practicing with throw ropes in a river rescue class.

As the Rescuer

An assumption is made that the rescuer is already in position with a throw rope at the ready:

1) Before the throw, pull a couple meters (~5–6ft) of rope out of the bag. This gives you some extra rope to work with should you need it. Also, remove any carabiners from the bag.[148]

2) Call the swimmer's name (or give a whistle blast) to get their attention. The swimmer needs to know that a rope is incoming.

3) While holding onto the rope, throw the bag. Avoid throwing the bag directly at the swimmer as it may fall short. Often, it's better to throw the bag right over their head.

4) If the first throw misses, reel in some rope and make a quick butterfly coil for a second throw. You don't have to pull in the entire rope; you only need enough to reach the swimmer.

When the swimmer grabs the rope, you'll have a few seconds before it comes under load. Brace yourself and keep your center of gravity low. Hold the line fast, and allow the swimmer to naturally pendulum in towards shore. Depending on the strength of the current, you may be able to reel them in simultaneously.

---

[148] Hitting the swimmer with the carabiner would be bad, but the situation can become worse if the carabiner were to accidentally get clipped to the swimmer.

Depending on how fast the water is moving, a surprising amount of force can come onto the rope. If the load is becoming unmanageable, try releasing rope to the swimmer. Moving downstream and/or further inland is another trick to reduce the load, although you may be limited by the local terrain, vegetation, etc.

- Never clip or tie the throw rope to yourself. Avoid wrapping it around your hands. If the force proves too much to handle, you need to be able to separate your connection to the rope instantly. The throw rope should never be held by more than one person.

- Other team members can assist by physically holding onto the thrower's harness, pack, or PFD. This will help keep the thrower from getting pulled in.

<u>As the Swimmer</u>

If the rescue rope lands near you, swim aggressively towards it. Try to grab the rope itself, not the bag.[149] Once you have a good grip, move to a defensive swimming position while holding the rope with both hands. In some cases, you may be able to shift your body into a ferry angle position to speed your way towards shore.

- Never wrap, tie, or clip the rope to yourself. If holding onto the rope is placing you in greater danger, let go of it.

---

[149] If the bag contains excess rope, all of it will need to come out before line comes under tension.

Becca Polglase on a guided rappel in Quicksilver Creek, Wash.
(Photo: Kevin Clark)

Chapter 20: Redirects & Guided Rappels

In this chapter, we'll take a look at a couple of advanced techniques that can be used to change the course of a rappel. These techniques might not be used frequently, but can be a good card to play under the right circumstances.

Avoiding Hazards

<u>Scenario</u>: Arriving at the top of a waterfall, the team discovers some hazard or obstacle below. Perhaps there's a strainer right in the middle of the drop, or the waterfall plunges into a deep turbulent pool. Another possibility: the flow is too high to run the falls directly.

Some options:

- Find another anchor to avoid the hazard.

- The leader rappels, setting a *redirect* on the way down. The course of the rappel is modified so as to avoid the hazard.

- The leader commits to overcoming the hazard. Once safely at the bottom, they set up a *guided rappel* for the rest of the team. The leader is the only person who commits to additional risk.

Rappelling the falls directly might not be safe.

Redirects (Directional Anchors, Deviations)

A *redirect* is an intermediate anchor located some distance down the pitch and laterally off to one side. By running the rope through a redirect, the course of the rappel below is modified. Redirection requires some forethought and planning. A directional anchor might be used to:

- ○ Keep rappellers away from high flow, obstacles, and other hazards.
- ○ Avoid a pendulum swing in places where the watercourse changes directions.
- ○ Keep the rope away rough surfaces and sharp edges.

Note that redirection increases the complexity of the rappel and will slow progression.

Natural Redirection

The easiest way to redirect a rope is to run it around a natural anchor or other terrain feature. For example, the rope could be set behind a rock knob or run behind a convenient tree located partway down the pitch. When using a natural redirect, the rest of the team will need to follow the same path as the leader. In some cases, the rope will need to be carefully repositioned by every rappeller.

- <u>Advantage</u>
  The rope can be redirected on the fly. There's no need to stop and build a directional anchor.

- <u>Disadvantage</u>
  Pulling the rope might be harder due to the additional friction.

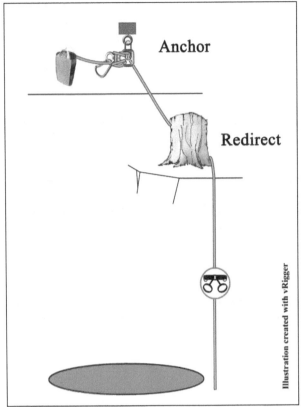

Anchor

Redirect

Using natural redirection to avoid the pool.

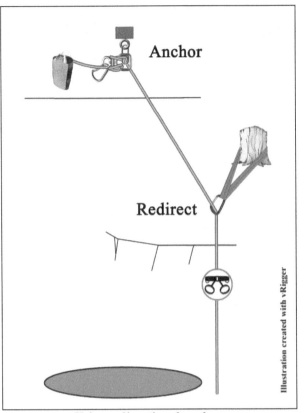

Anchor

Redirect

Using a directional anchor.

Redirect

Using a redirect to keep the rope away from abrasive rock.

Artificial Redirection

If the pitch doesn't lend itself to natural redirection, the leader will need to stop mid-rappel and build an anchor. Directional anchors don't need to be complicated. A simple sling girth hitched around a tree or rock horn might be all you need. Alternatively, try establishing a chock anchor in a crack in the canyon wall. In some canyons, you'll find bolts placed specifically for redirection.

- Ideally, the master point of a redirect should be situated where it's easy for rappellers to pass.

- Beware clipping into or weighting a directional anchor. The redirect's job is to change the course of the rappel, so it doesn't have to be a full-strength anchor. It may or may not be able to support full bodyweight.

<u>Rigging a Redirect</u>
1) Before rappelling, survey the pitch and make a plan for redirection. The leader will need sufficient material to build or replace the anchor. For the purpose of this example, let's imagine we plan to make use of a small tree located part way down the pitch.

2) Deploy the rope. The leader rappels and traverses laterally to the chosen feature. Use caution on the traverse to avoid a pendulum swing.

3) If there's a pre-existing anchor, you might be able to grab the redirect and pull yourself towards it. (Use caution, however, to avoid fully weighting the anchor.) Try to find a good stance. If necessary, you can lock off your descender to go hands-free.

4) As usual, pre-existing anchors should be thoroughly inspected prior to use. If a redirect were to fail, it could lead to a nasty pendulum swing. If no anchor exists, the leader will need to build one. Adjust the length of the anchor to avoid the hazard below and attach a non-locking carabiner to it.[150]

5) Clip the carabiner (i.e., the redirect's master point) to the rope above your descender.

6) Unlock and continue the descent, now on the modified rappel line.

<u>Passing a Redirect</u>
With a redirect in use, the rest of the team will need to pay attention during the descent. The goal is to avoid rappelling past the redirect as this would defeat the purpose of the rigging. In some cases, it's helpful for a team member below to apply a little tension to the rope (i.e. keeping it from getting pulled up through the redirect).

1) Rappel until about level with the redirect, then traverse laterally towards it. Generally, it's good to stay at (or slightly below) the level of the anchor. Use caution to avoid a pendulum swing. If necessary, you may be able to grab the redirect and pull yourself over to it.

2) Upon reaching the anchor, there are a couple of ways to pass it:

   o If you can find a good stance, clipping past is easy. While maintaining the brake with one hand, reach down and unclip the carabiner with the other. Clip it back to the rope above your descender.

   o If you need both hands, lock off the descender. While holding yourself in position with one hand, move the redirect with the other.

3) Unlock and continue your descent.

To avoid sacrificing a carabiner, the last person could swap it out for a quick link. Alternatively, they could clean the redirect and risk rappelling without it.

---

[150] A non-locking carabiner is preferred as they're cheaper to leave behind. If you need to leave a locking carabiner, leave it unlocked. This makes it easier for others to pass.

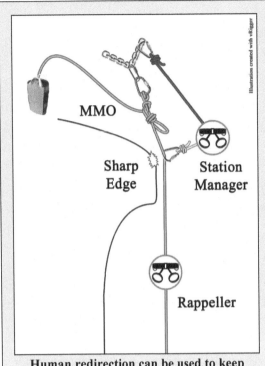

MMO

Sharp
Edge

Station
Manager

Rappeller

Illustration created with vRigger

**Human redirection can be used to keep
the rope away from a sharp edge.**

Human Redirection

The station manager can also use redirection to keep the rope away from abrasive rock. This technique works best from an anchor right on the edge.

Once a rappeller starts down the pitch, the station manager swings into position, straddling the rope. The station manager crouches and clips a short tether to the rappel line. Upon straightening up (i.e., using leg strength), the rappel rope is pulled away from the rock surface. Often, it only needs to be moved a matter of centimeters or inches.

- This method of redirection is a form of *vector pull* (i.e., a lateral force being applied to the tensioned rope). It doesn't take much effort to move the rope.

- Human redirection can also be used to reduce edge friction when hauling, or as a way to rescue a rappeller who's gotten a hand pinned under the rappel rope. (See the scenario "Pinned Hand or Arm" in Chapter 24.)

Guided Rappels

A guided rappel is another specialized rigging system that can be used to keep rappellers out of waterfalls and high flow. It can also be used to avoid obstacles in the middle of a pitch or the landing zone. It's a way to introduce horizontal movement into the rappel.

A guided rappel makes use of a separate tensioned rope, known as *the guide line*, that's anchored at both the top and bottom of the pitch. A rappeller starts down the pitch normally, but then clips into the guide line with a tether. As the rappeller descends, the tether eventually becomes taut and pulls them off the original rappel line. Essentially, it's rappelling down a zipline.

A guided rappel in Valhalla Canyon.

First Person at Risk
One obvious drawback to guided rappels: someone must to go down and set it up. This means the leader must commit to additional risk and overcome the hazard below. Once in a safe place, the leader builds the ground anchor and tensions the guide line with no one else present to inspect their handiwork. The leader should be one of the most experienced members of the team, and, in some cases, the strongest swimmer.

FAQ: "When would I need to use a guided rappel?"
A guided rappel might be a good card to play if you want to:

- Avoid an obstacle or hazard in the middle of the pitch. In aquatic canyons, rappellers can be kept out of high flow and waterfalls.

- Avoid an obstacle or hazard in the landing zone. Examples would include a rappel that exits into a hydraulic or jagged pile of logs. In the Desert Southwest, a guided rappel could also be used to avoid a cold pool at the bottom of the pitch, which is nice for that one person who forgot their wetsuit. Pools at the bottom of desert canyons can be very unpleasant, filled with rotting vegetation and dead animals. Only one person needs to take the plunge.

- Move beginners or injured party members through dangerous areas. Instead of rappelling, individuals could be lowered along the guide line from above.

- Desert Southwest: Ferry the team over a keeper pothole. Traveling over a pothole might be faster than requiring everyone to rappel in and escape out the far side.

How Much Rope is Required?
Guided rappels require more than twice the height of the pitch in rope. The exact amount depends on the location of both anchors and the tension system in use. In an emergency, additional rope may also be required for lowering. On short pitches, a guided rappel could be rigged with a single rope. Rigging with two ropes may be more common (i.e., one for the guide line and another for the rappel).

- Tip: Having two ropes of different colors is nice for visual clarity in the rigging.

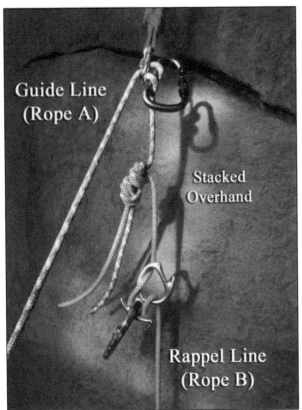

Rigging at the top of the pitch.

Rigging a Guided Rappel

<u>Scenario</u>: The team arrives at the top of a waterfall. Flow is high today and there's a turbulent pool at the bottom that we'd like to avoid. We have two ropes available (A & B). The leader will use Rope A to descend; it will then become the guide line. The rest of the team will rappel using Rope B.

Before doing anything, it's good to talk through the sequence as some coordination will be required between the top and bottom of the pitch. Note that the leader will need sufficient material (or rope) to build a ground anchor.

1) Establish an anchor atop the pitch with an appropriate rigging for the leader using Rope A.

2) The leader rappels, overcomes the hazard below, and drops off into the water. If the leader plans to swim while holding the end of the rope, the belayer should be prepared to feed out rope quickly. (See "Fast Release" in Chapter 11.)

    Alternatively, the rope could be thrown to the leader once they're in a safe place. In other situations, the rope could be deliberately set long, or the team could rig tail up and the leader rappels with the rope bag.

3) The leader pulls down most of Rope A and gets to work building the ground anchor.

4) Meanwhile, the belayer cleans the initial rigging and prepares for a guided rappel. The classic rigging is a tail up carabiner block, as shown above.[151] The ropes will be tied together with a stacked overhand.

5) When the belayer signals readiness, the leader tensions Rope A against the block. (We'll talk more about the tension system in a moment; there are a number of techniques that could be used.) Once sufficiently tensioned, the leader signals the team above.

    o   Be aware: the guide line generally doesn't need to be taut in order to accomplish the mission. Over-tensioning can actually be a bad thing in some cases as you'll end up stressing both anchors.

6) Deploy Rope B. An easy method is to zip the rope bag down the guide line. This is a nice way to deliver the bag directly to the leader and keep it out of whatever hazard exists below. Alternatively, the bag could be tossed down, or the first rappeller could take it down.

This completes the rigging for the guided rappel. To descend: rig the rappel normally on Rope B and start down the pitch. At a convenient location (either above or below the lip), clip a short tether to the guide line.[152] As you continue downwards, the tether eventually will become taut and change the course of the rappel. You're now performing a controlled descent along the guide line.

• As the first rappeller descends, the leader should watch and assess the system. Is it working? If necessary, the rope can be tightened as soon as the first rappeller is safely at the bottom. After this, no further adjustments should be required.

---

[151] It's possible to set a safety here, but isolating the rope strands will interfere with some rescue techniques.
[152] Make sure the carabiner at the end of the tether is locked.

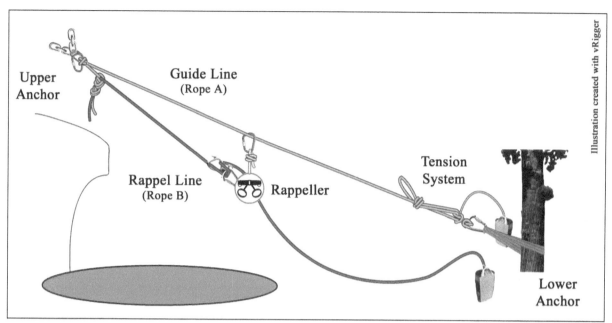

Upper Anchor

Guide Line
(Rope A)

Rappel Line
(Rope B)

Rappeller

Tension System

Lower Anchor

Rigging for a classic guided rappel.

Practicing guided rappels in Henline Creek, Ore.

The Anchors

WARNING! A tensioned guide line is a force multiplier and can place a load on the anchors that is considerably higher than your average rappel. The more horizontal the guide line, the greater these forces will be. Why is this happening? Think of a horizontal guide line as a giant two-point anchor with the rappeller suspended in the middle. From anchor physics, we know that the angle created between the legs of an anchor should be kept to 90-degrees or less. The wider this *critical angle*, the greater the force exerted on both ends. In this case, a horizontal guide line has an effective angle at close to 180-degrees. The force on the anchors will decrease as the guide tilts towards the vertical, but they can still be relatively high. (See also "The Critical Angle" in Chapter 4.)

Ideally, both anchors for a guided rappel should be bombproof and redundant. At a minimum, they should be capable of supporting a three-bodyweight load. Beware rigging a guided rappel on marginal anchors. Failure of the guide line could be catastrophic (i.e., the rappeller falling or going for a nasty pendulum swing).

Using a Human Anchor

If natural anchors are lacking at the bottom of the pitch, it may be possible to use a human anchor. The guide rope is run through the leader's descender and tensioned as much as possible. When ready, the team is sent down in sequence with the smallest and lightest rappellers going first. Once on the ground, each rappeller can join and strengthen the anchor. (See "Human Anchors" in Chapter 4.)

- The leader won't be able to apply as much tension to the guide line, but, sometimes, a small amount of tension is all that's needed to keep the rappeller away from the hazard.

- The leader should not hard lock their descender. If the load proves too much and they'd be at risk of getting pulled out of position, releasing rope may alleviate the situation. Being an anchor can be uncomfortable, but don't injure yourself.

The Floating Anchor

One advanced technique that we'll mention for familiarity is the *floating anchor*. These are used in swiftwater canyons for overcoming extreme obstacles. They require favorable terrain and strong current. A floating anchor has one big advantage: the leader gets to use the guide line too.

Here's how it works. Tie the rope to an empty rope bag (or pack) and throw it down the pitch to be caught by the current. By releasing rope at the anchor, the bag is allowed to float downstream and over the brink of the next waterfall. If the current is strong enough, water flowing into the bag will tension the rope. If additional tension is required, you can zip down a couple extra (full) packs. At this point, the guide line is ready for action. The lightest and most experienced team member goes first. Once the leader is safely down, the anchor can be improved, or a better one established for the rest of the team.

Tensioning the Guide Line

There are many ways to tension a guide line. As usual, it's good idea to use a releasable system. If a rappeller were to get into trouble (ex: jammed descender), the team has more options available. A stuck rappeller could be lowered to the ground or the canyon wall which makes rescue easier. Con: Lowering is not be a good idea if the rappeller would encounter the hazard we were trying to avoid.[153]

Whatever system is used, the trick is to get the tension just right. If there's not enough tension, the guide line will sag and rappellers may encounter the hazard. If there's too much tension, the load will be magnified on both anchors. Ideally, the guide line should be tensioned just enough to get the job done and no more. In many cases, the goal can be achieved with a surprising amount of slack still present in the guide line.

---

[153] One advanced rescue technique solves this problem by alternating a slow release of the guide line (Rope A) with a tensioning of the rappel rope (Rope B). This has the effect of pulling the stuck rappeller to the ground anchor.

<u>Other Notes</u>

- Guide lines should be rigged with the most static rope you have available. Semi-static and dynamic ropes are harder to tension due to their inherent stretch.

- The more horizontal the guide line, the less tensioning it should receive.

- Pay special attention to places where the guide line passes over abrasive rock or sharp edges. It's easy to damage a rope that's under tension. If possible, consider applying some edge protection.

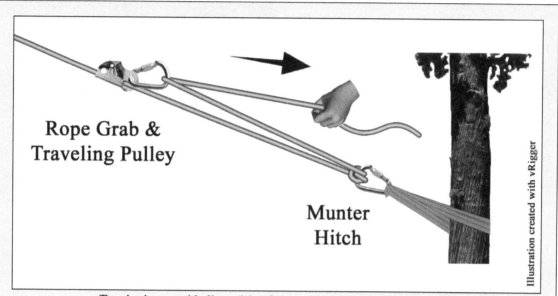

Tensioning a guide line with a 3:1 mechanical advantage system.

Tensioning a Munter Hitch

A simple releasable that we're already familiar with is the munter hitch. One major advantage: it requires minimal gear to rig. (See "The Munter Hitch" in Chapter 11.) Here's the sequence:

1) Clip a locking pear-abiner to the ground anchor. Tie a munter hitch on it, using the free end of the guide rope.

2) Install a rope grab a short distance up the guide line and attach a pulley (or carabiner) to it. This will be the *traveling pulley*.

3) Run the free end of the rope from the munter up through the pulley and back down again. This creates a 3:1 mechanical advantage system.[154]

4) Begin hauling to pull rope through the munter hitch.

5) Once sufficient tension (or slightly more) has been achieved, release enough slack to allow the hitch to flip back through the pear-abiner into the correct orientation for the load.

6) While maintaining tension, tie off the munter with a mule-overhand. This creates an MMO.

The guide line is ready for action. Leave the rope grab and pulley in place until you're sure the guide line requires no further tensioning.

---

[154] We haven't introduced *mechanical advantage* rigging yet, but it's coming in the next chapter.

Rappelling the Guide Line

It's a common misconception that guided rappels always cause rappellers to leave the wall and move out into open space. Whether or not this happens is actually a function of the local terrain and where the ground anchor is located relative to the base of the pitch. An anchor set laterally off to one side at the bottom will cause rappellers to descend along the canyon wall.

Before starting down a guided rappel, take a moment to envision yourself hanging on the guide line. Where will your descender and tether be located relative to one another? The goal is to avoid a situation where the rappel rope becomes tangled around the tether. Make any necessary adjustments before leaving the top of the pitch. Here are some tips:

Riding the guide line.

- It's best to use a short or medium-length tether to connect to the guide line. (Or shorten up a longer one.) This ensures the guide stays within easy reach. You might need to reach the guide if you stall out partway down, or you need to shepherd any stuck packs to the bottom.

- Long tethers may cause you to spin around during the descent which can cause problems.

- Your descender should be rigged with low friction, as you'll get some extra friction automatically from the carabiner at the end of your tether. (If you're connecting to the guide line with a pulley, use your standard friction settings.)

- Rappellers frequently clip themselves to the guide line before starting the rappel. This can make starting the rappel a little awkward. Sometimes, it's easier to get over the edge, rappel down a short distance, then clip to the guide line at a more convenient location.

- Try to avoid introducing slack into your tether until you're safely at the bottom.[155]

Pack Management

Packs and rope bags can be annoying on a guided rappel. They can pull you over backwards and throw you off balance. Quite often, it's better to send them down separately. One of the easiest methods is to zip them down the guide line.[156] The leader can leave their pack at the top and request a partner to send it down later.

- If a pack gets stuck in the middle of the guide line, the next person to rappel can go shepherd it down the rest of the way.

Dismantling a Guided Rappel

Once everyone is safely at the bottom, the tension system is released and dismantled. Next, the rappel rope is used to recover both ropes and the block. The ground anchor is also removed.

---

[155] Introducing slack might be unavoidable on a multi-tier drop. The real goal is to avoid shock loading the anchors.
[156] Alternatively, the rappel rope could be used as a zipline if a partner below provides some tension.

Pulling yourself along the guide line

Rappel rope has gone slack

If the rappel rope is slack and you're not yet on the ground, you can pull yourself along the guide line.

Stalling Out on a Guided Rappel

If the guide line is more horizontal than vertical, rappellers may reach a point where the rope sags into a V-shape, making it difficult to continue. Once fully supported by the guide line, maintaining the rappel brake is no longer necessary. Gently ease off and allow the rope to go slack through your descender. At this point, you can reach up to the guide line and pull yourself along it hand-over-hand (aka "commando mode"). Continue until you reach a place where you can stand up and disconnect.

- Beware going into "commando mode" too soon. If the carabiner at the end of your tether moves suddenly, fingers can get mashed. Sometimes, it might feel like you've stalled out, but you actually have too much friction to continue. Dial down the friction and you might start moving again. Don't reach up until the rappel rope has gone completely slack.

- Sometimes, a partner at the bottom can help a stalled rappeller by pulling down on the guide line (i.e., applying a *vector pull* to make the guide line a little more vertical). Be aware: this increases the force on both anchors. Rappellers may need assistance to unclip.

FAQ: "Should a person descending a guided rappel get a bottom belay?"
There's really no downside to providing a belay. On a long vertical guide line, the belayer can stop a rappeller who's lost control. On a more horizontal line, a belay might be useful near the top, but as the rappeller descends, more and more of their weight will be supported by the guide. Once fully on the guide line, the belay is no longer necessary.

Rodney Rodriguez descending Parkett Creek, Ore.
(Photo: Wade Hewitt)

Chapter 21: Mechanical Advantage

As a prelude to canyon rescue, let's take a look at *mechanical advantage* rigging. What is mechanical advantage? In a nutshell, it's a way of using a simple machine to leverage basic physics.

Suppose we have a large heavy object that we want to move, but moving it even a short distance would require a tremendous amount of effort. We can make the job easier with the clever application of ropes and pulleys. With a mechanical advantage system, the same object can be moved by applying a much smaller force over a longer distance. With strong anchors and the right rigging, a single person can move loads that, otherwise, would be beyond their ability. Mechanical advantage is a foundational skill for rescues.

Mechanical advantage (often abbreviated "MA") is a huge topic, so we'll confine ourselves to looking at systems that are most likely to be useful to canyoneers. In the canyon world, mechanical advantage might be used to:

- Lift a rappeller with a jammed descender.
- Haul an injured team member back up to the top of the pitch.
- Perform a *conversion*. For example, converting a static block to a releasable system.
- Pull down a stuck rappel rope.
- Assist team members in climbing up and over a mid-canyon obstacle (ex: out of a pothole).
- Tension a rope for a guided rappel.

MA rigging is used infrequently, so it's a great skill to practice. The best practice is done in a real-world environment with a real load on the system.

Illustrating Mechanical Advantage

The amount of leverage a given rigging provides can be worked out mathematically and is expressed as a ratio, such as 3:1. The first number in the ratio represents the load. The second number indicates how much force a person (the hauler) must exert in order to hold the load in place. Here are some examples of simple MA rigging:

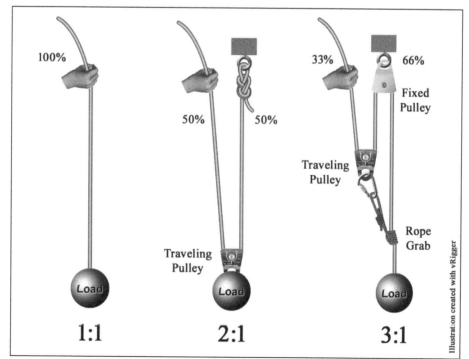

Examples of simple mechanical advantage.

Let's compare these three systems in a basic scenario. Suppose we want to raise a 100kg (~220lbs) load a total distance of one meter. These numbers are arbitrary but will help keep the math simple.

Ratio	Description
1:1	The load is attached to the end of the rope. It is supported only by the hauler. • To move the load, the hauler must exert enough force to raise 100% of the load a total distance of 1m. No advantage is gained.
2:1	Suppose, now, that one end of the rope is tied to an anchor. The rope passes through a *traveling pulley* attached to the load, then runs back up to the hauler. With the load shared between two points, the hauler only needs to support 50% of the load. • To move the load upward by 1m, the hauler must exert enough force to raise 50% of the load (i.e., 50kg (110lbs)) over a total distance of 2m.
3:1	The load is attached to the end of the rope. This time, the rope passes through a *fixed pulley* on the anchor, then runs back down through a *traveling pulley* on the load strand. From there, the rope runs back up to the hauler. With the load shared between three points, the hauler only needs to support 33% of the load. • To move the load upward by 1m, the hauler must exert enough force to raise 33% of the load (i.e., 33kg (~73lbs)) over a total distance of 3m.

Looking at the numbers above, a clear pattern is emerging. As the MA ratio increases, the hauler's job becomes easier, but the total distance they must haul is increasing.

Simple MA systems can also be linked together to increase the mechanical advantage. For example, a 3:1 system hauling on a 2:1 will have two pulleys moving at different speeds and becomes a 6:1 MA.[157] To raise the load by 1m, the hauler needs to exert enough force to raise 17% of the load (17kg (37lbs)) over a total distance of 6m.

So, the higher the MA the better, right? Not quite. There are some drawbacks and other considerations. We'll talk more about them in a moment, but, for now, here are two things to note:

- Traveling pulleys will increase the mechanical advantage.

- Fixed pulleys don't increase the advantage, but can be used to change the direction of pull. They're generally used to:

  o Allow hauling to take place in a better location (ex: a place further back from the edge).
  o Allow the haulers to pull in a more ergonomic direction (i.e., pulling downward instead of up).

Overcoming the Friction
The MA ratio represents the amount of force the hauler must exert in order to hold the load in place. In order to move the load, the hauler must exert more force … and, well, it's actually worse than that. Ratios represent a theoretical mechanical advantage in a world of zero friction, ropes that don't stretch, and 100% efficient pulleys. In reality, the hauler must overcome all the friction in the rigging, plus the edge friction.

If you need to raise a light load a short distance and have sufficient manpower, overcoming the friction generally isn't a big deal. However, if you're the only person hauling, or you need to raise a large load a significant distance, the overcoming the friction can be a serious problem.

---

[157] One simple MA system pulling on another is called a *compound system*.

Here are some tips for keeping your MA system as efficient as possible:

- Static ropes are preferred for hauling. The less stretch in the rope, the more efficient your system will be.

- If available, use efficient pulleys. If pulleys are in short supply, you'll need to use carabiners, although this will reduce the efficiency of the rigging.[158]

Type of Pulley	Efficiency	Notes
Quick Link / Rappel Ring	40–50%	This is the rope passing through the anchor's master point.
Carabiner	50–60%	Round stock carabiners are slightly more efficient.
Efficient Pulley	80–90%	Pulleys with plastic bearings are lighter in weight, but will be less efficient.

- Edge friction is both good and bad. It will work against you when hauling (i.e., it must be overcome), but the same friction makes it easier to hold the load in place (i.e., when resting).

  o A high-placed anchor will reduce how much contact the rope has where it passes over the edge atop of the pitch. Less contact means less friction. (See "Edge Friction" in Chapter 4.)

  o A fixed pulley directly atop the pitch can help reduce the edge friction. It could be a literal pulley attached to an anchor or a human redirect. (See "Human Redirection" in Chapter 20.)

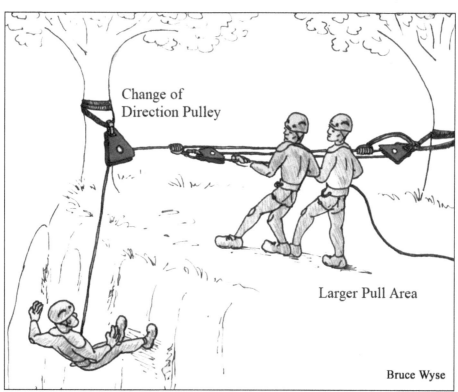

A fixed pulley atop the pitch can help alleviate edge friction.
It also allows the haul to take place in a better location.

---

[158] If you only have one efficient pulley, it should be placed closest to the haulers. This is the pulley that sees the most rope movement.

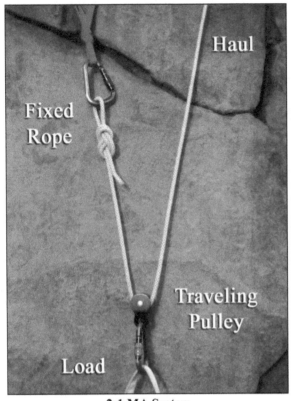

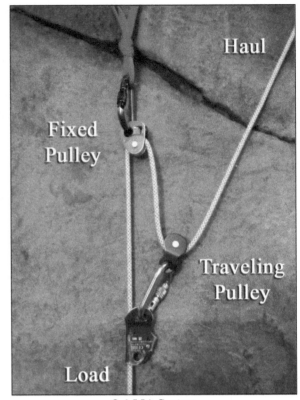

2:1 MA System   3:1 MA System

Preparing to Haul

When preparing for a haul, the first step is to find a good location. Ideally, you want a bombproof anchor and a safe pull area. Deep in the canyon, however, the local terrain may be uncooperative and your anchors limited. This makes it important to understand the pros and cons of MA rigging.

Choosing the Right Rigging

There are many ways to rig for mechanical advantage. The rigging that works best will depend on your situation and the resources at your disposal. The KISS principle comes into play here: keep it simple. Big systems are not always better. The larger the MA ratio, the more inefficient and complicated your rigging will be. By going right to a 9:1 system out of the gate (i.e., a 3:1 stacked on another 3:1), you may find it impossible to overcome the friction and you'll have wasted your time.

Instead, start with the simplest system that you think can achieve the goal. If the rigging proves inadequate, it's easy to increase the advantage. Both climbing and canyon experts agree that a simple 2:1 or 3:1 backed with sufficient manpower will probably suffice for most situations you're likely to encounter.[159] If you're hauling on your own, you might need bump it up to a 5:1 or 6:1. Beyond that, you're probably going to run into the law of diminishing returns.

- Don't rush when building haul systems. Taking a few extra minutes can help avoid many problems later on. The ideal MA system is one that's clean and easy to inspect.

- If pulling towards an edge, the haulers should be clipped into an anchor.

- Tensioned ropes can be easily damaged if dragged over sharp edges and rough rock. If appropriate, consider the use of edge protection.

---

[159] Tyson, A. & Loomis, M. *Climbing Self-Rescue – Improvising Solutions for Serious Situations*. Mountaineers Books, 2016.

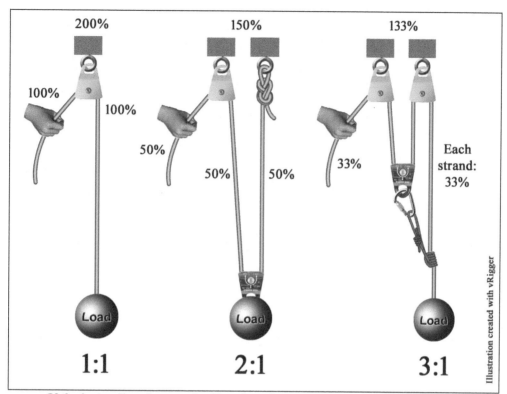

If the last pulley changes the direction of pull, a force multiplier is created.

Anchors for Hauling

WARNING! The force experienced by the anchor during a haul can be substantially higher than your average rappel. Hauling is a good time for strong/bombproof anchors. When in doubt: add redundancy, back up the anchor, or build a better one. Here are two questions to consider:

- What is the expected load?
  The anchor may need to support multiple individuals at the same time. Multiple haulers might need to be clipped into the anchor. In rare cases, you might be hauling both a subject and an attendant.

- Is this MA system a force multiplier?
  If the last pulley in the rigging (i.e., the pulley closest to the haulers) is fixed and changes the direction of pull, this will increase the load on the anchor. The following table shows the percentage of the load being held by the anchor and by the hauler with and without a final change of direction:

Ratio	Standard Rigging	... with a final change of direction
1:1	(no anchor) Hauler: 100%	Anchor: 200% Hauler: 100%
2:1	Anchor: 50% Hauler: 50%	Anchor: 150% Hauler: 50%
3:1	Anchor: 66% Hauler: 33%	Anchor: 133% Hauler: 33%

Again, these percentages represent the amount of force the anchor experiences while holding the load in place. So, if we have a 1:1 system with a final change of direction, the anchor could experience up to 200% of the load when the system is at rest. While the haul is underway, the force on the anchor could easily top 300%. With a standard rappel load of 1–2kN, this means the anchor could experience as much as 3–6kN when hauling. Clearly, this rigging would be a poor choice for a marginal anchor (ex: rock cairn), but it might be fine on a quality bolt station.

Backing up the Haul

A backup system is essential on longer hauls. Rope grabs can slip and it's easy to make mistakes under pressure. Mistakes are even more likely if you haven't practiced MA systems in awhile. One of the easiest backup methods is to give yourself sufficient slack and tie off the free end of the rope to an anchor. This provides an emergency backstop in the event of catastrophic failure.

- As the haul continues, excess rope will start to accumulate atop the pitch. Every so often, the backup will need to be adjusted.

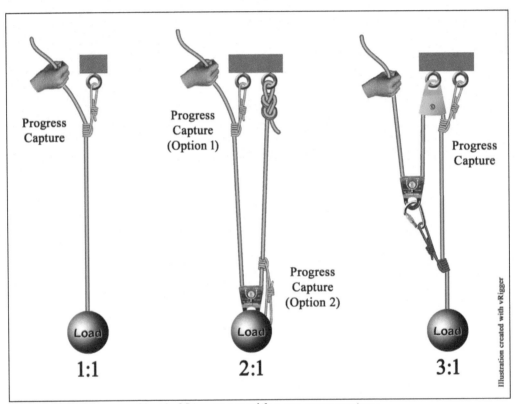

Simple MA systems with a progress capture.

Using a Progress Capture

On longer hauls, two other problems with MA systems become apparent:

1) Systems with traveling pulleys can run out of room. When the pulleys get too close to the anchor (or one another), they'll need to be reset in order for the haul to continue. A reset is not possible while the rope is under tension.

2) The haulers may need to rest. If they were to let go, the load would return to its original starting place.

Both of these issues are solved by incorporating a *progress capture* into the rigging. A capture, essentially, is a form of ratchet. It allows rope to move through the rigging in one direction, but not in the other. As the name suggests, its job is to capture progress made during the haul. When the haulers ease off, the load shifts and is held by the capture. This allows the haulers to take a break or reset the pulleys without losing any ground.

- Make sure the progress capture is holding before releasing the haul rope.

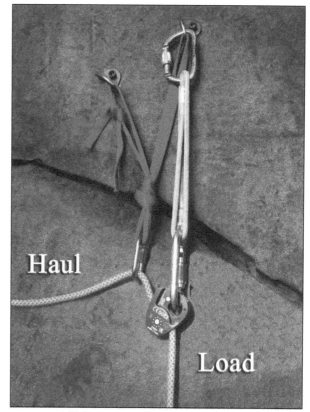

| Prusik as a progress capture. | Using a progress capture pulley. |

Rigging

Your typical progress capture is a rope grab that's clipped to the anchor. The rope grab could be a friction hitch or mechanical device. The progress capture is usually (but not always) installed on the load strand in front of the first pulley in the system. Quite often, the first pulley will be the master point of the anchor.

Not all progress captures are created equal. Some will take up rope automatically during the haul, whereas others must be manually tended. If you have sufficient manpower, someone could be stationed at the anchor to mind it. Otherwise, the haulers will need to adjust it periodically. When tending the progress capture, there are two things to watch out for:

1) If using a friction hitch, it may be in danger of getting sucked into the pulley and jamming.[160]

2) When the haulers are ready to ease off on the pull, the progress capture should be pushed down the load strand as far as possible. Otherwise, it'll need to stretch out to its full length before it engages on the rope. If the capture is not being tended, you'll lose some ground every time.

<u>Other Notes</u>

- In some cases, the capture will need to be set out past the rappel rigging (ex: MMO). A quickdraw or short sling can be used as a spacer.

- A progress capture pulley makes an efficient capture and pulley in one (ref: photo above-right). Once the capture has been installed, you can increase the efficiency of the system by removing the haul strand from the anchor's quick link. The pulley will become the new master point. One big advantage: a progress capture pulley requires no tending.

---

[160] A quick link or rappel ring at the anchor's master point might be sufficient to tend a friction hitch. Another way to avoid the problem is to use a prusik-minding pulley.

Direct Hauling

Having finished an overview of mechanical advantage, let's look at some rigging systems that might be used to rescue a canyoneer. First up, we'll look at *direct hauling*. This is when the rappel rope itself is used to haul.

> **About the Diagrams**
>
> The diagrams that follow depict the use of static blocks. Releasables are generally preferred in aquatic canyons, but static blocks were chosen here for visual clarity. The goal in these examples is to illustrate the various MA systems in a more realistic context. (The use of static blocks will also lead us into a discussion of *conversions* in Chapter 22.)
>
> - If the goal is to provide a temporary lift, the block can be left in place.
>
> - Pulleys may be in short supply deep in the canyon, so carabiners are shown.
>
> - In the following examples, the progress capture will self-tend against the anchor's quick link.
>
> - Several diagrams depict the use of a Petzl Basic as a rope grab. Side-loading ascenders are fast to install on the rope, but any rope grab will do.
>
> - The backup system is not shown for clarity. One option: give yourself sufficient slack and tie off the free end of the rope to an anchor.

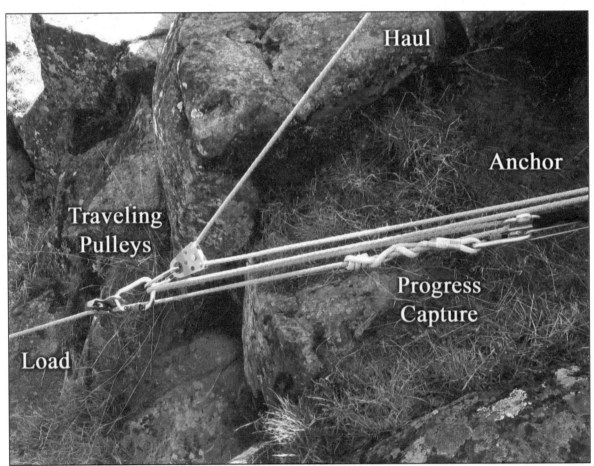

Rigging a 5:1 direct haul.

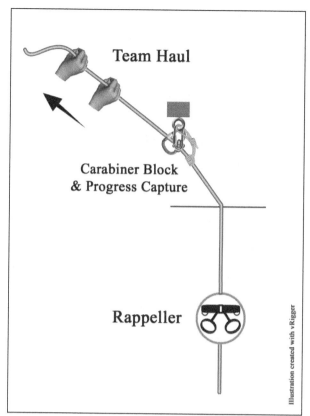

Simple 1:1 (direct haul).

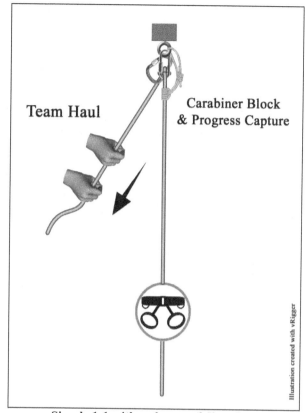

Simple 1:1 with a change of direction.

1:1 Direct Haul

With enough manpower atop the pitch, everyone hauls on the free end of the rope. This is a brute force technique that works best with lots of haulers, light loads, and on low-angle terrain. This method of hauling might be a good choice if you only need to raise the subject a short distance.

When might you use this technique? Imagine, a rappeller who has gotten their harness caught on a rock horn during a difficult rappel start. A quick lift with the rappel rope (a matter of centimeters or inches) is all that's needed to solve the problem. There's no need for any fancy rigging systems. (See also "Quick Lift" in Chapter 23.)

Advantage
- Fast to implement.

Disadvantage
- No mechanical advantage is gained. While the haul is underway, the haulers must support 100% of the load and overcome any edge friction. Hauling can be very strenuous.

1:1 Direct Haul with a Change of Direction

If the haulers were to pull from a different location, the same rigging becomes a 1:1 with a change of direction. Be aware: MA systems with a final fixed pulley will magnify the load on the anchor. The anchor must be bombproof.

- Tip: If the anchor is set well back from the top of the pitch, you might be able avoid overloading the anchor by performing the haul on the load strand (i.e., the rappeller's side of the anchor). In this case, another team member can be assigned to monitor the progress capture.

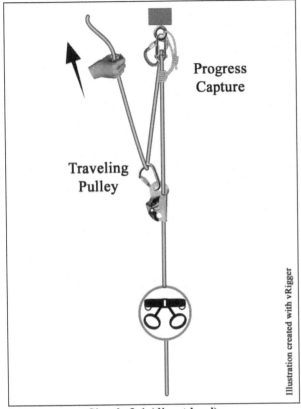

| Simple 3:1 (direct haul). | Simple 3:1 with a change of direction. |

3:1 Direct Haul

The 3:1 direct haul is the classic MA system for high angle rescue. It works well for raising moderate loads over longer distances. It's also known as a "Z-Rig" due to the shape the rope makes as it passes through the rigging.

<u>Rigging</u>

1) Set a progress capture. For a 3:1 direct haul, the capture is installed on the load strand in front of the first pulley. In the examples above, the first pulley is the quick link on the anchor.

2) Install a rope grab on the load strand a short distance down from the anchor and attach a pulley to it. This will be the traveling pulley.

3) Run the free end of the rope from the block down through the traveling pulley and back up again. This will be the haul strand.

4) Slide the traveling pulley as far down the load strand as you can. This will maximize the amount of rope that can be pulled through the rigging before a pulley reset is required.

5) (Optional) Install a final change of direction pulley on the anchor. This would allow hauling in a more ergonomic/convenient direction, but will magnify the load on the anchor.

6) Start hauling.

<u>Resetting the System</u>

When the traveling pulley reaches the anchor, the haulers ease off and allow the progress capture to take the load. Once the pulley is unweighted, slide it back down the load strand as far as you can. Continue hauling.

Converting 3:1 to 5:1

If the 3:1 system isn't working, here's a quick conversion to a 5:1. You'll need a change of direction on the anchor, then run the free end of the rope through a second traveling pulley on the same rope grab. Voilà! More power![161]

The 5:1 rigging is a good choice for raising large loads when the number of haulers is limited.

- Con: As with all high MA systems, a great deal of rope must be pulled through the rigging in order to raise the subject even a short distance. To raise the subject by 1m (~3ft), some 5m (~16ft) of rope must be pulled through the MA system. Get ready for a lot of pulley resets.

Hauling with a Drop Loop

Another method of hauling is to use a separate rope that is lowered to the subject from above. Hauling with a *drop loop* (or *drop line*) offers some advantages. For example: once the haul begins, the original rappel rope will go slack. This is a good way to help a rappeller with a jammed descender.

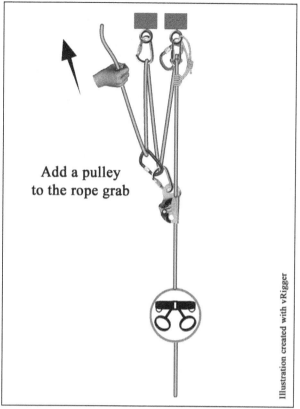

Add a pulley to the rope grab

Simple 5:1 (direct haul).

Illustration created with vRigger

General Limitations

- Drop loops (and drop lines) work best when the subject is relatively close to the top of the pitch. Getting the rope to the subject could be difficult if they're too far away, on a low-angle rappel, in high flow, or if the pitch is cluttered with obstacles.

- The subject must be conscious and capable of connecting the rope to their harness.[162]

- Beware the drop loop becoming tangled around the rappel rope. This could happen if the subject is spinning around on a free-hang. Tangling can interfere with your ability to haul.

About the Diagrams

The diagrams that follow depict hauling with a separate rescue rope. If there's sufficient rope available, the reserve atop the pitch (i.e., in the rappel rope bag) could be used. In this case, the rappel and MA systems should be isolated from one other. If the systems are not isolated, you might find yourself doing a direct haul when you meant to haul with a drop loop.

- Carabiners are shown, but pulleys are more efficient.

- In the examples that follow, the progress capture will require manual tending.

- Again, the backup system is not shown for clarity. Give yourself some slack in the rappel rope and tie it off to an anchor. Another option for supple ropes: move the static block closer to the anchor by adjusting the clove hitch.

---

[161] As the pulleys are moving at the same speed, the MA of the systems is added, not multiplied.
[162] In some cases, a rescuer could rappel down to deliver the rope to the subject. If you're going to the subject, it might be more efficient to perform a local lift or pick-off. (See "Contact Rescue" in Chapter 23.)

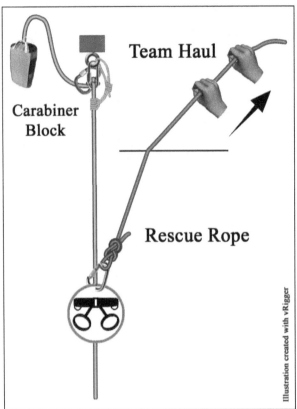

Carabiner Block

Team Haul

Rescue Rope

Illustration created with vRigger

Simple 1:1 (drop line).

1:1 Drop Line

A drop line is a figure-8 knot tied in the end of a rescue rope, that is lowered, with an accompanying carabiner, to the subject. The subject clips the carabiner to their harness and the team hauls from above. This is actually a 1:1 MA system again; it's just dressed up a little differently. Again, this is a brute force technique that works best with light loads and lots of haulers.

Other Notes

- No mechanical advantage is gained. While the haul is underway, the haulers must support 100% of the load and overcome any edge friction.

- In some situations, you might be able to deliver the drop line by clipping it to the rappel rope. As the team above pays out rope, the carabiner slides down to the subject.

- If hauling with the drop line isn't working, the next step would be to convert the system to a 3:1. As the subject is already clipped into the end of a rescue rope, re-rigging for a 2:1 drop loop would not make sense.

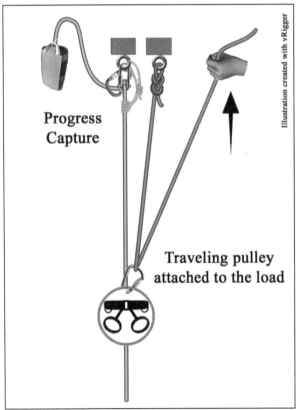

Progress Capture

Traveling pulley attached to the load

Illustration created with vRigger

Simple 2:1 (drop loop).

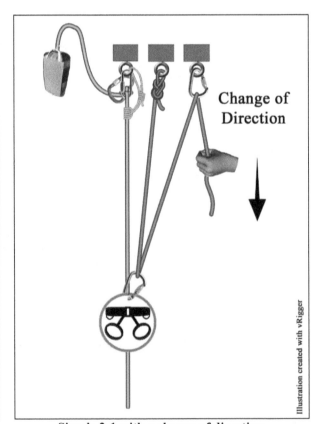

Change of Direction

Illustration created with vRigger

Simple 2:1 with a change of direction.

2:1 Drop Loop

A 2:1 MA system works well for temporary lifts and short hauls. A drop loop could also be used to help team members climb up and over a mid-canyon obstacle. A drop loop could also be used in reverse (i.e., lowering or belaying) to assist someone on a difficult rappel start.

Rigging

1) Tie a figure-8 knot in the end of the rescue rope and clip it to the anchor.

2) Create the drop loop. Form a bight in the rescue rope and attach a pulley (or carabiner) to it. The pulley is lowered to the subject who clips it to the load-bearing point of their harness. The free end of the rope will be used for hauling.

3) (Optional) Install a final change of direction pulley at the anchor. This allows hauling in a more ergonomic/convenient direction, but will magnify the load on the anchor.

4) Rig a progress capture. With a 2:1 MA system, you have some options. The progress capture could be:

   o Set on the rappel rope as shown in the examples.
   o Installed on the haul strand (or in front of the change of direction pulley on the anchor).
   o Attached to the subject (i.e., on the fixed side of the drop loop).

5) Start hauling.

Clever Tricks

If you have a progress capture pulley, it could be sent down to the subject on the drop loop. Make sure before lowering that: 1) it's attached to the rope in the correct orientation for the haul, and 2) the cam is locked out. Once clipped to the subject's harness and engaged, the device will function as an efficient pulley and progress capture in one.

- Tip: Need to perform a quick lift or haul? One team member sits down and becomes a human anchor. Another person lowers the drop loop and becomes the hauler.

Advantages

- Fast to implement.

- When the haul is underway, 50% of the rappeller's weight is supported by a fixed, unmoving line. This means the edge friction is similarly reduced, making the haul easier.

- If capable, the subject can assist by pulling themselves upwards on the fixed side of the drop loop.

- As the traveling pulley is attached to the load, no pulley resets are required. The haulers still might need to stop and rest, however.

- A simple 2:1 system (without a final change of direction) is a good choice when you only have marginal anchors to work with. The anchor will experience 50% of the load while the haul is underway and 100% when the haulers rest (i.e., held by the progress capture).

Disadvantage

- Drop loops require more rope for hauling. Take the distance between the subject and the anchor and multiply by two. You'll need at least that much rope.

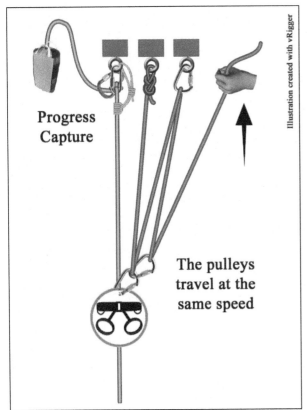

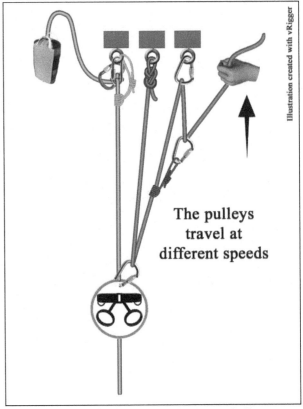

Progress Capture

The pulleys travel at the same speed

The pulleys travel at different speeds

Simple 4:1 (Block & Tackle).

Compound 6:1 (3:1 pulling on a 2:1).

Converting 2:1 to 4:1

If the 2:1 system isn't working, you'll probably want to jump right to a 6:1. Switching to a 4:1 is easy, but, in this case, it's impractical because it would require getting another drop loop to the subject. While the 4:1 isn't useful here, it definitely has applications elsewhere. (See "Hauling with a Pig Rig" below.)

To create a 4:1, you'll need a change of direction pulley at the anchor and then run the haul rope through a second traveling pulley attached to the load. You now have a pair of 2:1 systems acting in concert. This type of rigging is known as a *block and tackle*. As the traveling pulleys are moving at the same speed, the MA of the two systems are added together.

Converting 2:1 to 6:1

Switching to a 6:1 system is similar to the 4:1. You'll need a change of direction pulley at the anchor, then run the free end of the rope through a second traveling pulley attached to the previous haul strand. We now have a 3:1 system pulling on a 2:1. As the pulleys are moving at different speeds, the MA is multiplied.

<u>Disadvantages</u>

- Pulley resets are now required.

- As with all high MA systems, a great deal of rope must be pulled through the rigging in order to raise the subject even a short distance. To raise the subject by 1m (~3ft), some 6m (~20ft) of rope must be pulled through the rigging. Get ready for lots of pulley resets.

Hauling with a Pig Rig

A third type of haul uses a *piggyback rig* (or *pig rig*). This is an MA system that's attached to the load strand. It's similar to direct hauling, but has some other benefits. Pig rigs can be any type of MA system, but generally start as a 2:1 or 3:1. The diagram shows a 2:1 pig rig with a change of direction.

A pig rig might be a good choice if:

- You don't have enough rope atop the pitch for a direct haul or drop loop. Possibly the rappel rope is fixed (ex: tied off to an anchor with a bowline). A pig rig can be used to get the haul started, then you can switch over to direct hauling once enough rope has been pulled up.

- The rigging needs to be modified. A classic example is converting a static block to a lower. A short lift with the pig rig will unweight the static block, allowing it to be swapped out for a releasable system. We'll talk more about *conversions* in the next chapter.

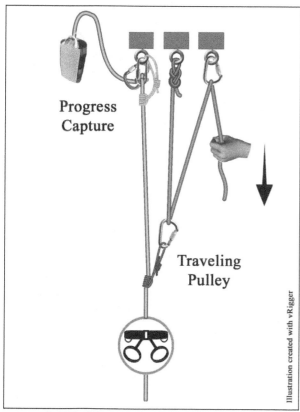

2:1 Pig Rig with a change of direction.

4:1 Pig Rig with a change of direction.

Advantages
- Pig rigs allow the use of 2:1 MA systems without needing to get a drop loop to the subject. This means a *block and tackle* systems (such as the 4:1) suddenly becomes more interesting.

- Compact. Pig rigs can be used to haul when real estate at the anchor is limited.

- Pig rigs don't require much rope for hauling. A short rescue rope, cordelette, or a long sling is all you need.[163] Alternatively, if there's sufficient reserve rope atop the pitch, it could also be used. When using the reserve rope, the rappel and haul systems should be isolated from one another.

Disadvantage
- Pig rigs are not a good choice for longer hauls. The hauling is going to be slow, your space is limited, and you'll need to perform lots of pulley resets.

---

[163] An elegant lift system can be created with a long Dyneema sling and two pear-abiners (see photo above right). Dyneema is lightweight, extremely strong, narrow in width, and low-friction.

Early season flow in the Oregon Coast Range.
(Photo: Wade Hewitt)

Chapter 22: Conversions

In this chapter, we'll look at another foundational rescue skill: the *conversion*. What's a conversion? Essentially, it's the ability to modify a rigging system that's fully under load (ex: there's a rappeller hanging on it). The modification could be anything from a simple fix to a total overhaul. A classic example would be converting a static block to a lower during a rescue.

There are many ways to perform conversions. The method you choose will depend on your situation, the rigging, and the resources at your disposal (manpower and gear). Some methods are more efficient than others. Conversions are performed infrequently in the real world, so this is another great skill to practice. As usual, the best practice is a safe place with a real load on the system.

Modifying the Rigging

Conversions usually take place atop the pitch. They're most often performed in the context of high-angle rescue because the current rigging is inadequate in some way.

Generally, rigging systems can't be modified while under load, so the secret is to move the load somewhere else first. A common solution is to create a new connection between the load and the anchor, known as a *bridge*.[164] The bridge serves as a temporary staging area. Once the load has been moved onto the bridge, the original rigging becomes unweighted. The team can then make any required changes. The entire rigging system could even be cleaned and rebuilt from scratch. Here are some possible conversions:

- o Fix a minor problem or error in the rigging (ex: tangled rope strands).
- o Convert the rigging to a lower or haul.
- o Move a knot past the anchor during a lower or haul.

Once the modifications are complete, the load is moved back. Moving the load on and off the bridge is just a series of load transfers. In a moment, we'll talk about how these transfers are achieved.

- We've introduced one type of conversion already in the previous chapter: hauling with a progress capture. When the haulers ease off to take a break, the load shifts and is held by the capture. When the haulers start up again, the load shifts back onto the MA system. In this case, the progress capture is the bridge. Some changes that might be made to the rigging would include:

  - o Performing a pulley reset.
  - o Increasing the mechanical advantage.
  - o Swapping out one or more carabiners (or the quick link on the anchor) for efficient pulleys.
  - o Resetting the backup.

- In rare cases, the load transfer might be one-way. Here are two examples:

  - o Moving the load onto a stronger anchor in preparation for a haul.
  - o *Cut & Lower*: a technique for lowering a rappeller in an emergency. (See Chapter 23.)

---

[164] The bridge might connect the load to the same anchor or to a different one.

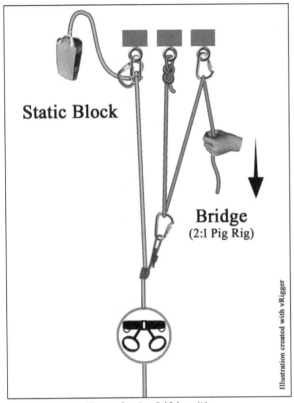

Transfer by Lifting #1:
A short lift with a pig rig unweights the block.

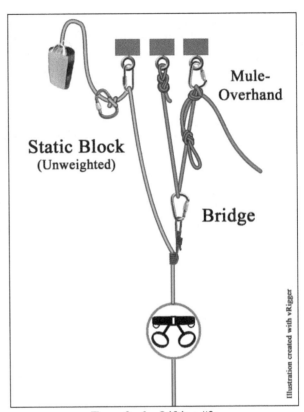

Transfer by Lifting #2:
The bridge is tied off with a releasable hitch.

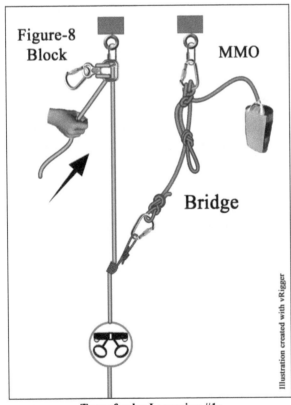

Transfer by Lowering #1:
With a releasable system in play ...

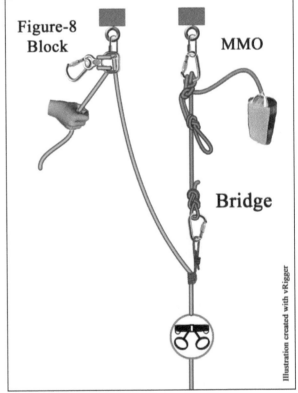

Transfer by Lowering #2:
... unlock and lower to weight the bridge.

Mechanisms of Load Transfer

Scenario: The rappeller gets stuck partway down the pitch (ex: jammed descender) and requests a lower. Unfortunately, this rappel was rigged with a static block.

Static systems, of course, cannot release rope while under load, so the block will need to be swapped out for a releasable system. To do that, the team must find a way to unweight the block. If there happens to be a nice, safe ledge (or similar location) where the rappeller can stand up, the problem is solved immediately. The team can convert the system without any fancy rigging. If no convenient ledges exist, however, the team will need to create a bridge to hold the rappeller while the conversion is carried out.

Moving the load on and off the bridge is accomplished by either lifting or lowering.

Lifting

There are a several ways to lift the rappeller and unweight the rigging:

- Pig Rig
  One method of load transfer is a short lift with a *pig rig*. In this case, the bridge has an integrated MA system. The load is raised enough to unweight the static block. The bridge is then tied off to the anchor with a *releasable hitch*. Once the new rigging is in place, the process is reversed. The team unties the releasable hitch and lowers. The rappeller is moved onto the new rigging.

- Direct Haul
  Another method is to perform a direct haul. The haulers set up an MA system with a progress capture (aka the bridge) and perform a short lift. Once the block has been unweighted, the haulers ease off (i.e., start to lower) and the load shifts onto the progress capture.[165] The load has been moved onto the bridge.

  Once the rigging has been converted, the load transfer is reversed. Using the same MA system, the haulers lift a second time to unweight the capture. The capture is manually tended to keep it from engaging as the haulers lower the rappeller onto the new rigging.[166]

- Drop Loop
  Lifting with a drop loop (or drop line) is another way to unweight the block. Con: This method is not very efficient as it may be tricky to get a drop loop to the rappeller.

Lowering

Let's consider another scenario. This time, the rappel is rigged with a figure-8 block. While lowering, we realize there's a problem: there's a knot in the rope (ex: core shot) that will not fit through the anchor.

Moving the knot past the anchor is another type of conversion. Again, we'll use a bridge to hold the load while the knot is being moved past the anchor. With a releasable system, moving the load onto the bridge is even easier. Once the bridge has been established, all we need to do is unlock the figure-8 and lower. The load will eventually shift onto the bridge and unweight the original rigging. (We'll cover this scenario in more detail later in the chapter.)

> **FAQ: "What's a Releasable Hitch?"**
> A releasable hitch (or "load releasing hitch") is a close cousin of releasable rigging. This is a category of tie-offs that can support significant weight, but that can also be untied and released while fully loaded. They're commonly used in hauling and load transfer systems. Some examples include the mule hitch, mariner's hitch, and the Valdotain Tresse. (See Appendix I for more information.)

---

[165] If the progress capture is right up against the first pulley, the lower may be so slight as to be imperceptible.
[166] Alternatively: if the capture has a releasable connection to the anchor, it can be released to move the load back.

Components of a Bridge

A bridge can be rigged with whatever materials you have available: a long sling, cordelette, accessory cord, webbing, or rope.[167] Depending on the rigging, you might need a few pulleys or carabiners as well. A typical bridge includes the following components:

Connection to the Load Strand	The bridge is usually connected to the load strand with a rope grab. It could be a mechanical device or friction hitch. (Alternatively, the bridge could be attached directly to the load.) • If you're converting the rigging to a haul, the bridge will likely become a progress capture.
Lift System (optional)	If lifting with a pig rig (or drop loop), the bridge will have an integrated MA system.
Connection to an Anchor	The bridge also requires a connection to an anchor. It's possible to use a static connection here, but a releasable connection often makes it easier to transfer the load back. There are several options: • The bridge could be tied off to the anchor with a *releasable hitch*. • The bridge could be attached to the anchor with a locked releasable rigging system (i.e., an MMO or figure-8 block). • The bridge could have a static connection to the anchor if the connection to the load strand is releasable (ex: Valdotain Tresse).

Performing Conversions

In the remainder of the chapter, we'll take a closer look at some selected conversions. As always, the method presented here is just one way to go about it. Your approach may be different depending on the situation, available resources, and personal preference.

- There's definite value in knowing multiple ways to convert a rigging system.

> **Backing up the Bridge**
> As with hauling, it's not a bad idea to have a backup when performing conversions. Try to avoid leaving the rappeller supported by the bridge alone. If the bridge were to fail (ex: it was rigged incorrectly), the outcome could be catastrophic. A quick backup method is to give yourself sufficient slack in the free end of the rappel rope and tie it off to an anchor.

---

[167] It might be the reserve rope atop the pitch or a separate rescue rope.

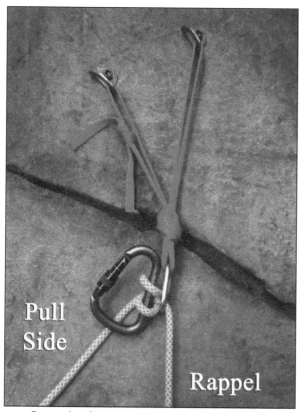

Pull Side

Rappel

Scenario: Convert a static block to a lower.

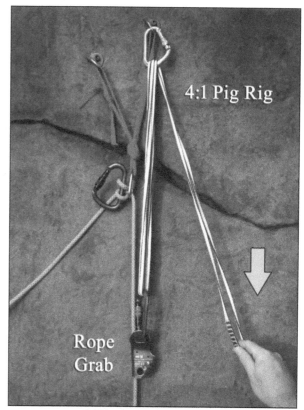

4:1 Pig Rig

Rope Grab

Lifting with a 4:1 pig rig.
The bridge is then tied off with a releasable hitch.

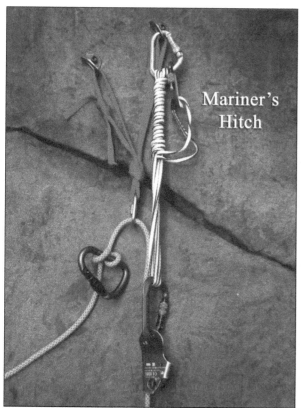

Mariner's Hitch

With the block unweighted, it can be replaced ...

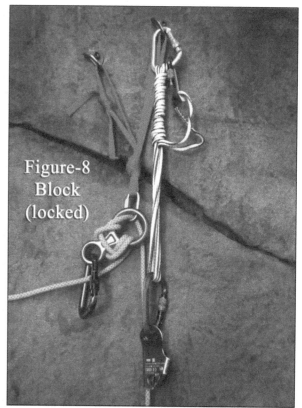

Figure-8 Block (locked)

... with a releasable system.

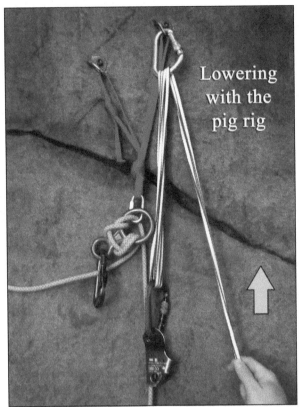

Lowering with the pig rig

Release the bridge to shift the load
onto the new figure-8 block.

Clean the bridge.
You can now unlock & lower.

Converting a Static Block to a Lower

<u>Scenario</u>: We need to lower a stuck rappeller, but, unfortunately, a static block was rigged on the anchor. It will need to be converted to a releasable system. This process is sometimes referred to as *breaking a block*.

1) Install a rope grab on the load strand (oriented for a haul) and clip a pear-abiner to it.

2) Clip a second pear-abiner to the anchor. Ideally, both carabiners should be situated on the opposite side of the anchor from the block. This will keep the lift system away from the block.

3) Create a lift mechanism. In the example above, a pig rig was created using a long Dyneema sling. To start, a 2:1 MA system was created by clipping the sling into the upper carabiner and running it through the lower one on the rope grab. Next, the sling was run one more time through both carabiners to create a 4:1 block and tackle. Pass the sling through the upper carabiner one more time for a final change of direction.

4) Transfer the load onto the bridge. Lift with the pig rig until the static block becomes unweighted. Often, this is just a matter of centimeters or inches. While holding the load in place, tie off the bridge to the anchor with a releasable hitch. In this example, a mariner's hitch (with an excessive number of wraps) was used. The final bight was clipped back to the anchor with another carabiner.

5) Set a backup. Loosen up the clove hitch on the static block and slip some rope through it to create slack between the block and the anchor. Don't remove the block yet. If the bridge should fail, the block will serve as an emergency backstop.

6) Once you have sufficient slack, rig a releasable system on the anchor (ex: figure-8 block) and lock it off. At this point, the static block can be removed. The figure-8 block is now backing up the bridge.

7) Transfer the load back. Untie the bridge and carefully lower with the pig rig to move the load back onto the modified rigging.

8) Clean the bridge.

With the rigging converted, the belayer can now unlock the figure-8 and lower.

Conversions in an Aquatic Canyon?
Next time you're breaking a block, get someone to time you. An expert can probably convert the rigging in a minute or two, but, for others (and those who haven't practiced in awhile), it may take quite a bit longer. On a dry pitch, a stuck rappeller can hang out and wait while the conversion is carried out. Getting stuck under a waterfall, however, could be a life-threatening situation.

Some faster solutions:

➢ With a releasable system, the rappeller can be lowered immediately,

➢ In Chapter 23, we'll introduce an emergency technique called *Cut & Lower*. This is a way to bypass a static system (or stuck releasable) using a separate rope.

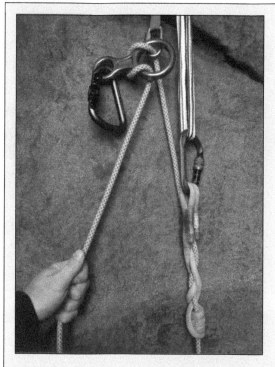

Clever Tricks: Valdotain Tresse
Instead of a static rope grab, a Valdotain Tresse could be used to connect the bridge to the load strand. Why would you want to do this? One advantage: the bridge no longer needs to be cleaned in order to lower. Once finished with the conversion, the Valdotain becomes a hands-free backup for the belayer.

• If time is of the essence (or the lower is short), you could even skip the figure-8 block. Once the load has been transferred onto the bridge, clean the static block. The rappeller can then be lowered immediately using the Valdotain Tresse. Con: The lowering will be jerky and awkward.

The Valdotain Tresse becomes a hands-free backup for the belayer.

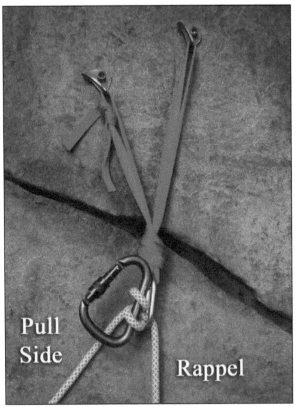

Scenario: Convert a rope block to a haul.

Add a progress capture (i.e., create the bridge).

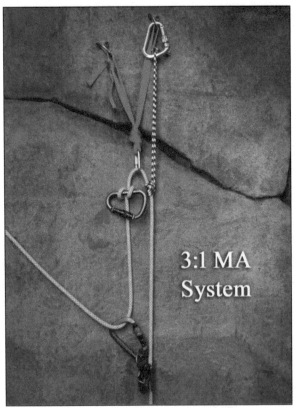

Create a 3:1 MA system and lift
just enough to unweight the block.

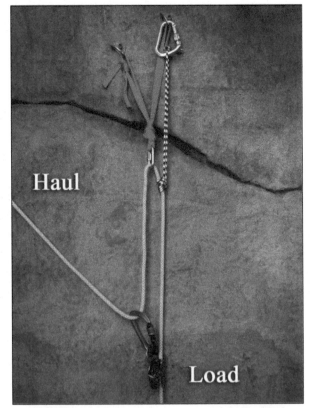

With the progress capture supporting the load,
the block can be removed. Continue hauling.

Converting a Static Block to a Haul

<u>Scenario</u>: The rappeller is stuck a short distance down the pitch and we want to bring them back up to the top. Again, a static block was used at the anchor. This time, we need to convert it to a haul system.

1) Create the bridge (aka progress capture). In the example opposite, a prusik loop was tied on the load strand and clipped to the anchor.

2) Install another rope grab on the load strand a short distance down from the anchor. Attach a pulley to it. This is the traveling pulley.

3) Run the free end of the rope from the block down through the traveling pulley and back up again. This becomes the haul strand.

4) Set a backup. Give yourself sufficient slack and tie off the free end of the rope to an anchor. This provides an emergency backstop. We now have a 3:1 MA system, but we're not done yet.

5) Transfer the load onto the bridge. When ready, begin hauling. As soon as the block is a short distance away from the anchor, ease off, and allow the progress capture to take the load. Make sure the capture is working before releasing the haul strand.

6) With the capture holding the load, the static block can be removed.

At this point, the haul system is complete. The capture is tended automatically by the quick link on the anchor.

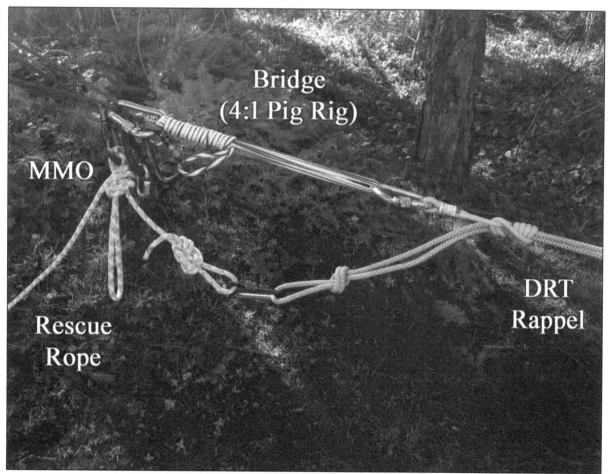

One way to convert DRT to a lower.

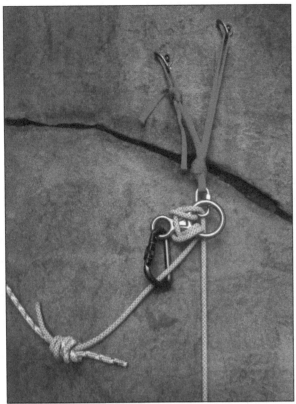

Scenario: We need to move a knot past the anchor.
When the knot gets close, lock off the rigging.

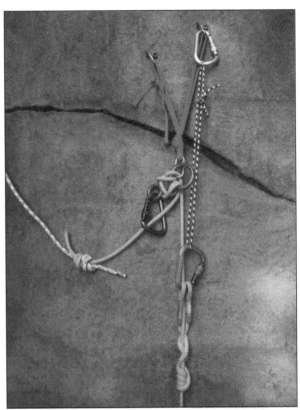

Create the bridge. In this case, we'll use a
Valdotain Tresse that's clipped to the anchor.

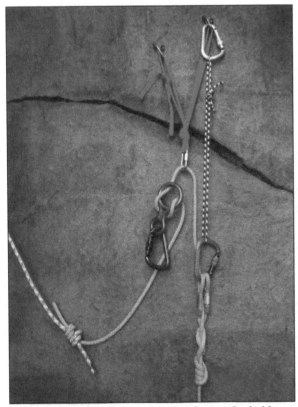

Unlock & lower to move the load onto the bridge.
Clean the figure-8 block.

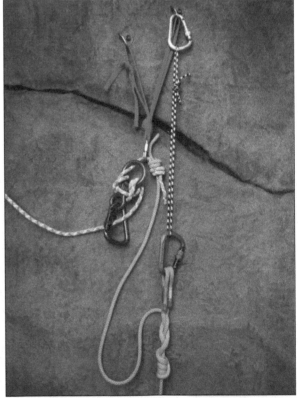

Move the knot past the anchor and
re-establish the figure-8 block on the new rope.

Release the Valdotain to weight the figure-8 block. | **Clean the bridge. You can now unlock & lower.**

Moving a Knot Past the Anchor

<u>Scenario</u>: We need to move a knot past the anchor during a lower. This might be necessary because two ropes were tied together or, perhaps, the rope was damaged (ex: core shot). A double fisherman bend is shown for clarity.

1) When the knot is 0.5m (~2ft) away from the anchor, lock off the figure-8.

2) Set a backup. Give yourself sufficient slack to work with and tie off the free end of the rope to an anchor. This provides an emergency backstop.

3) Create the bridge. In this example, we've tied a Valdotain Tresse on the load strand. (As the Valdotain is releasable, it's okay to have a static connection to the anchor.) The Valdotain should be situated some distance away from the anchor to give you some space to work.

4) Transfer the load onto the bridge. Unlock the figure-8 and lower until the bridge become weighted. Make sure the bridge is holding before releasing the brake. Clean the figure-8 block.

5) With the bridge supporting the load, the knot can be moved past the anchor.[168] Once accomplished, re-establish the block on the new rope (shown in green) and lock it. The knot should be situated as close as possible to the anchor's master point.

6) Transfer the load back by releasing the Valdotain Tresse. Keep moving slack through the hitch until the figure-8 block becomes weighted. This needs to happen before the Valdotain reaches the knot. Getting the spacing right here is key.

---

[168] If the quick link on the anchor can be opened, moving the knot is easy. If it can't be opened (i.e., rappel ring, bolts, or chains), you may need to untie the knot and re-tie it again on the load side of the anchor. Note: if you're untying the knot, this means the backup system is no longer in play.

7) Clean the bridge. The knot cannot pass through the Valdotain, so it'll need to be removed.

8) Clean the backup system.

The knot has been successfully moved past the anchor. You can now unlock and continue the lower.

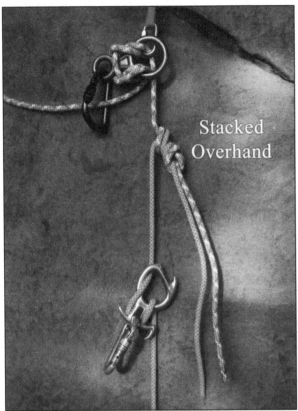

Stacked Overhand

The knot is pre-positioned on the rappel side.
(All lowering will be done using the green rope.)

Clever Tricks: Pre-Rigging

Moving a knot past the anchor is slow and tedious. On a dry pitch, the rappeller can hang out while this happens. If stuck under a waterfall, the rappeller may not have the luxury of time.

Here's one way to avoid needing to move a knot past the anchor. If your second rope (shown in green) is long enough for the lower, the knot can be pre-positioned on the rappel side of the anchor. If the rappeller gets into trouble, the belayer can respond immediately.

Pre-rigging is useful on exploratory rappels when you don't know the height of the pitch. The leader has full control of the rappel rope (yellow), while the team above retains the ability to release and lower (green).

Advantages
- There's no need to move a knot past the anchor.

Disadvantages
- The rope is not recoverable and must be re-rigged by the last rappeller. Use caution to avoid losing your ropes.

- When lowering, the knot has the potential to get snagged (ex: pinches, cracks, brush).

The Problem with Pre-Rigging
Be aware: with a block on one side of the anchor and a knot on the other, it's impossible to recover the rope. The last person must reconfigure the rigging. Here are some options:

➤ Clean the figure-8 block and rappel DRT.

➤ Open the quick link and move the knot past the anchor. The block can then be cleaned. The last person rappels SRT on the yellow rope using the knot as a block. (Alternatively, another static block could be rigged between the knot and the anchor.)

➤ Remove the figure-8 block and reinstall it on the opposite side of the anchor. The last person will rappel SRT on the green rope.

➤ Deploy the green rope and remove the figure-8 block. The team below establishes a ground anchor using the green rope. The last person will rappel SRT on the yellow rope. The team below retains the ability to lower the last rappeller.

Note that all of these options require the removal of the figure-8 block.

The dramatic final rappel in Big Creek, Wash.
(Photo: Wade Hewitt)

Chapter 23: Canyon Rescue

While we always strive to be safe and minimize risk, accidents can still happen. Mistakes, fatigue, bad weather, and bad luck can all play a role. In the canyon environment, outside help may be hours, or even days, away, so the importance of being able to fix problems and deal with emergencies cannot be understated.

Canyon rescue is another huge topic, so we'll narrow our focus to a set of common techniques which might be used to rescue someone on a vertical pitch. Later, in Chapter 24, we'll look at some specific problems and discuss what might be done to solve them.

High-angle rescues include some of the most complicated and least-practiced of all rigging systems. Reading about techniques and working through thought experiments is helpful, but nothing beats hands-on training and practice in a real environment.

Anticipation & Avoidance

While simple bad luck can play a role, most rappel accidents are due to human error.[169] Errors made during a rappel have the potential to be catastrophic, so we need do our utmost to avoid making mistakes. How can we do that? Through education, training, and practice. By anticipating problems and making good decisions, we can reduce the likelihood of accidents and avoid the need to be rescued. It's all about stacking the deck in your favor. Almost everything in this manual is about avoiding problems and reducing risk.

- Inadequate training, improper gear, and poor planning are all factors that can lead to accidents.

- Get to know your team before running the canyon. How experienced are they? When was the last time they practiced rescue techniques?

- What are the risks? What can be done to minimize them? By focusing on prevention, we can reduce the likelihood of accidents. "The approach to this anchor looks slippery. We're going to rig a traverse line here because the consequences of falling could be severe."

- When running a canyon, always try to be thinking ahead. "If someone were to get into trouble on this rappel, how would I rescue them?"

- Avoid taking unnecessary risks. It's better to err on the side of safety. Be paranoid.

Planning & Improvisation

Unfortunately, there's no one-size-fits-all solution that can be applied in an emergency. There are some general guidelines one can follow, but no set of rules can cover every scenario. There are too many variables. Instead, the team needs to assess the situation and come up with a rescue plan on the fly. The plan will depend on the team's training and experience, as well as the nature of the incident, local terrain, and available resources. The goal: fix the problem while minimizing the risk to the rest of the team.

The term *rescue* implies the subject has been injured, but there are many cases where the rappeller is fine and just needs some assistance. Some examples: a rope that doesn't reach the bottom of the pitch, discovering a core shot in the rope, a jammed descender, vertical foot entrapment, or assisting a scared beginner who's frozen up on the rope. The subject might need help, but doesn't require first aid.

---

[169] Hess, Robb. "Know the Ropes: Rappelling – Fundamentals to Save Your Life." *Accidents in North American Mountaineering.* (December 2015)

Priorities in a Rescue

In an emergency, the victim is not the highest priority. While there may be intense urgency to act, leaping in blindly has a high potential to make a bad situation worse. *Don't do it!* The first rule of rescues: don't create more victims. While it may be difficult in a moment of high stress, it's much better to have a considered and effective response.

The priority in a rescue should be as follows:

1) Yourself	Your first priority is always your own safety.
2) The Team	Make sure the team is safe. Everyone should be in a safe place, clipped into an anchor, etc. No one else is currently in danger.
3) Victim	Rescue the subject after seeing to your team and forming a plan.
4) Ropes & Gear	Recover gear once the subject is secure and if the risk to the team is low.

Leadership

In an emergency, it's important to have a single person to coordinate the response. If several people are all trying different things at once, it can create more problems than it solves. At the beginning of a trip, it's a good idea to appoint a leader. If there's no formal leader, it's common to defer to the person with the most experience or highest level of training. However, someone else may need to step up if the leader is the victim, or if the team is divided between the top and bottom of a rappel.

The leader's job is to develop a plan and supervise the rescue. What do we need to accomplish? What needs to happen in order to get us there?

- Being the leader doesn't mean you have to come up with the plan entirely on your own. If the situation permits, you could take a moment to solicit suggestions and critique from others. (In some cases, even the victim could be consulted.)

- If possible, try to delegate tasks to take advantage of the skills and experience of your teammates.

- A good leader tries to anticipate problems and think several steps ahead. "If the current effort is unsuccessful, what needs to happen next?" The leader should continue to re-evaluate the situation. Has anything changed? Are there other solutions that have not yet been tried?

Anatomy of a Rescue

Scenario

The team arrives at a vertical drop in the canyon. A rappel is rigged and, one-by-one, the team starts down the pitch. Two members of the team have successfully reached the bottom. A third person sets up to rappel and heads down the pitch. Suddenly, a continuous whistle blast is heard. An accident has happened …

Scene Survey

The first step in an emergency is to gather information. You need to know what's happening before you can take effective action. In aquatic canyons with significant flow, it's particularly important to have eyes on the rappeller as an immediate response may be necessary.

- If you have a clear line of sight down the pitch, it's easy to assess the situation.

- If the subject is not in sight, someone will need to get safely into a position to see what's happening. An observer might be able to move out along the rim to find a good vantage point. Other options would include self-belaying out to the edge, or rappelling down a short distance. The observer can relay their findings to the rest of the team.

Some things to determine:

- What happened? (Or: "What is happening?")
  What was the cause of the incident/accident?

- Is an urgent response required?
  If the rappeller is stuck in significant flow (or under a waterfall), an immediate response may be required. If the subject is stable and out of the water, the situation may be less urgent.

- What is the subject's condition?
  Is the subject responsive? Have they been injured? If so, what was the mechanism of injury? One other important piece of information: are they secure on the rope?

- What resources are available?
  How many team members are present and can assist? What ropes and gear are available? In some cases, the team's resources may be spread out between the top and bottom of the pitch. Rescues are almost always easier to conduct from above.[170]

How Do We Fix the Problem?

Using the information gathered in the scene survey, the leader must develop a plan for rescue. Draw upon your training and experience to come up with a solution. Coming up with a good plan under pressure is difficult, but a considered response is likely to go much better than a plan that's purely reactive in nature. When discussing accident management, the National Outdoor Leadership School (NOLS) puts it this way: "Go slow to go fast."[171]

- If the subject is in danger, seconds may count and there's no time for discussion. The leader should be prompt and decisive. The plan could be as simple as: "We're going to lower and get them out of the waterfall." Once the rappeller is out of immediate danger, the team can take a breath and figure out what needs to happen next.

- If the situation is less urgent, the leader might opt to quickly step through the plan with the team (i.e., "here's what needs to happen and why"). The goal is not to have a prolonged discussion, but to ensure that everyone's on the same page. This may also be an opportunity for others to provide suggestions and critiques to improve the plan. A good plan out of the gate can avoid wasting a lot of time later on.

Rescue Hierarchy

Rescues don't need to be complicated. It's actually best to start with the simplest and most low-risk solution that you think can achieve the goal. Simple techniques require less training and there are fewer things that can go wrong. If the effort proves unsuccessful, move on to a more complex solution.

Here's a list of rescue techniques in order of increasing complexity:

o	Self-Rescue	- The subject solves the problem on their own.
o	Quick Lift	- The rescuers give the subject a short, temporary lift.
o	Lower	- The subject is lowered from above.
o	Contact Rescue	- A rescuer descends to the subject to provide assistance.
o	Hauling	- The subject is raised all the way back to the top of the pitch.

The best course of action will, of course, be situationally dependent. If the subject is stuck under a waterfall or is already close to the bottom, lowering might be the best option. Similarly, if the subject is close to the top of the pitch or it'd be dangerous to lower, consider hauling to bring them back up. A quick lift might be used to help a rappeller with a jammed descender or trapped foot.

---

[170] Tip: In some cases, you might be able to use the reserve rope to haul any required gear back up to the top.
[171] Ostis, Nate. *NOLS River Rescue Guide*. Stackpole Books, 2015.

Limiting Factors

Here are some other things to think about when developing the rescue plan:

- Do you have sufficient resources (i.e., talent and gear) for this method of rescue?

- How long will the system take to rig? Do we have the luxury of time?

- What are the risks of using this technique? The rescuers are never expected to place themselves in danger. Don't make a bad situation worse by creating more victims.

- Does this technique require favorable terrain? What anchors are available? Ideally, all anchors in a rescue should be bombproof.

Other Notes

- Emergencies can be very stressful. Try to remain calm and focus on what you're doing.

- Stay within your training. Stick with techniques that you're familiar with and have practiced. A rescue is not the time to try out new tricks that you just learned on the internet.

- Good communication is key to a successful rescue. The rescuers may need to communicate with one another and the subject. Verbal communication, however, can be very difficult in aquatic canyons and on long/complex pitches. If possible, stay in contact with the subject and keep them updated.

Execute the Plan

Once a plan has been settled on, it should be put into action. The leader will delegate and supervise. If possible, they should avoid becoming involved in hands-on tasks (ex: building anchors, lowering, and patient care) and focus instead on the big picture. The leader might have to get involved, however, if manpower is lacking, or if they're the only person with a required skillset. Consider the case where everyone else present is a beginner.

Keep re-assessing the situation. If the current plan isn't working, it may be time to try a new approach. It's totally okay for the plan to change and evolve. Solicit input from others and keep trying.

- Anyone on the team can call for a halt at any time. If you see something that looks wrong, say something. It's easy to make mistakes under pressure.

Self-Rescue

If the subject is capable, individual self-rescue is often the preferred solution.[172] No action is required by the team and only the subject is at elevated risk. The team should still monitor the situation and be ready to respond. Depending on the situation, self-rescue can take many different forms. We'll look at some selected problems and what might be done to self-rescue in Chapter 24.

Here are some general solutions:

- If any convenient ledges or footholds are available, standing up and unweighting the rope momentarily might be all you need to solve the problem.

- If natural features are lacking, it might be time to break out the ascending gear. An ascender with an accompanying foot loop provides a quick place to stand up. In a worst-case scenario, you may need to transition and climb back up the rope a short distance.

Limitations

- Self-rescue might not be possible in high flow or if stuck under a waterfall.

- Beginners might not know how to self-rescue and others haven't practiced in awhile. In some cases, the team might be able to coach the subject through the process.

- Does the subject have sufficient gear for a self-rescue? If not, here are some options: 1) clip the required gear to the rappel rope and zip it down, 2) lower the gear using the reserve rope, or 3) a rescuer rappels to deliver the gear in person.

- In rare cases, the subject might know how to self-rescue, but is unable to do so. For example, the subject's hair or a beard is caught painfully in the descender. If the situation is severe, the subject will be doing their utmost to keep their hair from getting torn out by the roots.

Transitions, ascending, and knot-passing are all great ways to practice self-rescue. Ideally, all canyoneers should be fully proficient in mid-rope maneuvers.

Quick Lift

If self-rescue isn't feasible, the team will need to take action. One of the simplest things the rescuers can do is give the subject a quick boost upwards. This might be done with the rappel rope (i.e., direct hauling) or via a drop loop. Lifts are usually short and temporary. The idea is to raise the rappeller enough to fix the problem, then lower them back down to finish the rappel. Usually, lifts are short; often, a matter of centimeters or inches. Again, only the subject is at elevated risk.

A quick lift can be used to solve a number of problems:

- Entrapment. If the rappeller's foot is caught in a constriction, a quick boost upwards might enable them to escape. Lifting can also help someone who's caught on a terrain feature (ex: snagged harness or pack).

- Jammed descender. A quick lift with a drop loop (or drop line) will cause the rappel rope to go slack. With the rappel device unweighted, the rappeller can easily clear the jam.

- If the subject is close to the top of the pitch, a short lift could be used to bring them back up to the anchor.

---

[172] Confusingly, the term *self-rescue* is also used to describe a small recreational team performing their own rescue. If the team is unable to handle the problem on their own, they'll probably need outside assistance.

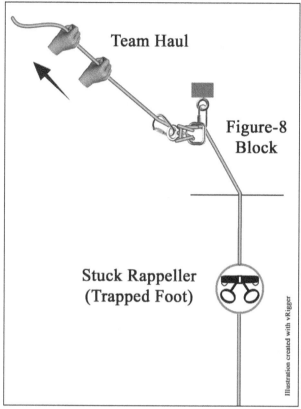

Team Haul

Figure-8 Block

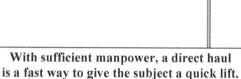

Stuck Rappeller
(Trapped Foot)

With sufficient manpower, a direct haul
is a fast way to give the subject a quick lift.

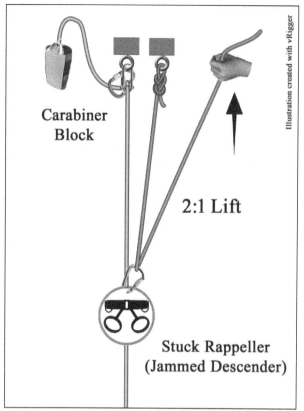

Carabiner Block

2:1 Lift

Stuck Rappeller
(Jammed Descender)

A short lift with a drop loop
will unweight the original rappel rope.

Other Notes

- A progress capture is probably unnecessary for a short, temporary lift.

- The above-right example shows a separate rope being used as a drop loop. If there's sufficient reserve rope atop the pitch (i.e., in the rappel rope bag), it could also be used. In this case, the two systems should be isolated from one another. (See "Hauling with a Drop Loop" in Chapter 21.)

- If lifting the rappeller isn't working, you might consider:

  o Increasing the mechanical advantage.
  o Lowering the rappeller instead. If a static system is being used, it could be converted to a lower.
  o Sending someone down to assist.

Limitations

- Lifting the rappeller will be harder in high flow. You'll also be fighting the force of the water.

- Beware lifting/hauling on marginal anchors. Ideally, anchors used for hauling should be bombproof. (See "Anchors for Hauling" in Chapter 21.)

- Jammed descender: Note that a direct haul will not unweight the rappeller's descender, so this is not a good technique if the intent is to help the subject clear the jam. A direct haul could be used, however, to bring someone with a jammed device back up to the top of the pitch.

- Drop loops (and drop lines) work best when the subject is relatively close to the top of the pitch. Getting the rope to the rappeller could be difficult if they're too far away, in significant flow, or the pitch is full of obstacles. The subject must also be conscious and capable of connecting the rope to their harness.

Lowering

Lowering is one of the most common forms of rescue. With a releasable system, it's easy to unlock and lower the rappeller. It's even faster if the system is unlocked and being manned by a belayer. During a lower, both gravity and edge friction are working in your favor.

Some reasons to lower:

- Aquatic canyons: Lowering might be the only solution if the rappeller is stuck under a waterfall.

- The subject is already close to the ground.

- Insufficient rope was paid out during deployment, or the rope was severed by rockfall.

- The rappeller encounters a core shot in the rope. In some cases (ex: inexperienced rappeller), it might be safer to lower rather than requiring them to pass a knot.

- An injured team member who cannot manage the rappel on their own.

The belayer might not need to lower the subject all the way to the bottom. In some cases, a short lower might be enough to move the rappeller out of danger. In the case of a jammed descender, a rappeller could be lowered to a safe ledge where they can stand up to fix the problem.

Limitations

In an emergency, it may be instinctive to lower immediately. Be aware: lowering can sometimes make the situation worse.

- Do you have enough rope to lower with? If you don't, lowering is not an option.

- Can you lower? If the rigging is static, it'll need to be converted to a releasable system.

- Where will the rappeller go if lowered? Lowering may not be a good plan if it would place the subject in greater danger (ex: lowering into a hydraulic). Also: how much rope is hanging below the rappeller? If the rappeller would be lowered into a turbulent pool, you may create an entanglement hazard.[173]

- If the subject is caught in a constriction (i.e. vertical entrapment), lowering could strand them in the middle of the pitch or invert them on the rope. Similarly, if the rappeller is caught on a terrain feature, lowering won't help.

- Lowering works best when the subject is aware and capable of action. An incapacitated or unconscious person may be prone to injury or getting stuck. Lowering an unconscious person into a pool is definitely a bad idea. If the subject is incapacitated, it may be better to send someone down to assist.

> **Lowering vs. Bottom Belay**
> If the subject is being held in place with a bottom belay, use caution when you start to lower. Once the lower begins, the rope below the rappeller will go slack. As a bottom belay only functions when the rope is taut, lowering could drop the subject. The belayer should quickly take in rope to prevent a fall. Good communication is key.

---

[173] If the subject is in danger under a waterfall (and raising is not an option), should we lower them into a turbulent pool? This is going to be a tough call to make. In the pool, at least the rope would be unweighted and the subject might have a fighting chance to escape. If other team members are already at the bottom, they may be able to assist.

Contact Rescue

If lowering isn't an option, a rescuer may need to descend to the subject. However, this should only be done if it's safe to do so.[174] In a contact rescue, multiple individuals are now at elevated risk. Fortunately, such rescues are quite rare. They also include some of the most complicated and least-practiced of all rescue skills.

Before sending anyone down, the team should have a plan. In some cases, coordination will be required between the rescuer and those atop the pitch. Again, follow the KISS principle. Don't go for a complex solution out of the gate if a simple one would suffice. Here are some options:

- General Assistance
  The rescuer might:
    o Provide support or coaching to an inexperienced rappeller.
    o Deliver a rope or needed gear to the subject, allowing them to self-rescue.
    o Assist the subject through a difficult area.
    o In the event of injury, apply immediate first aid (ex: staunch bleeding).

- Local Lift
  The rescuer gives the rappeller a quick boost upwards. This is a quick lift that's performed locally instead of from atop the pitch.[175] Once the situation, is resolved, the subject finishes the rappel.

- Assisted Lower or Haul
  The rescuer descends to the subject and remains with them while the team lowers or hauls from above. This might be done to help an injured or unconscious patient through difficult terrain.

- Pick-off
  The rescuer descends and transfers the subject to the rescue rope. Both individuals perform a *tandem rappel* to the ground.

Other Prerequisites

- The anchor must be able to support multiple individuals at the same time. A human anchor could still be used, however, to get someone down quickly to the subject.

- Does the team have sufficient ropes and gear for the operation in mind? Required gear can be sometimes be scavenged from the subject.

Approaching the Subject

Usually, the rescuer descends to the subject on a separate rope. The rescuer might rappel, downclimb (possibly on a belay), or be lowered from above. If time is of the essence, don't bother with any fancy rigging. Tie the rope to an anchor, rappel down, and worry about rope recovery later. (Yes, someone may need to re-ascend.)

- **WARNING!** If using the reserve rope, the rappel and rescue systems should be isolated from one another. Imagine the case where there's a block system at the anchor and a rescuer rappels down the unblocked side (i.e., with no safety in play). If the rappel rope were to become unweighted, the rescuer would fall.

- Don't hit the subject with the rescue rope or rope bag during deployment. It may be better to take the bag with you on rappel. Also, try to avoid knocking rocks on the subject from above.

---

[174] Possible hazards would include high flow, waterfalls, loose rocks, or an angry wasp nest.
[175] FAQ: "Why would we need to perform a local lift?" In some situations, a lift from above may not be possible. For example: if the rappeller has a jammed descender, a direct haul won't help, and a drop loop won't work if there's insufficient rope (or they're too far away). A local lift might be an option in such cases.

Secure the Subject

Upon arrival, the rescuer's first priority is to make sure the subject is secure on the rope. If the subject is capable, you can ask them to lock off their descender. Alternatively, you can clip a tether (or other pre-rigged sling) to their harness. This will keep the subject from going anywhere until you sort out the situation.

Local Lift

Once the subject is secure, the rescuer can provide a quick boost upwards. This is a contact rescue technique that might be used to help someone with a jammed descender. Unweighting the subject's rope momentarily might be all that's needed to clear the jam.

Here are several options for a local lift:

Hero Lift

A quick and dirty method is to grab both sides of the subject's harness and pull upwards. This is a brute-force technique that works best with smaller individuals on low-angle terrain. It's fast to implement and requires no other gear.

Provide a Foot Loop

Another simple solution is to install a rope grab on the subject's rope with an accompanying foot loop.[176] The subject can then step up to unweight their descender. It's an assisted self-rescue.

Lifting with a Pig Rig

If stepping up in a foot loop is not feasible for some reason, another option would be to lift the subject with a pig rig. This method requires a long sling, cordelette, or short section of rope. The slack rope hanging below the subject could even be used in a pinch.

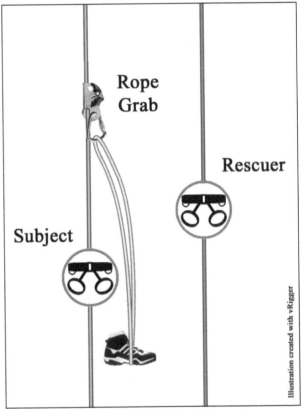

A simple contact rescue: give the subject a foot loop to step up in.

1) Rappel to the subject, stopping just above them, but still within reach. Lock off to go hands-free.

2) Verify that the subject is secure on the rope.

---

[176] The rope grab should be installed on the subject's rope due to rope stretch.

3) Install a rope grab with a locking pear-abiner on the subject's rope. This will be the high point for the lift system. Clip another pear-abiner to the subject's harness.

4) Create the bridge. Clip the sling, cordelette or rope into the high point. Run it down through the subject's carabiner, then back up again through the high point. This creates a 2:1 MA system with a change of direction as shown in the diagram. From here, the MA could be increased to 4:1 by passing the sling one more time through both carabiners.

   o (Optional) A foot loop could be added. This would allow the rescuer to add their bodyweight to the pull.

5) Lift the subject. The rescuer needs to raise the subject enough to unweight their descender; this might be a matter of centimeters or inches. With the descender unweighted, the jam is cleared. The subject then re-establishes their descender on the rappel rope and locks off.

   o The subject might be able to make the lift easier by pulling themselves up on the rappel rope.

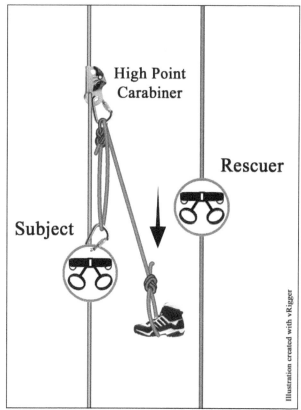

Lifting the subject with a 2:1 pig rig.

   o If the subject needs assistance clearing the jam, the rescuer can tie off the bridge (e.g., mule-overhand or mariner's hitch) to the high point and go hands-free.

   o If the subject is nervous about continuing the rappel on their own, the rescuer might opt to perform a pick-off instead. (We'll talk more about pick-offs momentarily.)

6) The subject is lowered back down to re-weight their descender. Once accomplished, disconnect the subject from the bridge. The subject can then unlock and finish the rappel on their own.

7) The rescuer cleans the bridge and high point.

Once the situation has been resolved, the rescuer could return to the top of the pitch or rappel to the bottom.

Pick-off Rappels

A pick-off is a contact rescue technique which might be used to rescue a nervous, incapacitated, or unconscious rappeller. It's a one-way load transfer, where the subject is moved onto the rescuer's rope. Once accomplished, both individuals perform a tandem rappel to the ground. There are many ways to perform pick-offs. We'll look at two methods here that are most likely to be useful in the canyon world.

> **FAQ: "If the rappeller's unconscious, why didn't they fall?"**
> Perhaps the rappeller is held in place with a bottom belay, an autoblock, or a fortunate kink in the rope that got stuck in their descender. Alternatively, the subject might have landed on a ledge or gotten their harness caught on a terrain feature.

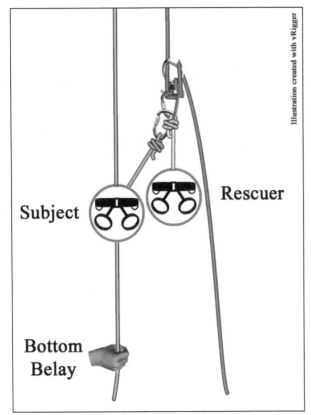

The belayer eases up on the subject's rope ...

... transferring them onto the bridge.
The subject is disconnected from their rope.

Method #1: Pick-off by Lowering

If time is of the essence, here's a quick way to perform a pick-off. The mechanism of load transfer is lowering.

1) Before leaving the top of the pitch, prepare for a tandem rappel. The rappel device should be extended on a short tether and rigged with friction for a two-person load.

2) Rappel until about level with the subject. Optional: lock off to go hands-free.

3) Verify the subject is secure on the rope. (This might be combined with the next step.)

4) Create a bridge. The easiest way to do this is to clip one of the subject's tethers to the master point of your descender (shown in blue above). Alternatively, you may need to improvise with an extra sling.

5) Transfer the subject to the rescue rope. This can happen in one of two ways:

   o If the subject is being held in place with a bottom belay, signal the belayer to ease off. The subject will be gently lowered onto their tether. Once accomplished, disconnect them from their rope.

   o Last resort: tension the bridge as much as possible, then cut the subject's rope. Tensioning the bridge will reduce the shock load to the system.

6) Unlock and perform a tandem rappel to the ground. A partner below might be able provide a bottom belay for extra security.

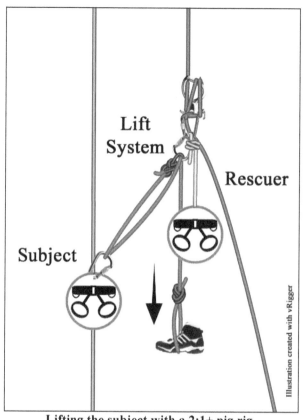

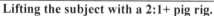

Lifting the subject with a 2:1+ pig rig.

When the rope goes slack, the bridge is tied off.
Next, the subject is disconnected from their rope.

Method #2: Pick-off by Lifting

This pick-off method has a few more steps and requires a sling, cordelette, or short section of rope. This time, the subject will be lifted to perform the load transfer.

1) Before leaving the top of the pitch, prepare for a tandem rappel. The rappel device should be extended on a short tether and rigged with friction for a two-person load.

2) Rappel to the subject, stopping above them, but still within reach.[177] Lock off your descender.

3) Verify the subject is secure on the rope.

4) Attach a locking pear-abiner to the master point of your descender. This will be the high point for the lift system. Clip another pear-abiner to the subject's harness.

5) Create the bridge. Establish a pig rig just as you would for a local lift. If needed, add a foot loop.

6) Lift and hold. The rescuer lifts until the original rappel rope goes slack. Once this happens, the pig rig is tied off to the high point. As this is a one-way load transfer, the tie-off could be static.

7) Back up the bridge. A quick backup method is to clip one of the subject's own tethers to the master point of your descender. (This step may not be necessary if you already clipped a tether to them in Step 3.)

8) Disconnect the subject from the now-slack rappel rope. (Or, as a last resort, cut the rope.) Unlock and perform a tandem rappel to the ground.

---

[177] Note that your rope will stretch when the subject is moved onto it, so getting the spacing just right is key.

Rescue from Below

Rescuing someone from the bottom of the pitch is one of the most complicated forms of contact rescue. It uses virtually every rigging system in the book. Note that this technique may not be feasible in high flow, or if the rope length was set and is not in reach. Here's the general sequence:

Ascend to the subject
- Tie a clove hitch in the tail of the rappel rope and clip it to a gear loop (i.e., bring it with you).
- Ascend to the subject and verify they're secure on the rope.
- Pass the subject like a human knot. Rescues are usually easier to conduct from above.[178]

Build a lowering system
- Add a high point carabiner to one of your rope grabs.
- Using the tail of the rappel rope, tie a figure-8 knot and clip it to the subject's harness.
- Run the rope up and tie a munter hitch on the high point. Remove as much slack as possible, then lock it off with a mule-overhand. This creates an MMO.

Move the subject onto the lowering system
- Create a separate lift system (ex: 4:1 pig rig) using the same rope grab or a different one.
- Lift the subject to unweight their descender. You'll need to tie off the bridge to go hands-free.
- Disconnect the subject from their rope.
- Release the bridge and lower to transfer the subject onto the MMO system.
- Clean the bridge.

Lower the subject
- Release the MMO and lower the subject to the ground.

Wrap up
- Clean all systems on the rope.
- Transition and rappel to the ground.

Hauling

Last on the list of rescue techniques is hauling (i.e., raising the subject all the way to the top of the pitch). Hauling is last because mechanical advantage systems are complicated and time consuming to build. With gravity and edge friction working against you, they're also slow and strenuous. Fortunately, needing to haul is quite rare. Some reasons to haul:

- The subject is already close to the top of the pitch. If the rappeller is only 3m down a 60m pitch, it might make more sense to bring them back up.

- There's not enough rope to lower with. Perhaps the beta was bad or we didn't bring enough rope.

- It would be dangerous to lower for some reason (ex: rappel exits into a dangerous water feature).

- There's some other advantage to be gained by bringing the subject up. Examples would include an opportunity to escape the canyon, or a better location to await rescue.

We've discussed haul systems quite a bit already in Chapter 21. Ideally, we want a large, safe pull area and bombproof anchors. Also, consider padding the edge to protect the rope.

---

[178] If the pitch isn't too high and time isn't a concern, another option would be to pass the subject, and ascend to the top of the pitch. Once at the anchor, convert the rigging to a lower.

Secure the Subject

Before hauling, the team must be certain that the rappeller is secure on the rope. If communication is difficult, a rescuer may need to go down and check. Ideally, the subject should also be made aware that, once the haul begins, rappelling may no longer be safe (e.g., the tail of the rope will rise further and further off the ground).

- If the subject is unconscious, a rescuer will definitely need to go down to assist. The rescuer could ascend in parallel, helping move the patient past any edges or obstacles.

Other Notes

- If the haulers can't see what's happening, an observer should be stationed at the edge to monitor and provide direction.

- It's very common to haul aggressively. A slow and steady pull is often better as the subject may need to negotiate rough terrain, obstacles, and edges.

- If the subject is capable and local terrain permits, they can assist the haul by climbing or stepping up on footholds. Beware outclimbing your haulers, however. Slack in the rope may not be safe.[179]

Limitations

- A complicated MA rigging is not a good choice if an urgent response is required.

- Forces during a haul can be substantially higher than your average rappel. Hauling on marginal anchors may not be safe.

- Hauling is harder in high flow. You'll be fighting the force of the water too.

- Use caution if the subject is being held in place with a bottom belay. If not paying attention, the haulers may find themselves playing an inadvertent tug-of-war game with the belayer.

---

[179] If the pitch is climbable, a top belay might be a better option.

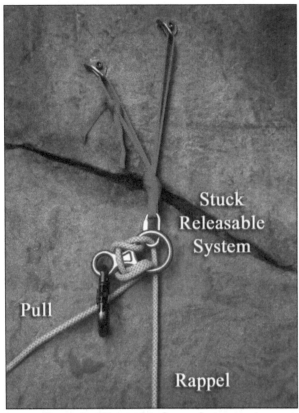

Stuck Releasable System

Pull

Rappel

Scenario: We need to lower, but cannot.
(Releasable system is stuck or the rigging is static.)

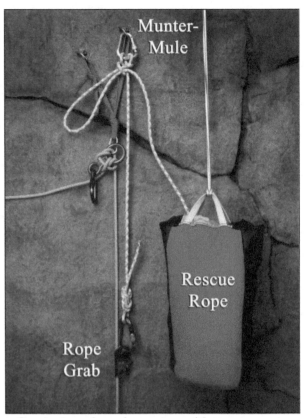

Munter-Mule

Rescue Rope

Rope Grab

Create a new lowering system with a rescue rope.
A munter-mule is tied on the anchor.

Cut the original rope and quickly tie a stopper knot.

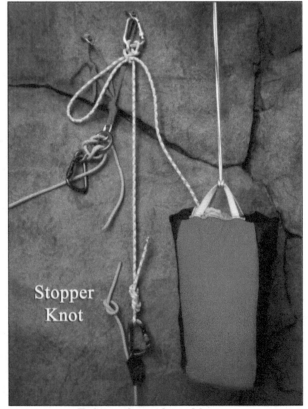

Stopper Knot

Release the mule and lower.

Cut & Lower: A Measure of Last Resort

Scenario: The rappeller is stuck under a waterfall and we're unable to lower for some reason. Perhaps the releasable system is stuck or the rigging is static (ex: static block or a fixed rope). The subject is unable to self-rescue, and the team is unable to lift or haul (possibly due to lack of ability, manpower, or gear). Sending someone down to assist is deemed too risky.

Cut & Lower is a final card to play when you're running out of options. The rescuers build a new lowering system and move the rappeller onto it by cutting the rappel rope. It's a fast one-way load transfer and requires a separate rescue rope equal to the height of the pitch. Here's the sequence:

1) Clip a pear-abiner to the anchor.

2) Tie a figure-8 knot in the end of the rescue rope and attach it to the load strand with a rope grab. A side-loading ascender is preferred for speed.

3) Run the rescue rope up and tie a munter hitch on the pear-abiner. Remove as much slack as possible and secure the munter with a mule. Don't bother with the overhand backup as seconds may count.[180]

4) Slide the ascender down until the rescue rope becomes taut. This will reduce shock load to the system.

5) **WARNING!** Cutting the wrong rope could be deadly. Triple-check everything.

6) Cut the rappel rope. The subject will drop slightly as they transfer onto the new lowering system.

   o Tip #1: Before cutting the rope, make sure you're holding the load strand just above the ascender. This will keep the cut end from getting away from you.

   o Tip #2: Cut the rope as close as possible to the anchor. The goal is to have enough slack rope above the ascender, so that you can tie a quick overhand knot. This knot becomes an emergency backstop in case the ascender should slip.

7) Release the mule and lower.

Limitations
- *Cut & Lower* has all the same prerequisites as releasable rigging. There must be enough rope atop the pitch to lower with or this technique will not work. (See "Prerequisites" in Chapter 11.)

- The ascender and knots have the potential to get snagged during the lower.

FAQ: "Couldn't we cut the anchor instead?"
In some situations, yes. Cutting a rope is never ideal. They're expensive and you might need that rope to get out of the canyon. Cutting the anchor, on the other hand, might not be the best choice if an urgent response is required. If the plan is to cut the anchor, you'll need a second one to lower from, and building anchors takes time.

- Sometimes, the anchor cannot be cut (ex: bolts or chains).

- If the anchor is cut, the original rappel rope will need to be fed out while the subject is lowered. This may complicate the situation.

---

[180] Alternatively: if a partner is present, skip the mule and ask them to hold the brake.

Chapter 24: Problems & Solutions

Continuing in the theme of canyon rescue, let's take a look at some selected problems. While nothing beats hands-on practice, working your way through thought experiments can help prepare you for contingencies in the real world. Some good questions to ask:

- What could be done to avoid the problem or reduce the odds of it happening?
- As the rappeller, what are your options for self-rescue?
- As a team member atop the pitch, how could you help the rappeller?

Each scenario that follows presents a set of possible solutions, although it's not a comprehensive list. Solutions will include skills and techniques covered in previous chapters.

Insufficient Rope Length

Scenario: Partway down the pitch, the rappeller realizes the rope is too short. The tail is hanging some 6m (~20ft) above the ground. The rope might have been poorly deployed or severed by rockfall.

This is a potentially dangerous situation as there's nothing to stop an inattentive rappeller from going off the end of the rope. Unfortunately, this is a common form of rappel accident.

Avoidance

- The first person to rappel should be one of the most experienced members of the team.

- Maintain situational awareness while rappelling. Try to get in the habit of looking down and confirming the rope length for yourself. If you can't tell (ex: the rope is hanging in a waterfall), stop and pull it up to confirm. If you need to go hands-free, lock off your descender.

- Brightly-colored ropes are good for visibility.

- A stopper knot tied in the end of the rope is one way to safeguard rappellers. They're not used frequently in aquatic canyons, however, due to the risk of getting stuck on the rope.

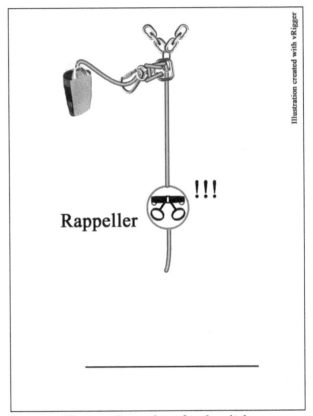

The rope is too short for the pitch.

Illustration created with vRigger

Self-Rescue

As the rappeller, some options for self-rescue would include:

- If the terrain and conditions permit, disconnect from the rope and downclimb the rest of the way.

- Signal the team above for a lower.

- Find a place nearby to build an intermediate anchor. (Possibly this will become a multi-pitch rappel?)

- Transition to ascending and climb back up to the anchor.

Team Rescue

With a releasable system, the rappeller can be lowered immediately. If the rigging is static, it could be converted to a releasable system. *Cut & Lower* could be used in an emergency. If there's insufficient rope for a lower, the rappeller could be hauled back up to the top.

- Let's say we lower until the rope reaches the bottom. Unfortunately, now the pull side is too short. To solve this problem, we could extend the pull side with any extra rope, cord, webbing, etc.

Trapped Rappeller

Illustration created with vRigger

The rappeller's hand is pinned under the tensioned rappel rope.

Pinned Hand or Arm

Scenario: The rappeller's free hand, arm, or glove has become trapped underneath the weighted rappel rope. Getting pinned is most likely to happen on an awkward or difficult rappel start.

- A similar problem can happen if your descender gets caught in a crack or snagged on a terrain feature while passing over the edge. This is more likely to happen when using rappel extension. The rappeller's own weight pins the device in place.

Avoidance

When rappelling, it's fine to hold onto the rope above your descender for balance, but try to avoid doing this on a difficult start. Instead, get as low as you can and lean back to weight the anchor. Use your free hand and knees to push yourself away from the lip. Take it slow as you pass over the edge. You'll need enough space to allow your descender to clear.

- Negotiating edges gracefully takes some practice.

- Use rappel extension only when necessary. Don't extend your device more than you need to.

- You can reduce the likelihood of anyone getting pinned by rigging for courtesy. Only the last person needs to perform the difficult start.

Self-Rescue

If you can't work your hand free, you'll probably need to unweight the rappel rope momentarily.

- If you can find a convenient ledge or foothold to step up on, the problem is solved immediately.

- If footholds are lacking, you may need to lock off and go hands-free. Locking off your descender, however, may be difficult with one hand. (Even a creating a leg wrap can be difficult.) If you're having a hard time, try a *quick lock*. This is another lock-off technique that works with most figure-8 style devices.[181] Once you're secure on the rope, reach up above the lip to see if you can find a handhold.

  If handholds are lacking, try installing a side-loading ascender with accompanying foot loop on the rope above your pinned hand. This creates a place to step up and unweight the rope.

---

[181] Quick lock: From the soft lock position, pull the brake strand up over the top of the descender. Squeeze it down into the gap between the rappel rope and the device itself. The rappeller's own weight holds the rope in place. Con: A quick lock is not secure if the descender becomes unweighted.

Team Rescue

- One solution is to provide a foot loop for the rappeller to step up in. A quick lift with a drop loop would also fix the problem. A direct haul could be used to pull the rappeller back up over the edge.

- Alternatively, you could self-belay out to the subject using either the rappel rope or the reserve. Near the edge, crouch down, and clip a short tether to the rope above the subject's trapped hand. Using leg strength, straighten up, and lift the rope just enough for the rappeller to slip free. This is a form of *vector pull*. (See also "Human Redirection" in Chapter 20.)

Jammed Descender

<u>Scenario</u>: Partway down the pitch, a foreign object becomes lodged in the rappeller's descender.[182] Getting stuck on the rope is an annoyance on a dry pitch, but could be life-threatening under a waterfall.

- A similar problem can happen if an autoblock rigged with too much friction engages on the rope. Once weighted, it can be very difficult to release.

Avoidance

Make sure the working area of your harness is clear prior to rappelling. Secure or tuck in anything that could get caught in your descender. Tie back long hair.

- Autoblocks are not used frequently in aquatic canyons due to the risk of getting stuck on the rope. You may be better off without one.

Self-Rescue

If the obstruction can't be worked free, the rappeller will probably need to unweight the descender in order to clear the jam. In a worst-case scenario, the device will need to be completely disconnected from the rope.

- If the pitch is low-angle or there's a convenient foothold nearby, standing up and unweighting the rope might solve the problem.

Getting stuck on the rope.

- Lacking footholds, you'll need to lock off and go hands-free. Install a rope grab and accompanying foot loop above the descender. This creates a place to step up and unweight the device.[183] You could also transition to ascending and climb back up a short distance.

- WARNING! It may be tempting to use a knife to cut yourself free, but use extreme caution. It doesn't take much to cut a rope that's under tension.

In extreme cases, self-rescue may not be possible. If the rappeller's hair or beard is caught in the descender, they may be contorted painfully, doing their utmost to keep their hair from getting torn out by the roots.

---

[182] Some things that can jam a descender: long hair, beards, ill-fitting gloves, fingers, loose clothing, pack straps, autoblocks, and vegetative scunge adhering to the rope.
[183] FAQ: "Could I create a makeshift foot loop with the rope hanging below me?" Unfortunately, this trick probably won't help as stepping up in the foot loop won't unweight your descender.

Team Rescue

If an immediate response is required, lowering might be the best option. If the situation is less urgent and the subject is relatively close to the top of the pitch, a quick lift with a drop loop lift would unweight the descender. (A drop loop might not work, however, if the subject is too far away or incapable of action.) If the subject is close to the top of the pitch, a direct haul could be used to bring them back up. If conditions permit, a rescuer could be sent down to assist (ex: provide coaching, a foot loop, or local lift).

- If there's a convenient ledge (or foothold) below, the subject could be lowered there. The rappeller can then stand up and clear the jam.

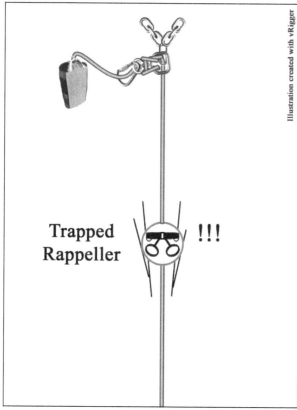

Illustration created with vRigger

Trapped Rappeller !!!

The rappeller is caught in a constriction mid-way down the pitch.

Vertical Entrapment

Scenario: Partway down the pitch, the rappeller's foot (or other extremity) gets caught in a constriction. Full body entrapment is also possible if passing through a tight squeeze. On a dry pitch, getting stuck might be an annoyance. Getting trapped under a waterfall has led to fatal accidents.

- A similar problem can happen if the subject's harness or pack gets caught on a terrain feature. This might happen on a difficult rappel start.

Avoidance

Part of situational awareness is watching where you're placing your feet. Beware cracks, constrictions, and leg-eating potholes. A narrow gap between boulders can also be an entrapment hazard. The best advice: try to stay out of constrictions. Take it slowly and watch where you're placing your feet. If possible, try to stem your way over or slide past the obstacle.

In aquatic canyons, entrapment hazards can also be hidden under the water. Use caution any time you see water pouring into a large crack or fissure. In high flow, consider using a different anchor or rappelling outside the watercourse.

- If the station manager observes slack (or a decrease in tension) in the rappel rope, this might mean the rappeller made it safely to the bottom. It also could mean that they landed on a ledge and momentarily unweighted the rope. A third possibility: they're trapped or have gotten stuck on a terrain feature. If the station manager can't see what's happening, an observer should be stationed at the edge.

Self-Rescue

If you get a foot stuck, don't allow any more rope to pass through your descender. Getting stuck is bad, but becoming inverted on the rope is worse. Hanging upside-down by your foot complicates everything.

- With your free hand, try to find a convenient handhold to pull yourself up with. In some cases, you might be able to use the rope itself. If you need to, lock off your descender.

- Try to work your foot free. While not ideal, jettisoning your footwear might work in some situations. The next rappeller can hopefully retrieve it for you.

- Stepping up in a foot loop might provide enough leverage to escape. A quick and dirty solution: use the slack rope hanging below you to create a makeshift foot loop. Alternatively, install a side-loading ascender and foot loop on the rope above. If stepping up doesn't work, you'll need to transition to ascending.

Team Rescue

In an emergency, there may be a strong instinct to lower the rappeller. This is a situation where lowering can actually make the situation worse.

The best option in this situation is probably a quick lift with the rappel rope. If you have sufficient manpower atop the pitch, a 1:1 haul might work in some situations. Otherwise, you'll probably need to build an MA system. The goal is to lift the subject just enough to escape.

- Note that lifting/hauling may be very difficult in high flow. The team's options for rescue in this situation are extremely limited. Sending someone down to assist may be too dangerous. If there's potential for entrapment, rappelling outside the flow may be the safer option.

Discovering a core shot in the rope.

Core Shot

Scenario: Partway down the pitch, the rappeller discovers a core shot in the rope.

Avoidance

Situational awareness includes watching the rope for damage. Try to get in the habit of looking down the pitch to see where you're going. Core shots are often encountered in places where the rappel rope passes over an edge.

- If the core shot is not spotted in advance, you're likely to encounter it first with your hand. Gloves may work against you here.

- Beginners are more likely to damage ropes due to inattention and poor rappel technique. Jumping, bouncing, and sudden stops should be discouraged.

- Beware straying too far off the rappel line. An inadvertent pendulum swing can damage a rope if it's dragged laterally over a sharp edge.

- Take precautions to protect your rope by choosing good anchors, padding edges (if appropriate), and rope creeping. Instead of a single long rappel, consider a series of shorter ones.

Self-Rescue

WARNING! Continuing to rappel past a core shot is risky. Ropes are strong, but a core shot is a big red flag. Try to lock off the descender before reaching the damaged area. Ideally, the core shot should be isolated by tying it off inside an alpine butterfly knot. This ensures the damaged section will no longer be loaded or rappelled on.

- If the rappeller is inexperienced (i.e., unfamiliar with knot-passing) or is close to the bottom of the pitch, signaling the team for a lower may be the fastest and safest option.

- If lowering isn't an option, you'll probably need to do one of the following:

  o Is it possible to downclimb? Or is there a place nearby to build an intermediate anchor?
  o Break out the ascending gear and climb back up.
  o Pass the knot and finish the rappel.

Once in a safe place, signal the team above that there's a problem. Hopefully, the team can re-rig at the anchor to avoid any further knot-passing. (For more information, see "Passing Knots: While Rappelling" in Chapter 18.)

Team Rescue
If there's sufficient reserve rope atop the pitch, lowering is an option. If reserve rope is lacking (or it would be dangerous to lower for some reason), the team could haul the subject back to the top. Once the rappeller is in a safe place, hopefully we can re-rig the system.

Rappelling through High Flow
<u>Scenario</u>: The team finds a great anchor atop the pitch, but the rappel line passes through a high-flow waterfall.

Avoidance
Just because someone left an anchor does not obligate you to use it. The anchor might have been left by a group who ran the canyon when the water levels were low. Are there any better anchors available? Could a redirect or guided rappel be used to keep team members out of the torrent?

If entering high flow is unavoidable, here are some things that can be done to improve safety:

- Make sure the working area of your harness is clear prior to rappelling. Secure or tuck in anything that might be liable to get caught in your descender or on terrain features.

- Send the packs down separately.

- The anchor should be rigged releasable and manned by a belayer. If the belayer's visibility is limited, an observer should be stationed at the edge to provide direction.

Rappelling in high flow.

Self-Rescue
Your options for self-rescue may be extremely limited in high flow. Before entering the danger zone, keep the whistle at the ready in your mouth. This avoids the need to go fumbling for it in an emergency.

- Be prepared to go back up. Side-loading ascenders are preferred in aquatic canyons as they're fast to install on the rope. Your ascenders should be ready on your harness before leaving the top of the pitch.

- Turn sidewise to the flow. By presenting a narrower profile to the torrent, you can reduce the amount of force acting upon you.

- Last resort: consider cutting the rappel rope. A broken leg is better than drowning while stuck on the rope.

Team Rescue

If the rappeller gets into trouble, lowering may be the fastest solution. (Be aware: In some cases, lowering can make the situation worse.) Lifting/hauling may be very difficult in high flow, and sending someone down to assist may be too dangerous.

- If the situation is severe, a ground contingency could be rigged for the last rappeller. If the last person gets into trouble, they can be lowered from the bottom of the pitch.

- Last resort: if the belayer is unable to lower for some reason (ex: a stuck releasable system), desperate measures may be called for. *Cut & Lower* is one solution. If the pitch isn't too high and there's a deepwater landing, another option is to cut the rappel rope. This is going to be a tough call to make.

Pulling the Rope

!!!

Illustration created with vRigger

Uh oh ... The rope is stuck!

Stuck Rope

<u>Scenario</u>: The team made it down safely, but the rope got stuck during the pull. Why is it stuck? Possibly, the last person forgot to remove the safety, the rope is trapped (ex: pull side pinching the rappel strand), or the block has gotten snagged somewhere.

- A similar problem can happen if a loop of rope falling down the pitch gets caught on a rock horn or other terrain feature.

Avoidance

There are many ways to reduce the odds of getting a rope stuck. Here are a few important ones:

- Try to find an anchor with a direct line of sight to the pull area at the bottom of the pitch.

- Before departing, the last person should verify that the rope can be pulled from below. Try a test pull. Double-check the safety has been cleaned.

- The last person should take special care to ensure the rappel and pull lines do not cross or tangle. Try to avoid situations where the pull line would cross and pinch the rappel rope. If the two lines must cross for some reason, try to position the pull side so as to be underneath the rappel line.

- Most important of all: when pulling the rope, watch the tail going up to make sure no knots or tangles get pulled up out of reach.

Move Back Further

When the pull becomes "sticky," don't apply too much force too soon. Try gentle tugs from different locations. Moving back from the base of the pitch and finding higher ground may also help. Teams frequently don't move back far enough before beginning the pull. The wider the angle the rope makes relative to the top of the pitch, the lower the edge friction will be. If you have a clear line of sight to the anchor, that's even better.

- Try giving the rope a strong circular whipping motion. This may be enough to get it to jump up out of a crack or pinch that it's caught in.

- If a block system is in use and you can reach both ends, you may be able to pull down on the rappel side to return the block to the anchor. If successful, try the pull again from a different direction.

- If a loop of rope is caught on a terrain feature (ex: rock horn) and both ends are within reach, try pulling one side, then the other. Flipping the rope up and away from the canyon wall might work too.

Increase the Force
If the rope remains stuck, slowly increase the amount of force applied. Here are some options:

- Start by attaching yourself to the rope (ex: an ascender on a tether). This allows you to add your leg strength to the pull. If this proves insufficient, attach a foot loop, and step up to load the rope with full bodyweight.

- Add more haulers to the pull.

- Build a ground anchor and rig an MA system on the pull side to retrieve the rope. You could also try a sudden release technique. Pull the rope until it's completely taut, then release it suddenly (ex: using a Valdotain Tresse as a progress capture). The sudden release might be enough to jar the rope free.

Ascending
WARNING! Ascending a stuck rope can be extremely dangerous; this has been the cause of fatal accidents. Whether or not the rope is safe to climb depends on the rigging and situation above. If you don't know what's going on up at the anchor, it's better to err on the side of safety.

- If both ends of the rope are within reach and the rope is still passing through the anchor, a ground anchor could be rigged on one side, allowing a climber to ascend on the other.

Measures of Last Resort
If you've given it your all and the rope is still isn't budging, it might be time to consider abandonment. Hopefully, you can come back and reclaim it another day. In a worst-case scenario with no hope of future recovery (or you're going to need all the rope you can muster to escape the canyon), consider cutting the rope and taking what you can.

- If you need to cut a rope, try to cut it as high as possible to maximize the amount you can salvage. If feasible, standing on the shoulders of a partner will give you a greater reach.

Wim Aarts and Ashley Drisoll at Covell Creek Falls, Wash.
(Photo: Wade Hewitt)

Chapter 25: Canyon First Aid

Deep in the canyon, outside help may be hours or days away and first aid skills can save lives. Patient care, splinting and evacuation techniques are beyond the scope of this manual, but classes are offered by many outdoor organizations. Your canyon training is incomplete without it. This chapter provides a high-level overview and we'll look at some special challenges posed by aquatic canyons.

- A typical Wilderness First Aid (WFA) class is 2–3 days in length, although hybrid courses (e.g., online learning) are also available that reduce the number of onsite hours. A Wilderness First Responder (WFR) course is much longer at 9–10 days, but is the standard for outdoor leaders, guides, and rescue teams.

- It's important to stay sharp and recertify your skills every few years.

Before Entering the Canyon

Get to know your team ahead of time and have a quick talk before entering the canyon. What level of first aid training, if any, do they have? Similarly, does anyone have any medical conditions that the group should know about? If, for example, you carry an inhaler or epinephrine kit (aka EpiPen), it's a good idea to let the team know in advance. Where do you keep it and what needs to happen in an emergency?

- Ideally, the team should have a designated person outside the canyon (usually a friend or family member) who knows where you're going and when you're expected back. If the team fails to report in by the appointed hour, the contact can initiate a rescue.

- Be aware: it's easy to underestimate how long it'll take to run a given canyon. If a team is overdue, it's often because it took longer than expected. You may want to build some extra time into your estimate to account for delays and communication failures (ex: dead phone battery).

- In North America (including the United States, Mexico, and Canada), the emergency phone number to call is 9-1-1. It's also a good idea for the team to have the contact information for the local land managers. As a precaution against dead phone batteries, multiple team members should have the numbers to call for help. Another good thing to know: where is the nearest hospital?

- To eliminate the possibility of losing car keys mid-canyon, they can be hidden on or near your vehicle. Make sure other team members know where the key is located.

First Aid Kit

While team members might carry a personal first aid kit as part of the *Ten Essentials* (i.e., for basic wound care, blisters, and personal medications), the team should bring a more comprehensive kit for emergencies. It's good to be prepared for common canyon injuries and environmental concerns. (See also "First Aid Kits" in Chapter 3.)

- The contents of a first aid kit can be tailored to your trip. A more comprehensive kit might be desired for remote canyons and multi-day adventures.

- A small dry keg makes a great waterproof container. Dry bags are lighter in weight, but can seep after prolonged immersion. Dry bags can also rupture on a hard impact, and may be prone to getting punctured (ex: by a writing implement inside the bag).

- It's good to go through your kit at least once a season and restock it. Check the expiration date on medications and other products.

Common Injuries

It's a well-known fact: canyons can be hard on both you and your gear. Cuts, scrapes, and bruises in unusual places are par for the course. Aquatic canyons may take the risk of personal injury one step further as everything underfoot is uneven and slippery. A simple slip on wet rock may be all it takes to sprain an ankle or twist a knee. Putting out a hand to stop a fall could result in a sprained wrist or broken finger.

Fortunately, more severe injuries are relatively rare when canyoning. Jumps gone wrong (i.e., the depth wasn't checked in advance) are likely to break ankles and legs. Falling may be the result of slipping near an edge (i.e., not clipped into an anchor), rigging mistakes, anchor failure, or a loss of control while on rappel. (See also "Anticipation & Avoidance" in Chapter 23.)

- According to *Rigging for Rescue* in Ouray, Colorado about one third of all canyon accidents take place while moving between rappels.

- Desert Southwest: Open injuries may be prone to infection if wading/swimming in stagnant water.

Thermoregulation

Another issue faced by canyoneers, particularly in aquatic canyons, is environmental exposure. Cold water saps heat quickly from the body and hypothermia can happen any time of year. Immersion in fast-moving water accelerates the heat loss. Having proper water protection is crucial.

Ironically, overheating can also be a danger when canyoning. It's often brought on by strenuous activity while wearing a wetsuit on a hot summer day. It's actually possible for the same person to suffer from both hypothermia and heat exhaustion on the same trip.

---

[184] Note that some models cannot send an *SOS* until a GPS position has been established.

If you're getting cold ...

If you're getting cold, take a moment out and do something about it. Cooling generally results from exposure to cold water. A secondary source is evaporative cooling (i.e. water evaporating from the outside of your wetsuit). This is why you can get cold while standing around, even if fully out of the water. Breezy conditions and spray will amplify the effect, turning your wetsuit into a full-body swamp cooler.

Adequate water protection makes a huge difference in your canyon comfort and the perceived fun factor of the trip. With sufficient layers/insulation, you'll be jumping in every pool you can find and floating around merrily while waiting for your turn on rappel. Inadequate water protection, on the other hand, will result in a cold, stressful experience while doing your utmost to stay out of the water. Your fun factor will plummet.

Some things you can do to warm up:

- Avoid large groups. The more people on your team, the longer it'll take to move through technical sequences. This often means more time waiting around and more opportunities to get cold.

- Find a place to get out of the water. Look for a dry sunny location where you can warm up for a bit.

- Stay active. Do some cardio exercises and keep moving around. Hike up and down the local canyon, climb up and down on nearby rocks, stuff rope bags, etc. Keep yourself busy.

- Add layers. Extra layers of neoprene might be worn for insulation. A hood or warm hat under your helmet will also help. A thin shell worn over your wetsuit helps block heat lost by evaporation.

- Keep snacking and have an occasional drink of water to keep your energy level up. A thermos with a hot drink or soup is wonderful on a cold day.

- Accelerate the team's progress down the canyon. Consider opening more rappel stations, using twin systems, or sending a rigging team ahead to set up the next rappel.

Hypothermia

Hypothermia is brought on by prolonged exposure to cold. Effectively, the body is losing heat faster than it can be produced. Inactivity, inadequate water protection (ex: an ill-fitting wetsuit), prolonged immersion (ex: long swims), and weather will all contribute. Note that hypothermia doesn't affect everyone the same way. Smaller individuals may be more susceptible. Fatigue, hunger, dehydration, and stress will also play a role.

Initial symptoms manifest as shivering and a loss of manual dexterity. As the subject deteriorates, decision-making and physical coordination is affected. The subject may become confused or irritable. They may begin to stumble. Once hypothermia sets in, action must be taken to keep the situation from becoming worse. If left untreated, hypothermia can be fatal.

If you're overheating ...

It sounds impossible in an aquatic canyon, but overheating can also be an issue. Neoprene doesn't breathe and, if your wetsuit's dry, you won't get an evaporative cooling effect. On a hot summer day, strenuous activity in a wetsuit can lead to heat illness. Early symptoms include headaches, fatigue, and muscle cramping. Dehydration can also play a role. Some things you can do:

- Hop in the nearest pool and get some cold water inside your wetsuit. Soak your head to cool off.

- Take frequent breaks in the shade or while lounging in a pool.

- Remove layers. If you have a long hike ahead, consider changing out of your wetsuit or, at least, unzipping the top and rolling it down to your waist. (Tie the sleeves together to keep them out of your way.)

- Stay hydrated. Carrying lots of extra water is usually unnecessary in Pacific Northwest creeks. Instead, bring a filter (or purification tablets) and tank up as needed.

- Salty snacks are good for replenishing electrolytes.

Patient Assessment

Before treatment is provided, the rescuers may need to assess the patient. This assessment will take different forms depending on the patient's condition and how much information the rescuers have. A full head-to-toe exam might not be needed if the patient slipped on wet rock in front of you and sprained their wrist. If the patient fell while rappelling, a more thorough examination would be called for. In the latter case, the patient may have suffered other injuries that are not immediately apparent.

The *National Outdoor Leadership School* (NOLS) has developed a mnemonic tool for patient assessment that has become the standard in wilderness first aid. It's a framework for gathering information in order to provide effective treatment.

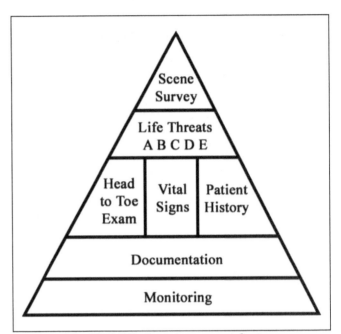

The NOLS Patient Assessment System

Scene Survey

The assessment begins with a quick survey of the situation. What happened? What was the mechanism of injury? Is it safe to approach the patient? What is their level of responsiveness? (See also "Scene Survey" in Chapter 23.)

Treat Immediate Threats

A quick assessment of the patient is carried out, looking for life-threatening issues that require immediate attention. If any are found, stop and treat them. These threats are referred to as the "ABCs" of first aid.

A – Airway	Is the patient's airway clear of obstructions?
B – Breathing	Is the patient breathing normally?
C – Circulation & Cardiac	Check their pulse and apply direct pressure to control major bleeding.
D – Decision on Disability	Are head, neck, or back injuries suspected? Consider spinal precautions.
E – Environment & Expose	Protect the patient from the environment and treat other injuries.

FAQ: "Can we move the patient?"
The party line says that the patient should not be moved until stable as there may be risk of aggravating their injuries. There are exceptions, however. The patient can be moved if they're in immediate danger, or it'd be impossible to administer first aid at the scene. For example, applying CPR in the middle of a rappel is not possible. The patient will need to be moved (raised or lowered) to a good working surface before chest compressions can be given.

- The patient will also need to be moved for environmental reasons. For example, pulling the patient out of a cold pool to prevent continued heat loss.

- Tip: A personal flotation device (PFD) will make it easier to move a patient across a deep pool while maintaining an airway.

Gather Information

Once any immediate life-threats have been dealt with, the rescuers can move on to a secondary assessment. If possible, start recording your findings on an accident form. This makes it easier to monitor the patient's condition and hand off care when outside help arrives. Try to gather as much information as possible.

- Check the patient's vital signs, including level of responsiveness, pulse, respiration rate, and skin condition.

- Consider a full head-to-toe exam to identify any additional problems. Other injuries may be less urgent, but still require attention.

- If the patient is conscious, they can provide any relevant information about their medical history. If, for example, the patient has allergies to certain medications, this would be important for the rescuers to know. Also, check for a medical-alert tag on the patient's wrist.

Once the secondary assessment has been completed, the rescuers should have a pretty good idea of what's going on with the patient. Treatment of non life-threatening injuries would take place at this time, such as splinting an injured limb.

- Stay within the scope of your training when providing first aid.

- Use the patient's gear in preference to your own. While one person is seeing to the patient, another could be going through their pack looking for dry layers, a personal first aid kit, medications, etc.

Continue to monitor and document the patient's condition. By taking the patient's vital signs at regular intervals, the team can track ongoing changes.

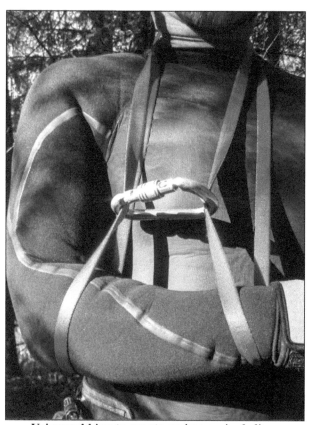

Using webbing to create an improvised sling.

Treatment

A few special notes about treatment when deep in the canyon:

- Bruising/Sprains
  In aquatic canyons, there's usually an abundant supply of cold water. If the patient has no open injuries, soaking an injured extremity might help to reduce pain and swelling. Con: This will expose the patient to cold water.

- Splinting
  In the backcountry, splints are generally fashioned from whatever materials are available. The goal is to immobilize the injury and pad it well for comfort.

  Branches found along the watercourse can be cut to size. Alternatively, some canyon packs can be disassembled for materials. The pack stays could be removed and used to create a rigid support. If necessary, consider cutting up a pack or rope bag for material.

  The team usually has plenty of webbing available. It could be used to create an improvised sling or tie up a splint. A flat overhand bend might be a good choice for tying a sling to size.

- Drowning
  If the patient is unconscious and less than an hour has elapsed, begin CPR immediately. Anyone who has inhaled water should be checked out later at a hospital, even if they recover and appear to be fine. Getting water in the lungs can result in infections which take several days to appear.

Protect the Patient

An injured patient may also need protection from the environment and shock. This is particularly important in aquatic canyons, where cold water and damp surfaces will continue to pull heat from the body.

If possible, move the patient onto an insulated surface to reduce heat loss through the ground. Even sitting on a pack or rope bag will help. Some backpacks have internals pads for support (or flotation) that can be removed. Another option is to lay out the ropes or a series of empty packs / rope bags to create an insulated surface.[185]

Wetsuit vs. Dry Clothing

The party line in wilderness medicine says to replace wet garments with dry ones. In an aquatic canyon, however, removing the patient's wetsuit may not be the best plan. Sometimes, leaving the wetsuit in place will keep the patient warmer. The rescuers will need to make a judgement call. Some things to consider:

- How much dry clothing is available? (Always use the patient's own clothing and layers first.)
- Weather conditions.
- Local environment. Can you find a dry, sheltered location nearby?
- How long will it take for outside help to arrive?

If the wetsuit is left in place, try to create a vapor barrier around the patient. An emergency blanket, rainshell, or trash bag can be wrapped around the patient. This will help block evaporative cooling.

- Wearing a wetsuit makes it harder to perform a thorough head-to-toe exam. Rescuers may be apt to miss areas of active bleeding.

- In some cases, a wetsuit left in place may function as a compression bandage.

Keep the Patient Warm

Do what you can to keep the patient warm and comfortable. Wrap the patient up in any available layers and huddle together for warmth.

- Chemical hand warmers can be used to generate heat, but, be aware, some varieties won't function if they get wet. These may be useless in an aquatic canyon.

- Emergency space blankets will block heat loss by convection. An emergency candle or tea light (used very carefully) underneath a space blanket is another way to generate/retain heat.[186]

- A tiny backpacking stove (such as the *MSR PocketRocket*) provides more options for heat (e.g., warm drinks and hot water bottles that can be tucked around the patient). These should be wrapped in a layer of clothing (or other insulation) to avoid scalding the patient.

- Is it possible to start a fire? Deep in a canyon, wood may be limited, and anything you find is likely to be wet. Consider sending some team members to see if they can find a way out of the canyon and search for dry tinder. Dryer lint or cotton balls swabbed in petroleum jelly (kept in an old film canister) are one way to get a fire going quickly. A smoky fire might be useful for helping rescuers pinpoint your position.

---

[185] Packs and gear should not be used if they'll be needed to send someone out of the canyon for help.
[186] Be aware: some mylar blankets should be kept away from open flames. Check with the manufacturer.

Shelter

If anticipating a long wait for outside help, try to find a dry place out of the water that's sheltered from airflow. The best location is one that's located away from waterfalls and spray.

For additional protection, a makeshift lean-to could be constructed. Stretch a tensioned rope over the patient, anchoring it to any convenient natural features nearby. Once in place, drape a space blanket over the rope. It could be guyed out or held in place by rocks and gear. The goal is to create a windproof enclosure that still allows the rescuers to easily check on the patient.

Protect the Team

While the patient is the center of attention in an emergency, it's also important to look out for the rest of your team. After a high-stress event, make sure everyone is doing okay. Even if no one was injured, it may be a good idea to take a break, have a quick snack and drink of water, and talk about what happened. It's a good way to take a mental step back from the event.

- If anticipating a long wait for outside help, other members of the team may want to change into dry clothing as well. Don't allow anyone to become hypothermic.

The Worst Possible Outcome

Serious injury and death are inherent risks of canyoning. No one wants to think about it, but if an accident leads to a fatality, the safety of the living always comes first. In most cases, it's probably best to exit the canyon and leave the body recovery to a Search and Rescue team. Document the accident as best as you can. Write everything down and take photos/video of the site, explaining what happened. Upon exiting the canyon, report the accident immediately and debrief as soon as possible.

Portland Mountain Rescue (PMR) conducting a mock canyon rescue.

Aftermath & Evacuation

Once the patient has been stabilized, the group needs to make a decision: can we self-evacuate, or do we need to send someone out of the canyon for help? The answer will depend on the patient's condition, local terrain, and the strength of the team. Some factors to consider:

- What's the fastest and safest way out of the canyon? Canyons are notoriously committing and, sometimes, the easiest way out may be to continue the descent. Once out of the canyon, how far is it back to the cars and civilization?

- Does the team have sufficient ropes and gear to exit the canyon?

- Can the patient to get out under their own power? An injured patient may need help overcoming technical obstacles. Is the team skilled enough to do this?

- If the team self-evacuates and the patient starts to deteriorate, is there a good place to stop?

- What environmental conditions are you facing? Weather, temperature (both air and water), and waterfall spray are all factors. Can you protect the patient from the elements?

- How much daylight is remaining? Is the team prepared to exit in the dark (i.e., sufficient headlamps), or would it be better to find a place to bivy for the night?

If the subject cannot walk, outside assistance will likely be required. Do not self-evacuate if a head, neck, or spinal injury is suspected. When in doubt, send someone for help.

Self-Evacuation

If the subject only has minor injuries, they may be able to walk out on their own. A sprained ankle or twisted knee may be tolerable. Sometimes, waiting and resting for awhile might allow the patient to recover. A person with a broken arm might be able to walk, but may need assistance getting past technical obstacles.

- The patient's gear may need to be divided up amongst the rest of the team.

- Scouts can be sent ahead to find the easiest way forward and clear away obstacles.

- Several team members can be tasked to walk with the patient. If necessary, they can provide physical support and/or short-rope the patient.

- Depending on the patient's condition, lowering might be preferred to rappelling. A guided rappel could be used to lower the patient past obstacles. A tandem rappel might be preferred in some cases.

There are a number of techniques for carrying a patient over short distances, but they're all slow and strenuous. Building a rope litter might be possible, but carrying someone over a significant distance is likely to be difficult-to-impossible. Moving a patient across fast-moving water can also be difficult or dangerous.

Remaining in Place

If the decision is made to await outside help, be patient. The group might consider moving to a better (drier) location nearby to await rescue, but, after that, stay put. Try to keep the patient as comfortable as possible, provide reassurance, and continue to monitor their vital signs at regular intervals.

- Depending on the situation, you might leave the patient's harness in place. It may be needed to get them out of the canyon. It could be loosened up for comfort, however.

Sending Someone for Help

Ideally, a minimum of two individuals should be sent for help; preferably the strongest and most experienced on the team. Don't send anyone out on their own unless absolutely necessary. (Similarly, don't leave the patient alone unless there's no alternative.) Before departing, the team should make sure those going for help have everything they need. A general list would include:

- Sufficient rope, gear, and anchor material to exit the canyon.
- Car keys. (If not hidden back at the vehicles.)
- A working cell phone or emergency beacon.[187]
- A copy of the map and canyon beta.
- A copy of the accident form. (Tip: Take a photo with a waterproof phone or camera.)
- If possible, the GPS coordinates where the patient is located.

The individuals going for help may feel pressured to move as fast as possible, but they should be deliberate and use caution. Any mistakes made while exiting will be detrimental to everyone. Don't take unnecessary risks.

- Getting all the way out to civilization may not be necessary. Just exiting the canyon might be sufficient to activate a beacon or obtain cell service. Alternatively, consider heading to a nearby high point which may increase the odds of reception.

- When placing a call for help, be sure to provide:

  - Nature of the emergency.
  - Patient's condition.
  - The patient's location (i.e., GPS coordinates).
  - Any pertinent information on how to reach the patient. How much rope is required?
  - Condition of others on the team and what gear/supplies the group has.
  - Your contact information and that of others on the team.[188] Also, your emergency contact.

- The individuals sent for help may be able to provide further assistance by meeting the rescue team and guiding them back to the group's location.

---

[187] Make sure those going for help know how to unlock/operate the device.
[188] It's good to provide multiple phone numbers for redundancy.

Afterword

At long last, you've reached the end … Or is it?

FAQ: "Where should I go from here?"

Continuing Education

While a good class or two can cover the basics of canyoning, don't stop there. There's a lot more to learn and tremendous value to be had in taking more classes. Additional training broadens your perspective, promotes safety and confidence, and will fill in any gaps in your background. You'll increase the number of tools in your toolkit, and learn to use the ones you have more efficiently. Even expert canyoneers can benefit from additional classes; both as a refresher and a way to pick up some new tricks. Keep learning.

- Seek out classes from different instructors. Everyone has their own style of teaching and different ways of doing things. You might come across a method that suits you better. In an emergency, there's definite value in knowing multiple ways to solve a problem. Don't assume you've seen everything.

- A number of canyon organizations have developed skill checklists. These outline a series of skills that one should master on the road to expertise. These lists are useful as a road map for future training.

- Try to get out and run canyons with more experienced canyoneers. This is a good way to get exposed of new techniques, different ways of doing things, and to build confidence.

- Desert Southwest: While the majority of canyons in the Pacific Northwest are aquatic, there's still value in taking dry canyon classes. There's definitely crossover in terms of techniques and it's good information to have for your next trip to the Colorado Plateau.

Support Skills

Don't limit yourself to canyon classes. Support skills are also valuable for increasing safety and self-sufficiency in the backcountry. Examples of such classes would include:

- Navigation
  Fine tune your map and compass skills, plus the ins-and-outs of GPS technology. These skills are critical for trip planning and navigation in the backcountry. Learn to use online mapping tools and other internet resources.

- Wilderness First Aid
  A multi-day wilderness first aid class is essential for canyoning. First aid skills can save lives.

- River Rescue
  River rescue classes are offered by many whitewater organizations. While boat-based skills may not be useful (except, perhaps, when pack-rafting), these classes are still a good way to learn the basics of swiftwater rescue and gain confidence in fast-moving water.

- High Angle Rescue
  Climbing organizations offer classes in mechanical advantage and high-angle rescue. While the scenarios may be different, the underlying concepts are all the same.

Continuing Practice

Even if you've taken a multitude of classes, skills will slip away if you don't practice. When was the last time you set up a guided rappel, rigged a 5:1 MA system, or practiced a pick-off? If the answer is "four years ago," it might be time for a refresher. If you don't practice, you're less likely to use these skills when the need arises in the real world. Practice is all about reinforcement and gaining proficiency with the tools in your toolbox. It's about dialing in your skills until they become second nature.

- The winter months are a great time to practice, but don't limit yourself to the off-season. When out running a canyon on a hot summer day, why not take thirty minutes to conduct a mock-rescue? How about planning a trip purely to practice your skills? If you find a nice drop in the canyon, consider setting up some ropes and running laps on it.

- Mix it up. Try practicing in a variety of locations, with different partners, different ropes, different gear, and different rigging systems. A dry pitch is a good place to start. Once you feel you've got it, try the same exercise again in a low-flow canyon.

- Going out and running canyons is practice to an extent, but it's even better when exercising skills that you don't use frequently. "We don't need a guided rappel here, but we're going to rig one anyway because we want the practice."

- Ask the "what if" questions. What if I didn't have this particular piece of gear? How would I solve this problem? If one of my ascenders were to become lost, how would I climb the rope? Can I rappel safely if I lose my descender? If this anchor wasn't here, how would we rappel? The more thought experiments you work through, the better prepared you'll be for problems in the real world.

- Canyon skill lists are great inspiration for practice. Take a look down the list. What skills haven't you worked on in awhile? Put those ones at the top of your priority queue.

A Few Final Words

Don't settle for where you are today, but keep challenging yourself to improve and become a better canyoneer. Continuing education and practice are the pathways to safety, expertise, and good decision-making. It's all about stacking the deck in your favor when running a canyon.

Pass on and share what you've learned. Seek out new canyons and new friends as you tackle new adventures.

Be safe out there and have fun!

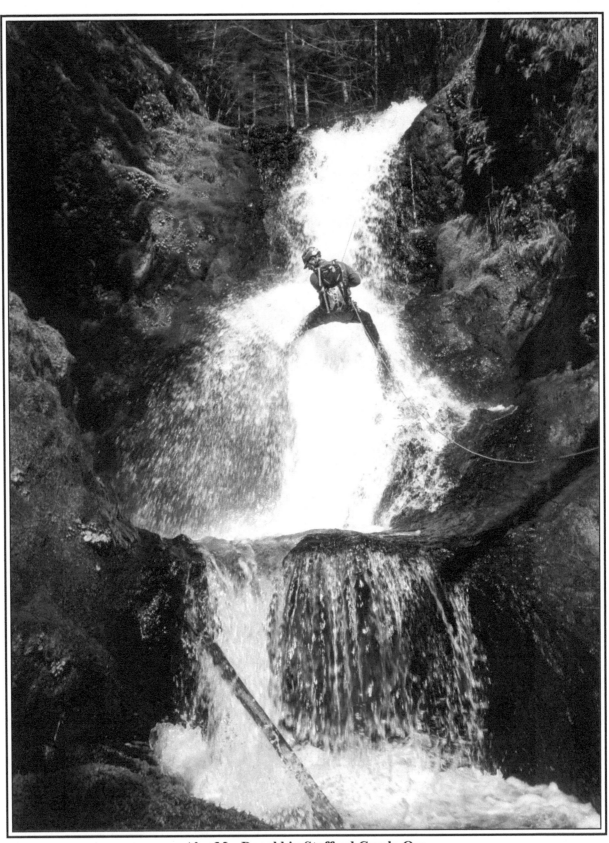

Alex MacDonald in Stafford Creek, Ore.
(Photo: Wade Hewitt)

Appendix I: Knotwork

Here's a selection of knots, bends, and hitches useful in canyoning. The golden rule of knots: make sure they're cinched and well-dressed. A well-dressed knot is stronger, safer, and easier to inspect. Knots should be practiced until proficiency is gained. They must be tied correctly every single time.

Flat Overhand Bend (EDK)

The flat overhand bend is used to join two ropes. The bend is also known as the *European Death Knot* (EDK), as it's almost too simple to be believable.

Lay out the ends of both ropes in parallel and tie an overhand using both strands. Leave about 30cm (~12in) of tail. Cinch it down to finish.

Advantages
- Easy to untie after being loaded.

- During the pull, the knot will ride up on top of the rope, making it harder to get stuck in cracks.

Disadvantages
- The knot must be well-dressed.

- The EDK can capsize and roll under large loads. If the knot were to roll off the ends, the result could be catastrophic. This has been a factor in several accidents.

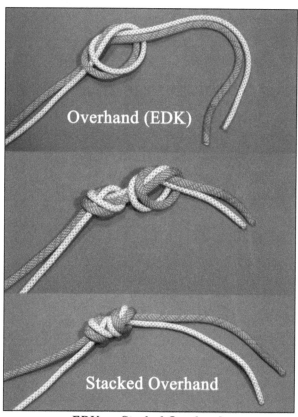

EDK vs. Stacked Overhand.

Variation: The Stacked Overhand
You can keep the EDK from rolling by tying a second overhand knot in sequence. It's tied exactly the same way as the first. This version of the bend is not as compact, but is substantially stronger.[189]

A standard EDK is appropriate for:
- SRT: attaching an unweighted pull line to a rope block system.
- DRT: only half the rappeller's weight will be suspended from the knot.

A stacked overhand is preferred if:
- The full weight of the rappeller would be suspended from the knot.
- Large loads are anticipated (ex: rescues).
- The ropes are stiff and difficult to tie.[190]
- Joining ropes of different diameter.

Summary
The stacked overhand takes a few extra seconds to tie, but is far stronger. It's good to get in the habit of using it when joining ropes. A stronger knot might be required during a rescue or if you need to lower.

---

[189] In testing, *Over the Edge Rescue* found that an EDK tied with 9mm ropes began to roll around 4-5kN, failing at around 6-7kN. The stacked overhand failed at about 9kN. (Prattley, Grant. "Which Bend for Joining Ropes?" *Over the Edge Rescue Blog. https://overtheedgerescue.com/rope-rescue/bends-joining-ropes-update*)
[190] If the rope is extremely stiff, a double fisherman bend might be a better option.

Flat Figure-8 Bend

WARNING! The use of a flat figure-8 bend for joining ropes is not recommended. This bend is surprisingly weak and, if poorly tied, has been known to roll with loads as low as 45–90kg (100–200lbs). A number of fatal accidents have been attributed to this bend.

The flat figure-8 looks quite similar to the Flemish Bend (see below), but, when placed under load, the knot is being pulled apart.

- A flat figure-8 might be tied by accident when intending to tie an EDK.

Double Fisherman

Flemish Bend

Double Fisherman Bend

Here's another classic knot for joining ropes. It's essentially a pair of barrel knots tied in opposition. It works well for joining ropes of different diameter. The tails should be at least 10cm (3–4in) long. It's easy to inspect, but the knot can be extremely difficult to untie after being loaded. It's often used for making prusik slings.

Flemish Bend (Figure-8 Bend)

The Flemish Bend is another good knot for joining ropes. To start: tie a simple figure-8 in one of the ropes close to the end. Once accomplished, "reweave" the tail of the other rope back through the figure-8 in the opposite direction. Leave at least 10cm (3–4in) of tail and cinch it down well. The bend is relatively easy to untie, but, as a slightly larger knot, it has higher odds of getting caught when it's time to pull the rope.

Barrel Knot (Double Overhand)

A barrel knot is essentially an overhand with one extra loop. Leave at least 10cm (3–4in) of tail. Some uses:

- A barrel knot tied near the end of the rope can serve as a stopper knot for narrow-aperture descenders. It also works well for pulling down a Friction Saver. (See "The Friction Saver" in Chapter 13.)

- You can also form a bight in the rope, then tie the knot back on itself. This might be used to hold a carabiner in securely in place at the end of a tether, or to tie a rope off to the inside of a rope bag.

- A double fisherman bend is two barrel knots tied in opposition. A barrel knot could also be tied to secure a bowline.

Two variations of the Barrel Knot.

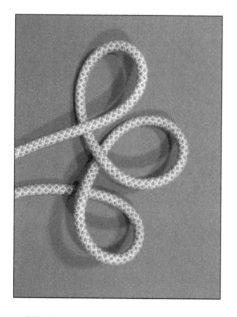

Triple Clove Hitch

The standard clove hitch can loosen up and slip under certain conditions (ex: stiff ropes and large loads). To avoid this problem, some canyoneers use a triple clove hitch when rigging a carabiner block.

The triple clove hitch is quite similar to the standard clove; it just has one more loop. Stack the loops sequentially and clip a large locking carabiner (or pear-abiner) through the center. Cinch the hitch down around the spine and pull on both strands to tighten. It's easy to tie and inspect.

- Always dress the hitch carefully. Don't rely on the weight of the first rappeller to cinch it.

Webbing & Overhand Knots

There are many ways to tie an overhand knot in webbing. Regardless of what method is used, always inspect the knot carefully. Nylon is an inherently slippery material, and it's easy to tie knots poorly. Some things to look for:

- o   Is the knot cinched and well-dressed? Pull on all opposing strands to tighten.
- o   Adequate tails. The tails should be at least 10cm (3–4in) in length.
- o   Is the knot is being loaded across its major axis? If the knot is being pulled apart, it may not be safe.

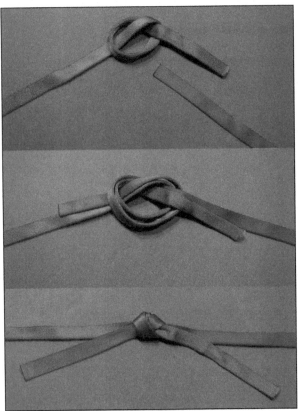

Water Knot

Water Knot (Ring Bend)

A *water knot* is actually a bend used to join two pieces of webbing. It's often used when tying slings and building anchors. To start: tie a simple overhand with no twists near the end of a piece of webbing (as shown in red). The other strand (shown in blue) is then "rewoven" in parallel all the way back through the knot in the opposite direction. Cinch down all strands.

- When placed under load, the tails will creep slightly into the knot. If a pre-existing anchor has tails less than 10cm, it should be re-rigged. Sometimes, you'll find water knots tied with extra long tails.[191]

- A water knot can loosen and slip under load if not well-tied. Always inspect the knot carefully to ensure it's securely cinched.

Overhand on a Bight

Create a bight near the end of a strand of webbing and fold it over on itself to create a loop. Push the end of the bight through the loop and cinch it down by pulling on all opposing strands. You now have a secure loop tied at the end of a piece of webbing.

Rewoven Overhand

<u>Scenario</u>: The team arrives at a drop in the canyon. There's a bombproof tree for an anchor here, but it's located 3m (~10ft) back from the top. We can build an anchor on the tree, but we'd like the master point to be situated over the edge to make the pull easier. Unfortunately, a single wrap anchor would require at least 6m (~20ft) of webbing. Is there any way to reduce how much webbing is left behind?

One option is to build an extended anchor with a *rewoven overhand*. To start: tie a simple overhand in the middle of a long piece of webbing. Run one end around the tree, then "reweave" it back through the same overhand in the opposite direction. Cinch it down well. We now have a loop of webbing tied around the tree, with one short tail and one long tail emerging from the same side of the knot. Next, run the long tail out to the edge and tie an overhand on a bight. This bight will house the quick link and become the master point for the anchor.[192] Voilà! We've built an extended anchor using about half the material that would normally be required. (Note: this anchor is not redundant.)

- If starting the rappel from the anchor's extended position would be difficult, consider rigging for courtesy. (See "Courtesy Rigging" in Chapter 4.)

---

[191] Long tails are sometimes tied off to the webbing on either side of the water knot with separate overhands.

[192] Tip: By making the bight a little larger, you can create a place for rappellers to clip in.

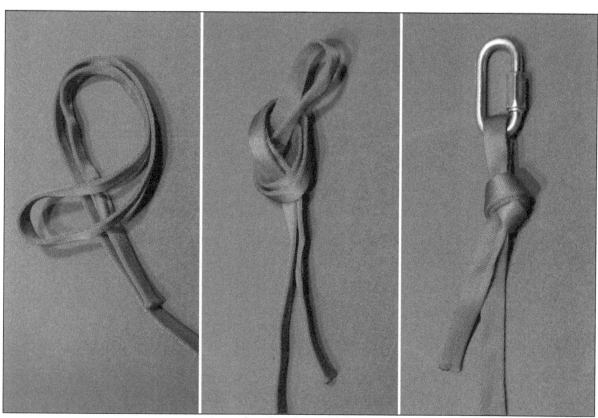

Overhand on a bight.

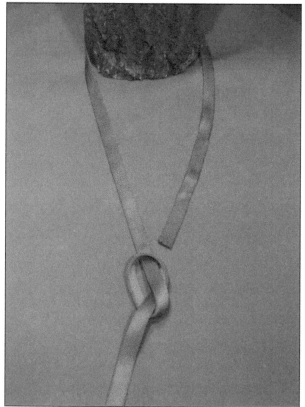

Tying a rewoven overhand.

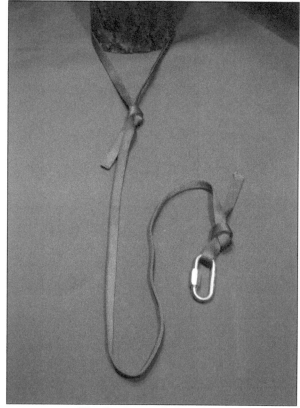

The final extended anchor.

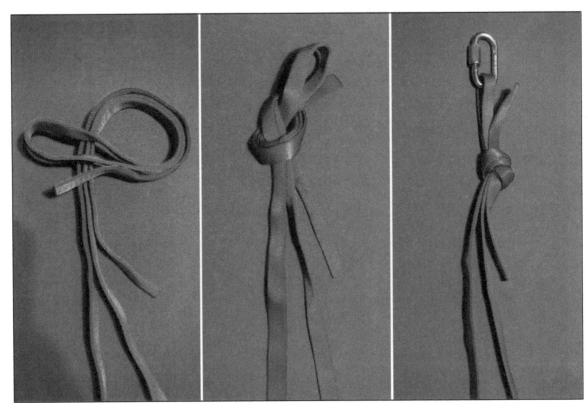

A quick way to tie a frost knot.

Frost knot tied around a tree.

Frost Knot

The frost knot is another overhand variation and a great way to build a simple anchor. It can be tied in several ways. One of the easiest is to treat it like an overhand on a bight. The only difference is an extra strand of webbing (shown in blue above for clarity) that comes along for the ride.

A frost knot can also be tied in a manner similar to a rewoven overhand. This time you're "reweaving" a bight of webbing back through the overhand instead of the tail.[193]

The final frost knot should have three strands of webbing emerging from each side.

Advantage
- You can get the anchor built, sized, and exactly where you want it before cutting any webbing.

Disadvantages
- The knot is harder to tie if you have a metal connection at the master point that can't be opened. It's easier to tie the knot, then add a quick link.

- Tying a frost knot requires more webbing than a standard water knot.

---

[193] This method is an elegant way to create an in-line master point for a courtesy anchor.

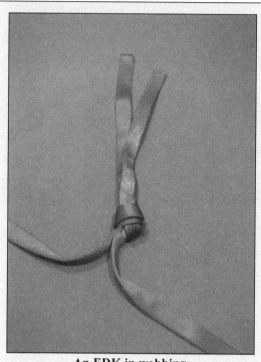

Flat Overhand Bend

Not recommended. Occasionally, you'll encounter pre-existing anchors tied with a flat overhand (i.e., an EDK in webbing). While the flat overhand is probably sufficient for a single-person load, its use in anchoring is not best practice for two reasons:

1) A standard water knot causes the anchor to lose about 30–40% of its strength, whereas a flat overhand loses about 50%.

2) Under heavy loads, the knot can capsize. If the knot should roll off the ends, the anchor will fail. A flat overhand tied with short tails has been the cause of several accidents.[194]

The chief argument in favor of the flat overhand is that it's faster to tie than a standard water knot. Adding two weaknesses to the anchor in order to save yourself a few seconds may not be the best of tradeoffs, however. If you find a pre-existing anchor tied with a flat overhand, consider replacing it as a community service.

An EDK in webbing.

---

[194] Gaines, B. *Rappelling: Rope Descending and Ascending Skills.* Falcon Guides, 2013.

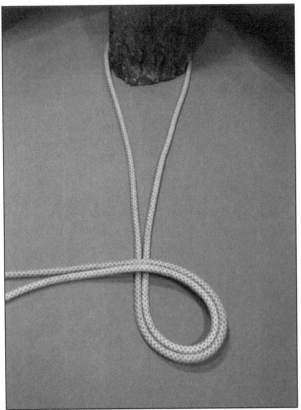

Scenario: Tying a stone knot. Create a loop.

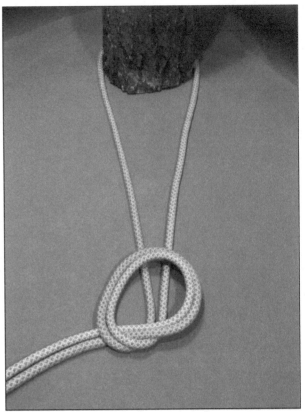

Fold the loop upwards.

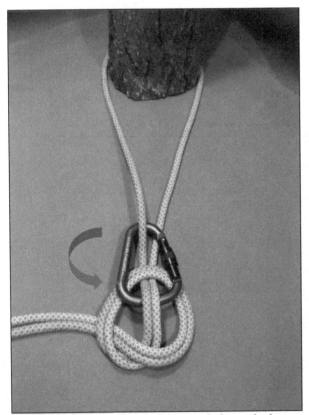

Clip a pear-abiner around a strand above the loop, then rotate it to pass under the central strands.

Cinch down all strands to finish.

Stone Knot [195]

The stone knot is generally used to attach rope to a natural anchor such as a tree, fallen log, or rock horn. It might be tied as part of a static twin system, or used in conjunction with a retrievable toggle. It's easy to tie and inspect.

- If the critical angle between the rope strands at the top of the knot is too wide, it can spread apart and become unstable. To fix this problem, move the knot further away from the anchor.

- The closed loop between the stone knot and the anchor is safe to clip into.

- A stone knot can be rigged any distance from the anchor.

Rigging

The stone knot comes in many variations. The example on the previous page shows how to rig a static twin system using an *upward overhand stone*.[196]

1) Start as if rigging the rope for a DRT rappel.

2) With one hand, grasp both rope strands with your palm down and thumb pointing away from the anchor. Rotate your hand upwards to create a loop with both strands. (See photo upper-left on the previous page.)

3) Fold the loop upwards once more, centering it over the two strands coming down from the anchor.

4) Clip a locking pear-abiner around one of the rope strands above the loop, then rotate it around to pass underneath the central strands of the hitch. Make sure it's locked.

5) Cinch the entire hitch down around the pear-abiner to finish.

---

[195] Technically, this is a marlinspike hitch. The greater canyon community seems to have adopted the term *stone knot*, however, so that's what I've chosen to go with in this manual.

[196] This same version of the stone knot is recommended for use with a retrievable toggle. It's been shown to release most reliably during testing. (Galyan, Luke. "Stone Knot aka Stein Knot." *BluuGnome*. http://www.bluugnome.com/cyn_how-to/gear/smooth-operator/smooth-operator_stoneknot.aspx)

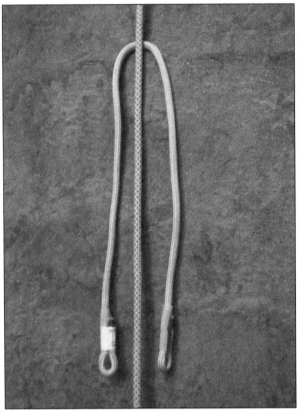

Scenario: Tying a Valdotain Tresse.

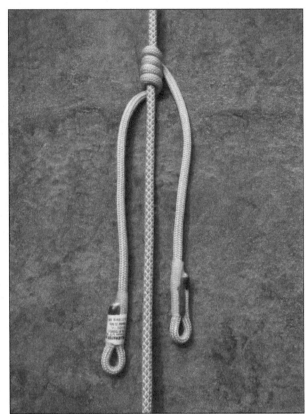

Create the initial spiral of 3–4 wraps.

Begin the braid, alternating over and under.

The completed Valdotain Tresse.

Valdotain Tresse (VT Hitch)

The Valdotain Tresse is a friction hitch that has the interesting property of being releasable under load. Tying it requires a *VT prusik*: a length of accessory cord that's about 80cm (~32in) long and 7–8mm in diameter. The VT prusik is not tied as a sling; it's a single length of cord with separate loops tied or sewn at both ends. Commercial versions are available or you can make your own.

The Valdotain Tresse can be tied on both SRT and DRT. Here are some uses for a releasable rope grab:

- o   Conversions and load transfers.
- o   A hands-free backup when lowering a rappeller.
- o   Progress capture in a haul system.
- o   Ascending.
- o   An autoblock rigged above the descender. (The hitch makes it relatively easy to pass a knot on rappel.)
- o   Descending a tensioned rope during a rescue.

Tying the Valdotain Tresse	1) Begin by placing the middle of the VT prusik on the rope. 2) Wrap one tail up and one tail down to create a tight spiral of three to four wraps. Three wraps is a good place to start, but you may need more or less depending on the load, the diameter of the rope, diameter of the VT prusik, etc. 3) Upon completing the spiral, even out the tails. 4) Next, crisscross the tails over and under to create a symmetric braid down the rope. Maintain a little tension and keep the strands close together. The hitch must be well-dressed or it won't function properly. 5) Continue braiding until you run out of material. When finished, clip both loops together with a locking carabiner.
Release	To release the Valdotain: gently compress the top of the hitch by pushing down on the initial wrap. Use caution as it can release quite suddenly. Try to find the sweet spot that allows for a controlled release.

Other Notes

- It takes a little practice to dial in the friction settings with a Valdotain Tresse. As always, practice in a safe place before using the hitch in the field.

- The Valdotain can be used for ascending, but it isn't terribly efficient as it needs to stretch out to its full length before it cinches down on the rope. Every time you slide the hitch upward, you'll lose about 10cm (3–4in) before it grips the rope. Lacking ascenders, an asymmetric prusik may be a more efficient option.

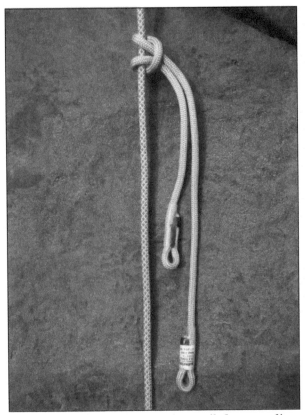

Scenario: Tying an asymmetric prusik for ascending. Start with a simple girth hitch.

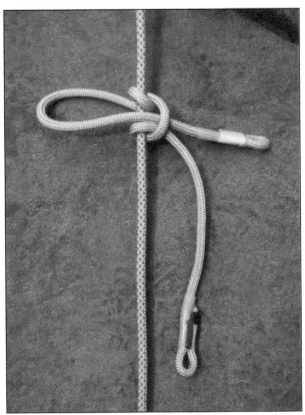

Thread the upper tail back through the hitch three more times.

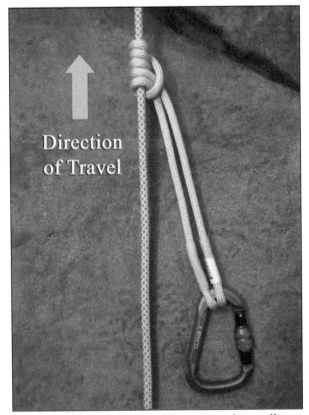

Direction of Travel

The completed "4-over-1" asymmetric prusik.

Asymmetric Prusik (Schwabisch)

Here's another friction hitch that can be tied with a *VT prusik*. It's generally used as a rope grab or progress capture, and can be tied on both SRT and DRT. It is not releasable under load.

Rigging

Start by tying a simple girth hitch on the rope with the VT prusik. If the goal is to climb the rope, the holding power of the hitch needs to be at the top. Adjust the VT prusik to make the upper tail a bit longer, then thread it back through the same hitch three more times. Cinch everything down to create a "4-over-1" asymmetric prusik. The number of wraps in the hitch can be adjusted for more or less friction.

If the goal is to haul (ex: raising a rappeller back to the top of the pitch), then the holding power of the hitch should be at the bottom. In this case, the lower tail would be lengthened. It's still a "4-over-1" asymmetric prusik; it's rigged on the rope in the opposite direction.

Advantage

- A standard prusik can be difficult to release after being loaded. The asymmetric prusik releases a little more easily.

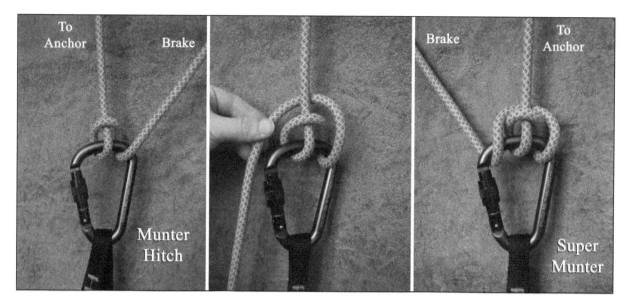

Munter Hitch (Italian Hitch)

The munter hitch is used for lowering, rappelling, and belaying. It makes a great backup rappel system in the event of a lost descender. It's easy to tie and can be rigged SRT or DRT. The munter is usually rigged at the wide end of a locking HMS carabiner (aka pear-abiner). The wide end allows the hitch to flip without interference.

- To test the hitch: pull first on one strand, then the other. The hitch should flip back and forth through the pear-abiner.

- Ideally, the pear-abiner should be situated so that the gate is opposite from the brake strand. This avoids any possibility of rope running over the gate and causing it to come open.

- Maximum friction is obtained when the brake strand is parallel to the load strand. This is opposite from most descenders. It is possible to brake from behind the pear-abiner, but it provides less friction.

- Hard lock: tie off the munter with a mule-overhand. (See "Mule Hitch" later in the chapter.)

Disadvantage
- The munter hitch introduces twists into the rope. If used once or twice on a short rappel, it's not a big deal, but it can become a problem when lowering. (See "The Munter Hitch" in Chapter 11.)

The Super Munter
Need more friction? The munter hitch is easily converted to a *super munter*. Wrap the brake strand around the load strand on the opposite side from the original hitch and clip it back into the pear-abiner.

Advantages
- The super munter is well-suited for skinny ropes (ex: rappelling SRT, and lowering large loads).

- The super munter does not place twists into the rope.

Disadvantages
- Belaying is not practical with the super munter. There's too much friction.

- The brake strand may end up on the gate side of the pear-abiner. While not ideal, this generally isn't as much of an issue as the super munter provides a lot more control.

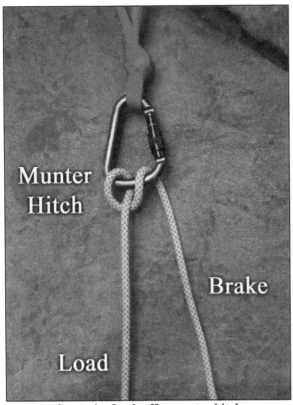

Munter Hitch

Brake

Load

Scenario: Lock off a munter hitch
with a mule-overhand.

Using the brake strand,
create a loop behind the load strand.

Form a bight, pass it in front of the load strand,
and push it through the loop. This creates the mule.

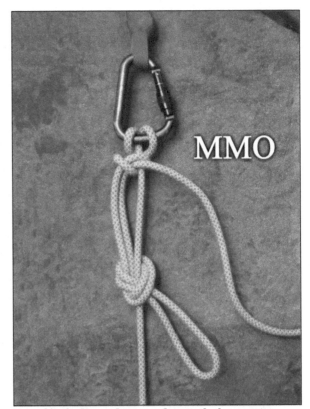

MMO

Cinch the mule up underneath the munter
and secure it with an overhand knot.

Mule Hitch

The mule is a releasable hitch that can be tied with rope, cordelette, or accessory cord. It can be untied even when fully under load. One caveat: the mule releases quite suddenly. For this reason, it's generally used to tie off some other type of friction system, such as a munter hitch or pig rig. This allows for a more controlled release of rope. Be aware: the mule requires a backup to be fully secure.

Some common uses include:

- Tying off a rigging system. A munter hitch rigged on the anchor could be tied off with a mule-overhand. This trio, the munter-mule-overhand, is referred to as an MMO. (See "The Munter Hitch" in Chapter 11.)

- Hauling and conversions. A mule-overhand could be used to tie off a pig rig or to connect a bridge to an anchor. (See Chapters 21 & 22 for more information.)

- A mule-overhand can be used to lock off most rappel systems (ex: descender or munter hitch).

The example on the previous page shows how to lock off a munter hitch using a mule-overhand. Before tying the mule, make sure the munter is in the correct orientation for the load.

Tying the Mule Hitch	1) Position both rope strands so that they exit the munter hitch in parallel. 2) Using the brake strand (i.e., the free end of the rope), create a loop behind the load strand as shown in the photo opposite. 3) Create a bight in the free end of the rope. Pass the bight around the front of the load strand and push it through the loop you created. This forms a slip knot (aka the mule hitch) that captures both rope strands where they exit the munter. 4) Cinch the mule up tightly underneath the munter hitch.
Backing up the Mule	The mule is complete, but we're not done yet. If the free end of the rope were to come under load, the bight could slip back through and the mule would fall apart. To keep this from happening, the bight must be secured. Here are two options: ➤ Lengthen the bight by pulling more slack through the mule. The bight can then be tied off to the load strand with a simple overhand knot. Ideally, the overhand should be tied as close as possible to the mule to prevent slippage. ➤ Alternatively, clip the bight back to the anchor with another carabiner. Con: This requires another piece of gear.
Release	Untie the overhand knot (or unclip the bight) and carefully pull the bight back through the mule, taking care that it doesn't get twisted up on itself. When the bight is as small as you can make it, pull the brake strand hard and fast. Use caution as the mule hitch releases quite suddenly.

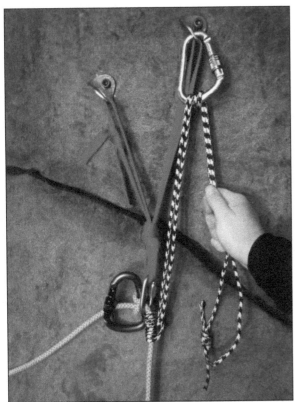

Scenario: Tying a mariner's hitch.
Wrap the bight twice through the carabiner.

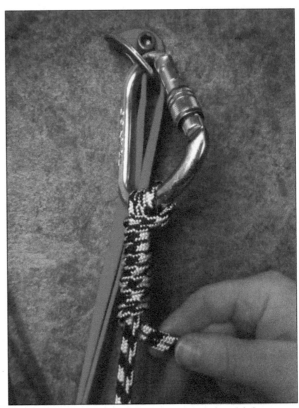

Continue wrapping the remaining bight
around the both original strands in a tight spiral.

After 4–6 wraps, thread the remaining bight
between the original strands.

Mariner's
Hitch

Complete the mariner's hitch by clipping
the bight back to the anchor.

Mariner's Hitch

Here's another releasable hitch that can be used to attach a bight of material (ex: webbing sling, accessory cord, or rope) to another object. The mariner's hitch is useful in haul systems and conversions. It might be used to tie off a pig rig or to connect a bridge to an anchor. It can be released when fully under load.

The example on the previous page shows the initial steps of converting a static block to a lower. Our plan is to create a bridge (i.e., progress capture), then haul to raise the subject and unweight the block. The progress capture is installed on the load strand in front of the anchor's master point. We'll attach it to the anchor with a mariner's hitch. This provides two advantages:

- It allows us to get the capture's length exactly right with no fiddling or guesswork.

- The progress capture is releasable. Once the rigging has been converted, it's easy to release the hitch and lower to weight the new system.

Tying the Mariner's Hitch	1) Using the end of the prusik loop opposite from the knot, tie a prusik on the load strand. (This will keep the knot out of the mariner's hitch.) 2) Give the prusik loop a little tension and wrap the bight twice through a carabiner on the anchor. Double-check that the carabiner is locked. 3) While maintaining tension, start wrapping the remaining bight around the two original strands in a tight descending spiral. Each wrap increases the friction and holding power of the hitch. You might start with 4–6 wraps, but having more doesn't hurt.[197] 4) Once you have a sufficient number of wraps, thread the remaining bight between the original strands of the prusik loop and cinch it upwards. 5) The mariner's hitch has potential to slip, so it must be backed up. The end of the bight can be tied off with a half hitch, or clipped back to the anchor with another carabiner.
Release	Untie (or unclip) the bight and pull the tail back through the original strands. Carefully start unwinding the spiral, while keeping tension on the bight. As each wrap is removed, the friction will decrease. If the hitch is under load, it'll eventually slip and permit a short controlled lower. - Be aware: the distance you can lower is limited by the length of the bight. During a conversion, however, a short lower may be all you need. If necessary, the bight could be extended by adding another sling (ex: girth hitch).

---

[197] A bight that's too long is better than one that's too short. If you don't have enough wraps, the hitch won't hold.

Appendix II: Simple Anchors

A *simple anchor* is exactly what it says on the tin. It's an uncomplicated anchor rigged on a single natural feature, such as a tree, fallen log, or boulder. A simple anchor is quite different from a *multi-point anchor* that shares the load between two or more independent points. It's worth taking a closer look at simple anchors as they're used quite frequently when canyoning. They can be rigged in a number of ways with varying levels of strength.[198]

> **Cinching Anchors**
> Some simple anchors are *cinching*, meaning that the anchor will tighten up around the natural feature when placed under load. This property is useful for high placements (ex: around the trunk of a tree).

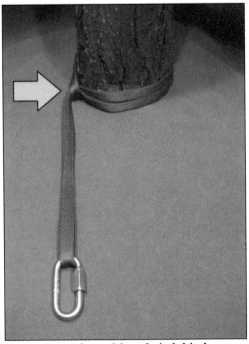

A poorly positioned girth hitch

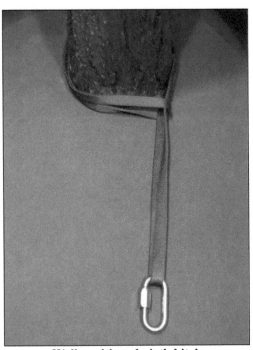

Well-positioned girth hitch

Girth Hitch

Wrap a sling around a natural feature and pass one end through the other to create a girth hitch. It's cinching, but not redundant. This is a quick way to build an anchor or create a convenient place to clip-in. (See "Temporary Clip-in Point" in Chapter 9.) A girth hitch has comparable strength to a single wrap anchor (~10kN).

Disadvantages

- Double-check the position of the girth hitch. If poorly positioned (ref: photo above left), the webbing will pass through two sharp turns instead of one. This places additional stress on the anchor. To fix the problem, rotate the anchor into a better alignment (ref: photo above right).

- Any movement of the anchor, such as that generated by rappelling, will cause the webbing strands to move against each other generating wear. This is not best practice for an anchor intended to be left long-term.

---

[198] CMC Rescue has published an excellent set of test data from pulling simple anchors to their breaking point. The percentages presented in this section were calculated using their test data. (CMC Rescue. *Rope Rescue Manual – 5th Edition.* CMC Rescue, Inc., 2017.)

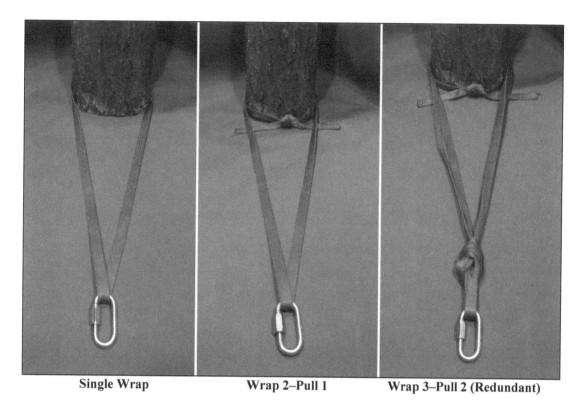

| Single Wrap | Wrap 2–Pull 1 | Wrap 3–Pull 2 (Redundant) |

Single Wrap (Wrap 1)

The single wrap is one of the most common types of rappel anchor. It's a length of webbing that's tied around a single natural feature (ex: bombproof tree). It is not cinching or redundant. Ideally, the knot should be situated on the opposite side of the tree from the direction of pull. In this location, it will experience the least amount of force due to friction. Previously, we estimated the breaking strength of a single wrap anchor at about 10–11kN. (See: "Is a single wrap anchor strong enough?" in Chapter 5.)

- Tying an overhand knot above the master point creates a shelf, but does not make the anchor redundant. The shelf could be used for other purposes, however.

Wrap 2–Pull 1

The webbing is wrapped twice around the tree and tied with a water knot. The knot should be positioned at the front of the tree (i.e., on the same side as the direction of pull) where it will experience the least amount of force. The other strand of webbing is pulled out to house the quick link. This anchor is 10–15% stronger than a single wrap (estimate: ~11–13kN). The anchor is cinching, but not redundant.

- Tying an overhand knot above the master point creates a shelf, but no redundancy.

Wrap 3–Pull 2

The webbing is wrapped three times around the tree and tied with a water knot. Again, the knot should be positioned on the same side as the direction of pull to minimize the amount of force it will experience. The other strands are pulled out to collectively house the quick link. The anchor is cinching, but not redundant.

- Tying an overhand knot above the master point creates a shelf and the anchor becomes redundant.

Advantage
- This anchor is 50–60% stronger than a single wrap (estimate: ~15–17kN) as the load is shared between four strands of webbing. This is great anchor for rescues and hauling, but is overkill for a typical rappel.

Disadvantage
- The anchor requires a lot more webbing to build.

Basket Hitch

Wrap a sling around the tree and attach a quick link (or locking carabiner) to both ends. With four strands sharing the load, the anchor is about 60–70% stronger than a single wrap (estimate: ~16–19kN). The anchor is not cinching or redundant.

- If you have sufficient webbing, it could be wrapped one more time around the tree. This makes the anchor cinching.

- The anchor can be made redundant by tying an overhand knot directly above the master point.

Advantage
- This is another fast way to build an anchor.

Disadvantage
- Beware an overly-wide angle between the strands at the master point. If the critical angle is too large, it can result in triaxial loading. As usual, it's good to keep the critical angle to 90-degrees or less.

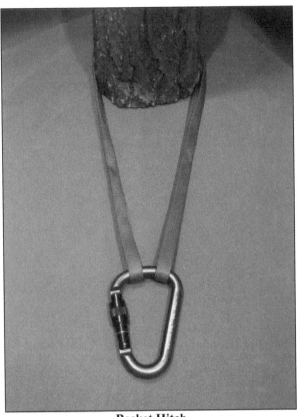

Basket Hitch

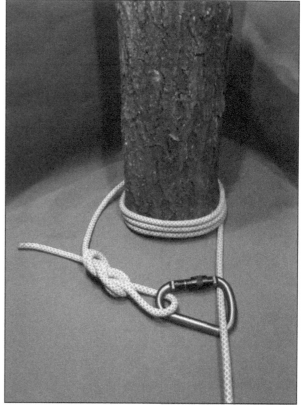

| **Bowline Knot** | **Tensionless Hitch** |

Bowline Knot

Here's another simple anchor that uses no gear other than the rope itself. Run the rope around a bombproof natural feature and tie it off with a bowline. A bowline can work its way loose after repeated loading and unloading, so it must be backed up with an overhand (or barrel knot) tied in the tail. (See also "Fixed Ropes" in Chapter 8.) Con: It's easy to tie the bowline incorrectly. Always inspect the hitch carefully.

- A bowline can be made cinching by wrapping the rope one more time around the tree before tying the knot.

- Variation: A bowline-on-a-bight can be used to set the length.

Tensionless Hitch

The tensionless hitch is another simple anchor that requires a rope and a locking carabiner. To tie: wrap the rope around any convenient natural feature about 3–5 times. Keep the wraps nice and tight. When finished, tie a figure-8 knot in the tail and clip it back to the load line with the carabiner.[199] The tensionless hitch is well-suited for tying on trees and fallen logs.

The tensionless hitch is quick to build and easy to inspect. With no knots, it retains almost the full strength of the rope, making it one of the strongest anchors out there. A terrific anchor for rescues.

- Variation: To set the length, the hitch can be tied using a bight in the middle of the rope.

---

[199] The carabiner is a safety precaution. If there are enough wraps, there should be no tension on the tail at all.

Appendix III: Rope Bags

In the canyon world, rope bags are used for the efficient management and transportation of ropes. They're usually quite burly, come in a variety of sizes, and are equipped with flotation to keep the rope from sinking in deep pools. Openings along the side allow the bag to drain quickly when lifted out of the water. A rope bag helps protect the rope and keep it contained.

- Tip: Any time you're bagging rope, it's a good opportunity to inspect it for damage.

Carrying Rope Bags

Rope bags can be carried by the handles, shoulder-strap, or worn like a backpack. Some canyoneers prefer to stow rope bags in their pack: either inside, or cinched down under the lid.

- When descending a canyon, your backpack is nearly empty (as almost everything is being worn), so your pack could be used as a rope bag.

- It's not a bad idea to attach a carabiner (sometimes with an accompanying sling) to your rope bag. This makes it easy to clip the bag to an anchor or hang it on your harness while rappelling.

Putting the Rope Away

The preferred method of stowing ropes will vary depending on where you are in the world. In aquatic canyons of the Pacific Northwest, we've found that having any rope sticking out of the bag is generally an invitation to get it caught on things. If the rope gets snagged and pulled out of the bag while hiking along the creek, it's annoying. If it were to happen while rappelling or swimming, it could become a dangerous situation.

Method #1: Individual Bagging

Here's a common method for putting the rope away. This method is usually a one-person operation, although a partner might help pull the rope and flake it into a neat pile for you.

1) Tie one end of the rope to an internal loop at the top of the bag with a secure knot (ex: barrel knot).[200] The interior loop should not be confused with the exterior handles.

2) Clip this same loop to the front of your harness. This will keep the bag positioned in front of you and helps hold it open for packing. Alternatively, a partner could hold the bag open for you.

3) The rope strand emerging from the bag is clipped into a high point carabiner. The high point could be a carabiner clipped to the shoulder strap of your pack or the chin-strap of your helmet. Alternatively, a partner could hold up a carabiner for you. The purpose of the high point is to elevate the rope and make it easier to pack into the bag.

   o A high point is unnecessary while pulling the rope from an anchor atop the pitch. As soon as the tail comes down, you could switch over to using a high point.

   o A high point carabiner could also be attached to an anchor. This might be done at the forward end of a retrievable traverse line or a hanging anchor.

---

[200] Tying it to a loop at the top is preferred as this allows anyone to see at a glance that the rope is tied securely to the bag. Tying it at the top also allows quick access to both ends of the rope. A secure knot will prevent the bag from becoming lost during deployment (ex: tossing the rope bag down the pitch).

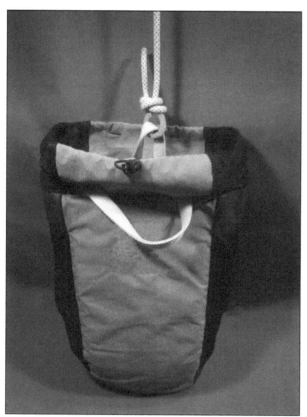

The rope is tied securely to an internal loop.

Using a high point carabiner to pack the bag.

4) Take hold of the rope below the high point, and begin stuffing it back into the bag. Every now and then, you'll need push the mass of rope down into the bag to compact it.

5) Other team members can help by flaking out the remaining rope into a neat pile and making sure it doesn't get caught on anything nearby. Feeding rope to the bag-stuffer usually isn't helpful.

6) Once finished, tie the tail of the rope to the same interior loop with a quick overhand knot. With two different knots, it's easy to identify which end of the rope is which.

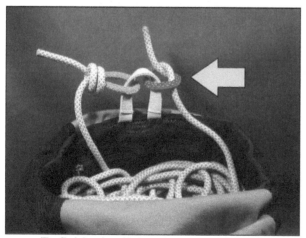

To finish: tie off the tail to the same loop with a simple overhand knot (shown in red).

7) Cinch the bag closed, and you're done!

Other Tips:

- Beware clipping the high point carabiner to the sternum strap on your pack. It's easy to forget it's there and you'll risk losing the carabiner the next time you take your pack off.

- Don't have an extra carabiner? Or you're not wearing a pack? Face away from the rope pile and pull the rope up and over your shoulder as a makeshift high point.

Make a coil of 10–12 small loops in your hand.
Multiple team members can all be coiling.

Stuff the coils carefully into the bag.
The tail is tied off with a quick overhand.

Method #2: Team Bagging

Here's another method of bagging rope that allows multiple team members to participate. With more people working together, putting the rope away is even faster.

This variation is essentially the same as the individual bagging method, except there's no need for a high point carabiner. Instead, make a small butterfly coil with loops about 10–15cm (~4–6in) long. Once you have a coil of about 10–12 loops, stuff it carefully into the bag, making sure the free end of the rope is positioned on top. Other team members can help by creating their own coils; each working at a different point along the rope. Every time a coil is completed, it's stuffed into the bag on top of the previous one. Continue until the entire rope is packed away.

When finished, tie off the tail of the rope to the same internal loop with an overhand knot. Cinch the bag closed to finish.

Appendix IV: The Pirana

The *Pirana* is one of the first modern descenders developed specifically for canyoning.[201] It's a variable-speed device intended for single-strand rappels (SRT). It can be used on two-strand rappels (DRT), although some of the friction settings may not be available with larger diameter ropes.

The Pirana requires a dedicated locking carabiner that's threaded through a hole in its base.[202] The device is held rigidly in place, which makes it harder to lose when disconnecting in deep water. The carabiner's gate should always face upwards, although the Pirana itself can be rigged in a left-handed or right-handed configuration. Note the small hand icon on the spur that identifies the brake side of the device. All of the photos that follow show the Pirana rigged for a right-handed rappeller.

- Tip: When not rappelling, the descender can be holstered by clipping the large opening to a carabiner on an adjacent gear loop. This keeps the device from hanging down and getting in the way.

Using a Pirana with a Climbing Harness
The Pirana is designed to be used on a harness with a horizontal attachment point. Unfortunately, most climbing harnesses have a vertical belay loop that causes the Pirana to twist out of alignment when loaded. It's still usable, but accessing some of the friction settings is a little trickier. One way to solve this problem is a short rappel extension (i.e., connecting the device to your harness with a 10mm quick link or small locking carabiner). See also "Rappel Extension" in Chapter 15.

- Extension via quick link
  The quick link should be climb-rated. Consider tightening it down with a pair of pliers. Prior to rappelling, check to make sure the gate has not accidentally come open.

- Extension via carabiner
  The carabiner should be checked prior to every rappel to ensure it's locked, and hasn't accidentally become cross-loaded.

---

[201] A new version of the Pirana was released in 2019. Photos here show the original design.
[202] Check with the manufacturer as not all carabiners will fit.

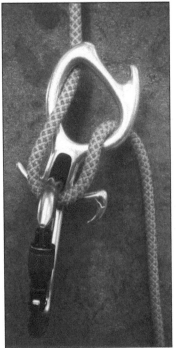 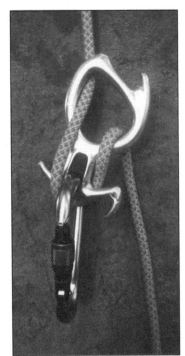 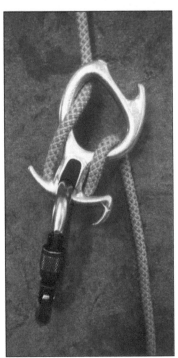

Initial settings: the friction increases from left to right.

Increasing the Friction

The lowest friction setting is a bight of rope passing up through the large opening of the Pirana and around the dedicated carabiner. (See photo above-left.) The more horns the rope passes around, the greater the friction produced. The photos above show the device's base settings with the friction increasing from left to right.

Danger!

- Be aware: these base settings are not easily changed on the fly. In order to change them, you'll need to find a safe place along the rappel where the device can be unweighted momentarily.

- Use caution on difficult rappel starts and whenever the rope is unweighted. If the rope is not under tension, it can sometimes pop out from behind the horns, causing the friction settings to change unexpectedly.

- WARNING! Wrapping the rope directly over the upper horn (as shown in the photo left) appears a tempting way to increase the friction. To reach this setting, however, the rappeller must move the brake strand upwards. This means that the friction is momentarily reduced en route to the higher setting. This has been a factor in at least one accident. Use with caution.[203]

Left: Direct use of the Pirana's upper horn is not recommended.

---

[203] Any figure-8 style device with horns above the large opening may be subject to this problem.

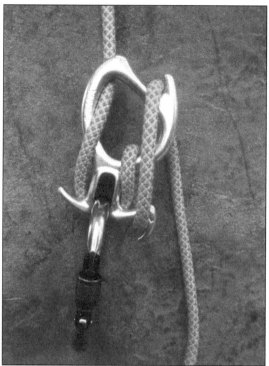

Soft Lock

Here's a better way to use the upper horn. Start by pulling the brake strand downward and pass it around the lower-right spur of the device. The rope can then be run back up over the upper horn (see photo left). This setting increases the friction enormously and is usually enough to bring most rappellers to a stop. Rope can still slip through the device, however, so the brake must be maintained. This position is known as a *soft lock* (aka static position).

Hard Lock

There are several ways to go hands-free with a Pirana. Here's an easy method:

1) Starting from the soft lock: feed a bight of the brake strand through the dedicated carabiner and create a half-twist as shown below.

2) Fold the twisted bight back up and over both the horn and spur on the brake side of the device. Cinch this cleat firmly into place. The rope is secure and you've gone hands-free.

To inspect the hard lock: double-check that the brake strand (shown in red) is being pinched or captured where it exits the rappel device. If the brake strand is not being pinched, the hard lock is not rigged correctly.

Soft lock—the brake must be maintained.

Pass a bight through the carabiner with a twist.

Completed hard lock.
(Note the red brake strand is captured.)

Appendix V: The Critr

The *Critr* is another modern canyon descender. It was originally developed by *Canyon Werks* and is currently available from *Imlay Canyon Gear*. While similar in many respects to the Pirana, the Critr has more friction options and is easier to lock off. The following photos show a Critr rigged for a right-handed rappeller.

Advantages
- The rope is less likely to slip off the Critr's legs when the device is unweighted. This means that rappel extension is probably unnecessary when using a climbing harness.

- The aperture at the center of the device can be used as a sticht plate for belaying.[204]

- Desert Southwest: The Critr is symmetrical, giving the descender greater longevity in sandstone environments. The manufacturer recommends flipping the device over after every rappel.

Disadvantages
- The Critr's legs are more prone to catch on things and snag the rope.

- The Critr is slightly larger than the Pirana, meaning the rope travels over a greater surface area. Smaller canyoneers may find the Critr provides too much friction out of the gate.

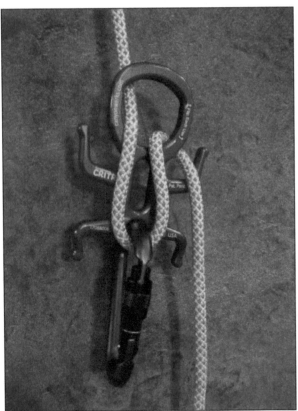

Increasing the friction by a "half step."

Increasing the Friction

The lowest friction setting is a bight of rope passing up through the large opening of the descender and around the dedicated locking carabiner. Like the Pirana, the base friction can be increased by running the rope around one or both of the Critr's lower legs. These initial settings are not easily changed on the fly.

- Friction on Demand

   One nice feature of the Critr is the ability to dial up the friction by a "half step." For a right-handed rappeller, this is done by running the brake strand over the device's upper right leg. This gives you a slight increase in friction, which may be all you need.

---

[204] The slot is designed to accept up to a 10mm rope. Note, however, that the Critr is not rated for taking lead-falls.

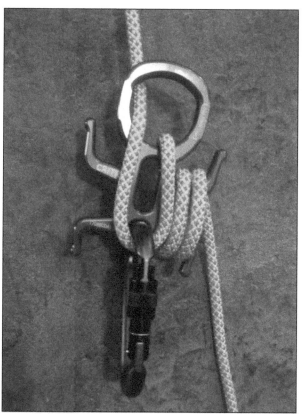

Soft Lock

For a *soft lock*, wrap the rope once or twice around both legs on the brake side of the descender. Rope can still slip through the device, so the brake must be maintained.

Hard Lock

From the soft lock position, pass a bight of rope through the descender's dedicated carabiner and give it a twist. Pull the twisted bight up and over both legs on the non-brake side of the Critr and cinch it down. This quick cleat secures the rope, enabling you to go hands-free.

To inspect the hard lock, check that the brake strand (shown in red below) is pinched or captured where it exits the device. If the brake strand is not being pinched, the hard lock is not rigged correctly.

Soft lock—the brake must be maintained.

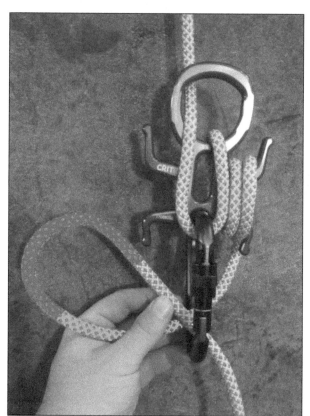

Pass a bight through the carabiner with a twist.

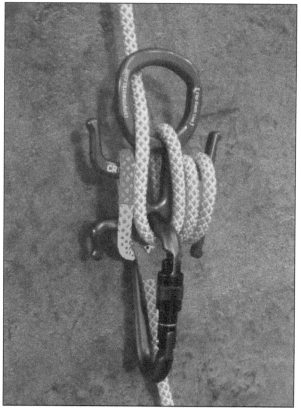

Completed hard lock.
(Note the red brake strand is captured.)

Appendix VI: Canyon Gear List

Here's a gear list for a typical day outing in the Pacific Northwest. Your kit will vary with the season, current conditions, your experience level, personal preference, and other factors.

Proper Attire
- [ ] full body wetsuit
- [ ] synthetic quick-dry clothing
- [ ] neoprene or wool socks
- [ ] canyoning shoes or light hiking boots
- [ ] rainshell or dry top

Packs & Water Protection
- [ ] backpack (40–50 liter) with drainage
- [ ] dry bags or kegs
- [ ] dry box (camera, electronics, etc.)

Technical Gear
- [ ] helmet (with signal whistle attached)
- [ ] harness
- [ ] cowstails (i.e., safety tethers x 2)
- [ ] descender with dedicated locking carabiner
- [ ] locking carabiners x 3–4
- [ ] ascension system (ex: Frog Rig)
- [ ] rescue knife
- [ ] VT prusik
- [ ] extra descender (ex: classic figure-8 device)
- [ ] webbing for anchors (5–10m (20–30ft))
- [ ] quick links (or rappel rings) x 2–3

Group Gear
- [ ] ropes & rope bags
- [ ] group first aid kit
- [ ] emergency beacon or cell phone (charged)

Essentials
- [ ] maps, canyon beta & compass
- [ ] GPS-enabled device (charged)
- [ ] headlamp (waterproof)
- [ ] personal first aid kit, medications & TP
- [ ] sunscreen & lip protection
- [ ] lunch & snacks
- [ ] water bottle (1 liter) or filter
- [ ] emergency space blanket

Extras
- [ ] hat with brim
- [ ] gloves (sturdy leather or synthetic)
- [ ] kneepads
- [ ] swim mask or goggles
- [ ] camera (check batteries)

Winter Additions
- [ ] thicker wetsuit
- [ ] extra layers (neoprene, rash guard, etc.)
- [ ] thermos with hot beverage
- [ ] small stove & fuel; lighter

Leave in the Car
- [ ] full change of clothes & footwear
- [ ] tarp to change on
- [ ] towel
- [ ] post-canyon water & snacks
- [ ] garbage bag for wet gear

Notes
- Wetsuits: minimum full-body 4/3mm with long pants/sleeves.
- Backpack: large enough to carry a rope bag secured under the lid or stuffed inside.
- All quick links / rappel rings should be climb-rated.
- Always leave a change of dry clothes back at the car.

Acknowledgements

Writing this manual has been an enormous multi-year effort with input from a great many individuals. A huge thank you to everyone who has contributed in large and small ways to move this project forward. I couldn't have done it without you. My sincere apologies to anyone I've inadvertently left out here, but I'd like to thank:

- Wim Aarts
- Scott Allred
- Sarah Bradham
- Sean Brady
- Jason Breaker
- Scott Brown
- Sarah Busse
- Keith Campbell
- Anna Cranmer
- Jay Chambers
- Hereward Cooper
- Annalisha Cox
- Alex Danielson
- Erin Devlin
- Tim Donner
- Ashley Driscoll
- Alexey Dynkin
- Daniel Elson
- Ian Farquhar
- John Godino
- Madeline Hwang
- Kendra Kallevig
- Vandy Hall
- Karl Helser
- Chelsea Heveran
- Wade Hewitt
- Deb Hill
- Jake Huddleston
- Heather Johnston
- Julia Jordan
- Zach Kiefer
- Keith Langenwalter
- Tiffanie Lin
- Alex MacDonald
- Vaqas Malik
- Nick Maslen
- Ellen McClure
- Tara Meyer
- Karin Mullendorff
- Michelle Nilles
- Bradley Noren
- Keith Occeña
- Becca Polglase
- Lisa Ripps
- Rodney Rodriguez
- Brent Roth
- Kaitlin Rupert
- Andy Sorensen
- Leah Sorensen
- Tom Ulrich
- Brian Wellman
- Jeremiah West
- Bruce Wyse

I'd also like to thank the *Mazamas*, the *Mountaineers*, *Portland Mountain Rescue*, and the *V7 Academy*.

Special thanks to all the great instructors I've had the good fortune to take a class or three with over the years: Jason Bowman, Rich Carlson, Luca Chiarabini, Logan DeGrand, Klaus Gerhart, Dusty Gold, Andrew Humphreys, Tom Jones, Dean Kirchner, Kevin Koprek, Ben Lewis, Richard Metawi, and George Yates. Any errors in the text are all mine and not the result of their excellent training.

I'd like to give special thanks to Sarah Bradham, who undertook the heroic task of editing and reviewing the manual. I really appreciate the time and effort that you put into it. You're the best.

Also, big thanks to Wade Hewitt for allowing me to use some of his excellent photos. My own photography skills are inadequate for capturing the beauty and wonder of our local canyons.

And, finally, thank you to Keith Campbell, who, in a random conversation in 2015, sparked this project.

References

Technical References

- Beschdel, L. & Ray. S. (2009). *River Rescue–4th Edition*. CFS Press.

- Black, David. (2013). *Canyoneering: A Guide to Techniques in Wet and Dry Canyons–2nd Edition*. Falcon Guides.

- CMC Rescue (2017). *Rope Rescue Manual–5th Edition*. CMC Rescue, Inc.

- Connally, Craig. (2005). *The Mountaineering Handbook*. Ragged Mountain Press.

- Denissot, Michael. (2015). *Assistant Instructor Manual–v2*. ICOPro.

- Denissot, M. & Poublan, L. (2017). *Canyoneer Level 1 Manual–v3*. ICOPro.

- Denissot, M. & Poublan, L. (2017). *Canyoneer Level 2 Manual–v3*. ICOPro.

- Denissot, M. & Poublan, L. (2017). *Canyoneer Level 3 Manual–v3*. ICOPro.

- Gaines, Bob. (2013). *Rappelling: Rope Descending and Ascending Skills*. Falcon Guides.

- Jeffrey, D. & McDaniel, T. (2010). *Canyoneering Anchors and Basic Rope Systems*. AuthorHouse.

- Kirkpatrick, Andy. (2020). *Down: The Complete Descent Manual for Climbers, Alpinists and Mountaineers*. Independent Publisher.

- National Safety Council Wilderness Medical Society (2004). *Wilderness First Aid: Emergency Care for Remote Locations*. Jones & Bartlett.

- Ostis, Nate. (2015). *NOLS River Rescue Guide*. Stackpole Books.

- Prattley, G. & Clearwater, D. (2020). *Canyoning Technical Manual*. Over the Edge Rescue. Maxim Print.

- Rescue 3 International (2015). *Water and Flood Rescue Manual–v4.2*. Rescue 3 International.

- Smith, B. & Padgett, A. (1996). *On Rope – North American Vertical Rope Techniques*. National Speleological Society.

- The Mountaineers (2010). *Mountaineering: The Freedom of the Hills–8th Edition*. Mountaineers Books

- Tilburg, Christopher V. (2000). *Canyoneering: Beginning to Advanced Techniques*. Mountaineers Books.

- Tyson, A. & Loomis, M. (2016). *Climbing Self-Rescue–Improvising Solutions for Serious Situations*. Mountaineers Books.

- Warild, Alan. (2008). *Vertical – A Technical Manual for Cavers–5th Edition*. Independent Publisher.

Articles

- American Alpine Club (2017). "Anchors." *American Alpine Club Blog*. https://americanalpineclub.org/resources-blog/2017/7/31/anchors

- Canyon Magazine (2016). "Canyoning Hydrology & Water Hazards." *Canyon Magazine*. https://canyonmag.net/technical/safety/hydrology/

- Delaney, Richard (2016). "Munter Hitch." *RopeLab*. https://www.ropelab.com.au/munter-hitch

- Delaney, Richard (2018). "Redundancy in Rope Systems." *RopeLab.* https://www.ropelab.com.au/redundancy-in-rope-systems

- Fraser, Shanan. (2017). "NZCA Bolting Code of Practice–v1.9." *New Zealand Canyoning Association.* http://nzcanyoningassociation.org/wp-content/uploads/2019/11/NZCA-Bolting-Code-of-Practice-v1.9-2017.pdf

- Hess, Rob. (2012). "Know the Ropes: Rappelling. Fundamentals to Save Your Life." *Accidents in North American Mountaineering, December 2012.*

- Humphreys, Andrew. (2017). "Indirect Anchor Cutting." *Canyon Magazine.* https://canyonmag.net/explore/indirect-anchor-cutting

- Galyan, Luke. "Smooth Operator Retrievable Rappel Anchor." *BluuGnome.* http://www.bluugnome.com/cyn_how-to/gear/smooth-operator/smooth-operator.aspx

- Kovach, Jim. (2004). "The Effectiveness of a Bottom Belay on Long Drops." *Nylon Highway #49.*

- Petzl. "Forces at Work in a Real Fall." *Petzl Tech Tips.* https://www.petzl.com/US/en/Sport/Forces-at-work-in-a-real-fall

- Prattley, Grant. "Webbing in Hangers." *Over the Edge Rescue Blog.* https://overtheedgerescue.com/canyoning/webbing-in-hangers

- Prattley, Grant. "Which Bend for Joining Ropes?" *Over the Edge Rescue Blog.* https://overtheedgerescue.com/rope-rescue/bends-joining-ropes-update

- Snider, L. & Haas, J. (2015). "Too Important to Fail: The Problem of Aging Bolts." *Vertical Times–The National Publication of the Access Fund, Vol 104.*

- Stephanides, S. & Vohra, T. (2007). "Injury Patterns and First Aid Training Among Canyoneers". *Wilderness & Environmental Medicine, Issue 18.*

- Woods, John. (2008). "Comparisons of the Frog & Mitchell Ascending Systems." *Nylon Highway #54.*

Internet Resources

- Achelis, Steve. "Rope Rescue Training." Basic overview of rescue systems, including mechanical advantage. https://roperescuetraining.com

- Bristol, Derek. "Cave Exploration–Caving Techniques–Caving Equipment." Instructional videos. https://www.derekbristol.com

- Carlson, Rich. *Canyons & Crags.* Instructional videos. https://canyonsandcrags.com/knowledge-base

- Humphreys, Andrew. *Canyoning Colorado.* Online class: "Indirect Rescue Workshop." https://learn.canyoningcolorado.com/course

- International Canyon Accident Database (ICAD). https://canyonaccident.org/

- Jones, Tom. *Canyoneering USA.* "Tech Tips." https://www.canyoneeringusa.com/techtips

- Ropewiki. Crowd-sourced beta-base. One of the best sources of information on Pacific NW canyons. http://ropewiki.com/Pacific_Northwest

- Smiley, Mark. "Rappelling for the Modern Climber." Online class. https://www.mtnsense.com/p/rappel

- Yates, George & Humphreys, Andrew & et. al. *V7 Academy.* Online classes in aquatic canyoning https://learn.v7academy.com

Index

About the Author

Aha, you've arrived at the least-interesting page in this manual. (There's a reason they put these things in the back, right?) Why would you want to know about me, when you could be out canyoning?

I came into canyoning from an alpine climbing background and have been a volunteer climb leader for the *Mazamas* (a non-profit mountaineering organization in Portland, Oregon) for over fifteen years. I've led numerous climbs and outings throughout the Cascades, although it wasn't until 2007, when planning a trip to Zion National Park, that I became aware of this thing people did called "canyoning." I didn't know it at the time, but that was the beginning of the slippery slope.

Since then, I've become an avid canyoneer and have been taking just about every class I can find. I've run hundreds of canyons over the last ten years, both here and in the Desert Southwest. There's nothing quite like dropping into a canyon for the first time and not knowing what challenges lie ahead. In 2015, I helped launch a canyon program for the Mazamas and have been coming back every year to help teach. My hope is that this manual will prove a useful reference for others on their canyon journey.

Currently, I live in Portland, Oregon. When not canyoning (or scouring maps for new adventures), I'm probably out climbing, backpacking, hiking, adventure thrashing (aka bushwhacking), or cross-country skiing.

It's a pretty exciting time in the Pacific Northwest as the Cascades are only just being assessed for canyon potential. There's a ton of exploration going on with new discoveries and first descents being made every year. We still don't entirely know what's out in the backyard. I'm looking forward to helping find out!

- Find something egregiously wrong (or out of whack) in this manual? While it has undergone many revisions, it's possible that errors lurk out there still. Or, perhaps, something's not presented as clearly as it could be? Let me know. I'll get it fixed in an erratum or updated edition down the road. *Thanks!!*

- Send any questions, comments, or suggestions to: *pnw.canyoning@gmail.com*